Mordy Golding

John Ray

Sams **Teach Yourself**

Adobe®
Creative
Suite 3

All in One

 SAMS   800 East 96th Street, Indianapolis, Indiana, 46240 USA

Sams Teach Yourself Adobe® Creative Suite 3 All in One

ISBN-13: 978-0-672-32934-0

ISBN-10: 0-672-32934-4

Library of Congress Cataloging-in-Publication Data:

Golding, Mordy.

  Sams teach yourself Adobe Creative Suite 3 all in one / Mordy Golding, John Ray.

      p. cm.

  Includes index.

  ISBN 978-0-672-32934-0 (pbk.)

  1. Computer graphics. 2. Web sites–Design. I. Ray, John, 1971- II. Title. III. Title: Teach yourself Adobe Creative suite 3 all in one.

T385.G63933 2007

006.6'86–dc22

                              2007031093

Printed in the United States of America

First Printing September 2007

Trademarks

All terms mentioned in this book that are known to be trademarks or service marks have been appropriately capitalized. Sams Publishing cannot attest to the accuracy of this information. Use of a term in this book should not be regarded as affecting the validity of any trademark or service mark.

Warning and Disclaimer

Bulk Sales

Sams Publishing offers excellent discounts on this book when ordered in quantity for bulk purchases or special sales. For more information, please contact

U.S. Corporate and Government Sales
1-800-382-3419
corpsales@pearsontechgroup.com

For sales outside of the U.S., please contact

International Sales
international@pearsoned.com

Acquisitions Editor
Betsy Brown

Development Editor
Songlin Qiu

Managing Editor
Patrick Kanouse

Project Editor
Mandie Frank

Copy Editor
Heather Wilkins

Indexer
Ken Johnson

Proofreader
Williams Woods Publishing Services, LLC

Technical Editor
Prospect Hill Publishing Services

Publishing Coordinator
Vanessa Evans

Designer
Gary Adair

Composition
Mark Shirar

Contents at a Glance

Table of Contents

Sams Teach Yourself Adobe® Creative Suite 3 All in One

Part II: The Applications

About the Author

Mordy Golding has played an active role in the design and publishing environment since 1990. A production artist for both print and the Web for many years, Mordy, an Adobe Certified Expert and Adobe Certified Print Specialist, has served as a hands-on trainer and has spoken at worldwide events and seminars including The Creative Suite Conference, Macworld, Seybold, NAB, and PhotoshopWorld.

Mordy worked at Adobe as the product manager for Adobe Illustrator 10 and Adobe Illustrator CS, and is currently a consultant specializing in the Adobe Creative Suite through his company, Design Responsibly (www.designresponsibly.com).

You can often find Mordy at his blog (http://rwillustrator.blogspot.com), hanging around the Adobe User to User forums (www.adobeforums.com), or at the Print Planet forums (www.printplanet.com), and you can reach him at mordy@mordy.com. Other books published by Mordy Golding include *Real World Adobe Illustrator CS3* (Peachpit Press, 978-0321496218, 2007), *Sams Teach Yourself Adobe Illustrator in 24 Hours* (Sams Publishing, 0-672-32313-3, 2003), and *The Web Designer's Guide to Color* (Hayden Books, 1-5683-0354-8, 1997). Mordy is also the author of several video training titles, which you can find at www.lynda.com.

About the Contributing Authors

John Ray is a senior business analyst and developer for The Ohio State University Research Foundation. He provides custom network, security, and programming solutions for clients across the country, including the National Regulatory Research Institute and the Brevard Metropolitan Planning Organization in Florida. In his spare time, John has written a number of books, ranging from IT security to operating systems to web development, and serves as a course writer for many online institutions.

Robyn Ness holds a master's degree in quantitative psychology with a specialization in judgment and decision making from The Ohio State University. She currently works as a web developer, focusing on issues of usability and content design, and has also written books on Mac OS X and digital media. In her spare time she tests the bounds of iPhoto by taking a ridiculous number of digital photographs, the best of which can be seen at www.floraphotographs.com.

Dedication

To Zaidy, who always wanted to know what you could do with a computer anyway.
I still miss you.

Acknowledgements

Books don't just appear on the bookshelves by themselves. Thanks to all the folks at Sams Publishing, and to Betsy Brown, Songlin Qiu, Heather Wilkins, and Mandie Frank for their professional and untiring help in publishing this book. Words simply cannot describe the admiration and appreciation I have for John Ray, who assisted in updating most of the book for this CS3 version. John's knowledge and personality show in his work. Simply put, this edition would not be possible without his dedication and support. Special thanks to Kate Binder, who not only helped make sure this book was technically accurate, but offered valuable advice as well.

This book is a work that finds its words shaped from years of experience and friendship. Thanks to Sharon Steuer, Sandee Cohen, David Blatner, and Bert Monroy for your continued support.

There's no way that I could have possibly completed a project of this magnitude without the support from my friends at Adobe. While it's impossible to list everyone, there are some folks for which a blanket "thanks to everyone at Adobe" statement simply won't do. Thank you to Ginna Baldassarre, Lydia Varmazis, Will Eisley, John Nack, Addy Roff, Kevin Connor, Lynn Grillo, Whitney McCleary, Phil Guindi, Terry Hemphill, and Julieanne Kost.

I can't offer enough thanks to Dave Mainwaring and the entire membership of the Print Planet forums. It's a fun place to be, and I guarantee that I learn more from you guys than what you learn from me.

To the Wrotslavsky family, who welcomed me as one of their own over 12 years ago (and who still willingly admit to that fact today).

For all the times I asked him silly questions, like why the sky is blue, my father has forever earned the right to ask me how to create a mask in Photoshop (and other assorted technical support questions). My mother continues to serve as my role model for everything I do.

Of course, this book would not have been possible without the love and support of my wife, Batsheva, and my children, Chayala, Simcha Bunim, and Chavi. I'm one lucky man.

Mordy

We Want to Hear from You!

As the reader of this book, *you* are our most important critic and commentator. We value your opinion and want to know what we're doing right, what we could do better, what areas you'd like to see us publish in, and any other words of wisdom you're willing to pass our way.

You can email or write me directly to let me know what you did or didn't like about this book—as well as what we can do to make our books stronger.

Please note that I cannot help you with technical problems related to the topic of this book, and that due to the high volume of mail I receive, I might not be able to reply to every message.

When you write, please be sure to include this book's title and author as well as your name and phone number or email address. I will carefully review your comments and share them with the author and editors who worked on the book.

E-mail: graphics@samspublishing.com

Mail: Mark Taber
            Associate Publisher
            Sams Publishing
            800 East 96th Street
            Indianapolis, IN 46240 USA

Reader Services

Visit our website and register this book at www.samspublishing.com/register for convenient access to any updates, downloads, or errata that might be available for this book.

Introduction

Welcome to *Sams Teach Yourself Adobe Creative Suite 3 All in One*. This book is designed to give you a fast and easy start with the Design Premium edition of Adobe's powerhouse of creativity, design, and production tools. Adobe Creative Suite 3 Design Premium brings together Photoshop, Illustrator, InDesign, Flash Professional, Dreamweaver, and Acrobat software; an innovative file-management tool called Version Cue; and an image browser called Bridge. Together, these tools can create a smooth workflow for professional print or web design, taking into account all aspects of the design and production processes.

A recent search at Amazon.com came back with several pages of books on Photoshop alone. Considering that Adobe Creative Suite contains the fully functional versions of Photoshop, Illustrator, InDesign, Flash, Dreamweaver, and Acrobat, it's a wonder this book is anything smaller than *War and Peace*. The goal of this book isn't to overwhelm you with needless information about every single feature in every application, but rather to help you learn how to use Adobe Creative Suite as a whole to get your work done.

Organization of This Book

I've broken the book down into three parts, each taking a different approach to Adobe Creative Suite 3:

Part I: The Suite—An overall introduction to the different applications in the Creative Suite, as well as an overview of each application's strengths and weaknesses. You'll learn when to use which application, as well as get an understanding of how each application works with the others to produce a complete product. You'll also see how each application in the suite integrates with the others and how certain features are similar across the entire suite.

Part II: The Applications—An in-depth look at each individual application in Adobe Creative Suite 3 Design Premium. Part I of the book gave you an understanding of when to use a particular application, and now Part II goes into detail about the features, functionality, and uses for Bridge, Photoshop, Illustrator, InDesign, Flash, Dreamweaver, and Acrobat.

Part III: The Projects—A collection of projects you can re-create using all the tools in Adobe Creative Suite 3 Design Premium. After becoming familiar with the workflow process and the applications themselves in Part I and Part II, you will now create a series of projects that will not only give you real-world working experience with the

Creative Suite, but also offer tips and tricks you can apply as you are working on the projects themselves. All art and files necessary to complete the projects are readily available (see below), so you can follow along to create a corporate identity, a brochure, an ad campaign, a web ad banner, and a website.

If you have some familiarity with the applications in the suite, you can read Part I and then jump to Part III to work on the projects, using Part II as a reference when you need more information about a particular feature in an application. In either case, the three sections will present the Creative Suite in a way that is not overwhelming, and before you know it you'll be creating professional-quality art and having fun at the same time!

Where to Download the Project Images

The projects in Part III of this book are all step-by-step in nature, written with the intention that you follow along on your own. You'll be creating files from scratch, getting the true feel of what it is like to work "in the real world" and all of the fonts that you'll be using already come installed with Adobe Creative Suite 3.

The fine folks at iStockPhoto.com have been kind enough to set up a specific page where you can download all of the images that you'll need to complete the projects in this book. To access and download these images, point your favorite web browser to http://www.istockphoto.com/teachyourselfcs3.php.

Conventions Used in This Book

This book uses the following conventions:

▶ Keyboard shortcuts are listed as [Macintosh key combination] (Windows key combination). Simply press the key combinations to access the menu item.

▶ New terms are in *italic* text when they are defined.

▶ CSS and HTML elements and snippets of code are set in `monospace` text.

▶ Text that you are to type is in **`bold monospace`** text.

This book also presents information in the following sidebars:

> ## By the Way
>
> **By the Way** notes present interesting information related to the discussion.

> ## Did You Know?
>
> **Did You Know?** tips offer advice or show you easier ways to do something.

> ## Watch Out!
>
> **Watch Out!** cautions alert you to a possible problem, and give you advice on how to avoid it.

PART I

The Suite

CHAPTER 1

Overview:
The Creative Process

Every child is an artist. The problem is how to remain an artist once he grows up.

Pablo Picasso

We're all creative.

It doesn't matter what job we do, but we all manage to be creative in one way or another—either in our job or just as a hobby. You don't have to be a graphic designer or an artist to be creative, either. Lawyers put together graphic presentations to demonstrate a part of a case in court. Doctors use diagrams to describe medical procedures to patients. Business professionals create snazzy charts and graphs to demonstrate future growth of their company. Parents create scrapbooks for their kids about their trip to Disney World, and grandparents distribute cute photos of all the kids to the family.

It wasn't that many years ago that professional layouts for books and magazines could be set only on special expensive typesetting machines and then mechanically put together using X-Acto blades and wax or rubber cement. Photo retouching was a costly expense that required the use of an airbrush, and printing your final art required a lengthy task of creating film color separations manually.

These days, the process is quite different. Pages for magazines are now completely laid out on a computer, incorporating high-end typography. Photographs can be combined or adjusted to just about anything, and digital presses can take files directly from the screen to the printed page. Additionally, the emergence of the Internet brings a new level of publishing and creativity to the forefront.

Technology plays a large part in the way people are creative. There are digital cameras, scanners, computers, digital printers, pressure-sensitive graphics tablets, and more. These technologies open the door to allow people to explore new ways of expressing their creativity. We all have a creative mind inside of us, and these items—along with the software that takes the most advantage of them—can help us to not only express those ideas, but do it faster and more efficiently, and maybe even have some fun in the process.

The catch, of course, is learning how to use the technology available to you to express your creativity. Think of design software as a set of tools you can use. Just as an artist may have paintbrushes, pastels, pencils, erasers, scissors, glue, or glitter (my favorite messy creative item), the Adobe Creative Suite serves as the tools to express your creativity on your computer. As a creative individual, you'll find that this knowledge gives you an edge over the competition.

Throughout this book, you'll learn what these tools are, when you should use them (and when you shouldn't), and how to use them.

The Dream Team

Adobe Creative Suite 3 Design Premium is made up of several components, each with its own set of tools that excel at specific tasks. To get a better understanding of what's included in Adobe Creative Suite 3, let's discuss each of the components and what its primary function is.

Adobe Bridge CS3

Adobe Bridge is an application that enables you to browse files visually (see Figure 1.1) and perform certain tasks that span several Creative Suite applications. From setting global color-management settings across all Suite applications at once, to performing scripts and automated tasks on files, to purchasing and downloading stock photos, Bridge acts as a central access point to all of the applications in Adobe Creative Suite 3.

Adobe Photoshop CS3

Photoshop is a pixel-based program (we'll talk more about this in Chapter 2, "So Many Applications: Which One to Use?") that excels at working with photographs and illustrations with painterly effects. Most noted for its capability to manipulate photos (see Figure 1.2), it is also used for designing web graphics.

FIGURE 1.1
Viewing document thumbnails from within Adobe Bridge.

FIGURE 1.2
The original photograph on the left, and the final photograph on the right after it was edited in Photoshop.

Adobe Illustrator CS3

Illustrator is a vector-based program (more on this in Chapter 2) that excels at creating illustrations (see Figure 1.3), logos, maps, signs, and more. Illustrator can also serve as a single-page layout tool for creating ads and posters, and for designing web pages.

FIGURE 1.3
A logo created
with Illustrator.

Adobe InDesign CS3

InDesign is a page-layout program that enables you to composite or put together entire brochures or booklets (see Figure 1.4) and even author-interactive PDF files. Robust tools such as table editors and master pages enable designers to easily compose pages and designs.

FIGURE 1.4
A typical page
layout designed
in InDesign.

Adobe Flash CS3 Professional

Flash is an interactive design program that allows you to build animations, online games, and websites (see Figure 1.5). Equipped with a timeline and a full scripting language called ActionScript, Flash has become extremely popular not only for developing cool content for the Web, but also for online games, user interfaces, and cell phone graphics.

FIGURE 1.5
A typical animated banner designed in Flash.

Adobe Dreamweaver CS3

Dreamweaver is a web-publishing program that allows you to publish and manage websites (see Figure 1.6). You can use the HTML editor to lay out individual pages of a site, as well as set up complex database-driven pages. Server-management tools and FTP functionality enable you to easily update and maintain your websites.

FIGURE 1.6
A typical web page designed in Dreamweaver.

Adobe Acrobat 8.0 Professional

Acrobat is a tool used for working with PDF (Portable Document Format) files. You can mark up and review PDF files with useful annotation tools, making it easy to get feedback from clients or co-workers (see Figure 1.7). Acrobat can also be used for filling out forms, applying digital signatures, preflighting files for printing, and previewing color separations onscreen. In addition, a new component called Acrobat Connect allows you to have meetings by sharing your screen with others over the Internet.

By the Way

The Acrobat family (as Adobe likes to call it) actually includes several programs, which is always a cause for confusion. Each product has different levels of functionality, but here are the three main versions you need to be aware of:

Adobe Reader 8 (once called Acrobat Reader) is a free program and browser plug-in that allows anyone to view and print PDF documents. This is the version most people have—with close to a billion downloads worldwide. In fact, whenever you hear people say, "Yeah, I have Adobe on my computer," they are most likely referring to the free Adobe Reader.

Adobe Acrobat 8 Standard gives users the capability to mark up and review PDF files, as well as fill out forms, apply digital signatures, and perform some other basic functions. This version is useful for people who often work with PDF files but usually do the same kinds of simple tasks. Basically, it's a scaled-back version of Acrobat Professional.

Adobe Acrobat 8 Professional is the version that ships in the Creative Suite and offers the most robust toolset of all the versions listed here, including everything mentioned previously, plus preflight tools, onscreen separations preview, editing tools, and more.

FIGURE 1.7
A marked-up PDF with comments in Acrobat.

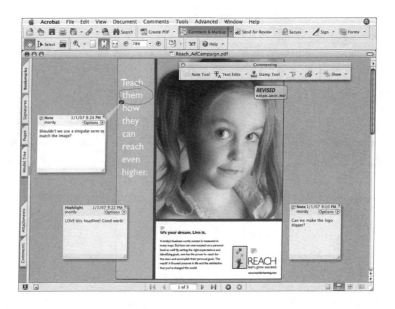

In Chapter 3, "The Game Plan: Developing a Workflow," we'll talk a lot more about PDF files and how they are used.

The Different Versions of Adobe Creative Suite 3

Adobe Creative Suite 3 is available in a variety of configurations. This book covers Adobe Creative Suite 3 Design Premium and Adobe Creative Suite 3 Design Standard, although you might find much of the content useful in other versions of the suite as well. Here is a short description of each of the available configurations.

Adobe Creative Suite 3 Design Premium

Containing full versions of Bridge, Photoshop Extended, Illustrator, InDesign, Flash Professional, Dreamweaver, and Acrobat Professional, Adobe Creative Suite 3 Design Premium is a jam-packed collection of tools used for print and web-based publishing.

Adobe Creative Suite 3 Design Standard

Containing full versions of Bridge, Photoshop, Illustrator, InDesign, and Acrobat Professional, Adobe Creative Suite 3 Design Standard is focused on serving the needs of print-based publishing.

Adobe Creative Suite 3 Web Premium

Containing full versions of Bridge, Photoshop Extended, Illustrator, Flash Professional, Dreamweaver, Fireworks, Contribute, and Acrobat Professional, Adobe Creative Suite 3 Web Premium is a complete collection of tools for web development and publishing.

Adobe Creative Suite 3 Web Standard

Containing full versions of Bridge, Flash Professional, Dreamweaver, Fireworks, and Contribute, Adobe Creative Suite 3 Web Standard is focused on serving the needs of web-based publishing.

Adobe Creative Suite 3 Production Premium

Containing full versions of Bridge, Photoshop Extended, Illustrator, Flash Professional, Premiere Pro, After Effects, and Soundbooth, Adobe Creative Suite 3 Production Premium is a robust collection of tools for video publishing.

Adobe Creative Suite 3 Master Collection

For those who "do it all," Adobe Creative Suite 3 Master Collection combines the full versions of Bridge, Photoshop Extended, Illustrator, InDesign, Flash Professional, Dreamweaver, Fireworks, Contribute, Premiere Pro, Encore, After Effects, Soundbooth, and Acrobat Professional.

Summary

Now that we understand what Adobe Creative Suite is used for and what each of its basic components are, let's take a closer look at what each application in the Suite actually does. More importantly, we'll learn the specific tasks that each application excels at performing.

CHAPTER 2
So Many Applications: Which One to Use?

Quality is never an accident; it is always the result of high intention, sincere effort, intelligent direction and skillful execution; it represents the wise choice of many alternatives.

William A. Foster

I recently began playing golf. (I've come to realize that up until a certain age, golf is the most boring, idiotic sport in the world, but suddenly one day you become infatuated with getting this little ball in a hole.) As a beginner, here I was with a bag full of different golf clubs, all with different numbers or names, and I had absolutely no idea when I was supposed to use which one. I also had no idea whether I was supposed to use all of them in any specific order. It was actually quite confusing.

As it turns out, each golf club is made for a specific purpose. A sand wedge is used to hit golf balls out of sand traps, drivers are used to hit balls long off the tee, and various irons can be used to give the ball just the right amount of lift or distance. A good golfer knows exactly which club to use in each situation.

Likewise, when using Adobe Creative Suite, a good designer knows exactly which program to use for each situation or task.

Some jobs call for using all the tools you've got. Yet some projects might require only one or two of them. The important thing to realize is that just because you have all of these tools, you don't have to use all of them for every project. Knowing each and every feature of each and every program is also something you might not need (at least, not right away), so don't get frustrated if learning all these applications seems like an insurmountable task. Getting a basic understanding of what each of these applications can do for you is enough to get you started—the rest will come in time.

Before you can start making decisions about which application to use for each kind of job, you have to know how each application works, what tools it has, and what its strengths are. The more you know about the tools you use, the easier it will be for you to decide how best to use them to your advantage.

In this chapter, we focus on each application by itself and the tasks that each can (and can't) do. In Chapter 3, "The Game Plan: Developing a Workflow," we discuss how to use all the Adobe Creative Suite applications together to complete full projects.

Adobe Bridge CS3

Adobe Bridge is in its second version (although it's now named CS3 to better align with the rest of the products in the suite). It is released as a part of Adobe Creative Suite, although it is also included if you purchase individual versions of most Adobe applications.

Where Bridge Came From

Way back when Photoshop 7 was released, Adobe added a feature to Photoshop called the File Browser, which enabled users to quickly find the files they needed by using a visual interface. Turns out that people who used Illustrator, InDesign, and other Adobe applications wanted a way to easily browse files as well, and so Adobe completely pulled the file browser out of Photoshop and turned it into its own application, called Bridge.

What Bridge Does

Bridge acts as a hub for all the applications in the suite and actually goes far beyond simple image browsing. Adobe Bridge can perform complex searches, view and edit the metadata (descriptive information) of files without opening them, and perform time-saving tasks using scripts and functions across multiple files and applications.

You can launch Bridge as you would any other application, or you can launch it by clicking on the Go to Bridge button that appears in each of the suite applications (see Figure 2.1). Here's a small sample of the kind of functionality you'll find in Bridge CS3:

FIGURE 2.1
The Go to
Bridge button
appears in the
upper-right
corner of the
Control panel
in each
Creative Suite
application.

▶ Use a variety of preview methods and settings so you can visually browse different file types, like a lightbox (see Figure 2.2).

▶ Perform powerful searches across files using multiple criteria and file metadata. In addition, you can save searches as Collections so you can perform the same search again quickly.

▶ Use a variety of workflow scripts to perform time-saving tasks such as batch processing files, tracing images, and building customized contact sheets.

▶ Use Bridge Home to find tutorials, podcasts, and other valuable resources.

▶ Synchronize color management settings across the applications in Adobe Creative Suite.

▶ Set up and work with Version Cue servers and projects.

▶ Search, browse through, and purchase royalty-free stock photo images with the Adobe Stock Photo service.

FIGURE 2.2
Browsing
images
in Adobe
Bridge CS3.

Now that you have a better understanding of what Bridge can do, let's discuss when you should use it.

When to Use Bridge

Bridge is perfect for a variety of tasks, including the following:

▶ You just received a CD full of images from a photographer you've hired. Or you just downloaded all of the content from your digital camera. Now it's your job to find just the perfect image for the project on which you're working. With Bridge, you can narrow down your choices using hi-resolution previews and the capability to both rate and group images—all without having to physically open each file.

▶ Just last week, you were working on some files, and now you can't remember where you saved them. Using metadata as your search criteria, you can find all files that match a particular job number, font, or even a particular color.

▶ You're late for a meeting and have a folder full of images that need to be traced and converted to vectors in Illustrator. You can use Bridge's workflow scripts to have your computer do the work for you while you head out to the meeting.

▶ You're working in InDesign and need to place some images into your layout. Rather than try to figure out what files you need from your hard drive or server, drag images directly from Bridge right into your InDesign layout.

▶ You're looking for a little bit of help using a feature with which you're unfamiliar. Bridge can point you to the right resources, be it a tutorial, a movie clip, or even a podcast.

▶ You're working on a design piece and need the perfect image to convey your message. Through Bridge you can access Adobe Stock Photos where you can find, download, and purchase royalty-free images (see Figure 2.3).

Bridge CS3 is certainly faster than its predecessor, but it still isn't as quick as navigating through files in Mac OS X Finder or Windows Explorer. So while there are tremendous benefits to using Bridge, there are times when you might choose to use your desktop instead.

FIGURE 2.3
The Adobe
Stock Photos
service for
royalty-free
images is
integrated
into Bridge.

Adobe Photoshop CS3

Adobe Photoshop CS3 would have been Photoshop version 10 if Adobe had not
renamed it for the Creative Suite.

Where Photoshop Came From

What started out as a personal project for Thomas Knoll and his brother John in the
late 1980s turned into Adobe Photoshop, an image-editing program that has since
redefined how we look at computer graphics. Photoshop has since become a verb ("I
just Photoshopped his head in the picture"). And Adobe has created other products,
such as Photoshop Elements (a consumer version of Photoshop) and Photoshop
Album (a digital photo album), an endeavor that almost makes the name
Photoshop into a franchise itself.

What Photoshop Does

Adobe Photoshop is what's generally called a pixel-based (or raster-based) paint program. A raster is a matrix of dots, called *pixels*, that form to make a picture or an
image (see Figure 2.4). The number of pixels in a raster image defines the *resolution*
of that image. The resolution is usually specified as dpi (dots per inch) or ppi (pixels
per inch); you've probably heard of images being described as 300dpi, for example.
This means that for every inch in the raster image, there are 300 pixels or dots.

Think of it as a level of detail: To fit 300 pixels in 1 inch, you have to make them a lot smaller than the size of pixels you would need to fit 72 pixels in an inch. Having more and smaller pixels gives you better detail (see Figure 2.5). That's why when you hear people talk about professional-quality images, they refer to them as high-resolution images.

FIGURE 2.4
A low-resolution raster, each square representing one pixel.

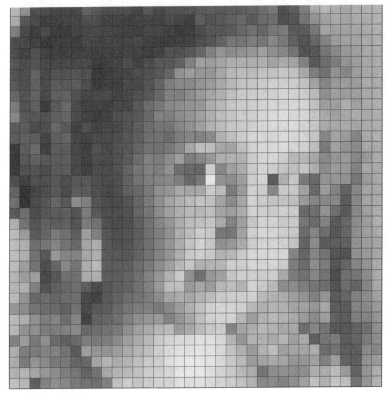

I know what you're thinking: If higher-resolution images look better, let's crank up the resolution to something like 1000dpi everywhere. Well, it's a bit more complicated than that. First, the resolution of an image is determined when the image is created. When you scan an image using an image scanner, it gets scanned at a resolution that you set; when you take a photo with a digital camera, the photo is taken at a specific resolution; and when you create a new Photoshop document, you're asked to determine what resolution you want the document to be (see Figure 2.6). After a resolution is set for an image, it can't be changed. This means that if you enlarge a 300dpi photo to be twice its size (200%), the resulting image will be 150dpi. The pixels themselves get enlarged when you scale the photo, resulting in

FIGURE 2.5
The more pixels, the better the detail.

bigger pixels. What you get is usually less than ideal, resulting in a blocklike, jagged-edge image. When an image is such that you can see the individual pixels, it is called *pixelated* (see Figure 2.7).

FIGURE 2.6
Setting the document resolution in Photoshop's New dialog box.

Okay, so I lied. You *can* change the resolution of an image using a process called resampling. Luckily, you have the best tool to resample with: Photoshop. *Downsampling* an image means you're reducing the number of pixels, such as reducing a 300dpi image to 72dpi for use on the Web. Basically, extra pixels are thrown out of the image to bring the resolution down. *Upsampling* occurs when you increase the number of pixels in an image. Photoshop uses a process called interpolation to create the necessary extra pixels—but increasing the number of pixels won't increase the level of detail or make for a better image.

By the Way

Photoshop might rely on resolution, but its power lies in how it can manipulate those individual pixels. A wide range of pixel-based tools and effects gives you com-

FIGURE 2.7
A pixelated
image.

plete control over any image. By *control,* I mean the capability to change each and every pixel in your image. The following is just a sample of the kinds of tools and effects Photoshop provides:

▶ Color correction and tonal filters to adjust the overall look of an image or to add special color effects, such as sepia tones

▶ Cloning tools to manipulate or retouch images, such as adding or removing items from a photo

▶ Blur and smudge effects to smooth out parts of an image or to add a sense of motion

▶ Layers and alpha channels to assist in compositing multiple images into a single image, as in a photomontage or collage

▶ Optimization settings and Web previews to easily specify image formats such as GIF, JPEG, and SWF

▶ Slice tools to cut up images into HTML tables for better and more flexible design options

▶ An animation palette to help create graphics that move for the Web

▶ A Quick Selection tool and other selection tools to choose which parts of an image you want to adjust or work with

If any of the terms listed here—HTML, GIF, and so forth—aren't familiar to you, don't worry; we cover each of these in detail in Chapter 6, "Using Adobe Photoshop CS3."

I'd like to focus on that last item for a moment. The one thing you'll do most often within Adobe Creative Suite is select things. Until the day comes when computers can read our minds (and I constantly live in fear, knowing that day will come), we have to tell Photoshop—or any program, for that matter—what we want to do. More specifically, we need to indicate what part of the image (or the page, the illustration, and so on) we want to work with. As you'll come to see, your options for the kinds of functions you can apply depend on your selection. It's hard to change the font for some text if you have a blue circle selected. We discuss how to make selections as we cover each of the programs in Part II, "The Applications."

Now that you have a better understanding of what Photoshop can do, let's discuss when you should use this tool.

When to Use Photoshop

Photoshop is perfect for various tasks, including the following:

▶ If a photograph is too yellow, too dark, or too blurry, or just needs adjustments in the highlights or shadows, you can access all kinds of tools and functions to make it just the way you want it—such as the cool Shadow/Highlight feature, for example. Likewise, blemished photos (ones with fingerprints, scratches, or cracks) or old, damaged photographs can be repaired with cloning tools or Photoshop's spectacular Healing Brush tool.

▶ Photo compilations such as collages and montages are perfect for Photoshop. With layers, masks, alpha channels, and more, Photoshop is well equipped to combine multiple images into single compositions.

▶ Photoshop excels at web design. Many of the websites you see every day are designed using Photoshop. Because Photoshop allows for such precise control over the individual pixels of an image, designers can tweak pixel-based web graphics to perfection.

▶ Web design is only half the job. Preparing graphics for the Web, such as optimizing, slicing, and adjusting the number of colors (otherwise called Web production) is just as important. Photoshop is perfect for this kind of work.

▶ Do you consider yourself an artist? Photoshop is often used for digital painting and fine art. Attach a pressure-sensitive graphics tablet (such as a Wacom tablet) to your computer, and you can take advantage of Photoshop's powerful brush engine to create paintings and original art.

▶ Final art preparation and production is a necessary task in just about every project. Whether it's resizing a photo, converting an image from RGB to CMYK or from a JPEG to a TIFF, or specifying spot colors for a duotone, Photoshop is up to the task. A perfect utility tool, Photoshop can both open and export a wide range of file formats.

As you can see, Photoshop can be used to perform a wide range of tasks, but keep in mind that there are certain things you don't want to use Photoshop for. Because it's pixel-based, you want to avoid using Photoshop for art that will be scaled to different sizes (logos, for instance). Things that might require a lot of editing or changes, such as text headlines, should also be avoided because it's time-consuming to make those changes in Photoshop.

Adobe Illustrator CS3

Adobe Illustrator CS3 would have been Illustrator version 13 if Adobe had not renamed it for the Creative Suite.

Where Illustrator Came From

After inventing PostScript, a computer language specifically tailored for printing graphics on printers, John Warnock devised a program that would enable people to draw in PostScript. This became Adobe Illustrator. The first software program that Adobe sold, Illustrator was released in 1987 and has since come a long way from being a simple vector drawing program. It now does great 3D effects, transparency, web graphics, vector tracing, and more.

What Illustrator Does

Described as a vector-based drawing program, Illustrator uses mathematical outlines (called Bézier curves) to define paths and shapes. Unlike Photoshop, which works with individual pixels, Illustrator is object based, meaning that you work with things such as shapes, lines, and text objects instead of a bunch of little dots. Don't get the idea that Illustrator is a kids' drawing program, though—nothing could be further from the truth. Illustrator has the capability to create art that is so photo-realistic, you'd think it was created in Photoshop (see Figure 2.8).

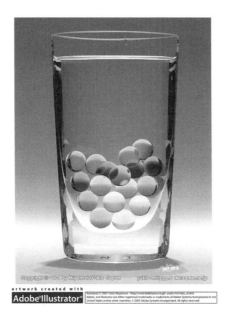

FIGURE 2.8
This photo-realistic vector artwork was created in Adobe Illustrator (it's included as a sample file with Illustrator).

Let's take a deeper look at what vector graphics are and how they work. In the early 1960s, a fellow by the name of Pierre Bézier developed a computer drawing system that consisted of points and paths to help design aircraft and cars (those paths would come to be known as Bézier paths). Think of the points and paths like those connect-the-dots exercises you did as a kid (although, if you're anything like me, you still enjoy doing them). There are dots, which we call anchor points, and the lines that connect them, which we call paths. In the world of vectors, there are two kinds of paths, closed and open (see Figure 2.9). A closed path is one in which the path starts at one anchor point and then finishes at that same anchor point, whereas an open path doesn't.

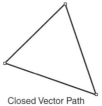

Open Vector Path   Closed Vector Path

FIGURE 2.9
An open vector path and a closed one.

At a basic level, every vector object has two attributes, a fill and a stroke (see Figure 2.10). The fill is the part that fills up the area inside the path, and the stroke is the actual path itself. You can apply colors and settings to the fill of an object, the stroke, or both.

FIGURE 2.10
The stroke and fill of a vector object.

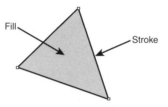

You're probably asking yourself how Illustrator can create complex artwork if all it does is connect straight paths among all these anchor points. Good question. Well, it turns out that not all anchor points are created equal. In fact, Illustrator employs three kinds of anchor points (see Figure 2.11): corner points, smooth points, and combination points. Each kind controls how the paths that connect to it are drawn.

FIGURE 2.11
The three kinds of anchor points.

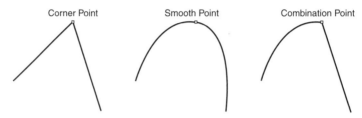

A good way to quickly grasp the concept of drawing with Bézier paths is to understand that you don't draw the paths. What you are really drawing are the anchor points, the dots. Illustrator does the rest, automatically connecting the dots with paths, based on how you place those anchor points.

A vector shape can be made up of any combination of anchor points, so you can already get an idea of how precise vector graphics can be (see Figure 2.12). Illustrator's Pen tool enables you to draw these vector shapes, as well as edit existing vector paths.

FIGURE 2.12
A complex vector path made of different kinds of anchor points.

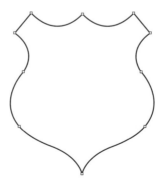

You'll find a lot more than just the Pen tool in Illustrator, however. Here's a small sample of the kinds of tools and features you'll find in Illustrator:

▶ Illustrator has spectacular 3D and artwork-mapping capabilities, making it easy to create not only the coolest art, but also realistic packaging mockups.

▶ Many designs utilize parts of artwork repeatedly (logos, design elements, and so on), and Illustrator manages these artfully with the Symbols palette. Special tools let you spray symbols on your page, taking creativity to a new level.

▶ A tracing feature enables you to convert pixel-based images into vector artwork.

▶ A Save for Web feature enables you to export web graphics in just about any web format you might need, such as GIF, JPEG, SWF, or SVG.

▶ A seemingly endless supply of vector drawing tools makes it as easy as possible to help you draw art, including Pen, Pencil, and Brush tools. There is also a Polygon tool, a Line tool, an Arc tool, and a Grid tool—even a vector Flare tool.

▶ You'll find a wide range of what Illustrator calls Live Effects, such as Drop Shadow for adding those nice soft shadows, Feather for giving vector shapes a soft edge, and many other effects—even Photoshop ones such as Gaussian Blur.

▶ Illustrator's Pathfinder palette makes editing vector shapes a breeze by giving you a plethora of options that let you combine shapes, cut holes in them, and more, all at the click of a button.

▶ Illustrator contains a wealth of text options that enable you to set the perfect line or paragraph of type, as well as have text run along a free-form path.

▶ Powerful Enveloping, Warp, and Liquefy tools enable you to twist, squeeze, bend, and distort art to your heart's desire.

▶ A Mesh tool and a Blend tool enable you to achieve painterly effects and smooth blends and gradations between colors—all vector, all the time.

▶ Illustrator has an innovative Variables palette for helping to generate artwork automatically using scripting and a database.

Now that you have a better understanding of what Illustrator can do, let's discuss when you should use it.

Did you Know?

> You'll also find the vector Pen tool in Photoshop, Flash, and InDesign. In fact, many of the applications in Adobe Creative Suite share similar tools, which we discuss in detail in Chapter 4, "The Key That Makes It All Work: Integration."

When to Use Illustrator

Illustrator is perfect for various tasks, including the following:

▶ Most people use Illustrator for logo design and corporate identity. Because logos are continually scaled to different sizes (anywhere from a button on a website to a highway billboard or the side of a blimp), creating them as vector artwork is a must.

▶ As if the name of the program wasn't enough of a hint, Illustrator is the tool of choice for fine art and illustration. Illustrator's diverse and flexible toolset allows for a wide variety of stylized artwork. Many of Illustrator's tools also have support for pressure-sensitive tablets, to allow artists to put their ideas on screen easier, with more control.

▶ With a full selection of text tools and the capability to place raster images into a file, Illustrator is a great single-page layout tool for creating flyers, advertisements, or sales sheets.

▶ Walk down the aisle of your favorite supermarket and take a look at all the packages on the shelves. Chances are, just about every package you see was created with Illustrator. Package design demands unlimited creative options, custom color support, and reliable printing—all attributes of Illustrator.

▶ Because most graphics on the Web are rasters, most people don't think of Illustrator when they think of web design. The truth is, Illustrator is a great tool for designing web graphics. Illustrator's Save for Web feature lets you export optimized web graphics directly, or you can bring art directly into Photoshop or Flash. An added benefit is that if you ever need to use those graphics for print, you don't need to re-create the art at a higher resolution— you can use it right from Illustrator for just about any task.

▶ In Illustrator, you can open and edit Illustrator files, EPS files (PostScript), PDF files, SVG (Scalable Vector Graphics) files, DXF/DWG files (AutoCAD)—even native FreeHand and CorelDRAW files. Illustrator can also export files in all kinds of formats, making it a valuable production and utility tool. Between Photoshop and Illustrator, you'll be able to open and work with just about any kind of file you might get your hands on.

▶ Graphs and charts are used to graphically represent numbers or other data that might be hard to grasp just by looking at a bunch of numbers. Illustrator's Graph tool enables designers to quickly create eye-catching and appealing infographics that can be incorporated into annual reports, newsletters, and business presentations.

▶ Going beyond the static image, Illustrator can convert layered and blended art into art that animates or moves when exported as a Flash (SWF) file. Illustrator is also used for creating art that is used in traditional animation such as television cartoons and animated motion pictures.

▶ Maps, environmental graphics (such as signs), and architectural drawings require Illustrator's precise vector tools and unique capability to structure art using layers, sublayers, groups, and subgroups.

It quickly becomes obvious that Illustrator is a powerful application that can perform a wide range of tasks. Keep in mind, however, that Illustrator can contain only one page per document, so it isn't ideal for layouts such as newsletters, books, magazines, and other documents that require several pages. Although you can place raster images into an Illustrator document, you can't edit the individual pixels, such as taking red eye out of a photo.

Adobe InDesign CS3

Adobe InDesign CS3 would have been InDesign version 5 if Adobe had not renamed it for the Creative Suite.

Where InDesign Came From

There is a lot of history behind InDesign. It started way back in 1986, when a company called Aldus introduced PageMaker, a ground-breaking program (most likely responsible for the era that would define the term *desktop publishing*) that enabled users to lay out pages on a computer screen and set type. As PageMaker evolved, it lost ground in the professional design community to competitor QuarkXPress. Adobe took ownership of PageMaker in 1994, but the technology that it was based on was limited in what it could do. Adobe began work on what it dubbed "the Quark Killer," which was code-named K2. When K2 was finally named InDesign 1.0 and launched in 1999, it was greeted with little fanfare. Sure, there was hype, but being a version 1.0 product, it simply had too many issues that prevented people from using it. When Adobe released InDesign 2.0 in January 2001, it was a whole new ballgame.

Fast-forward to the present, and the battle ensues between QuarkXPress and InDesign—although, if you read the press reviews or the various forums on the Internet, Adobe already seems to have won the battle. There is a definite turn of the tide in today's industry, as both designers and printers continue to move to adopt InDesign.

What InDesign Does

InDesign is generally called a page-layout program. Also dubbed an aggregate tool, InDesign basically enables you to gather content that was created in other applications and position the elements on a page to create a completed design. For example, to create a page of a catalog, you'd set up a page in InDesign, place a product photo you touched up in Photoshop, place the company logo you created in Illustrator, and import some text from Microsoft Word (see Figure 2.13). When you had the elements on the page, you could experiment with your design, moving the items around and adjusting them to complete your page design.

FIGURE 2.13
Working with different elements on a page in InDesign.

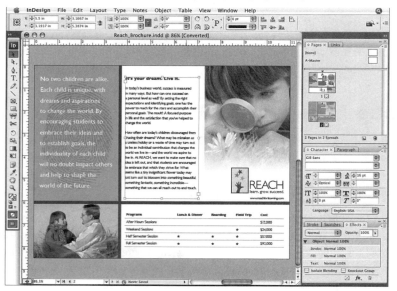

Whether you're producing a magazine, a newsletter, or a brochure, nothing is more important than the way the text looks on your page. InDesign has many strengths, but typography is definitely first on that list because it was built to set perfect type quickly and consistently.

A professional designer pays close attention to how a paragraph of text reads. Things such as kerning and tracking (the amount of spacing between letters and words), justification (how text lines up to the margins), leading (pronounced "led-ding," the amount of space between lines), and the number of hyphens can make the difference between a block of text that's easy to read and one that gives the reader a headache (see Figure 2.14). Various special characters such as curly quotes and ligatures (special character combinations such as fi, ffi, fl, and ffl) can really make an impact on the visual appearance of text as well.

> It was the last day of summer and the weather couldn't have been nicer. Labor Day was always crowded at the beach and so we loaded up the minivan and headed for the shore. After liberal helpings of sunblock, off we ran to the hot sand and cool, crashing waves. We got the perfect spot too, and before you knew it, there were everywhere. Laughing, smiling, giggling, running, or just sitting — everyone was enjoying the sun and the last day of summer.
>
> It was the last day of summer and the weather couldn't have been nicer. Labor Day was always crowded at the beach and so we loaded up the minivan and headed for the shore. After liberal helpings of sunblock, off we ran to the hot sand and cool, crashing waves. We got the perfect spot too, and before you knew it, there were people everywhere. Laughing, smiling, giggling, running, or just sitting — everyone was enjoying the sun and the last day of summer.

FIGURE 2.14
The difference between good (right) and bad (left) typography.

Adobe InDesign offers features such as paragraph styles that enable you to store all the information we just talked about, as well as specify font attributes, size, color, and more—all in a setting you can apply with one click of a button. For example, you can have paragraph styles (see Figure 2.15) set up for how you want a headline, body text, or a caption to look and have any text in your document match those attributes instantly.

FIGURE 2.15
InDesign's Paragraph Styles panel.

What really makes InDesign shine above the competition is how it fits with all the things you need to do in the design process (something called workflow), which we talk about in intimate detail in Chapter 3. But just to give you an idea of what we're talking about, InDesign understands native files from other applications in the Creative Suite, so you can easily drop native Illustrator, Photoshop, and PDF files into your InDesign layout. InDesign also exports PDF files directly, letting you effort- lessly send proofs to clients or co-workers for review and approval.

Of course, InDesign contains a lot more than professional type tools. Here's a sam- ple of the kinds of tools and features you'll find in InDesign:

▶ InDesign has a powerful table editor for quickly laying out tables that can flow from one page to another.

▶ Text-wrap controls can help create designs in which text follows the irregular shape of images, as well as other creative options.

▶ InDesign's Story Editor enables you to make quick edits by displaying text in a word processor–like window, while it updates live in your layout.

▶ To make it easy, fast, and reliable to set type consistently, InDesign has para- graph and character style sheets.

▶ You don't have to worry about how good your spelling is because InDesign contains a handy spell checker.

▶ InDesign offers the capability to apply such transparency effects as Photoshop- style blend modes and soft drop shadows.

▶ OpenType is a new standard for type, and InDesign can take full advantage of all the features that OpenType brings. InDesign also has a handy Glyph palette to help you find just the glyph (or character) you need from any font.

▶ InDesign saves you time with an innovative Edit Original feature, which enables you to quickly edit and update art that was placed into a layout.

▶ When it comes time to print your file, InDesign has a full-featured Print dialog box that enables you to print color separations. InDesign even has an onscreen Separation Preview feature.

▶ InDesign features an Export command for quickly creating PDFs that you can send to others for review.

Now that you have a better understanding of what InDesign can do, let's discuss when you should use it.

When to Use InDesign

InDesign is perfect for various tasks, including the following:

- ▶ Product brochures and folders are perfect layout tasks for InDesign. These types of jobs normally include placing content from Photoshop and Illustrator, and demand consistent typography and table layouts.

- ▶ InDesign has specific long-document support that makes it great for designing and laying out books. Besides all the benefits you get with professional-looking typography, InDesign can generate a table of contents automatically, can assist in generating indexes, and has a feature that will "stitch" several files together (individual chapters) to create an entire book with correct page numbering throughout.

- ▶ Magazines and newspapers usually require quick assembly but also demand the capability to create eye-catching designs that will generate interest in subscribers and readers. InDesign gives designers creative features such as transparency effects, resulting in more creative options.

- ▶ Most advertisements you see don't have much text (people just don't seem to have time to read anymore), but that doesn't mean you can't use InDesign to design great ads. InDesign can export files directly in the PDF/X-1a standard, which is used in the advertising industry.

- ▶ Some documents, such as newsletters and periodicals, are based on templates and are published very often, which makes them perfect for the powerful text features in InDesign. The built-in Story Editor makes these specific tasks easy to do because you don't need to scroll through complex layouts to change a few words of text.

- ▶ Catalogs—you know, the ones you receive in the mail almost daily—utilize just about every aspect of what InDesign can do (complex layouts, tables, text treatments, and more). And InDesign's high-resolution preview mode enables you to position photos and art precisely, and gives you a better idea of what the entire page will look like when printed.

- ▶ Whether you're designing a CD cover for the latest best-selling pop sensation or creating a DVD cover for your recent family vacation to San Jose (to visit Adobe, of course), InDesign helps you specify custom page sizes, bleeds, trim marks, fold marks, and more to ensure that your job prints as it should.

- ▶ As technology pushes the publishing industry forward, standards such as XML are becoming even more important. InDesign's capability to automatically flow and maintain structured content makes it perfect for XML-based workflows.

▶ At the end of the day, printing your job flawlessly is most important. InDesign contains a wealth of features to ensure quality output every time, including the capability to preview color separations. InDesign makes for a wonderful print production tool.

After discussing how InDesign is used, you should have a better understanding of why it's called an aggregate tool, gathering content from different sources to complete a layout. Although InDesign is also capable of handling complete projects from scratch on its own, it is usually better to use InDesign's Edit Original feature to link graphics and edit them in the apps that handle specialized tasks better. Don't mistake InDesign for a web design tool though—web design is better left to applications like Dreamweaver.

Adobe Flash CS3 Professional

Adobe Flash CS3 would have been Flash version 9 if Adobe had not renamed it for the Creative Suite.

Where Flash Came From

In the mid 1990s, the Web was almost completely pixel based. The most common image formats were low-resolution GIF and JPEG files, making for low-quality printouts of web pages, and few options for interacting with those images on screen. A company called FutureSplash created a web-browser plugin to allow for the display of vector-based images on the Web. More importantly, the format was also interactive, allowing designers to create animations.

In the late 90s, Macromedia bought FutureSplash and named the product and the technology Flash. Flash quickly grew in popularity because of its capability to create interactive animations with sound while keeping file sizes relatively small. In addition, Flash had a scripting language called ActionScript, which allowed designers and developers to create highly interactive content, such as online games and complex interfaces. It is rumored that one of the driving forces behind the merger of Adobe and Macromedia was Adobe's desire to acquire Flash and its technology.

What Flash Does

At the core, Flash is a web-based animation tool. But defining it as such would be overlooking what Flash really offers, which is a development platform for interactive design. That means Flash can be used to develop content for all kinds of uses—and not only for the Web, either. Flash is being used today to drive user interfaces and applications on cell phones and in cars. Tomorrow it could be your microwave or your wristwatch. And many components of Flash and what it supports, including video capabilities, help drive popular sites such as YouTube. But before we go too far, let's begin with a basic understanding of what Flash itself actually does.

Flash uses a frame-based animation model. That means there's a timeline with keyframes that determine how content changes and moves (see Figure 2.16). Because Flash uses vectors for its art, you can easily manipulate objects and layers much like you can in Illustrator. In fact, you can even draw elements in Illustrator and then bring them into Flash to make them move. After you've created your artwork, you can also specify how users will interact with your artwork. For example, you might use ActionScript to determine that when a user clicks and drags on an object, a music clip starts playing. You can even use Flash to develop an online gaming experience.

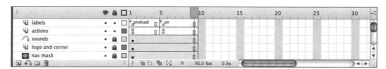

FIGURE 2.16
The timeline in Flash CS3.

In reality, Flash is an application that serves two kinds of people. Designers look at Flash as a way to extend their creative vision, and to create artwork that goes beyond the capabilities of the printed page. On the other hand, developers see Flash as a powerful platform that they can use to develop interactive applications (see Figure 2.17), interfaces, and a new generation of Rich Internet Applications (commonly referred to as RIAs).

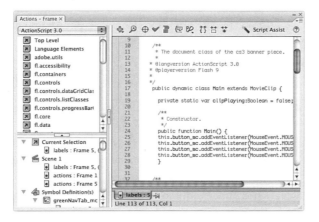

FIGURE 2.17
The Actions panel in Flash provides a powerful coding environment where developers can write ActionScript.

Flash content (.swf files) does require the Adobe Flash Player to view it. The player is included in the installers of today's most popular web browsers, however, and recent data released by Adobe shows that 98% of computers have the player installed. To take advantage of the latest Flash files and ActionScript 3.0 though, users must download and install the latest version of the Adobe Flash Player (a free download from Adobe's website). Adobe was also recently awarded an Emmy for its Flash Video technology, as many networks have moved to the Flash platform to deliver their TV shows and broadcast content online and on mobile devices.

With this introduction, let's take a look at some of the features and functions that are available in Flash:

▶ The vector-based drawing tools in Flash allow you to create content that can be scaled in a web browser without loss in quality or detail.

▶ Flash is built on a powerful scripting language called ActionScript, which allows you to develop logic and higher levels or programmatic interactivity. Flash CS3 features the new ActionScript 3.0 language, which is more powerful and easier to use than previous versions.

▶ Flash enables you to build animated content via the use of a frame-based timeline. This allows you to determine how elements move, when they should appear in a scene, and how the elements should interact with each other.

▶ At the core of its graphics engine, Flash utilizes symbols, which is a way to create a graphic once in a document, and then to have all other instances of that graphic simply reference that one original copy. In this way, you can create complex designs that take up little file space.

▶ Symbols can contain all kinds of attributes including animation, rollovers, links, and even sound. So user interface elements can animate and make sounds as you interact with them.

▶ You don't have to create all of your content in Flash. You can create artwork in both Photoshop and Illustrator, and then seamlessly move that content into Flash. For example, symbols can be defined in Illustrator first, and then be copied and pasted, with all settings intact, directly into Flash.

▶ Flash can import video content and contains a variety of encoding options so you can set your video to play back as you specify.

Now that you have a better understanding of what Flash can do, let's discuss when you should use it.

When to Use Flash

Flash is perfect for various tasks, including the following:

▶ When you want to give your website the perfect touch, you can use Flash to design and create a fully interactive user interface, with features such as animated buttons and elements that hide and show themselves as the user moves the mouse pointer around the screen. Most importantly, you can also integrate music and sounds to make a truly complete experience.

▶ Flash does a wonderful job when it comes to creating interactive web banners. When you need to create ads that are small in file size and that need to grab people's attention, Flash offers the tools to make it happen quickly and easily.

▶ Just because Flash can create complete interactive experiences doesn't mean you can't use it to create small, simple illustrations. Flash is perfect for adding helpful and interesting graphics to your website, especially if you consider that graphics and text print out looking much better when using Flash than they would if you were using, for example, animated GIFs.

▶ A Flash-based presentation is a great way to promote yourself, your business, or your project. Flash presentations can be viewed over the Web or offline, giving you the ability to create highly interactive content that goes far beyond an ordinary slide presentation.

▶ The Internet is filled with online games. Using Flash and ActionScript, you can design and develop interactive games.

Although it's easy to get started using Flash, learning to take advantage of advanced features and to write ActionScript code can be daunting, especially if you've never written scripts before. Flash does offer an incredible array of features and options, but there are also times when you might find it easier to export Flash content directly from Illustrator or Photoshop instead. As with anything, it all depends on the needs of the particular job.

Adobe Dreamweaver CS3

Adobe Dreamweaver CS3 would have been Dreamweaver version 9 if Adobe had not renamed it for the Creative Suite.

Where Dreamweaver Came From

Whether or not you believe that the Internet was invented by Al Gore, the World Wide Web has pushed professional publishing and design to a new level. The tools to help publish rich web experiences have evolved as well. Back in the day (um, like several years ago), creating web graphics and publishing websites of any kind required an intimate knowledge of HTML, Unix-based systems and commands, and more. Hypertext Markup Language (HTML) is the code that defines how a web page should appear. (We talk in more detail about HTML later in this book.) At the time when Internet IPOs meant instant wealth and early retirement, a slew of WYSIWYG (what you see is what you get) HTML editors were released. Similar in concept to PageMaker or QuarkXPress, these programs, such as Adobe PageMill, attempted to allow designers to easily lay out pages without having to learn or know how to code HTML. There weren't many success stories. A promotional QuarkXPress poster at the time proclaimed, "HTML is just like typesetting—yeah, like typesetting from 20 years ago."

Macromedia set out to change that by introducing Dreamweaver—an application that was geared toward the development of websites. Quickly becoming the industry-standard website tool because of its support for web standards and professional coding features, Macromedia Dreamweaver became Adobe Dreamweaver when the two companies merged.

What Dreamweaver Does

At first glance, Dreamweaver seems like an incredibly complex program, but on closer inspection, it begins to make a lot of sense. That's because Dreamweaver takes care of just about every aspect of the process, from planning a website to designing it and publishing it to the Internet. If you had to make a comparison with a program such as InDesign, you'd have to give InDesign storyboards for planning your entire project, and then you'd need to add a printing press, to boot.

Let me explain. One of the most incredible aspects of the World Wide Web is how quickly you can distribute information. The Web is a medium that offers the capability to publish information so quickly—even in real time—to anywhere in the world. This can happen because the information is electronic; publishing information on the Web is as simple as copying a file from your computer to another computer (a server or "host"). Dreamweaver possesses the tools to perform all the steps involved in this process. There are site-layout tools to help you plan your website, a full range of web page layout tools, and a complete set of tools to upload your site to a server.

Much like Flash, Dreamweaver lives a double life. As a design tool, it allows you to lay out and design pages for your website. On the other hand, Dreamweaver is an extremely powerful web development tool that allows developers to write scripts and code (see Figure 2.18). Even more important, however, Dreamweaver embraces open standards like Cascading Style Sheets (CSS), Dynamic HTML (xHTML), and a new Spry Framework that allows increased website interactivity with little upfront work. Dreamweaver also features an impressive browser check feature so you can be sure that your site will appear correctly on any web browser. And Dreamweaver is linked to Adobe's new CSS Advisor website, so even if you aren't familiar with some of the latest web standards, you can quickly learn what you need (in addition to what you're already learning in this book, of course).

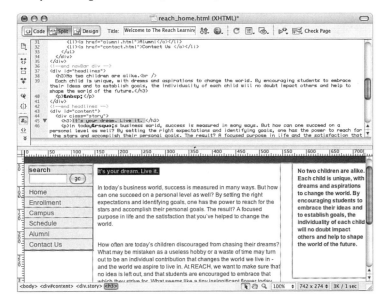

FIGURE 2.18
The Split view mode in Dreamweaver allows you to see and edit both your code (top) and your design (bottom) simultaneously.

The final part of the web publishing process involves uploading your website to a server, a process called taking your site "live." Dreamweaver has a full range of site-management features (see Figure 2.19) that make it easy to track changes across your entire site, as well as manage updates and modifications. Basically, Dreamweaver knows exactly what needs to be uploaded when you modify your website and can do so at the click of a button. Dreamweaver also makes it easy to administer a site so that you can have several people contributing to or updating different parts of your site simultaneously.

FIGURE 2.19
The Files panel keeps your local files and your server in sync.

It's important to realize that some web design firms break up these processes into completely different departments. Site designs are done by information architects, web designers create the look of the site, and web developers oversee the technical aspects of coding and maintaining the site. Dreamweaver can handle all these tasks if you're a department of one, but if you are part of a team, you can focus on just the part of Dreamweaver that you need. Of course, Dreamweaver has a whole range of features, some of which we mention here:

▶ To help more and more people develop their sites with the added benefit of CSS, Dreamweaver contains a wealth of CSS-based templates and starter documents. Not only do these files help you get started quickly, the templates contain a wealth of comments that explain how to customize the settings to your exact needs and specifications.

▶ With an added level of integration, you can copy and paste content from Photoshop directly into your page design in Dreamweaver. And if changes need to be made, you can double-click the art to edit the original layered image content right in Photoshop.

▶ Dreamweaver's Insert bar makes it easy to add all kinds of elements to a site. As an example, you can add Spry elements, like sliding buttons or accordions, to jazz up a web design and improve the page's usability simply by dragging an icon into your page.

▶ For publications published simultaneously to print and to the Web, Dreamweaver and InDesign can share XML content.

▶ A Browser Compatibility Check feature checks your page and identifies any issues that might exist on specific browsers. For example, Dreamweaver might inform you that a page won't look correct when viewed in Internet Explorer 6 on Windows. Dreamweaver will not only show you exactly where in your code the problem exists, it will even offer advice via the CSS Adviser website on how to solve the issue.

▶ Dreamweaver has full File Transfer Protocol (FTP) capabilities, enabling you to upload your site directly to your web server.

▶ A website has many components, such as HTML pages, scripts, and linked graphics. Dreamweaver enables you to keep track of all of these in a single place.

▶ Paired with Adobe Contribute (available as part of Adobe Creative Suite 3 Web Premium software or as an individual product), you can set up administration rights and have other people perform updates to the website.

Now that you have a better understanding of what Dreamweaver can do, let's discuss when you should use it.

When to Use Dreamweaver

Dreamweaver is perfect for various tasks, including the following:

▶ Management is an extremely important part of maintaining a website. Dreamweaver does this exceptionally well by keeping track of links. For example, say that you change the name of a web page. Any link that might already link to that page needs to be updated with the new name. Dreamweaver automatically updates these links for you (free of charge, I might add).

▶ As alluded to earlier, Dreamweaver excels in giving the designer the capability to lay out web pages, allowing for the placement of images copied right out of Photoshop. This makes it possible to quickly implement your web designs.

▶ Although you can use Photoshop, Flash, and Illustrator to create high-impact designs for the Web, you can use Dreamweaver alone to create more straightforward and simple web designs. This is helpful for creating quick sites for internal purposes or for websites for which getting a specific look isn't a requirement.

▶ Have a website already? Dreamweaver can create new websites from scratch, or it can import a website that already exists, enabling you to take advantage of Dreamweaver's site-management features.

▶ For those who still like to write their own code, Dreamweaver can serve that purpose very well. Dreamweaver is a great tool not only for HTML coding, but for writing scripts as well.

▶ Dreamweaver has a full complement of tools for creating online forms, including adding value fields, pop-up lists, submit buttons, and more, making it a snap to create feedback forms, order forms, and the like.

If you've never been involved with web design, it might take some getting used to. Overall, though, the concepts are similar to those you've seen in the print world. Of course, just because Dreamweaver can design pages doesn't mean you should use it to design your next print brochure. As a specialized tool for all that the Web brings to the table, Dreamweaver will fit your needs today and for the future as well.

Adobe Acrobat 8 Professional

Adobe Acrobat doesn't have the same CS3 moniker as the other applications in the Suite, mainly because it plays a large role as an enterprise-level business application as well as a graphics tool. In addition, while Acrobat Professional is an integral part of Adobe Creative Suite, it was developed according to a different timeline and was actually released several months before Adobe Creative Suite 3 was even announced.

Where Acrobat Came From

In an effort to be able to view a document—as it was carefully designed—on just about any computer in the world, John Warnock and the folks at Adobe came up with the *Portable Document Format* (PDF). Acrobat would be the name of the product that could display these PDF files, which would look right, fonts and all, on any computer. Adobe created a version of Acrobat called Acrobat Reader, which it gave away free of charge. The full version of Acrobat was still needed to *create* PDF files (a process called *distilling*), so the company made money selling the full version of Acrobat—and people who created these documents were assured that anyone could view those documents with the free reader. Nice concept, eh?

What Acrobat Does

Chances are, you've seen a PDF file before. Of course, the initial benefit of working with PDF files is that you're safe knowing that what you are creating on your screen will look right on someone else's computer. There are many other benefits, such as the capability to password-protect your PDF file so that only the people who are supposed to see it are able to. Adobe Acrobat 8 Professional basically enables you to take control of your PDF files.

Let's start from the beginning. Acrobat enables you to create PDF files in several ways:

- ▶ You can print your file from any application to an Acrobat Printer, which was installed when you installed Acrobat.

- ▶ You can use the Distiller part of Acrobat (it's a separate application that comes with Acrobat) to create PDF files from any PostScript file.

▶ You can open just about any kind of file in Acrobat Pro and export it as a PDF. You could open existing PDF files as well if you wanted to save the PDF with different settings than it already had.

Of course, you can also export or save PDF files directly from any of the other applications in the Adobe Suite.

When you have a PDF file, Acrobat can do many things with it. What's interesting to note is that many people aren't aware of even half the things Adobe Acrobat can do (see Figure 2.20). Most people use it like the free Adobe Reader, to view and print PDF files.

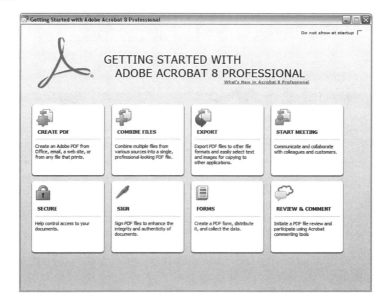

FIGURE 2.20
The Startup Screen gives you fast access to just some of the things you can do with Acrobat 8 Professional.

But let's explore how we use PDF files today and see how you can use tools such as Acrobat Pro to make your life easier (I'm sure you've heard *that* one before...). You create a PDF to send to a client or a co-worker for approval. Inevitably, there will be corrections, comments, changes, and such, so the one reviewing the document prints the file, makes some comments, and faxes it or hand-delivers it back to you. Or the person might send you an email describing the desired changes. This process might repeat itself several times before the job is ready to go. But who are we kidding here? If your job is anything like mine, at least 5—maybe even 10—people need to review that document. The next thing you know, you have emails and faxes out the wazoo, and you can't even keep track of who said what.

Acrobat has a set of commenting and reviewing tools that enables users to make comments directly in the PDF file (see Figure 2.21). For example, you can highlight or strikethrough text, add sticky notes, draw arrows, and add scribbles, as well as add dynamic "stamps" such as *Approved* or *Rejected*, with time and date stamps that note exactly when the file was approved or rejected. The client simply indicates changes in the PDF and sends the file back to you. What's better is that Acrobat lets you merge the comments of several files into a single file. So if your document is being reviewed by 10 people, you can look at a single PDF file that has comments from everyone. Each comment is identified by who created it and when it was created (see Figure 2.22). You can even print a summary of all the comments in a specific PDF—great for billing purposes.

FIGURE 2.21
Acrobat's
Annotation
toolbar.

FIGURE 2.22
Comments are
identified by
who made them
and when.

By the Way

Comments are stored in a separate "layer" on a PDF file, called Annotations. This not only keeps the original data intact, but it also enables you to save the comments into a separate file (called an FDF file). This is extremely useful when dealing with large PDF files. For example, say you send a 10MB PDF file of a catalog to a client for comments. The client can make comments and then send back just the FDF file (see Figure 2.23), saving the time it would take to keep sending that 10MB file back and forth over email.

FIGURE 2.23
The icon of an
Acrobat PDF file
(left) and that
of an FDF file
(right).

Commenting and reviewing are just a sample of the many features you'll find in Adobe Acrobat 8 Professional. Here's a partial list of the tools and features you'll soon find yourself using in Acrobat Pro:

▶ Acrobat has a fantastic feature that enables you to kick off a review process via email that automatically tracks comments and makes it easier for people who prefer to do things via email.

▶ With a full-featured Print dialog box, Acrobat can print any PDF file (with correct authorization), including creating color separations for prepress.

▶ Acrobat Pro has a Preflight tool that helps ensure that your PDF file is ready for print and that highlights the problematic areas based on preset criteria.

▶ For electronic forms and to indicate approvals, Acrobat has the capability to add digital signatures to a file.

▶ You can export PDF files to conform to any of several PDF standards, such as PDF/X-1a and PDF/X-3.

▶ Acrobat contains *touch-up* editing tools that enable you to modify text and perform certain edits to PDF files.

▶ For creating eForms, Acrobat has the capability to create form fields, buttons, and more.

▶ Acrobat has the capability to link or even embed interactive content into your PDF files, such as QuickTime movies and Flash (SWF) files.

▶ A Search tool enables you to quickly find the text you're looking for throughout an entire PDF file.

▶ Acrobat can encrypt files with passwords that enable you to control whether the document can be printed or changed. You can even use a process called Certification that enables you to specify even higher levels of security.

Now that you have a better understanding of what Acrobat Professional can do, let's discuss when you should use it.

When to Use Acrobat

Acrobat is perfect for various tasks, including the following:

▶ Acrobat is used for viewing PDF files (of course).

▶ Acrobat is the best tool for creating or resaving PDF files for various purposes, such as for PDF/X-1a or PDF/X-3 compliance, or for web-optimized viewing.

▶ With the capability to select and edit text as well as art elements, Acrobat is a great tool for making small edits or for "touching up" PDF files.

▶ As mentioned earlier, Acrobat is just the tool you need for commenting and reviewing, getting approvals, and more. The email–based review process makes it easier than ever to get people involved in the process as well.

▶ How can you be sure that your PDF files are ready to print? You can create your own Preflight profiles and check each PDF, as well as use Acrobat's onscreen Separation Preview feature to ensure that your color separations are correct. Of course, you can (and should) use Acrobat to print all your PDF files.

▶ As eForms become more popular, you can use Acrobat to fill out PDF-based forms. Not only is Acrobat a great way to work with internal forms in your company (job tickets, for example), but you also can use Acrobat to fill out forms online, such as with tax and insurance forms.

▶ Use Acrobat to digitally sign documents or authorize PDFs by certifying them. In the United States, laws have been passed to allow such signatures to be legally binding, enabling people to digitally sign mortgage documents, contracts, tax forms, and more.

▶ Protect your files by assigning passwords to limit how your PDF files can be used. Different levels of security allow for either printing the file only as a low-resolution proof, or not allowing printing or copying at all.

Chances are, you're probably a bit surprised at (if not overwhelmed by) just how much Acrobat Pro can do. Don't worry, we go into a lot more detail about each of these features in Chapter 11, "Using Adobe Acrobat 8 Professional." Although Acrobat can perform certain edits to PDF files, if you have more complex editing to do, you'll want to make those changes in the application the file was originally created in, if at all possible. As a last resort, you can always open a PDF in Adobe Illustrator (one page at a time).

Summary

We've discussed each application in Adobe Creative Suite in detail, noting where each one came from, the specific features that each can be relied on to perform, and examples of some of the key features they possess.

You should now have a clear understanding of what each of the individual applications in Adobe Creative Suite 3 Design Premium does. In the next chapter, we discuss how all these programs work together to help you complete projects (and spend your weekends at home instead of at the office).

CHAPTER 3
The Game Plan: Developing a Workflow

If you can't describe what you are doing as a process, you don't know what you're doing.

W. Edwards Deming

While you can certainly purchase Adobe Creative Suite and use just one of the applications within the collection, the real value of the Suite becomes visible when using each of the applications together in concert. One of the ways to describe the process of using multiple applications to get your work done is by defining a workflow. However, the word workflow can mean a variety of different things.

In this chapter, we'll discuss exactly what a workflow is, in the context of designing and producing artwork with Adobe Creative Suite applications, and we'll see how different types of design projects rely on the broad shoulders of Adobe Creative Suite.

What Is a Workflow?

A workflow is a process of how something gets done. It's a map that gets you from point A to point B. In other words, it's the roadmap for a project. In most cases, there are several ways to get to where you're going. Some ways might have more traffic, others nice scenery—but they all basically get you to your destination. In the business world, though, you want to get to your destination in the shortest amount of time, using the least amount of gas, and having a bit of fun at the same time—which makes your job rewarding, successful, and, most important, profitable.

In graphic design, a workflow comprises all the necessary steps that have to happen for a particular job to be completed. Obviously, whatever your final result is supposed to be will determine what the workflow is. If you're designing a piece that will be output to the Web, it will have a different workflow, or process, than a project that will end up on a printing press.

Right off the bat, it's important to realize that every workflow is different—mostly, of course, because every project has different goals, but also because there is usually more than just one way to accomplish a task. Workflows are also affected by factors you might not necessarily think about. For example, if you're a designer who is putting together a newspaper, you might be incorporating some photographs into your layout that came from prints from your local photographer. Another paper might have overseas photographers who need to submit their images digitally.

More so, there are organizations or design firms that handle nearly all the aspects of a project, and there are designers who might work on only one portion of a project. Some firms offer services from concept all the way through design. Some people are just photographers. Even so, photographers who understand the entire workflow not only can provide better services to their clients, but also can be more efficient and can avoid having to redo work later in the process.

Traditionally, a designer was required to possess and learn several software tools, each of which worked differently. A tremendous amount of work was required to make sure that all these tools worked together in some useful way. And maintaining them was challenging (to say the least) because each of the tools had different upgrade cycles, causing constant workflow changes.

The Adobe Creative Suite is unique because it provides all the tools necessary for a design workflow. Because of the integration among the applications in the Suite, it's easy to move your project along each step of the process. And because these applications all work in the same way, you don't have to tear your hair out learning about all kinds of programs to get your work done. Most important, Adobe has aligned each of the products in the suite to release at the same time, making it easier to develop and maintain a workflow.

The workflows you find here are guidelines to give you a better idea of how the applications work together and what the process might be for different kinds of projects. They work in a majority of cases; however, specialized tasks or functions might require a modified workflow. By all means, feel free to customize and expand on the workflows mentioned here to achieve the workflow required for your particular needs.

As you read through the rest of this chapter, you might feel the urge to skip particular areas because they don't pertain to the kinds of things you are doing today. For example, you might want to skip anything related to the Web because you work primarily in print-related materials. My advice is to at least get a basic understanding of other workflows because you never know what might come your way. This way, if you end up getting an opportunity to do such work—even if you're going to out-source it—you'll have a complete understanding of the process and what needs to happen. If I had a nickel for every time I've heard someone say "I lost so much money because I told them I could do it, but I had no idea how much work was involved," I'd have enough money for one of those fancy shmancy 30-inch flat-panel displays.

Understanding Print, the Web, and Beyond

In the 1980s, computer technology redefined print publishing. In the 1990s, the Internet and the World Wide Web took center stage as a powerful medium for com-munication. As we begin to settle into this new millennium, wireless technologies are pushing design and communication even further.

> Another workflow that is becoming more common as bandwidth increases is creat-ing content for video. Adobe Creative Suite 3 Production Premium contains the tools that can be used to create this content. The good news is that these tools, including Premiere Pro (video editing), After Effects (special effects and composit-ing), and Soundbooth (sound editing), are all applications that integrate with the apps you now have. Should the day come when you need to dive into the world of video, you'll already have some of the tools—and the knowledge—to get you started.

By the Way

As we look at the workflows specific to these different media, I'm going to focus pri-marily on the aspects that involve working with the Creative Suite directly. Obviously, many different things need to happen to communicate your (or your client's) message. For example, concepts are discussed, copy is written, sketches are drawn, and meetings with the client are endured (oh, the agony)—all before you even start working on the project. This book, however, focuses mainly on the techni-cal aspects of doing your job, not necessarily the conceptual ones. I'm going to assume here that the initial concept is done and that you have copy written.

Designing for Print

Say what you want about the future of print, but find me another medium that can provide a designer with the prospect of using an exquisite paper with embossing, foil stamping, custom die-cutting, varnishing, or various other effects that pulls a reader in and delivers a message all its own. I've seen art directors who sometimes spend days picking out just the right paper for an annual report. Use of custom inks such as metallics, pastels, or even magnetic inks (such as what's used for account numbers on bank checks) takes print a step further.

That being said, when you are designing for print, you have to be mindful of such things as image resolution, custom spot colors, transparency flattening, bleed and trim areas, folds, fonts, and color separations. Some jobs also require knowledge of government or postal regulations. Following are three workflows that are common in the area of print design.

Corporate Identity

Corporate identity projects include the creation of a logo and other materials used to identify a company or an organization. Examples are business cards, letterheads, envelopes, notes, and the like. Most corporate identity projects also focus on the branding and positioning of the company. Common applications used in this workflow are Photoshop, Illustrator, and InDesign (see Figure 3.1, shown on page 52).

Brochure

A brochure is used as an informational and marketing tool for businesses and organizations. The simplest type of brochure is printed on a letter-size page and folded into three panels (commonly referred to as a trifold or a "slim jim"). Common applications used in this workflow are Photoshop, Illustrator, and InDesign. Microsoft Word (or any other word processor) is also commonly used (see Figure 3.2, shown on page 54).

Advertising Campaign

An advertising campaign is an organized effort to publicize a company or an organization. Integrated campaigns often feature a series of ads that share a similar concept and might include print advertising, direct mail, or other methods of distribution. Common applications used in this workflow are Photoshop, Illustrator, and InDesign. Acrobat also can be used for campaign reviews (see Figure 3.3, shown on page 56).

Designing for the Web

Two approaches to web design exist: create something the same way you would for print, but adapt it to work on the Web; or create a true interactive experience from the ground up. In the early days of the Web, most sites you went to were of the former kind—page after page of large static images, garish colors, and illegible text. Granted, two main reasons for that were a lack of powerful web authoring tools and a general lack of understanding of the technical capabilities of the medium.

I should note that today's dynamic design environment has also caused a reverse of this effect. Many designers specialize in web design but have almost no knowledge of what it takes to create a quality printed piece. Those who have tried going to press with a 72dpi RGB image know what I'm talking about.

A good web designer thinks about what size monitor he expects users to have, how best to build a page that can be updated quickly and easily, how to add interactive elements to draw a reader's attention, how to provide useful navigation and links to help readers find what they're looking for, and, most important, how to communicate all of it with a design concept that delivers the right message. Some jobs also require knowledge or interfacing with back-end systems and databases. Following are three workflows that are common in the area of web design.

Web Banner

A web banner is an advertisement that appears on a website. Ever since the Internet became a place that people frequent, companies and organizations have found the Web to be an effective medium to advertise their products and services. Most web banners have to conform to specific sizes and formats. Common applications used in the creation of web banners are Photoshop, Illustrator, and Flash (see Figure 3.4, shown on page 58).

Website

What started out as a "fad" in many people's eyes has become a way of life today. Websites are used to sell products, provide information, display family pictures, and present just about anything else you might want to share with other people around the globe. Common applications used in the creation of websites are Photoshop, Illustrator, Flash, and Dreamweaver (see Figure 3.5, shown on page 60).

Designing for Both Print and the Web

Most people say that print and the Web don't mix. They might be right, but it does-n't mean that print and the Web can't coexist together peacefully. By carefully plan-ning a workflow, you can save significant time developing content that will be pub-lished both in print form and electronically on the Web.

Obviously, the goal is to create content once and then share that content between the Web and print elements you are producing. In this way, you avoid having to create and manage two sets of identical content (one for print, one for the Web). More important, if changes need to be made (show me one job in which they don't), you have to change only one set of assets instead of two. Save time, make more money, go home early. Nice, eh? Following are two workflows that are common in the area of cross-media (or mixed-media) design.

Print/Online Newsletter

Companies often create newsletters to distribute news to all the employees of the organization. With the advent of the "I need it now" mentality in today's fast-paced world, companies offer online versions of these publications as well. Cross-media (web and print) workflows are quickly becoming the norm in today's business envi-ronment. Common applications used in a cross-media workflow are Photoshop, Illustrator, InDesign, Flash, and Dreamweaver (see Figure 3.6, shown on page 62).

Interactive PDF

In a relatively short period, PDF has become a standard in the industry for distribut-ing published information. Lately, capabilities have been built into the PDF format to support interactive content. Businesses and organizations can now deliver rich media content—including hyperlinks, interactivity, and movies—in a single file that nearly everyone can view. Common applications used to create interactive PDF files are Photoshop, Illustrator, Flash, InDesign, and Acrobat (see Figure 3.7, shown on page 64).

Moving to a PDF Workflow

Undoubtedly, you've seen both Acrobat and PDF appear quite often on the work-flows listed here. In fact, one of the biggest benefits of using the Adobe Creative Suite is that you can take full advantage of PDF—mainly because support for PDF is built into the Creative Suite at almost every level. From creating PDF files and plac-ing them into your layouts, to opening PDF files, setting up PDF review cycles, and using PDF as a final delivery format, the Creative Suite ensures that it all works and fits seamlessly into your workflow.

Think about it. In the past, client reviews consisted of expensive color comps, unclear faxes, low-resolution JPEG images, and forgotten phone conversations. Today email–based PDF reviews make for an experience that's welcome to clients because they can review materials faster than ever before, as well as to designers, who can save money and track issues and make changes more efficiently than ever.

This isn't to say that moving to a complete PDF workflow is easy. There are still issues that have to be dealt with, including color-management issues (making sure that what you see on *your* screen is the same as what the client sees on *his* screen), software compatibilities (making sure that clients are using the right version of Acrobat), and more.

Switching to PDF overnight probably won't happen, but one thing is sure: After you establish a workflow and get comfortable with using the Adobe Creative Suite, you'll be able to help yourself and your clients by taking advantage of PDF where you can. Before you know it, you'll have more PDF files in your inbox than emails that promise instant huge stock investment profits (okay, maybe not...).

Summary

So many tasks can be done in any of several programs. People are always asking when Photoshop and Illustrator will combine to become one program, or when Illustrator will support multiple pages (making for less of a need for InDesign). Now that the Creative Suite is out there, it should be obvious that each tool is necessary for certain tasks. No one tool can do it all—nor should it. An arsenal of integrated tools such as the Creative Suite offers far more power and options than any single application ever could.

In the next chapter, we'll talk about integration and how all the suite applications work together as one complete graphics solution.

Workflow: Corporate Identity

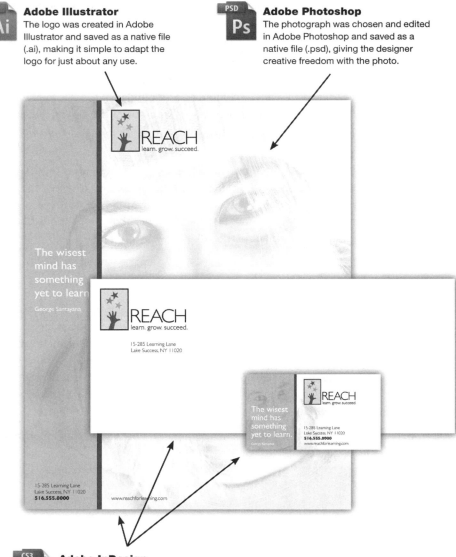

Adobe Illustrator
The logo was created in Adobe Illustrator and saved as a native file (.ai), making it simple to adapt the logo for just about any use.

Adobe Photoshop
The photograph was chosen and edited in Adobe Photoshop and saved as a native file (.psd), giving the designer creative freedom with the photo.

Adobe InDesign
The letterhead, envelope and business cards were assembled in 3 separate documents inside InDesign. The photo (.psd) and the logo (.ai) were placed into the layouts, and additional text and elements were then added to complete the design.

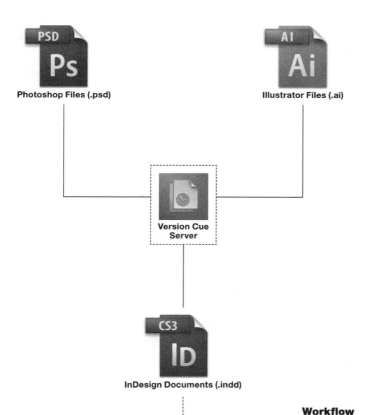

Photoshop Files (.psd)

Illustrator Files (.ai)

Version Cue
Server

InDesign Documents (.indd)

Acrobat Documents (.pdf)

Workflow

Photoshop and Illustrator files are checked into the Version Cue database. The native files are then placed into an InDesign document and positioned on the page. Other design elements, including text, are added inside InDesign. A PDF is then created and sent for client approval or to the printer for final output.

————— Standard Workflow
- - - - - - - - Optional Workflow

FIGURE 3.2
An example
of a brochure
workflow.

Workflow: Brochure

Adobe Photoshop
Several photographs were chosen and edited in Adobe Photoshop and saved as a native file (.psd), giving the designer creative freedom with the photos.

Adobe Illustrator
The logo for REACH was created in Adobe Illustrator and saved as a native file (.ai), making it simple to adapt the logo for just about any use.

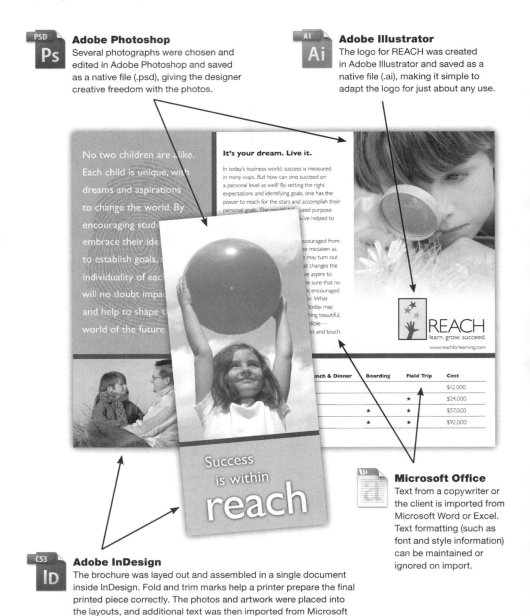

Microsoft Office
Text from a copywriter or the client is imported from Microsoft Word or Excel. Text formatting (such as font and style information) can be maintained or ignored on import.

Adobe InDesign
The brochure was layed out and assembled in a single document inside InDesign. Fold and trim marks help a printer prepare the final printed piece correctly. The photos and artwork were placed into the layouts, and additional text was then imported from Microsoft Word and styled to complete the design.

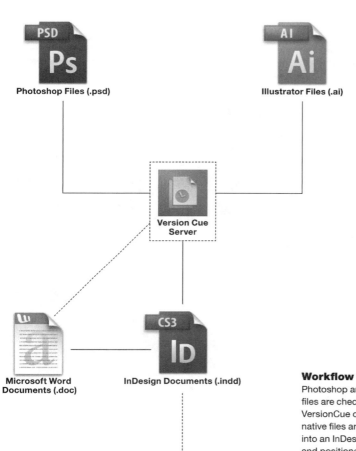

Photoshop Files (.psd)

Illustrator Files (.ai)

Version Cue Server

Microsoft Word Documents (.doc)

InDesign Documents (.indd)

Acrobat Documents (.pdf)

Workflow

Photoshop and Illustrator files are checked into the VersionCue database. The native files are then placed into an InDesign document and positioned on the page. Copy is imported from Microsoft Word or Excel and positioned on the page and styled. (Alternatively, these files can be managed in Version Cue as well.) A PDF is then created and sent for client approval or to the printer for final output.

———	Standard Workflow
--------	Optional Workflow

FIGURE 3.3
An example of
an ad campaign
workflow.

Workflow: Advertising Campaign

Adobe InDesign

The ads were assembled in a single InDesign document, where the designer can specify trim sizes as well as a slug area — a place to include specific job and client information in an area that won't print. The photos (.psd) were placed into the layout and cropped, copy was added, and the logo (.ai) was dropped in place.

Adobe Photoshop

This ad campaign relies on the powerful photos that were carefully chosen. Adobe Bridge helps designers and photographers choose the right photo for the job, and Photoshop makes them perfect.

Adobe Illustrator

The logo was created in Adobe Illustrator and saved as a native file (.ai), making it simple to adapt the logo for just about any use.

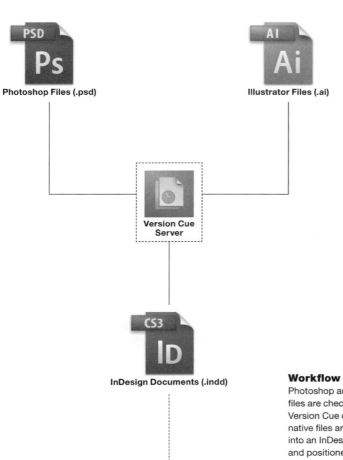

Photoshop Files (.psd)

Illustrator Files (.ai)

Version Cue Server

InDesign Documents (.indd)

Acrobat Documents (.pdf)

Workflow

Photoshop and Illustrator files are checked into the Version Cue database. The native files are then placed into an InDesign Document and positioned on the page. Other design elements, including text, are added inside InDesign. A PDF/X-1a file is then created (a PDF standard now adopted by many magazines and newspapers) and sent for client approval or to the publisher.

——————— Standard Workflow
- - - - - - - Optional Workflow

FIGURE 3.4
An example of a web banner workflow.

Workflow: Web Banner

Adobe Photoshop
Stock photography was chosen and edited in Adobe Photoshop. Photoshop files (.psd) can then be opened or placed into Illustrator or Flash.

Adobe Illustrator
The ad banner was designed in Illustrator, allowing elements of the design to be repurposed for print projects easily if necessary. The file was saved as a native Illustrator file (.ai) and opened in Flash.

Adobe Flash Professional
Once the design is created in Photoshop and Illustrator, the art is brought into Flash to add interactivity and animation. ActionScripts may also be added for additional functionality.

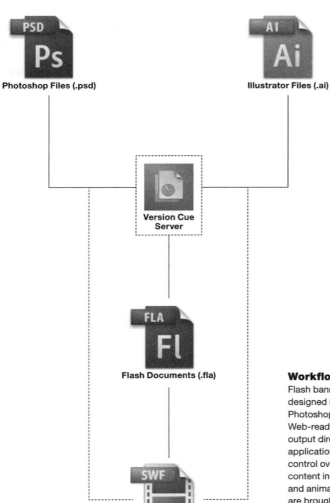

Photoshop Files (.psd)

Illustrator Files (.ai)

Version Cue Server

Flash Documents (.fla)

Flash Files (.swf)

Workflow

Flash banners can be designed in Illustrator, Photoshop, or Flash. Web-ready content can be output directly from these applications. For complete control over interactive content including rollovers and animations, designs are brought into Flash and modified. Photoshop can also export animated GIF files, but interactivity is then limited to simple animation.

——— Standard Workflow

-------- Optional Workflow

FIGURE 3.5
An example
of a website
workflow.

Workflow: Website

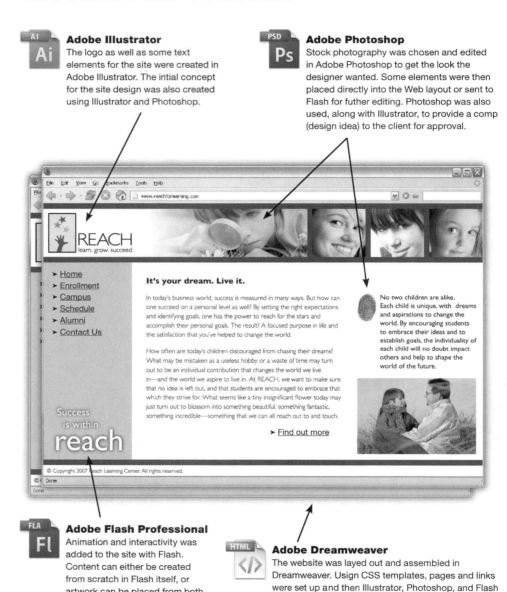

Adobe Illustrator
The logo as well as some text elements for the site were created in Adobe Illustrator. The intial concept for the site design was also created using Illustrator and Photoshop.

Adobe Photoshop
Stock photography was chosen and edited in Adobe Photoshop to get the look the designer wanted. Some elements were then placed directly into the Web layout or sent to Flash for futher editing. Photoshop was also used, along with Illustrator, to provide a comp (design idea) to the client for approval.

Adobe Flash Professional
Animation and interactivity was added to the site with Flash. Content can either be created from scratch in Flash itself, or artwork can be placed from both Photoshop and Illustrator.

Adobe Dreamweaver
The website was layed out and assembled in Dreamweaver. Usign CSS templates, pages and links were set up and then Illustrator, Photoshop, and Flash content was added. Dreamweaver also handled the website management, including uploading the site to the server and checking all of the links.

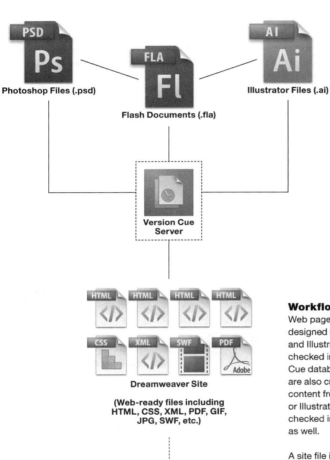

Photoshop Files (.psd)

Flash Documents (.fla)

Illustrator Files (.ai)

Version Cue Server

Dreamweaver Site

(Web-ready files including HTML, CSS, XML, PDF, GIF, JPG, SWF, etc.)

FTP
(upload to web server)

Workflow

Web pages layouts are designed in Photoshop and Illustrator, and files are checked into the Version Cue database. Flash files are also created using content from Photoshop or Illustrator, and those are checked into Version Cue as well.

A site file is then created in Dreamweaver. Using the assets from the Version Cue database, pages are assembled and generated. Dreamweaver creates web-ready files and then uploads them to the web host (server).

——— Standard Workflow
-------- Optional Workflow

FIGURE 3.6
An example of a cross-media newsletter workflow.

Workflow: Print/Online Newsletter

Adobe Illustrator
The logo for as well as the masthead was created in Adobe Illustrator making it simple to adapt the logo for just about any use.

Adobe Photoshop
Several photographs were chosen and edited in Adobe Photoshop, giving the designer creative freedom with the photos.

XML Content
Structured XML is used for both the print version and the Web version of the newsletter, allowing you to make changes once, and see both publications updated.

Adobe InDesign
The newsletter is layed out and assembled in InDesign. The photos and artwork were placed into the layouts, and additional text was then placed from a structured XML file, allowing the text to be shared with Dreamweaver.

Adobe Dreamweaver
The website was layed out and assembled in Dreamweaver. Pages and links were set up and then Illustrator, Photoshop, and Flash content was added. Assets, including XML content was shared between the printed newsletter and the online version.

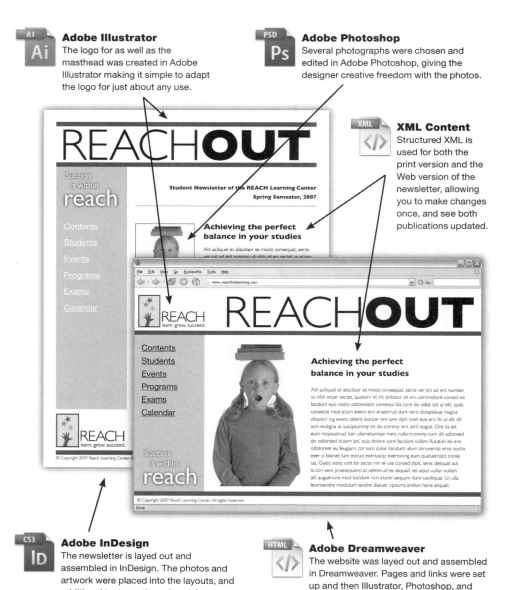

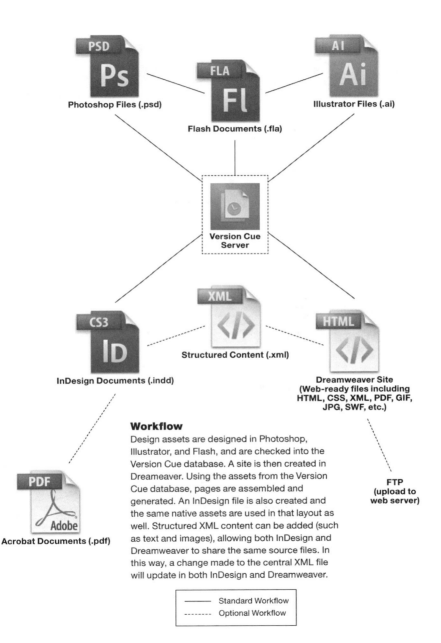

Photoshop Files (.psd)

Flash Documents (.fla)

Illustrator Files (.ai)

Version Cue Server

InDesign Documents (.indd)

Structured Content (.xml)

Dreamweaver Site
(Web-ready files including
HTML, CSS, XML, PDF, GIF,
JPG, SWF, etc.)

Workflow

Design assets are designed in Photoshop,
Illustrator, and Flash, and are checked into the
Version Cue database. A site is then created in
Dreameaver. Using the assets from the Version
Cue database, pages are assembled and
generated. An InDesign file is also created and
the same native assets are used in that layout as
well. Structured XML content can be added (such
as text and images), allowing both InDesign and
Dreamweaver to share the same source files. In
this way, a change made to the central XML file
will update in both InDesign and Dreamweaver.

Acrobat Documents (.pdf)

FTP
(upload to
web server)

Standard Workflow
Optional Workflow

Workflow: Interactive PDF

 Adobe Illustrator
The logo was created in Adobe Illustrator and saved as a native file (.ai), making it simple to adapt the logo for just about any use.

 Adobe Photoshop
Photographs were chosen and edited in Adobe Photoshop and saved as a native file (.psd), giving the designer creative freedom with the photos.

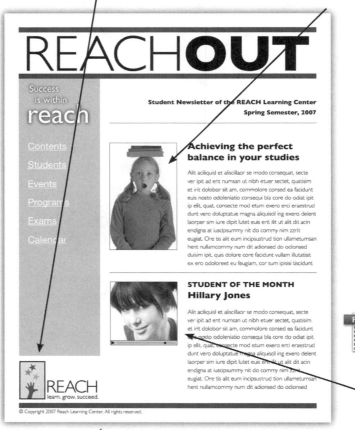

 Video Content
Place video directly into InDesign and specify playback settings. The PDF 1.5 format supports the embedding of movie files, so your movies play back when viewed in Acrobat.

 Adobe InDesign
The document was layed out and designed in InDesign, pulling elements from Illustrator and Photoshop. Using structured XML text files means that text will reflow correctly even if the PDF is viewed on alternative devices like PDAs and cellphones. InDesign can also add interactive elements like buttons, rollovers, and hyperlinks.

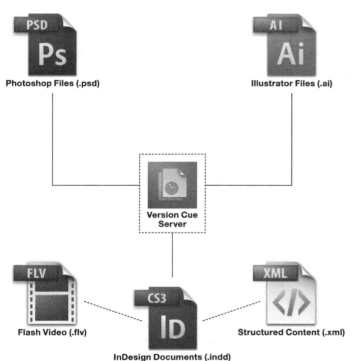

Photoshop Files (.psd)

Illustrator Files (.ai)

Version Cue Server

Flash Video (.flv)

Structured Content (.xml)

InDesign Documents (.indd)

Acrobat Documents (.pdf)

Workflow

Photoshop and Illustrator files are checked into the Version Cue database. The native PSD and AI files are then placed into an InDesign document and positioned on the page. Copy from XML files and interactive files, such as movies, is placed into InDesign as well. Hyperlinks and bookmarks are added, and a PDF is then created and opened in Acrobat Pro for any final editing.

————	Standard Workflow
--------	Optional Workflow

CHAPTER 4

The Key That Makes It All Work: Integration

"It is not a question of how well each process works; the question is how well they all work together."

Lloyd Dobens and Clare Crawford-Mason

It's hard enough keeping track of all of my kids' names, let alone trying to remember how to use the Pen tool in all of the applications I use to get my work done. So it's of great comfort for me to find that the Pen tool works in the exact same way in all Adobe applications. This is just a small example of what integration means, and as you begin to use Adobe's applications more, you'll appreciate these "little things" to no end.

This chapter discusses many of the things that define integration as it pertains to the Creative Suite applications. As we walk through the applications in this chapter, we talk mainly about Illustrator, Photoshop, InDesign, and Flash. Even though Dreamweaver and Acrobat are a part of the Creative Suite, they don't share the same interface as the other applications. We cover Dreamweaver in detail in Chapter 10, "Using Adobe Dreamweaver CS3," and Acrobat in Chapter 11, "Using Adobe Acrobat 8 Professional."

Getting Started with the Creative Suite

So you know what each application in the suite is supposed to do. You also have a pretty good understanding of where each application fits in the workflow and when you would use each of them. Now you'll take a look at how the applications work and how they are used.

As you'll find out, many tasks and concepts apply to all the applications in the suite. One thing that Adobe does extremely well is make its applications look and feel the same way. The different applications also play very well together. These combined aspects of the Creative Suite are referred to as *integration*. One of the main benefits of working with the suite is this high level of integration, and we talk about many of these aspects in this chapter.

Before we get to the applications themselves, I want to spend a few moments talking about your computer setup. After all, it's what you'll be using to run the Creative Suite.

Real World System Requirements for Running the Creative Suite

Adobe puts a list of system requirements on the box, but those should be treated as an absolute bare minimum. What I list here are items that I feel are important for the needs of the graphic designer. Use this only as a guideline, of course—your budget most likely dictates what you have at your disposal.

▶ **Computer**—I'm not even going to touch the whole Mac versus Windows issue because I believe that you should use whatever you're most comfortable with (my own personal preference is a Mac). What's important, though, is that you have a system that can handle whatever you have to throw at it. Hard-drive space (storage memory) is always important because graphics files tend to be quite large. It would also be wise to have at least 2GB of RAM (working memory) on your machine because that will enable you to run several applications at the same time (instead of having to continually open and close them). If you're planning to use a digital video camera, you need to get a system with a FireWire (also called IEEE 1394 or iLink) port.

▶ **Monitor**—Your monitor is your workspace and can prove to be a very important factor as you design. Remember that, as a user of the Creative Suite, you'll have several applications running at the same time, and Adobe's user interface is panel-happy (we talk more about panels later in the chapter); the more screen real estate you have, the better.

▶ **Input devices**—No doubt your computer came with a mouse and a keyboard, but depending on what kind of work you'll be doing, you might want to explore other options as well. Photoshop and Illustrator both have built-in support for pressure-sensitive tablets (such as those offered by Wacom) for such tasks as photo retouching, painting, and drawing. Trackballs offer a different feel than a mouse, and mouse devices are available that offer a scroll wheel, several programmable buttons, and other features (one such example is the Logitech NuLOOQ Professional Series).

Being comfortable with your input devices is essential if you make your living working on a computer. Ergonomic input devices are more than just hype—they can mean the difference between having fun at your job and having painful wrists, a sore neck or back, stressed eyes, headaches, and more. I'm not suggesting that you buy every product out there with the word ergonomic on the box, but doing some research (trying things out at stores or at a friend's workspace) can prove to be very helpful. I've personally found that switching between a mouse and a pressure-sensitive pen every so often relieves the pressure on my wrists.

By the Way

▶ **Internet connection**—A DSL or cable connection is essential for many reasons. The Internet has much to offer today's designer. The Adobe Stock Photos service, which enables you to quickly find just the images you're looking for and use them for comps and to download high-resolution versions instantly, requires a broadband Internet connection. User forums and websites offer a tremendous resource for tips, tricks, or even help. And of course, there are plenty of blogs and podcasts that offer great information as well. If you're the type who loves fonts, you can purchase just about anything your heart (or client) desires on demand, and more. Most important, with a high-speed connection, you can easily download software updates and patches. A fast Internet connection also makes it easier to email PDF proofs to clients.

▶ **Scanner**—A scanner is important for several reasons. You'll always need to scan photo prints or logos for design jobs. Many people also like to start their designs as sketches on paper (or napkins over a lunch meeting with the client) and might want to scan those in and work from there. Finally, I've found that a scanner can be very useful for experimenting with scanning fabrics and materials for interesting backgrounds, or even from other sources (when it's legal to do so, of course—I'm not advocating copyright infringement). Some scanners require a FireWire connection; most also offer a (slower) USB connection.

▶ **Digital camera**—A digital camera can do a lot more than just take pictures of the family. It's a great way to get quick concepts onto your screen. You can scout out scenery, take photos for comps to show clients and photographers—even take simple product shots. Just about any camera with at least 2 megapixels should work fine for these tasks.

▶ **Archiving**—When a job is done, you'll want to keep it somewhere that's easy to find and get to (a client will always ask for a small update to a job they did several months ago). I find that copying jobs to CDs or DVDs can be the easiest and cheapest, although there are plenty of other methods. Choose a system that you can be comfortable with and that you can track easily. I like the

CD or DVD method because most computers come with drives that can easily record these, the media is cheap enough, and the technology won't become obsolete anytime soon (remember SyQuest drives?). If possible, it's also a good idea to keep copies in a separate location, to avoid a catastrophic loss (such as burglary or fire).

▶ **Backup**—Nothing could possibly be worse than losing your data just when you need it the most. You've invested a lot into your work, and the only way to protect it is with a decent backup system. You'll find many different solutions out there (DAT, AIT, CD, DVD, and so on), and you should use whatever fits your budget and your work patterns. As an alternative, some companies are offering the capability to back up your files over the Internet. Although it is a bit more expensive, the backups happen automatically and are safely on a server, away from your office. The files are also accessible from anywhere if needed. Check out www.mozy.com and www.carbonite.com for a sampling of these offerings.

▶ **Work area**—Sometimes you have no control over where you'll be working— be it a cubicle in an office, a small desk tucked into the corner of your bedroom, a home office, or a decked-out design studio. But you should take some things into consideration. Bright sunlight can make it difficult to see your computer screen and can make colors look different on a sunny day than on a cloudy one. Desk space is also important. If you can, try to use as large a workspace as possible. Cramped work areas are the main cause for repetitive strain injuries (such as carpal tunnel syndrome), to say nothing of making it harder to find that fax the client sent you yesterday (one of the reasons I fill my fax machine with yellow paper, by the way).

Quick Tip for Launching the Suite Applications

Even though all the applications in the suite were installed at the same time, you still have to launch each one individually. In other words, if you need to do a task in Photoshop only, there's no need to launch the rest of the applications in the suite.

You launch any of the Creative Suite applications the same way you launch just about any other application. You might want to create shortcuts (or aliases) for your applications on your desktop (on Windows, you can place them in the Quicklaunch toolbar). On a Mac, you might want to put the applications in your Dock so that you can find and launch them easily.

To create a shortcut in Windows, right-click the application's icon and choose Create Shortcut. On a Mac, drag the application's icon to the Dock.

So what are we waiting for? Let's get started by examining some of the Creative Suite applications and learning about the similarities among them.

Common User Interface

You bought this book (or "borrowed" it from your friend) because you wanted to learn how to use Adobe Creative Suite 3. It would be a pain if you had to spend time learning how to use a photo-editing program, only to realize that you have to learn a whole new way of using your computer for working in a page-layout application. So it's of comfort to know that the applications in the suite share a brand new user interface.

> In case you aren't familiar with the term, *user interface* describes how a person uses or interacts with software. Examples of these kinds of elements can range from buttons, panels, and dialog boxes to tools and how they work.

By the Way

In fact, the interfaces of the suite applications are so alike that it's sometimes easy to forget which application you're using. Because so many things work the same way in all the individual applications, it's possible to focus on *doing* your work rather than trying to figure out *how* to do it.

The user interface really comprises many things, and we're going to discuss some of them here, including panels, tools, and more.

> Remember that although Adobe Creative Suite promises untold integration among its parts, applications such as Flash and Dreamweaver are appearing in the Creative Suite under the Adobe umbrella for the first time, so there might be certain elements or functions that aren't exactly the same. Throughout the book, I point out where such differences exist and why. I imagine that with each release of the suite over the years, the applications will become more alike.

By the Way

Panels and Docks

If you've ever used an Adobe application before, you know what a *palette* is. Now in Adobe Creative Suite 3 applications, palettes are referred to as panels. Certain functions and tools are always at your disposal, and these "float" on top of your document and are called floating panels. Panels can be shown or hidden, and some panels can expand or contract to show more or less information.

As you'll quickly find out, there are a lot of panels in each application, and your entire screen can quickly get filled with panels, leaving you with little or no space to view or work with your document. But don't worry—there are plenty of ways to adjust panels so that you can best take advantage of them.

Panels have several attributes. The part where the name of the panel appears is called the tab. On the upper-right corner of the panel is a little icon. Clicking on it opens the *panel menu* (see Figure 4.1), where you can choose from several additional options or functions. At the bottom of a palette is usually a row of palette buttons that provide more functionality as well.

FIGURE 4.1
The Color Guide panel in Adobe Illustrator CS3.

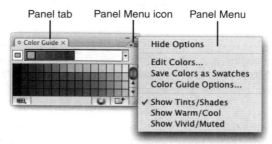

You can move panels around by grabbing their tabs, and you can resize some of them by grabbing their edges. You'll notice that panels "snap" to each other and to the edges of your screen.

Showing/Hiding Panels

The simplest way of working with panels is showing and hiding them. You'll find all the panels listed in the Window menu for any of the suite applications. A check mark next to an item means that the panel is open, or showing (see Figure 4.2).

Double-clicking on a panel's tab collapses the panel so that it takes up less space (see Figure 4.3). Whenever you need the panel again, double-clicking on the tab reveals the contents of the panel.

FIGURE 4.2
A check mark
indicates that
the panel is
already open on
your screen.

FIGURE 4.3
A collapsed
panel.

Notice that some panels have little arrows in front of the name in the tab (see
Figure 4.4). Those arrows indicate that the panel has multiple *states* or ways it can
be displayed, each showing fewer or more options. Clicking once on the arrows
changes the state of the panel. Clicking repeatedly on the arrows cycles through all
the states of the panel (see Figure 4.5).

FIGURE 4.4
You know that a panel has multiple states when you see the up and down arrows in the panel tab.

FIGURE 4.5
The three states of the Color panel in Illustrator.

Did you Know?

Press the Tab key to quickly clear your entire screen of panels. Press Tab again to restore your panels onscreen. If you press Shift+Tab, all of your panels become hidden except for your Tools and Control panels (which we cover in detail later in this chapter).

Adjusting Panels

Panels can be manipulated, giving you even more control over how they display (and take up space) on your screen. We discussed before how clicking on and dragging the title bar of the panel lets you move it around your screen. You'll notice that when you drag it around, you see a "ghost" of your panel.

You can drag this ghost into the upper portion of another panel (where the tab appears) to create a *group* of panels. Notice that as you drag the ghost into another open panel, that panel gets a thick blue outline around it (see Figure 4.6). In a group of panels, clicking once on the palette tab brings that palette into focus. For example, if you have the Swatches, Brushes, and Gradient panels in the same group, clicking on the Swatches panel tab brings that panel to the front (see Figure 4.7). Of course, you can still access the different states of each palette, as mentioned earlier. The benefit of creating a cluster of palettes is that you can have multiple palettes on your screen, but have them take up the screen space of just one palette.

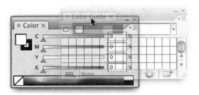

FIGURE 4.6
The highlighted outline indicates that you're about to create a panel group.

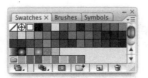

FIGURE 4.7
The Swatches, Brushes, and Symbols panels grouped in Illustrator, with the Swatches panel in front.

If you drag the ghost of a panel to the very bottom of another panel, you'll notice that only the bottom of the receiving panel gets a blue outline (see Figure 4.8). This indicates that you'll be *attaching* the panels instead of grouping them. Attaching a panel to another makes the two act as one (see Figure 4.9). Double-clicking on the panel tab of the upper panel collapses all the attached panels in one fell swoop. Some panels enable you to use the keyboard to navigate through them. The Color panel is one such panel in which you can enter CMYK values and tab between them. When you have panels attached to each other, you can also tab between the panels. So if you had the Stroke panel attached to your Color panel, you could tab through the CMYK values and then press Tab again to edit the stroke weight value.

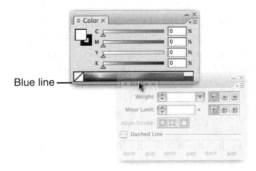

Blue line

FIGURE 4.8
A blue line at the bottom of the panel indicates that you're about to attach the panel.

FIGURE 4.9
The Color panel
and the Stroke
panel in
Illustrator,
attached.

Docking Panels

Sure, collapsing, grouping, and attaching all of your panels can be fun and even helpful in making room on your screen, but Adobe is always known for making even cooler features—and you won't be disappointed with this one. It's called docking, and it really helps you control all of your panels.

Here's how this feature works. Grab a panel by its tab and drag it towards the left or right edge of your screen. You'll notice that as you approach the edge, a bar comes out to meet the panel (see Figure 4.10). When you let go of the mouse, a panel dock is created and the panel appears within it (see Figure 4.11). Click once on the little white arrows that appear at the top of the panel dock and the dock is reduced in size, with each panel displaying as an icon (see Figure 4.12). You can drag additional panels into the dock, and clicking on an icon in the dock displays that panel so you can access it (see Figure 4.13). Click away from the panel and it disappears back into the dock, conveniently getting out of the way. It's a totally cool way to free up some valuable space on your screen while keeping panels close at hand. You can actually create more than one panel dock, and Flash can even dock panels to the bottom of the screen as well.

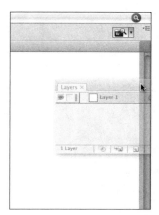

FIGURE 4.10
The highlighted tab indicates that you're about to create a panel dock.

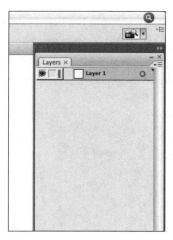

FIGURE 4.11
A single panel, as it appears when viewing the panel dock in its expanded state.

FIGURE 4.12
A single panel, as it appears when viewing the panel dock in its collapsed state (also called icon mode).

I know that you're having *way* too much fun right now with panel docks (I'll admit that it can be quite addictive), but I want to direct your attention to a feature that takes everything you've learned about panels so far and brings it to the next level: Custom Workspaces.

FIGURE 4.13
Viewing the Layers panel in Illustrator when the panel dock is in icon mode.

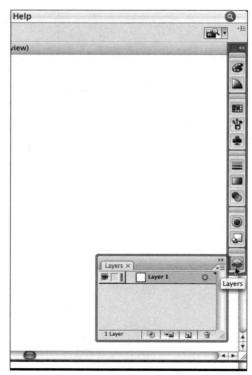

Custom Workspaces

No doubt by now you're overwhelmed with the plethora of panels in any one of Adobe's applications. Besides having to understand what each of those panels is for, you can already tell that your screen is going to be a mess of panels. Many people spend precious time moving their cursor around the screen looking for a panel. And when you're actually working on your document, all those panels can get in the way (see Figure 4.14). Life would be so much easier if there was just a way to control or manage all of these panels.

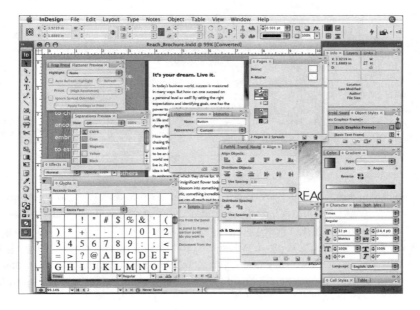

FIGURE 4.14
"Panels Gone Wild"—a daily occurrence on my computer.

Luckily, there's a feature in the suite called Custom Workspaces that enables you to save the position of all your panels and reset your screen to that setting at any time. In fact, you can keep multiple workspaces so that you can easily switch among them.

Using this feature is really quite simple. Start by opening the panels you want, and then position them to your liking on the screen. Group them, attach them, dock them—all to your heart's content. When you have everything perfectly positioned and set up, choose Window, Workspace, Save Workspace (see Figure 4.15), and give your new workspace a name. You can create as many workspaces as you like by repeating the process.

FIGURE 4.15
Saving a work-
space in
Photoshop.

Whenever you want to switch workspaces, all you have to do is choose one from the Window, Workspace submenu, and, like magic, your screen will adjust to the new panel configuration. Just in case you go crazy and define totally wacky workspaces, the kind and thoughtful people at Adobe included a default workspace allowing you to quickly get back to normalcy (see Figure 4.16). Most of the applications in the Suite also ship with a variety of workspaces that are already created, each optimized for specific workflows.

By the Way

If you're using two monitors, this feature can be extremely helpful in arranging different palette layouts for different tasks. And if you're using a laptop that is sometimes connected to a desktop monitor, Custom Workspaces enables you to easily arrange your palettes for optimal use when you're just on the laptop or attached to the monitor.

FIGURE 4.16
Choosing
the default
workspace.

Tools

These tools aren't the kind you buy at the Home Depot, but rather the kind that help you select objects, draw shapes, create graphs, and perform other functions with Adobe Creative Suite. Although each application contains a whole slew of tools, the good news is that many of them are the same across applications. We discuss these tools here, but before we do, let's first take a look at where the tools live.

The Tools Panel

Basically a panel on its own, the Tools panel is where you'll find all the tools for any of the suite applications. With the exception of Dreamweaver (which doesn't have tools), the Tools panels are extremely alike across the rest of the suite (see Figure 4.17).

FIGURE 4.17
The Tools
panels in
Photoshop,
Illustrator,
InDesign,
and Flash.

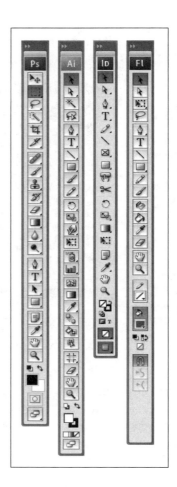

By the
Way

As you'll see later, Dreamweaver doesn't use tools because the interface is extremely context sensitive. As you click on parts of your page, your options automatically adapt and change to the needs of the object selected. Dreamweaver does use a special Insert bar (similar to the Control panel in other applications) for adding objects to your page, making it at least similar in look and feel to its sibling applications.

As with other panels, you can grab the Tools panel from the top and position it to your liking. The top part contains a pretty graphic that helps identify which application you're in (sometimes the apps look so similar that you need to look at this image to tell which of the apps you're actually in). Some applications also enable you to change the look or format of the Tools panel to make it easier to position on your screen. Double-clicking the white arrows at the top of the Tools panel toggles between a single-column and a double-column configuration of the tools. The single-column view saves a few valuable pixels on your screen, but you should choose whatever is more comfortable for you.

If you take a closer look at the Tools panel, you'll notice that some of the tools have a miniscule triangle or arrow at the lower-right corner of the tool's button. This icon indicates that more tools are "hidden" behind that one. As you'll quickly come to realize, Adobe applications have many tools, and it's impossible to display all of them at once without taking up a tremendous amount of screen real estate. Instead of trying to display them all, Adobe combined them into logical groups. Consider Illustrator's Type tool, for example. Hidden under it are five additional tools that are used to work with text. To access these tools, simply click a tool with your mouse and keep the button pressed until the other tools pop up (see Figure 4.18). You can then choose one of the other tools.

FIGURE 4.18
Accessing the hidden text tools in Illustrator.

> Later in the chapter, we talk about keyboard shortcuts that can assist you in selecting tools quickly. One of the great things about keyboard shortcuts is that you can use them to select a tool that's hidden behind another one.

By the Way

Sometimes you're continually jumping between tools that are grouped together (such as the Symbolism tools in Illustrator), and it can be quite tedious to continually access the hidden tools. Using a feature found in Illustrator (not in the other suite apps), if you look to the far right when you click and hold down the mouse to see all the tools in the group, you'll see a narrow button with an arrow in it, called Tearoff. When selected, it actually creates a mini Tools panel with all the grouped tools in a row. You can position this anywhere on your screen, as needed (see Figure 4.19).

FIGURE 4.19
A "mini Tools panel" of the text tools in Illustrator.

Selection Tools

Back in Chapter 2, "So Many Applications: Which One to Use?" I mentioned the importance of selecting things. I'd like to clarify that here and explain some of the methods of selections in the suite apps.

As you use your computer, you'll find that you're basically doing one of two things: creating content, when you're using tools or functions to add elements to your document; or editing content, when you're adjusting or modifying elements in your document. Here's a quick example of what I mean: When drawing a star in Illustrator, first you draw the star itself (creating content), and then you choose a color for it and position it just where you want it (editing content).

To edit content, you need to indicate what exactly you want to edit. This process is called making a selection. Depending on the program, there are many ways to achieve this. For the most part, Illustrator, Flash, and InDesign are object-based programs, so making selections in those programs is very similar. Photoshop has similar selection tools for its vector shapes, but because it's mainly a pixel-based program, it also has a range of other selection tools specific to selecting pixels themselves. Dreamweaver does enable you to select objects by clicking on them, but it's also unique, in that you don't necessarily need any specific tool to select things—it has more of a context-sensitive interface. We discuss each of these methods when we focus on each of the applications, but I wanted to touch on a few important concepts here.

Selections in Illustrator, Flash, and InDesign

Illustrator, Flash, and InDesign are primarily object-based programs, so you're usually selecting one of the following:

- ▶ An object
- ▶ Part of an object
- ▶ A group of objects
- ▶ Text

Illustrator, Flash, and InDesign have two primary selection tools: the black arrow and the white arrow (okay, so that's what I like to call them; their real names are the Selection tool and the Direct Selection tool; Flash calls the latter the Subselection tool). For the most part, the black arrow is used to select objects and groups of objects. The white arrow is used to select parts of objects. In all applications, the Type tool is used to both create and edit text, so you use the Type tool to select text as well.

There are two basic ways to select objects (see Figure 4.20) with the arrow tools. You can either click on the object you want to select, or click and drag over an area to select any objects that fall within that area—a method called marquee selection.

FIGURE 4.20
When an object is selected, it is highlighted (right), indicating so.

Let's start simple and talk about the first method. Using the black arrow, click once on an object to select it. You can then move the object around using the black arrow as well. Click on any empty space on your screen to deselect the object. Click on it again to select it. To select more than one object, you can press and hold the Shift key while clicking on additional objects (see Figure 4.21). You'll notice that with each click, you're adding objects to your selection, and you'll be able to move all the selected objects together at once. If you Shift-click on an object that's already selected, that object is deselected.

FIGURE 4.21
Multiple objects
selected in
InDesign.

When you think about it, the Shift key toggles a selection on or off. If you Shift-click an object that is not selected, the object becomes selected; if you Shift-click an object that is already selected, it becomes deselected.

If you want to select several objects, you can use the marquee method by clicking the mouse button on a blank area of the screen and holding the button down while dragging. As you drag the mouse, you'll notice a box being drawn (this is the marquee). When you let go of the mouse, whatever objects fall within the boundaries of the marquee become selected (see Figure 4.22).

When you're marquee-selecting, it's important not to click directly on an object, or you'll simply be selecting and moving that object (as we discussed in the first method).

FIGURE 4.22
The three steps to marquee selection: Click the mouse outside the objects, drag over the objects, and release the mouse.

Sometimes it's useful to use both methods to make your selections. For example, say you have a group of 10 objects and you want to select them all except for one in the middle. Using the first method, you might try to select one and then Shift-click each of the other eight objects to select the ones you want. However, you could use the marquee method to select them all and then Shift-click on the one object you *don't* want, to get the same selection much faster.

Selections in Photoshop

Photoshop is primarily a pixel-based program, so most of the selection tools are focused on selected pixels instead of objects. In other words, you can't just select the "sky" in a photograph because Photoshop doesn't see it as a single object, but rather as a collection of many individual pixels. The primary selection tools in Photoshop are the Marquee selection tool, the Lasso tool, the Magic Wand tool, and the new Quick Selection tool. I'm sure you're sitting at home thinking to yourself, "A magic wand? This guy is pulling my leg...." Well, before you put down this book to pick up the latest copy of the *National Enquirer* instead, let me explain.

The Marquee selection tool selects a range of pixels in much the same way we discussed marquee selections before. You drag a box, and whatever pixels fall inside the box become selected (see Figure 4.23). Several variations of the Marquee tool exist in Photoshop—one for making ellipse-shape selections, one for selecting a single vertical row of pixels, and one that does the same for horizontal rows of pixels. To add to your selection, press the Shift key to marquee more pixels (see Figure 4.24); to remove pixels from your selection, press the (Option) [Alt] key as you draw your marquee.

The Lasso tool acts exactly like the Marquee selection tool, with one major difference: It lets you select pixels by drawing a free-form path. Remember that with the Marquee tools, you can select only with rectangular- and elliptical-shape boundaries, but the Lasso tool lets you draw an irregularly shaped path. For example, the Elliptical Marquee tool might be perfect for selecting the sun in a sky, but the Lasso tool would be perfect for selecting branches of a tree (see Figure 4.25). To use the Lasso tool, you simply click and drag to draw a path around the area of pixels you want to select. If you let go of the mouse before you get back to the point of the path where you started, Photoshop draws a straight line from the last point your cursor was to the point where the path started, completing the shape for you.

FIGURE 4.23
An area of pixels selected.

FIGURE 4.24
As you press the Shift or (Option) [Alt] keys, the cursor indicates whether you are adding to or removing from your selection.

FIGURE 4.25
An area of
pixels selected
with the Lasso
tool.

In addition, Photoshop has a Polygonal Lasso tool, which enables you to mark boundaries by clicking repeatedly (almost like connect the dots), as well as a Magnetic Lasso tool, which "magically" detects edges as you drag along them. We discuss these in detail when we get to Chapter 6, "Using Adobe Photoshop CS3."

Then there's the Magic Wand tool. Because of the nature of pixel-based images (photographs), colors are usually painterly, or what we call continuous tone. So if there's a blue sky in your picture, each blue pixel is probably a slightly different shade of blue. The Magic Wand tool selects regions of the same color, but with a tolerance. That means you can control how close the colors have to match to be selected. For example, you click on the blue sky, as we just mentioned, but you don't want white clouds selected, right? The Magic Wand tool can differentiate the colors and select just the blue sky (see Figure 4.26). Why the folks at Adobe called this the Magic Wand tool is beyond me.

FIGURE 4.26
An area of pixels selected with the Magic Wand.

Photoshop CS3 also adds a brand new Quick Selection tool. This tool is based on the Magic Wand tool and is more intuitive and easier to use when making selections. To use the tool, simply click and drag over the areas you want to select. As you drag, the tool detects and selects areas of similar color and composition.

Drawing Tools

The world of design was forever changed with the introduction of Adobe Illustrator in the late 1980s. Since then, drawing on a computer has become an art form in itself. Illustrator introduced the world to the Pen tool, and since then Adobe applications have added many more such tools, each for specific tasks. Rectangle, Ellipse, Polygon, Star, and Line tools all give users the ability to quickly and easily draw basic shapes. The Pen, Pencil, and Paintbrush tools give users the freedom of creating more free-form and natural renderings. Many of these tools appear across the apps, and they all work in much the same way.

By the Way

Because applications address particular tasks, there might be some differences in how the same tool is used among the applications. For example, the Paintbrush tool in Photoshop has different settings and options because it's a pixel-based tool. Illustrator's Paintbrush has other options available pertaining to the object-based nature of vector graphics.

Drawing a rectangle in Photoshop, Illustrator, Flash, or InDesign can be accomplished in exactly the same way. You start by selecting the Rectangle tool, and then you click and drag (see Figure 4.27). We go into specific details about each of these tools when we talk about the applications themselves, but I wanted to point out how learning even one application in the suite can give you the basics on using the other apps as well.

FIGURE 4.27
Drawing a rectangle in any of the suite applications.

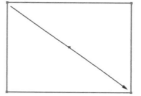

Keyboard Shortcuts

The mouse is a wonderful thing (I'm not referring to the squeaky kind that likes cheese), but it can be inefficient for many tasks. For example, to choose the Print command so that you can print your document, you would move the mouse to the File menu, and then scan down the list of items and choose Print. Printing can be something you do quite often, and having to navigate back to that File menu each time can be time-consuming.

The good news is that there are keyboard shortcuts—or keys you can press on your keyboard to perform specific tasks or functions—that can save a whole lot of time. In the example I gave previously, simply pressing (Cmd-P) [Ctrl+P] invokes the Print command. In fact, there are hundreds of keyboard shortcuts for many different tasks. Power users take advantage of keyboard shortcuts to execute tasks quickly. Keyboard shortcuts can even be used to switch between different tools, enabling you to focus more clearly on the work at hand. You'll find that as you become more adept at using keyboard shortcuts, switching between tools and performing certain functions will become second nature—almost to the point that you won't be consciously aware that you are doing it.

It's easy to find out what the keyboard shortcut is for a function or a tool. Menu items have the keyboard shortcut listed to the right (see Figure 4.28), and tools list their shortcut in the ToolTip (see Figure 4.29).

By the Way

FIGURE 4.28
Keyboard short-cuts indicated in the File menu of Photoshop.

FIGURE 4.29
Keyboard shortcuts indicated in the Tools panel of Photoshop.

Now, obviously, if you consider that each program can have a ton of keyboard shortcuts and there are several applications in the suite, that's a lot of shortcuts to try to learn and remember. It's no coincidence, then, that most of the keyboard shortcuts are consistent across the suite applications. This means that you can press the P key in Photoshop, Illustrator, Flash, or InDesign and expect to get the Pen tool.

Clearly, learning even one of the applications in the suite gives you a head start on learning all the others. Even if you've never used Flash, simply being familiar with Illustrator or Photoshop serves as an introductory course to using these other tools.

But there's more....

Making Your Own Shortcuts

Adobe realizes that its users are unique and that just about every designer wants a keyboard shortcut assigned to the feature or tool that he personally uses most often. At the same time, there are several hundred menu items, tools, and functions in each application, and there are a limited number of possible key combinations you can use on your keyboard. Above that, certain key commands are reserved for use by functions outside the applications. For example, (Cmd-Tab) [Ctrl+Tab] is a shortcut used by the operating system (both Windows XP and Mac OS X) to switch between open applications.

Photoshop, Illustrator, and InDesign all enable you to customize keyboard shortcuts. That means you can decide to assign your own shortcuts to functions or tools that *you* use most often.

By the Way

> It's important to point out that there are certain keyboard shortcuts that are not consistent among the applications, and there are usually good reasons for this. For example, (Cmd-F) [Ctrl+F] in InDesign is the shortcut to bring up the Find and Replace dialog box. However, in Illustrator, that same shortcut is used for the Paste in Front command. This is because Find and Replace is something that might be used quite often in InDesign, but not nearly as often in Illustrator. At the same time, Illustrator users might use Paste in Front all the time. Of course, customizable shortcuts now let you make all of these decisions on your own.

Customizable keyboard shortcuts is one of those cross-product features that hasn't been "sweetened" yet (sorry, couldn't resist the pun), in that the implementation is slightly different depending on which application you're in.

From Photoshop, InDesign, and Illustrator, choose Edit, Keyboard Shortcuts (see Figure 4.30). You can change or assign keyboard shortcuts to any tool, any menu item, and some panel menus as well. If you try to assign a shortcut that already exists (say, for another tool or function), you'll get a warning telling you so, with the option to keep the older assignment or to adopt the new one you just defined.

Most important of all, you have the capability to save your custom keyboard shortcut settings as an external file. This means you can secretly change all the keyboard shortcuts on your co-worker's computer—um, I mean, you can easily distribute custom sets to co-workers or take your own sets with you if you regularly work on different computers or share a different computer with others.

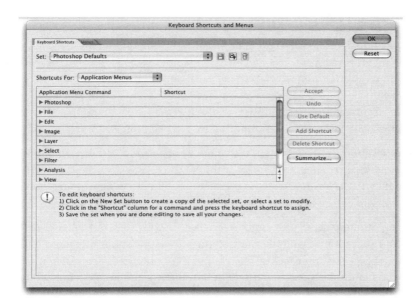

FIGURE 4.30
The Keyboard
Shortcuts
dialog box in
Photoshop.

Moving Data Between Apps

As you use the individual applications in the suite, you'll realize increasingly that you have to move information between them—and other applications outside the suite as well. There are several ways to do this, each method having its own pros and cons.

Copy and Paste

One of the quickest ways to move data between applications—be it text, images, or artwork—is via the copy and paste command. But like most things in life, the quicker way isn't always the best way. In most cases, information is lost when copying and pasting between applications, including text formatting, color information, image resolution, metadata, and more. However, many times a simple copy and paste will save time and provide you with what you need. For example, you might want to draw a shape in Illustrator, taking advantage of the precise drawing tools in that application, and then copy and paste just the path into Photoshop or InDesign.

One example of when copy and paste does work well is between Illustrator and Flash. Adobe has done a lot of work with Flash to make it understand Illustrator information even via copy and paste.

Exporting/Importing

The applications in the suite can both import and export different file formats. Depending on where your files and documents have to go, you can choose from various formats—each with its own particular strength or use. Some of the more common formats used for print workflows are PDF, TIFF, and EPS. Popular web formats are GIF, JPEG, SWF, and SVG. Illustrator also has the capability to save files in Photoshop (PSD) format and contains a Save for Microsoft Office command.

Most applications in the suite can also place or open these formats—along with a long list of other formats, such as Microsoft Word or Excel documents, FreeHand files, and QuarkXPress files—giving you the capability to work with just about any file that might come your way.

Exporting and importing files might seem like an extra step, but the formats are richer and support more file information (including important metadata, in many cases—we cover this topic later in the chapter). It's also a necessary step when working with other applications that aren't in the suite (yes, there *is* a whole other world out there).

Native File Support

One of the strengths of using the Creative Suite in your workflow is that all the suite applications can support the native file formats of each other. This means that you can easily place a native Illustrator file into Photoshop, InDesign, or Flash, and even open it in Adobe Acrobat. Other non-Adobe applications might require that you export a specific file format, such as EPS, from Illustrator.

Of course, this is an extremely valuable benefit. As we discussed back in Chapter 3, "The Game Plan: Developing a Workflow," this enables you to keep just one version of your file (instead of native files as well as EPS, TIFF, and JPEG versions, and so on) and also enables you to take advantage of the rich format that these file formats support. For example, you can access all the layers in a Photoshop file when you open it inside Illustrator. You can view and hide layers from both InDesign and Illustrator files when you're in Acrobat. You can access Photoshop layer comps when you place native Photoshop (.psd) files into InDesign and Illustrator.

When possible, it's best to use native file formats because those file formats retain the most information. An added benefit to this method is that you retain the individual files, making it easy to quickly update different elements in your design. Using the Edit Original command found in each of the applications, you can easily make changes to a graphic—and have that graphic automatically updated throughout all the documents that it is placed in. We discuss how to do that from each of the applications in Part II, "The Applications."

Creating PDF Files

One of the biggest time-savers the suite offers is the capability to create PDF files directly and *consistently*. PDF files are commonly used to get client and manager approvals, and to create proofs. PDF files are also accepted by a large majority of printers and service providers, and the format is now accepted by virtually every magazine or newspaper publisher for submitting advertisements.

> In reality, consistent PDF creation is only half the story. All Adobe Creative Suite applications can also open or place PDF files.

By the Way

The truth is, many different settings are available when you save a PDF file. For example, you can choose from different compression settings, color settings, print-specific settings (such as crop marks and bleeds), and even password security settings. To avoid having to go through all the settings each time you wanted to create a PDF file, Adobe added PDF Presets, which was a way to save your PDF settings. However, these presets weren't consistent across applications.

In previous versions, each individual Adobe application had different PDF settings, making it confusing and difficult to get consistent PDF creation across all the applications. For example, a PDF saved from Illustrator could be very different than a PDF saved from InDesign. And because the PDF settings themselves were different, you couldn't even try to create similar PDF presets yourself within each application.

With Adobe Creative Suite, all applications now share the same PDF presets. This means that you can open Illustrator and save a PDF preset, and then open InDesign and use that very same preset (see Figure 4.31). Settings are now similar, allowing for consistent and reliable PDF creation.

FIGURE 4.31
Defining a PDF Preset in InDesign makes that preset available from within other suite applications.

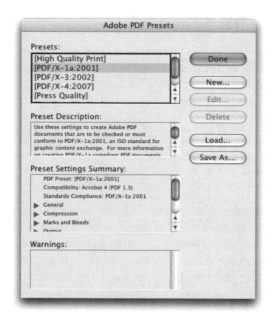

Enhancing Integration with Metadata

Meta-*what?* If you're not familiar with the term, *metadata* refers to data that resides inside a file that provides extra information about the file itself. For example, a file might contain information about who created the file, when it was created, what client or job number it was created for, and so on. Digital photos might contain copyright information and even data about what kind of digital camera was used and what the camera settings were (called EXIF metadata) when the photo was taken. When you think about it, metadata makes files smart because the files themselves know more about what's in them.

Some metadata is added automatically to every file (such as which application created it), but you can also add your own. In any of the Adobe Suite applications, you can choose File, File Info to access the File Information dialog box, where you can add specific information to your file (see Figure 4.32). In fact, Adobe applications can automatically add metadata to files. For example, when you download comp images using the Adobe Stock Photos service (which we talk about in Chapter 5, "Using Adobe Bridge CS3"), metadata is added so that InDesign knows the image is a low-resolution comp image. When you preflight the file in InDesign, this metadata enables InDesign to alert you that the image isn't a high-resolution image that's fit to print at high quality.

FIGURE 4.32
The File Information dialog box in InDesign.

Adobe helped to publish an open-standard platform for metadata called Extensible Metadata Platform (XMP), which is basically a way to describe metadata using XML. All Adobe applications write metadata into an XML header in the files they save. This information is available to any application or system that can read it. And although metadata is pretty cool on its own, it takes on a whole new meaning when you consider what Adobe Bridge can do with that information. We'll talk more about that in Chapter 5 as well.

Summary

By now you have a solid understanding of what all the applications are for and when they should be used, along with a general understanding of how they work hand in hand with each other. All you have left to do now is actually learn each of the applications. Have no fear—if you've gotten this far, you're going to do just fine. In the next part of the book, we jump into each of the applications one by one and fully understand the strengths and uses for each of them.

PART II

The Applications

CHAPTER 5

Using Adobe Bridge CS3

Way back when Photoshop Version 7 was released, Adobe added a feature called the File Browser, which enabled users to quickly find the files they needed by using a visual interface. Over the past few releases, this tool was greatly enhanced and eventually turned into its own application, called Bridge.

Bridge acts as the hub for your digital media assets. It can track the locations of the files that you're using and creating in the CS3 suite, as well as files created outside of CS3 that are supplemental to your projects. Think of Bridge as the ultimate media file browser for your system that just happens to also include

- ▶ An integrated browser for accessing online resources
- ▶ A photo downloader for your camera
- ▶ An advanced file tagger and search engine
- ▶ A control center for the Version Cue system

This chapter will look at many of the features of the Bridge application and how you can use it to better manage your digital files.

Finding Your Way Around in Bridge

The easiest way to figure out how Bridge can help you organize your digital assets is to start using it. So go ahead and launch Bridge now, either by opening it from the Macintosh Finder or Windows Explorer, or by choosing Browse from within one of the Adobe CS3 applications.

> If you find yourself using Bridge frequently, you might want to start it and leave it running as you work with the core CS3 applications. This enables you to quickly use Browse within Photoshop, Illustrator, and so on to jump back and forth into Bridge without it having to launch each time.

Bridge, seen in Figure 5.1, looks a bit different from the other CS3 applications. With such a specialized purpose, the interface is a bit more stylized and "fun" than the core suite. Let's start by looking at the default Bridge window browsing a few photographs on my computer.

FIGURE 5.1
Welcome to the Bridge workspace.

Did you Know?

If you don't like the modern white-on-gray appearance of the Bridge interface, you can use the General settings under the Bridge preferences to adjust the appearance to black on white, or anywhere in between!

Understanding the Bridge Window

Along the top of the Bridge window is the toolbar, with simple buttons and menus for navigating through your file system, similar to what you'd see in the Finder or Windows Explorer.

Along the sides are additional panels for quickly jumping to your favorite locations, navigating the folder structure on your computer, specifying filter criteria for image search, and viewing/previewing any information about files that you have currently selected.

In the center of the Bridge workspace is the primary content area, called the Content panel. When you select a folder from the Favorites or Folders panel, this area refreshes to show thumbnails of all the files within a selected folder. Alternatively, if you perform a search, the Content panel shows the search results.

At the bottom of the Bridge window is the status bar. A double-arrow icon at the left side of the status bar enables you to quickly expand and collapse the panels on the sides. On the right side of the status bar, you'll notice a slider bar; this controls the size of the thumbnails within the content area. For example, in Figure 5.1, the thumbnails were sized at the default setting. In Figure 5.2, the slider has been changed to show significantly more detail.

FIGURE 5.2
Use the slider in the status bar to increase the size of the Bridge thumbnails.

At the far right of the status bar are three buttons that represent different workspace presets that you might want to use.

> Macintosh users might notice some similarities between Bridge and Apple's iPhoto. Although these applications have different audiences, they actually share many of the same features and controls.

By the Way

Managing the Bridge Workspace

A *workspace*, in case you haven't encountered that term, is just a way of referring to the current organization of all the panels onscreen. For example, you can expand and collapse the onscreen panels by clicking and dragging their sides, or you can move them around by clicking and dragging their tabs. To hide a panel entirely, either right-click on its tab and choose Close, or deselect it from the Windows menu. As you change the panels, you are customizing your workspace.

You can always add a panel back to the workspace by right-clicking where you want it to appear and choosing its name from the menu that appears, or by reselecting it in the Window menu.

We're going to be using the default workspace (the initial setting for the first workspace button), but you might want to explore or set workspaces for the other buttons by clicking them, or clicking and holding to choose a specific workspace preset.

All of the same features and panels are available regardless of what workspace you use—they might just be organized differently to emphasize different features or to hide options that aren't relevant to your current project. If you come up with a particular arrangement that you like better than the presets, you can click and hold any of the workspace preset buttons in the status bar and choose Save Workspace to save your very own workspace variation.

Browsing Your Files

After you're up and running in Bridge, the first thing you'll probably be asking yourself is "Okay, where are my files?!" This is a natural reaction, as Bridge doesn't quite behave like a standard file browser on the Mac or Windows. If Adobe decides to make its own operating system, we might get used to it, but it's okay if it feels a bit "alien" to you starting out.

The Folders Panel

The easiest way to start using Bridge to browse and manage your files is by using the Folders panel, shown in Figure 5.3.

FIGURE 5.3
Use the Folders panel to navigate through your files.

This panel displays a hierarchical list of the folders on your computer, as well as any network connections that you have in place. Using the icon in front of each folder, you can expand and collapse your directory structure and dig as deeply into your system as you'd like.

The Content Panel

While you're working your way through the folders, you'll notice that the Content panel updates to show the contents of the folder you currently have selected. You can use the icons in the Content panel to open files (or navigate to other folders) by double-clicking the icons.

If you'd prefer to view more details about the files in the content area (rather than a simple icon), choose View, As Details from the menu bar. This displays additional metadata for each of your files, in addition to the thumbnail, as demonstrated in Figure 5.4.

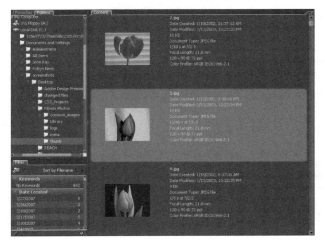

FIGURE 5.4
The Details view presents more information about each file.

A cool way to quickly step through and rate large collections of images is to use Bridge's slideshow feature. Choose View, Slide Show to see images in full-screen mode. Press the H key to view all the keyboard shortcuts for the things you can apply to images as they appear on your screen, such as rating them.

Did you Know?

As you browse your files, you might want to direct your attention to a few options in the toolbar. The arrow buttons can take you forward and backward through your browsing history, while the pop-up menu can jump to specific folders. Using buttons on the right side of the toolbar, you can create new folders (the folder icon), rotate a selected image (the curved arrows), delete a selected file or folder (the trash can), or collapse the window into a tiny "mini" browser view.

The Favorites Panel

Navigating to your most commonly used folders using the Folders panel (or Content panel) *works,* but is hardly efficient. To speed things up, you can create shortcuts using the Favorites panel.

This panel lists several icons that provide quick access to different functions, services, and locations, as seen in Figure 5.5. For example, clicking on the Version Cue item enables you to access files in Version Cue projects right from Bridge (we talk more about this a little later), while clicking the Adobe Photographers Directory connects you to a live directory of national photographers.

FIGURE 5.5
The Favorites panel provides shortcuts to commonly used services, files, and folders.

Items that appear below the divider line in the Favorites panel are specific folders or files that you access frequently. You can add your own favorites simply by dragging any folder or file into the panel. To delete a favorite, either drag it to your system trash or choose File, Remove from Favorites. You can also specify what does or does not appear in the Favorites panel in the General panel in Bridge Preferences, as seen in Figure 5.6.

FIGURE 5.6
Control what is visible within the Favorites panel using the General preferences.

Viewing Files, Setting Metadata, and Filtering Content

To this point, we've been focusing on the Folders, Favorites, and Content panels. As you've clicked through these areas, you've probably noticed that there are other things changing on your screen as well. These other panels provide previews of your files' content, as well as a means of setting metadata for each file and filtering your file view based on metadata.

What Is Metadata?

Metadata is, simply, data about data. For example, when you take a picture, you have certain exposure settings on your camera. These settings can be used to help describe the picture. Similarly, a time and date stamp for a picture would also be considered metadata. For a song file, the artist, song name, and album name could be stored as metadata.

Metadata isn't the content of a file itself, but is information that helps you identify or describe the file.

The Preview Panel

The first new panel that we're going to take a look at is the Preview panel. This panel provides (surprise!) a preview of the content that you have selected. What might actually surprise you is that the Preview panel does more than just display pictures; it can also provide playback of audio and video files, as demonstrated in Figure 5.7.

FIGURE 5.7
The Preview panel previews the contents of files that you have selected— even video or audio files! In this example, the animated QuickTime logo movie is shown.

Did you Know?

Clicking on an image in the Preview panel opens a very cool magnifying glass that you can position anywhere you'd like over the image to get an enlarged view.

The Metadata Panel

Directly below the Preview panel (in the default workspace) is the Metadata panel (shown in Figure 5.8). Here you can view all of the information about your currently selected file, including camera settings, file sizes, resolutions, color space, and more things than we can possibly mention here.

FIGURE 5.8
The Metadata panel shows data about your... data.

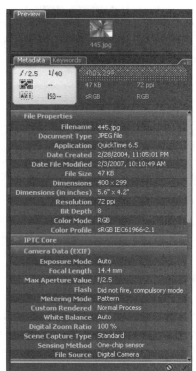

For some types of files, you'll notice that there is a pencil to the right of certain metadata field names. This means that the metadata is editable. To enter your own information, click the pencil and you can type into the field—it's as simple as that!

To save the changes, click the check mark in the lower-right corner of the panel. To cancel your modifications, click the circle with the line through it.

This is a bit off-topic, but if you have a collection of music and don't have all the artists or song titles set correctly, using Bridge and the Metadata panel is a quick and very simple way to edit the information yourself.

Did you Know?

The Keywords Panel

Sometimes there is metadata that you want to set for a file, but it isn't part of the metadata available for the file type. In these cases, you can create custom keywords and apply them to files however you'd like. To access the keyword feature of Bridge, open the Keywords panel, as seen in Figure 5.9.

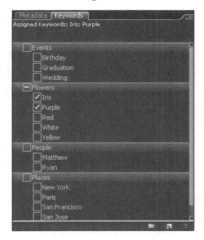

FIGURE 5.9
The Keywords panel enables you to tag files with your own keyword metadata.

Keywords are organized by sets and, within each set, multiple keywords can be set.

By default, there are several example categories and sample keywords. You can delete the categories or keywords by clicking their label in the panel, and then choosing the trashcan icon in the lower-right corner.

To add a new keyword, click the paper-pad button at the bottom of the panel. This adds a new keyword to a set called Other Keywords. If you want to add a new set, click the folder button. You can move keywords between sets by clicking and dragging their labels.

To assign a keyword to a file, make sure the file is selected in the Content panel, and then click the box beside the keyword label. All assigned labels are displayed at the top of the panel. To quickly assign all the labels to a set, just use the check box for the set itself, rather than the individual keywords.

Additional Metadata Settings

Believe it or not, you can set even more pieces of metadata for a file. Using the Label menu, you can set labels for selected files or select star ratings to denote your preference for one file versus another.

You can also set ratings directly from the content view. Click on a file, and five small dots appear beneath the image thumbnail. Clicking on the dots enables you to rate the images with anywhere from zero to five stars.

Advanced users might want to look at the Metadata Template Creation tools found under the Tools menu for even *more* options related to metadata.

Filtering Based on Metadata

One of the nicest features of Bridge is the capability to filter the files you are viewing based on the metadata that has been set for a given file. By default, all files are shown when you view a folder. At the same time you're viewing a folder of files, the Filter panel (shown in Figure 5.10) is being populated with metadata information about the files.

FIGURE 5.10
The Filter panel can be used to limit what files you see in the content area.

To limit your view to specific metadata attributes, scroll through the Filter panel and check or uncheck the items you want to use as filter criteria. As you activate or deactivate filter items, the Content panel updates accordingly.

At the top of the Filter panel are two additional functions. On the left side is a folder icon. Clicking this button applies your filter criteria across *all* files, not just the selected folder. Note that this can take quite a bit of time! On the right side of the panel is a pop-up menu that can be used to set how the files in the Content panel are sorted.

Finding Files Based on Metadata

Choose Edit, Find to run a search within Bridge. Use the Criteria section of the dialog box to specify exactly what you're looking for, again, based on metadata.

That's not the best part of it. After you perform a find, you can click the Save As Collection button (see Figure 5.11). This creates what Bridge calls a *collection*, which you can access by clicking on the Collections icon in the Favorites panel. Collections are like live searches and can be very useful when you need to perform functions on the same kinds or groups of files. As you add or remove files that match the criteria of your collections, they are automatically added to or removed from the collection itself.

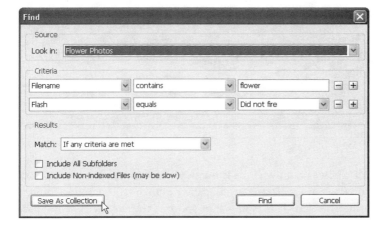

FIGURE 5.11
Use the Find feature to locate files based on metadata and to create collections of search criteria.

Accessing Professional Photography Services

Bridge features two innovative services that can help you locate photos and photographers. The Stock Photos service enables you to browse and search several leading royalty-free image libraries, download watermark-free compositions (called "comps" in designer-land), and even purchase high-resolution images—all from within the application itself. The Adobe Photographers directory, on the other hand, provides an easy way to locate photographers in your area or around the world.

Adobe Stock Photos

Adobe doesn't have its own library of images; instead, it has partnered with stock photo giants Photodisc (Getty images), Comstock, and others that make managing the process of using stock photos easier and more efficient.

You can access the Adobe Stock Photos service by clicking on the Adobe Stock Photos icon in the Favorites panel. You can then perform searches (across all partners simultaneously) and download watermark-free comps without having to even launch a browser or log into a site, as shown in Figure 5.12.

FIGURE 5.12
Accessing the Adobe Stock Photos service in Bridge.

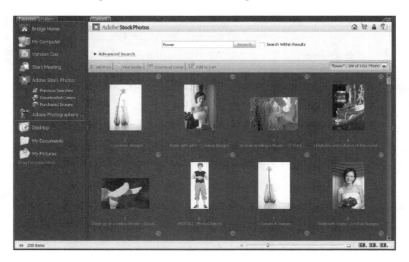

Adobe Stock Photos actually embeds metadata into each comp that you download that contains the image ID, the partner site from which the image came, and other important information. This means that you can change the name of a downloaded comp (they always have meaningless names such as AA45900012.jpg anyway), and InDesign or Illustrator is still capable of identifying the image as a low-resolution comp. In fact, from either of those two applications, you can select the comp image and purchase the high-resolution version of the file right from the Links palette.

Adobe makes purchasing stock photo images easy because you can set up a single shopping cart account (accessible right from within Bridge) that enables you to purchase images all at once, even if they are from multiple partner libraries. Adobe has also negotiated with all the partners to offer a single consistent license agreement for all images.

Adobe Photographers Directory

Few of us are professional photographers. Although the stock photo library might come in handy for common types of images, there are times when you might need to find a photographer to take the perfect picture for your project (try saying that five times fast!). Thankfully, Bridge now includes direct access to an online directory of photographers through the Adobe Photographers Directory link in Favorites.

Through this interface, shown in Figure 5.13, you can search for photographers by location, specialty, and name.

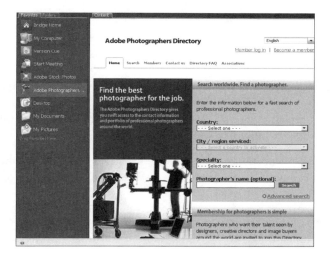

FIGURE 5.13
Locate professional photographers for your projects.

Other Bridge Functions

As we finish up our look at Adobe Bridge, there are still a few more features that you might be interested in trying—specifically, Bridge Home, Adobe Connect, Get Photos from Camera, Version Cue, and Color Settings. Let's review these remaining items now.

Bridge Home

Adobe's Bridge Home, found at the top of your favorites list, is a great place to get information about the products in the CS3 suite. Seen in Figure 5.14, Bridge Home gives you direct access to training, conference information, and other resources.

FIGURE 5.14
Use Bridge
Home to find
information
about your CS3
suite products.

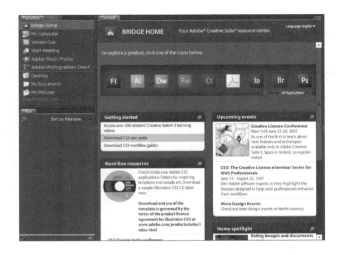

Acrobat Connect

Acrobat Connect is Adobe's cross-platform conferencing solution. Based on the Flash engine, Connect is a great tool for collaborating with others across distances. If you have a Connect account, you can initiate a conference from directly within Bridge by clicking the Start Meeting link within the Favorites panel.

Visit http://www.adobe.com/products/acrobatconnect/ for more information on Acrobat Connect and the option to sign up for a free trial account.

Get Photos from Camera

As mentioned earlier, Bridge can serve as your digital camera download application. To use this feature, simply plug in your camera, and then choose Get Photos from Camera from the File menu. You are prompted about whether you want Bridge to start each time you plug in your camera (this can be reset in the Bridge General preferences). Bridge displays the Photo Downloader dialog, as seen in Figure 5.15.

After making your settings, click Get Photos and your images are transferred from your camera.

FIGURE 5.15
Configure the settings for downloading your photos.

Version Cue

Version Cue is a product that is built into CS3 that enables groups of people to create and collaborate on products over a network. It can be used to manage multiple versions of files, and it acts essentially as a mini file server for your local network. To activate Version Cue, you can click the Version Cue item in Favorites, and then click the Start Server button. You are guided through a configuration process in your web browser where you are prompted to set up user accounts and server-type information.

After a server is up and running, you are able to browse it directly from the Version Cue shortcut in any CS3 application, as well as Bridge itself.

Creative Suite Color Settings

You've heard people say it before: "Never trust your monitor." Getting consistent color on your desktop has always been an issue with designers, and, at some point, we've all believed in all the gadgets, plug-ins, and utilities that promised to deliver computer color nirvana (like those emails I get that promise you can lose weight by eating chocolate).

So here comes Adobe saying that, with one click of a button, you can get consistent colors on your screen. Let's see how true that is. Choosing Creative Suite Color Settings from the Edit menu opens the Suite Color Settings dialog box, seen in Figure 5.16.

FIGURE 5.16
Manage your color settings across CS3.

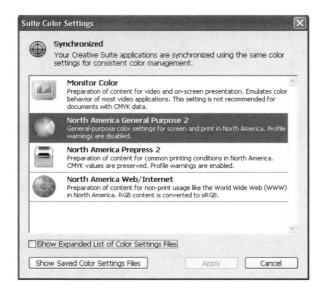

From here you can choose a color setting that will be synchronized across all your suite applications. And that's the key concept to focus on: *consistency across the suite*. The way I see it, there are two levels to color management. The first level is having what you see on your screen match perfectly to proofs, press sheets, and anywhere else your files need to go. This first level is the most complex when you consider that so many different devices and technologies exist, in addition to all the external physical factors.

The second level of color management is consistency across the applications that you use. I don't care as much about how close my screen is to my press proof. I do care that my colors look consistent among Illustrator, Photoshop, InDesign, and Acrobat.

Adobe promises this second level of color management with the Creative Suite Color Settings setting in Bridge. With one click, you can synchronize your color settings across the entire suite, ensuring that a color displayed in Photoshop looks exactly the same when displayed in Illustrator, InDesign, or Acrobat. Overall, that makes me happy.

Summary

This chapter introduced Adobe Bridge and the features that it provides across the CS3 suite. What started as a simple file browser is now a full-featured file organization, search, and preview utility. Although it is different from the browser built into your operating system, you'll appreciate the consistency across Windows and Macintosh platforms.

In addition to the file-browsing features, Bridge also acts as a camera image download utility, a central hub for managing color settings, a way to locate professional photographers and download stock photos, and even a multimedia conference program. How (and if) you use it is entirely up to you, but you'll definitely be surprised at the number of features you can access from a single application.

CHAPTER 6

Using Adobe Photoshop CS3

Over the past few versions, Photoshop has gotten an impressive face-lift, helping to make the traditionally complex program a bit easier to use. Photoshop CS3 certainly continues this trend by introducing a customizable user interface that enables you to turn off the features you don't want or need. In this chapter, you'll learn how to use Photoshop and get familiar with its tools and features.

What's New in Photoshop CS3?

By the Way

Photoshop CS3, as with the rest of the CS3 suite, sports a more consistent interface that should feel comfortable as you move from application to application. CS3 also features Device Central, where you can preview your graphics on a variety of different handheld devices; new export formats; a Refine Edge feature for controlling selections; non-destructive Smart Filters; and the capability to work directly with camera RAW files. Advanced new features include video and 3D layers for working with complex multimedia projects.

In CS3, Adobe is no longer shipping ImageReady, so Photoshop is now the primary image manipulation application for your web graphics.

Introduction to Photoshop CS3

When you first look at Photoshop (see Figure 6.1), you'll see the standard menu bar across the top of the screen.

FIGURE 6.1
Welcome to the
Photoshop CS3
interface.

Menu bar

Tool Options bar

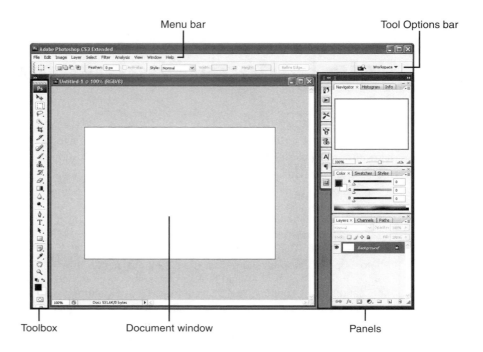

Toolbox   Document window   Panels

Directly under the menu bar is the Tool Options bar, which is context sensitive. That means the options listed in this area change depending on what tool you have selected. To the far right of the Tool Options bar is the button used to access Adobe Bridge and a button to access common workspaces and create new workspaces.

Unlike other CS3 applications, Photoshop does not provide a welcome screen when it first starts. You can access a wide range of help documentation from the Help menu, including many how-to documents encompassing a wide range of common tasks.

Along the left side of the screen is the toolbox, which contains all of Photoshop's tools, as well as several other functions. The color proxies indicate the foreground and background colors (you can also choose colors by clicking on the proxies), and the two icons surrounding the proxies enable you to set the colors to the default black foreground and white background, and to swap the foreground and background colors. Directly below the proxy icons are the Quick Mask mode buttons— we'll talk more about these useful mask buttons later in "Working with Masks"— and under those are the different view modes: Standard, Full Screen with Menu Bar, and Full Screen. You can toggle through the view modes by repeatedly pressing the F key on your keyboard (the letter *F*, not a Function key).

Some useful keyboard shortcuts to remember and get used to are the X key, to swap the foreground and background colors, and the D key, to set the colors to their default settings.

Did you Know?

Along the right side of your screen are some of Photoshop's panels. We discuss the primary panels and how to use them as we go through this chapter.

We talked about custom workspaces in Chapter 4, "The Key That Makes It All Work: Integration," and discussed how you can save your screen setup (including panel locations), which palettes are open or closed, and so forth.

By the Way

Finally, the document window is where you work on your file. The gray area is the part of the window that falls outside the image area. Photoshop lists the filename, the view percentage, and the color mode right in the title bar of each file. Along the bottom left of the window you'll find the status bar, including a zoom indicator and save status indicator.

Hold down your (Cmd-Option) [Ctrl+Alt] keys and click the status bar to see additional information on image dimensions, resolution, color depth, and so on.

Did you Know?

Opening, Creating, and Importing Files

You have to start with something, right? With Photoshop, you have various options: You can open existing files, whether Photoshop files, JPEG images, or any other of Photoshop's enormous list of supported image types; you can create a new file from scratch (basically a blank document); or directly import files from another source, such as a scanner or a digital camera.

The Open Dialog Box

As with just about any computer program, you can open a file by choosing File, Open or by pressing (Cmd-O) [Ctrl+O] to bring up the standard system Open dialog box. In Photoshop CS3, Adobe's own file picker is shown by default on a fresh install, as seen in Figure 6.2.

FIGURE 6.2
Adobe's File dialog provides more features than your built-in OS browser.

Using the pop-up view menu on the right side, you can show thumbnails or tiles of the files you are browsing. You can also use the Version Cue icon on the left side of the window to directly access files in Version Cue.

When you've located the file you want to open, click the Open button to open the file. Photoshop also lets you open several files at once by holding the (Cmd) [Ctrl] key as you click the different files. You can also open files in Photoshop directly from Adobe Bridge.

If you're more comfortable with the file browser built into your operating system, just click the "Use OS Dialog" button in the lower-left corner of the Adobe file browser and you'll revert back to the native file handler of your OS.

Creating a New File

To start from scratch and create a new file, choose File, New or press (Cmd-N) [Ctrl+N] to access the New dialog box (see Figure 6.3). Here you can give your file a name (you can do this later when you actually save the file, too) and choose a size and resolution for your file. In the Presets pop-up menu, Adobe has also included many common canvas sizes, and you can choose one of those (for example, a 5×7-inch file). Choosing the right resolution is very important when you create a

Photoshop file because changing the resolution in the file later could cause degradation or distortion in your file.

You can also create your own new document presets by choosing the options you want and then clicking on the Save Preset button.

Did you Know?

There's an option to choose what the default background of your file will be (White, Background Color, or Transparent), as well as the Color Mode (we'll cover these in just a moment). To view Advanced options, click the disclosure arrow. Here you can set a color profile or specify a nonsquare pixel aspect ratio for video content. The full expanded New File dialog can be seen in Figure 6.3.

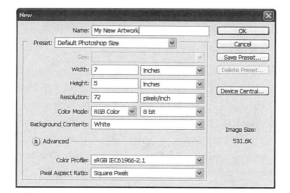

FIGURE 6.3
Choose the settings for your new file.

Color Modes

Photoshop lets you create files using any of several color modes, and it's important to know which one to choose. Although you can change color modes later in the process, just about any such change will cause color shifts. Each color mode has a *gamut*, or range of colors that can be produced. Some gamuts are wider, or can contain more colors, than others. For example, certain colors can be displayed in RGB that simply can't be reproduced in CMYK (for example, bright greens, oranges, or pastel colors). So converting an RGB file to CMYK might cause some colors to become dull or to change color altogether because those colors don't exist in CMYK. Let's take a look at each of the supported color models:

▶ **Bitmap**—Also called one-bit, a one-bit bitmap image can contain only two colors—usually black and white (like my favorite kind of cookie). It's useful for certain workflows, such as screen printing or specialized newspaper techniques. Some other programs (Illustrator or InDesign, for example) can change the black color of a bitmap to a different color, so scanned logos are also sometimes saved as bitmap images.

▶ **Grayscale**—The Grayscale color model is a range of grays, from white to black. The number of grays is determined by the bit depth, which we'll look at shortly. Mainly used for single-color artwork such as black-and-white photographs, the Grayscale model is also used to create monotones, duotones, tritones, and quadtones—all of which we cover later in "Monotones, Duotones, Tritones, and Quadtones."

▶ **RGB Color**—RGB (red, green, and blue) is a color method used to display color on televisions, computer monitors, and video screens. In RGB, you start with black (when your TV is off, the screen is black), and adding values of red, green, and blue results in white. When you're working on files that will be used in video, for broadcast, on the Web, or for onscreen presentations, RGB is the format you should use.

▶ **CMYK Color**—CMYK is a color method used to print color on paper. Unlike RGB, if you mix all the colors together in the CMYK color space, you get black, but if none of the colors is present, you get white. Anything you see in print uses CMYK (a blank piece of paper is white), so obviously when you're designing content that will be printed in color, CMYK is the color model of choice. CMYK stands for cyan (a shade of blue), magenta (a shade of red), yellow, and key (black). Black is referred to as key because that is traditionally the key color; it reinforces and invigorates the other colors (or so a printer once told me).

By the Way

As I mentioned earlier, the CMYK gamut isn't nearly as wide as most designers would like, so designers use spot colors (for example, Pantone colors) that allow designers to pick a specific color ink (including metallic inks, pastels, and the like).

▶ **Lab Color**—Almost scientific in nature (as if the other color models weren't), the Lab color model contains a Luminance level called L and two channels of color, called a and b (hence the name Lab). Lab has the widest color gamut of all those listed here, and Photoshop uses this model internally to calculate operations. For example, when you convert an image from RGB to CMYK, Photoshop first internally converts the RGB data to Lab and then converts the Lab data to CMYK. Because very few—if any—applications can use or understand Lab files, I suggest that you choose this color model only if your image isn't going to be placed into other applications or printed on a press.

Bit Depth

Along with color modes are bit depths. The bit depth is the number of bits used to store information about the components that make up a color model. For example, in a grayscale image, there are only shades of gray, ranging from white to black, so only a single value is used to represent the image. In an 8-bit grayscale image, there are 2 to the power of 8, or 256, levels of gray. In a 16-bit grayscale image, there are 2 to the power of 16 levels, or more than 65,000, shades of gray.

In other color models, the bit depth is applied to the values that make up the color. In 8-bit RGB, for example, there are a total of 256 levels of red, 256 levels of green, and 256 levels of blue that can be used and mixed. In general, the higher your bit depth, the smoother your gradients and the better your image quality will be.

Importing Images

Another way to bring images into Photoshop is to import them from another hardware source. Plenty of scanners, traditional cameras with digital film backs, fully digital cameras, video capture devices, and the like can be used to capture images that can be directly imported into Photoshop. Each of these devices usually comes with a plug-in for Photoshop to allow this use. For example, my Epson Expression 1600 FireWire scanner has a plug-in that enables me to access my scanner from the File, Import submenu.

> Check with your hardware manufacturer for the latest driver and plug-in updates. You can usually download them free from the Internet.

Did you Know?

More popular than almost anything these days are digital cameras. It seems as though just about everyone has one. Some cameras let you import pictures directly into Photoshop as JPEG images; others simply copy the files to your hard drive. Additionally, some cameras support something called camera raw format.

> For organizing and cataloging photos, you can use Windows Vista Photo Gallery, or Macintosh users can use iPhoto (part of Apple's iLife software package).

Did you Know?

Camera Raw Image Support

Many of the newer digital cameras have the capability to shoot in "raw" format. This means that the camera preserves the image in an uncompressed and unmodified format instead of storing it as a JPEG file and/or applying enhancements, such as color saturation (as most cameras do). The benefit, of course, is that the image is unadulterated and contains every aspect of the data that the camera can capture. You can open raw files directly in Photoshop or through Bridge.

Customizing Your Interface with Workspaces

With so many features for hundreds of different tasks, there are many different menus and commands to choose from when using Photoshop. If you work for a news media agency and aren't allowed to alter images using features such as the Vanishing Point filter, you might want to create a Photoshop environment that has less clutter.

Choose Edit, Menus to open the Keyboard Shortcuts and Menus dialog box. Clicking on the eyeball icon next to a menu command determines the visibility of that menu item, as shown in Figure 6.4.

FIGURE 6.4
Customize which menu items are visible.

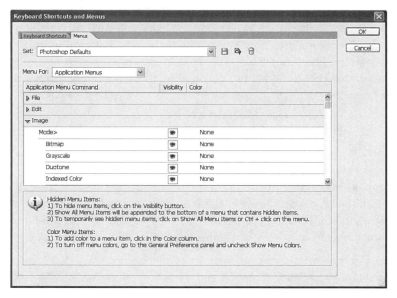

Besides showing or hiding menu items, you can apply specific colors to each menu item. This is helpful if you want to make an item easier to find. Any changes you make to menu items are stored in custom workspaces, accessible through the workspace button in the Tool Options bar.

In addition to menu items, panel groupings and arrangement are also saved in custom workspaces. To save your current workspace in a custom workspace, choose Save Workspace from the Workspace pop-up menu.

Adobe has included several workspaces by default, including a very useful workspace called What's New in CS3, shown in Figure 6.5. When chosen, the What's New in CS3 workspace highlights all of the features that are new in Photoshop CS3.

FIGURE 6.5
What's New in CS3 shows the new features in Photoshop CS3; here the new features are highlighted in the menus.

Working with Selections

Selections are especially important in Photoshop due to the pixel-based nature of the program. With a few exceptions, such as text and vector shapes, everything in Photoshop is just a mass of pixels. If you have a photograph with a blue sky, don't think of it as a sky that's colored blue, but rather many, many blue pixels that together form the image of a sky. If you want to change the sky to a different color, you can't just select the sky; you have to select all the individual pixels that form the sky. At a basic level, if you want to manipulate only *part* of your image, you need to isolate that part so other parts of your image aren't affected.

By the

    Way

Selections can also be called masks. When professionals used an airbrush to edit photographs in the past, they didn't want to accidentally affect other parts of the photo as they worked, so they cut masks (called friskets) that allowed them to use the airbrush on a specific part of the photo.

It might all sound a bit confusing, but as we go through the individual selection tools and the methods used to work with selections, everything will begin to make sense.

Marquee Selection Tools

The Marquee selection tools are used whenever you want to select a rectangular or elliptical range of pixels. For example, say that you want to darken a rectangular area of a photo so you can overlay some text. You would use the Rectangular Marquee tool to select an area that you will darken.

You have various options when using the Marquee tools:

▶ Holding the Shift key while dragging constrains the marquee area to a square or a circle.

▶ Holding the Option (Alt) key while dragging makes the point where you clicked the center of the marquee rather than the corner of the marquee.

▶ Holding the spacebar freezes the marquee and lets you drag it anywhere in your image with the mouse.

The options for the Marquee tool can be found in the Tool Options bar. By default, if you currently have a selection on your screen and then you draw a new marquee, you get a new selection and the previous marquee is discarded. You can change this behavior by clicking one of the Add, Subtract, or Intersect buttons, shown in Figure 6.6.

FIGURE 6.6
Choose the options for multiple marquees.

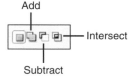

For example, if you draw your first selection, click the Add button, and then draw another marquee, both areas are selected simultaneously. If your new marquee overlaps the previous one, they are joined together to form a single larger selection.

I personally find it tedious to have to navigate up to the Tool Options bar to specify Add, Subtract, or Intersect mode, so naturally, I use the keyboard shortcuts. Holding the Shift key adds to your selection, holding (Option) [Alt] subtracts from your selection, and holding both Shift and (Option) [Alt] together uses the Intersect mode.

Notice that the Marquee icon in the Tool Options bar is actually a pop-up menu button in itself. See the sidebar "Tool Options for Everyone" later in this section.

At times you might want to draw a marquee that is a specific size. Rather than guessing as you draw the marquee, you can choose one of the options from the Style pop-up menu in the Tool Options bar: Fixed Aspect Ratio (which resamples the file) or Fixed Size. When either of these two options is chosen, you can enter a Width and Height value, and you'll notice that as you draw with the Marquee tool, your selection will be created or constrained to the dimensions you've specified.

After you've drawn your selection, you can move the selection around as you like by positioning your cursor anywhere inside the marquee and then dragging it. You'll notice that only the selection itself moves, not the pixels that are inside it. To move the pixels, switch to the Move tool or press and hold the (Cmd) [Ctrl] key before you start dragging the selection. To drag a *copy* of the selected pixels, press and hold (Cmd-Option) [Ctrl+Alt] before you click and drag.

Lasso Tools

Although the Marquee selection tools can be quite helpful, chances are, there will be plenty of times when you'll need to select something that isn't rectangular or elliptical in shape. The Lasso tool enables you to make irregularly shaped selections. Simply choose the Lasso tool and press the mouse button. As you drag, you'll see a line appear. When you release the mouse button, Photoshop closes the path and turns it into a selection. All the options we spoke about for the Marquee tools (adding, subtracting, moving, and so on) are available here as well.

If you're not as comfortable using a mouse, it can be difficult to make clean selections using the Lasso tool. Don't fret, though—Photoshop has two variations of the Lasso tool that might help:

▶ **Polygonal Lasso tool**—I personally use this selection tool more than any other, and I find it extremely useful for many tasks. Instead of having to press the mouse and drag it all over your screen, you can click once and then move your cursor to the next spot and click again. A "rubber band" follows your cursor around to give you visual feedback of where your selection path will be drawn, as demonstrated in Figure 6.7. You can either click the original point to close your path and turn it into a selection or simply double-click to have Photoshop automatically close the path for you.

FIGURE 6.7
Use the Polygonal Lasso tool to select areas using straight lines.

Did you ___
Know?

Holding the (Option) [Alt] key while using the regular Lasso tool makes it act just like the Polygonal Lasso tool.

▶ **Magnetic Lasso tool**—You spent enough money on your computer and on the software you're using, so why are *you* left doing all the work? Shouldn't the computer be doing the work for you? Well, the Magnetic Lasso tool does its part: It automatically detects edges as you use it. An edge here is defined as a shift or change between one color and another. As you drag along an edge with the Magnetic Lasso tool, it automatically detects the edge and draws a path along it (shown in Figure 6.8). Double-clicking with the tool automatically closes the path and turns it into an active selection.

FIGURE 6.8
The Magnetic Lasso tool does the work for you!

If you look at the Tool Options bar when you have the Magnetic Lasso tool selected, you can see various options that control the sensitivity of the tool. Width refers to how far the tool will look for an edge from where your cursor is. Edge Contrast controls how sensitive the tool is with regard to differences in color. A higher number finds only an edge that is a high-contrast one, whereas a lower number looks for more subtle shifts in color. The Frequency value determines how many points the tool uses to draw out the path. A higher number yields a path that is more precise, and a lower number results in a smoother path. The button at the right enables you to use a pressure-sensitive tablet to change the Width setting.

Did you **Know?**

With Caps Lock turned on, Photoshop displays the cursor for the Magnetic Lasso tool as the size of the Width setting, making it easier to trace over edges of color. Pressing the right or left brackets on your keyboard increases or decreases the Width setting by one pixel.

Magic Wand

For selecting areas of similar color, you can use the Magic Wand tool. By default, the Magic Wand selects all pixels of similar color adjacent to the area that you click. Simply click an area of your image. If you uncheck the Contiguous option in the Tool Options bar, Photoshop selects all similarly colored pixels throughout the entire document.

You can control how sensitive the Magic Wand tool is by adjusting the Tolerance setting in the Tool Options bar. A low tolerance number means the Magic Wand selects only pixels that are closer to the color that you clicked. For example, if you click a dark blue color with a low tolerance, the Magic Wand selects only dark-blue pixels— but with a higher tolerance, other shades of blue are selected as well. You can see this setting in Figure 6.9. As with the other selection tools, you can use the Add, Subtract, and Intersect options with the Magic Wand tool.

Low Tolerance (20)   High Tolerance (100)

FIGURE 6.9
Use higher tolerances to select a wider range of colors.

Watch Out!

> If you don't see the Tolerance setting in the Tool Options bar, it means you haven't selected the Magic Wand tool from the toolbox.

Did you Know?

> Another way to make a selection is by using a feature called Quick Mask, which we cover later in "Quick Mask Mode."

Selecting a Range of Colors

Although the Magic Wand tool is cool, it doesn't really provide the user (that's you) with any useful feedback. It's basically hit and miss—you click, see what is selected, deselect, change the Tolerance level a bit, and then try again.

Let me direct your attention to the Color Range feature (Select, Color Range). Here you can use an eyedropper tool to click parts of an image and get a preview so you can see what will be selected before you actually make the selection, as seen in Figure 6.10.

FIGURE 6.10
Use the Color Range feature to fine-tune selections of colors.

Above that, you have options such as Fuzziness, which can control how sensitive the feature is to color shifts. Using the Select pop-up menu, you can choose to automatically select ranges of predefined colors, highlights, shadows, midtones, and even out-of-gamut colors.

For even better previewing, you can choose to preview your document window itself with different viewing options that are found in the Selection Preview pop-up menu. Clicking on the OK button closes the Color Range dialog box and returns you to your document, with your new selection waiting for you.

The Quick Selection Tool

New in Photoshop CS3 is the Quick Selection tool. This tool makes selecting an area as easy as painting inside of it. Grouped with the magic wand, the selection tool looks like a wand over an oval shaped selection. Like the magic wand, the tool uses similarities in color to make selections, but, unlike the magic wand, it does so in a more natural way.

To use the Quick Selection tool, simply choose it, then use it to "paint" inside the area that you want to select. As you paint, the selection will spread out from the tool until it reaches an edge. You can control the size of your selection "brush" using the brush size selection in the options bar. You can also choose whether or not the tool is creating a new selection (the default), adding to a selection, or subtracting from a selection by using the three quick selection tool icons in the options bar (immediately to the left of the brush size indicator).

The quick selection tool offers one of the easiest and most precise ways to make accurate selections within an image. Although long-time Photoshop gurus may turn to the magic wand through habit, the Quick Selection tool will likely become your first stop for complex selections in the future.

Feathering

Ever see a nice vignette photograph with a soft edge and wonder how they did that? Wonder no more. Until now, you've been creating selections that have hard edges. Using a technique called *feathering*, you can specify a gradual edge for your selection instead of a hard one. You can specify how soft your edges are by indicating how many pixels you want your feather to be. For each of the selection tools, you can specify a feather amount in the Tool Options bar. Doing so applies the feather to your selection as you make it. Alternatively, you can apply a feather by making a selection, choosing Select, Modify, Feather, and then entering a feather radius, demonstrated in Figure 6.11.

When you apply a feather to a selection, it stays until you discard the selection. Additionally, the feather isn't editable, meaning that you can't change the value. So if you apply a five-pixel feather to a selection, you can't then decide to change it to an eight-pixel feather. You basically have to discard the selection, create a new one, and then apply an eight-pixel feather (or use Undo if you applied the feather after making the selection).

FIGURE 6.11
Feather your
selections to
create soft
edges.

When you're unsure of how much of a feather you want, save your selection before you apply a feather (saving selections is covered later in "Saving and Loading Selections"). This way you can always reapply the feather, if necessary.

Once you understand feathering, you'll want to switch to the Refine Edges feature (discussed in the next section) to preview your edge options before you make them.

Here's an important fact: Feathers are calculated using pixels, not units that are absolute. Because the size of a pixel is dependent on the resolution of your file, a 10-pixel feather might be very soft in a 72ppi file, yet barely recognizable in a 300ppi file. As you get experience in working with feathered selections, you'll get a better feel for how much is right for each file.

There are many uses for feathering selections. As we mentioned earlier, they can be used to help create soft-edged masks to create vignettes, as seen in Figure 6.12. They can also be used for creating soft cast shadows, for glow effects, for blending photos into each other, and more. I find that they are most useful for selections that you make for purposes of photo retouching. If you have an area that needs an adjustment such as a color shift, doing so with a regular selection creates a visible line that shows where you made the correction. Using a feathered selection, however, results in a seamless correction that no one will be able to see.

FIGURE 6.12
Feathering can
be used to cre-
ate soft-edged
masks.

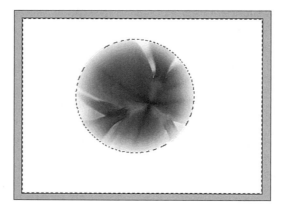

Tool Options for Everyone

The Tool Options bar is useful and gives quick access to the most commonly used options for each Photoshop tool, but the most brilliant part of it is something called Tool Presets, which enable you to save different settings that you use often. For example, say you often use a feathered 4×5 aspect ratio setting for your Rectangular Marquee. You can save that as a tool preset and access those settings with one click of a button. You can store many of these tool presets, saving you valuable time as you work on your files.

Of course, these presets aren't limited to the selection tools—you can save tool presets for just about any Photoshop tool. You do so by choosing the settings you want in the Tool Options bar, clicking on the tool icon (the one that looks like a pop-up button), and then clicking on the Create New Tool Preset button. Alternatively, you can choose New Tool Preset from the fly-out menu, visible in Figure 6.13.

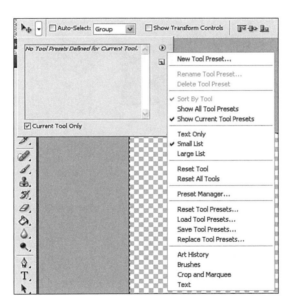

By the Way

FIGURE 6.13
Create new presets with commonly used settings.

Give your new tool preset a descriptive name (otherwise, you won't remember what each one is), and it will appear in the list from now on. These are application preferences, meaning that even if you close the file you're working on or open a new or different file, your tool presets will still be present.

Modifying Selections

You can modify a selection after it's created in several ways. One of the most useful is by using the Select, Inverse command or pressing (Cmd-Shift-I) [Ctrl+Shift+I], which basically selects whatever you *don't* have selected (and deselects everything that was selected). Sometimes it's easier to select the one part of an image that you don't want and then invert your selection. You can also transform your selection. These transformations that you make (by choosing Select, Transform Selection) apply only to the selection itself, not the pixels inside them. For example, you might use the Rectangular Marquee tool to create a square selection, and then use the Transform Selection command to rotate the square to effectively get a diamond-shape selection, as seen in Figure 6.14.

FIGURE 6.14
Transform your selection using the transformation tools.

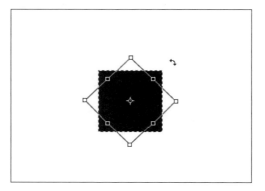

Under the Select, Modify submenu, you can adjust your selection in four additional ways. All of them are useful, and it would be a good idea to experiment with them to fully understand what each one does. In each of these cases, you'll lose your original selection, so you might want to save it before you modify the selection. These are the additional options:

▶ **Border**—Use the Select, Modify, Border command to specify a pixel width border to add around the edge of your selection. This command yields a round-cornered border, which is not appropriate in all cases.

▶ **Smooth**—Not everyone can draw with a mouse as well as they can with a pencil (myself included), so when you're creating selections with the Lasso tools, it's nice to know that you can smooth out your selections by choosing Select, Modify, Smooth. This is also useful when you're making selections with the Magic Wand tool because it can sometimes create selections with jagged or uneven edges.

▶ **Expand**—At times you will want to enlarge or expand your selection by a specific number of pixels. One such example is if you want to have a border or background around the edges of text. Although you can instead scale your selections using the Transform Selection command I mentioned earlier, many times simply scaling your selection won't work (especially with odd-shape selections).

▶ **Contract**—Rather than expanding your selections, sometimes you'll want to contract them. You can do so by choosing Select, Modify, Contract and then specifying the number of pixels you want your selection to shrink.

Refining Edges

In addition to the Modify options for selections, you can also refine them using the Refine Edge button in the Tool Options bar. The Refine Edge dialog, shown in Figure 6.15, provides control over how the selection is actually made. You can choose edge softening, the radius of the edge (usually just a single pixel), whether the edge should be expanded outward or contracted in on itself, and so forth. By clicking the Preview button, you can see exactly what each setting will do.

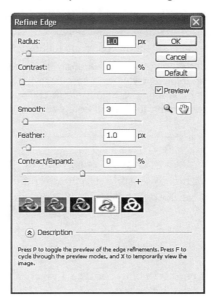

FIGURE 6.15
Refine Edge helps you fine-tune how your selection behaves.

Saving and Loading Selections

A quick selection is easy enough to make, but many times getting just the perfect selection for your needs can take quite a bit of time (and a double dose of patience). The last thing you want in that case is to accidentally click somewhere and lose your selection. Or you might want to continue to make adjustments to that selection later. You can save your selections so you can retrieve them later by choosing Select, Save Selection (shown in Figure 6.16). It's best to give your selections a descriptive name; otherwise, if you have several of them, it might be difficult to find the right one.

FIGURE 6.16
Save selections for later use.

If you want to access the last selection you made, choose Select, Reselect.

In general, it's a good idea to name things carefully because one day you'll have to edit the file, and you'll go crazy trying to remember what you named it. You also never know who else will be working with your file (a coworker, prepress operator, or client, for example), so naming things will help people quickly find what they are looking for.

When you have selections already saved in a file, you can either continue to save new selections or add to or modify existing selections from the Save Selection dialog. Alternatively, you can load selections by choosing the Select, Load Selection command.

Channels

Channels can be thought of as selections because, in reality, that's what they are. You can find them in the Channels panel.

Every file has at least one channel by default, and three or more if it is a color file. For example, an RGB file starts with three channels: one each for red, green, and blue. Photoshop also displays a composite, one for all of the channels combined, although this composite isn't actually a channel itself. You can view and edit each channel individually by accessing the Channels panel, which gives you total control over your image, as seen in Figure 6.17.

FIGURE 6.17
Each component of the color file has a channel as well as selections.

But the real strength here is that you can create your own channels. When you save a selection (as mentioned earlier), Photoshop is creating a channel, and that is how the selection is stored. Channels that you create can contain 256 levels of gray. Certain file formats can use the information in channels as well. For example, you can specify that a channel should be a transparency mask when you export a file as a PNG from Photoshop. In contrast to clipping masks (which we discuss in "Creating a Clipping Path") that you might save in EPS format, an alpha channel transparency mask can utilize 256 levels of gray.

Rather than having to load selections via the Select menu, you can simply (Cmd-click) [Ctrl+click] on a channel in the Channels panel to load that selection. This is true with any layer—you can create a selection based on all of a layer's contents this way.

Paths

If you've used Illustrator before, you know what a Bèzier path is. You'll learn more about it in Chapter 7, "Using Adobe Illustrator CS3," but at a basic level, it's an object-based path (defined by its shape rather than a set number of pixels) that you can draw using the Pen tool, demonstrated in Figure 6.18. It just so happens that Illustrator, InDesign, Flash, and Photoshop all have Bézier Pen tools—mainly because these tools are basic drawing tools.

FIGURE 6.18
Bézier tools are
a staple of
most drawing
programs.

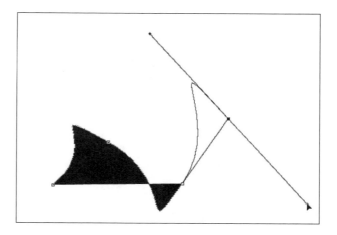

The selection tools we've discussed until now aren't really precise drawing tools at all. When you want to draw a high-quality selection, the Pen tool is the way to go. You can also use a variety of vector shape tools to create paths, including the Rectangle, Ellipse, Polygon, Line, and Rounded Rectangle tools. When you select one of these Shape tools, you need to be aware of three options in the Tool Options bar that control the behavior of the paths you draw. The Shape Layers option creates vector layer masks (covered in "Creating a Clipping Path"), the Paths option creates free-standing vector paths, and the Fill Pixels option (not available for the Pen tools) immediately commits paths to pixels as you draw. For making selections, the Paths option (the default) gives you the results that you expect. These options are located immediately to the left of the Shape tools.

As you draw a path, you see it appear in the Paths panel. From the Paths panel, you can choose Save Path from the panel fly-out menu to save the path for future use. At any time you can also (Cmd-click) [Ctrl+click] on the path in the Paths panel to create an active selection from the path.

You can also use paths in the reverse context. You start by creating a selection using any of the methods we've discussed. Then, with the selection active, choose Make Work Path from the Paths panel fly-out menu (shown in Figure 6.19) to turn that selection into a vector path; at that point, you can use the Pen tools to further edit that path, if necessary.

FIGURE 6.19
Use the Paths
fly-out menu to
save paths and
create paths
from selections.

Creating a Clipping Path

A clipping path is basically a mask for an exported EPS image (although the newer TIFF format supports clipping paths as well). You can save a path with an image that will define how the image appears in a page-layout application, such as InDesign or QuarkXPress.

In Chapter 3, "The Game Plan: Developing a Workflow," we discussed how InDesign can understand Photoshop's native transparency, so clipping paths aren't really necessary in a full Adobe workflow. Regardless, it's important to know about clipping paths in case you need to work with QuarkXPress or send files to other people.

Begin by creating a path. If you're uncomfortable using the Pen tool, use the inverse method mentioned earlier, in which you start with a selection and then convert it to a path. After the path is created, save it. Then choose Clipping Path from the Paths panel fly-out menu and choose the path you saved.

Finally, for the path to be recognized in a page-layout application, choose to save your file in either Photoshop EPS or TIFF format. See " Saving and Printing Files" later in this chapter for information on how to save files.

Layers and Effects

Trying to imagine what Photoshop would be like without layers is like trying to imagine what a peanut butter and jelly sandwich is like without the bread (everything is just one gooey, sticky mess).

Imagine painting in the traditional method. As you use the brush on the canvas, you're adding paint. If you decide to paint a white cloud over a blue sky, the white paint covers the blue paint under it (some paint might show through, and we'll get to the subject of opacity soon). Theoretically, if you wanted to move that cloud to a different part of the sky, you'd have to cut it out and then glue it elsewhere, leaving a gaping hole in your canvas. It's no different in Photoshop. Let's say you create a blue sky and then draw a white cloud over a part of it. If you try to select and move that cloud elsewhere, you'll have a hole cut out of the sky where the cloud was originally. You can see this effect in Figure 6.20.

FIGURE 6.20
If you cut and paste without layers, you leave a hole in your canvas!

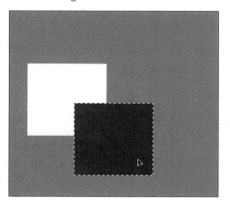

Now let's talk about layers. Going back to the canvas, imagine that you first painted the sky and then covered your painting with a clear sheet of acetate (plastic). You then painted the white cloud on the acetate. Think about it: You'd see the same composite result, but if you moved the acetate around, you'd be able to position the cloud independently of the sky under it. In Photoshop, think of a layer as a sheet of acetate—only better. Layers can have opacity values, blending modes, and even special effects such as drop shadows and bevels. As you'll see, Photoshop uses layers extensively to make files editable and easier to work with.

Layers 101

Let's start with the basics. Layers are controlled via the Layers panel. Every Photoshop file starts with one layer, called a Background layer, which can be only the bottom-most layer in the document. This layer does not support any kind of transparency—think of it as the canvas under a painting.

To convert the Background layer so it acts like any other layer, double-click it to rename it Layer 0 and click OK.

To add a layer to a file, click the Create New Layer button (the dog-eared page icon) in the Layers panel. Alternatively, you can drag an existing layer on top of the Create New Layer icon to create a duplicate layer. You can drag layers up and down to shuffle them within the hierarchy of the Layers panel, shown in Figure 6.21. Layers at the bottom of the panel are stacked behind those that appear at the top of the panel.

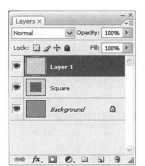

FIGURE 6.21
Create and manage layers in the Layers panel.

Viewing, Linking, and Locking Layers

Besides being able to shuffle the stacking order of objects by moving layers up and down in the Layers panel, you can choose to show or hide any layer at any time. The little eye icon to the left of each layer's entry in the Layers panel indicates whether a layer is visible (shown in Figure 6.22).

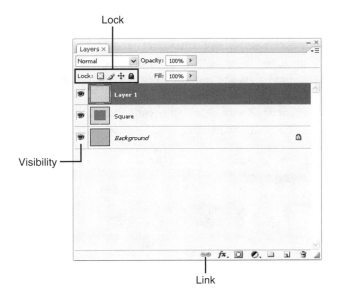

FIGURE 6.22
The eye icon sets the visibility of a layer.

Click once on the eye to hide the layer; click again to show the layer. If you (Option-click) [Alt+click] an eye, Photoshop automatically hides all the other layers in your document, enabling you to see and work on just the layer you clicked.

Using the Move tool (the arrow with a + at the lower-right corner), you can move the items on a layer, but sometimes you'll want to move several items together at once—and those items may be on different layers. Photoshop enables you to Shift+click layers to select them so you can move them or apply transformations to them. You can (Cmd-click) [Ctrl+click] to select noncontiguous layers as well. If you are constantly moving several layers as a single unit, rather than having to select them each time, you can link them by first selecting the layers and then clicking on the Link button at the bottom left of the Layers panel. When you do so, a link icon appears on those layers, indicating that the transform edits you make will occur to those layers as a unit. Transform edits consist of moving, scaling, and rotating, as well as using the Free Transform tool.

If you'd like to lock a layer so no changes can be made to it, simply select the layer in the Layer panel, and then click the Lock you want to use. You can also use the icons to the right of the Lock button to lock specific parts/attributes of a layer. From left to right, these layer lock options are locking transparent pixels, locking image pixels, locking the layer location, and, finally, locking everything.

Layer Opacity and Blending Modes

As mentioned earlier, you can apply opacity levels or blending modes to a layer that affect the appearance of the pixels on the layer. For example, changing the opacity of the top layer of your document, demonstrated in Figure 6.23, enables you to see through that layer to the layer underneath—basically allowing the lower layer to show through. Blending modes enable you to specify how the pixels from the upper layer and those from the lower layer mix with each other. For example, if you had two layers and Layer 1 was filled with blue and Layer 2 was filled with yellow, you could set Layer 2 to use the Multiply blending mode to give you a green result.

FIGURE 6.23
The opacity and blending mode determine how your layer visually interacts with layers under it.

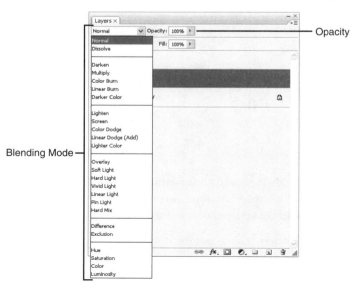

Layer Groups

Managing a lot of layers can be difficult, and having to scroll through a large number of them is time-consuming as well. Similar in concept to Illustrator, Photoshop has the capability to create groups. A group is like a folder that has several layers inside it. You can also put a group into another group (up to four levels deep), giving you even more control.

Create new groups by clicking on the Create a New Group button (the folder icon) at the bottom of the Layers panel, and you can add other layers into a group by dragging them into the group, as seen in Figure 6.24.

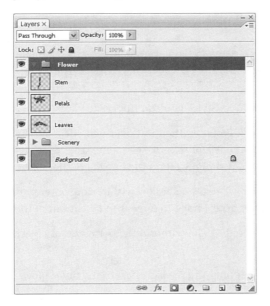

FIGURE 6.24
Use layer groups to group large numbers of layers.

Layer Styles

Each layer can have several effects applied to it, which Photoshop refers to as *layer styles*. You can access the Layer Style dialog box by choosing Blending Options from the Layer panel fly-out menu. Alternatively, you can double-click the layer itself (just not on the actual name of the layer), or choose Layer, Layer Style.

To apply a particular effect, check the box for it along the left side of the dialog box, demonstrated in Figure 6.25. For each effect, you can use specific settings to control how that effect is applied. A layer can have any combination of these effects.

FIGURE 6.25
Layers can have multiple effects applied to them.

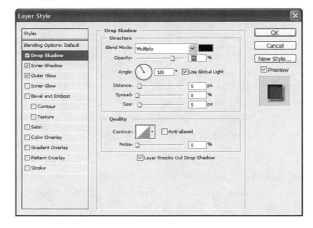

Did you Know?

Double-click a layer's name in the Layers panel to edit the name of the layer. Double-click elsewhere in the layer's entry to open the Layer Style dialog box.

Here are some of the layer styles you can apply:

▶ **Drop Shadow**—Probably the most overused effect ever created, the drop shadow is still very useful to make elements seem to pop off the page. This effect creates a soft shadow along the outside of the objects on your layer.

▶ **Inner Shadow**—Creates a shadow within transparent areas on your layer. The effect causes your image to appear to be cut out of the page.

▶ **Outer Glow**—Adds a glow around the perimeter of objects on the selected layer.

▶ **Inner Glow**—Applies the reverse effect of the outer glow.

▶ **Bevel and Emboss**—Contains several settings that make an image appear as if it were three-dimensional by adding highlighted edges. Used often for making web buttons.

▶ **Satin**—Adds shadows and highlights to make the image appear as if it has the pillowed waves or ripples of satin.

▶ **Color Overlay**—Simply adds a color over the entire layer. Colors can be set with an opacity, and this can be used to create color casts or special effects.

▶ **Gradient Overlay**—Same as Color Overlay, but uses gradient fills.

▶ **Pattern Overlay**—Same as Color Overlay and Gradient Overlay, but with pattern fills.

▶ **Stroke**—Can be used to simulate a stroked outline around the objects on your layer.

Saving and Reusing Styles

When you've defined settings for a layer style that you like, you can save it as a style by clicking the New Style button. You can then easily apply that style to other layers. After you save a style, it appears in the Styles panel, shown in Figure 6.26. Alternatively, you can create new styles directly from the Styles panel.

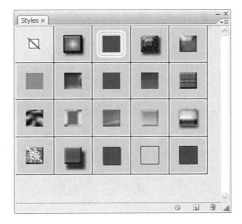

FIGURE 6.26
Define and manage reusable styles.

Photoshop actually ships with several sets of styles you can use. More important, you can reverse-engineer these styles by seeing how they were created by applying the style, then opening up the Layer Style dialog to see the settings. You can access these sets from the Styles panel fly-out menu.

Layer Comps

Because layers can be manipulated so easily in Photoshop and because they are nondestructive, designers often use layers to create different variations of a design. By hiding or showing different layers, they can quickly preview several design ideas—either throughout their own process or to show a client several design possibilities.

Continually hiding and showing layers can be tedious—especially when you're trying to remember which layers were used for which design concept. So the wonderful folks at Adobe added a feature called layer comps, which manages this entire process quite well. Layer comps can save the visibility, position, and appearance (layer style) of each layer in your document. You can then quickly step through different layer comps to see how your designs look. Photoshop is simply remembering the "state" of each layer, so if you change an item on a certain layer, that change is automatically made on all of your layer comps, which makes this a great time-saver as well.

To create a layer comp, begin in the Layers panel and hide or show your layers as necessary to show your first design. Then open the Layer Comps panel and click the Create New Layer Comp button. You're presented with a dialog box (seen in Figure 6.27), where you can name your comp, choose which attributes Photoshop will save, and add a comment (always helpful for those of us who forget easily). Where was I again? Oh, yes, you can create additional layer comps by repeating the process.

FIGURE 6.27
Create layer comps for different concepts or arrangements within a single file.

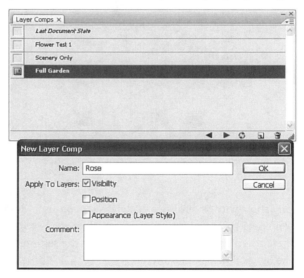

To preview each of your comps, simply click the icon along the left side of the Layer Comps panel, visible in Figure 6.27, or use the arrow buttons at the bottom of the panel to step through the different layer comps.

You might want to get used to creating layer comps because Illustrator and InDesign have the capability to choose between layer comps when you import the file into your layouts. That means you can create several design ideas in a Photoshop file using layer comps and then place a single file into your layout, at which time you'll be asked to choose which design idea you want to appear in your layout for that use.

Did you Know?

Working with Masks

A mask hides some parts of an image and lets other parts show through. This is extremely useful when you want to hide parts of an image but you don't want to lose any data in your file by having to delete parts of it.

Earlier, we discussed one kind of mask: creating a clipping path for placing images into page-layout applications. But there are also needs for masking inside Photoshop itself—such as when you want to have one photo blend into another, or when you want to make a quick selection.

Layer Masks

When it comes to creating a mask for a layer, Photoshop makes the task easy. Using your selection method of choice, choose the layer in the Layers panel, select the area of the image that you want to remain visible, and click the Add Layer Mask button (a white circle in a gray box) at the bottom of the Layers panel. This does two things right off the bat: First, it masks the image in your document; second, it creates a second thumbnail in your layer, as demonstrated in Figure 6.28. In fact, let's take a closer look at what's going on in the Layers panel.

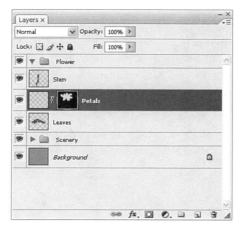

FIGURE 6.28
After applying a mask, a second thumbnail (showing the mask) can be seen in the Layers panel.

You'll notice that a masked layer has two thumbnails with a link icon between them. The thumbnail on the left is the image itself, and the thumbnail on the right is the mask. To edit and work with your image, click the left icon to highlight it. Any edits you make to that layer will occur to the image itself. If you click and highlight the thumbnail on the right, you can edit the mask itself.

If you're unsure of whether you're in the image-editing mode or the mask-editing mode, take a quick look at your document's title bar.

As you move the image with the Move tool, the mask moves along with it because the link icon between the two thumbnails indicates that they are linked to each other. If you click the link, it disappears, enabling you to move the image and mask independently of each other.

To remove a mask, drag the mask thumbnail to the Layer panel's Trash icon (in the lower right of the panel). You'll get a dialog box asking whether you want to apply the mask (which will delete the parts of the image that are masked) or discard it (the image will return to its full view).

Vector Masks

Although Photoshop has vector tools, it's not a vector-based drawing program. Photoshop uses vector outlines to create masks filled with color. For example, when you draw a rectangle using Photoshop's Rectangle tool with the Shape Layers option chosen in the Tool Options bar, a mask (which is the vector path) is created, filled with the color of your choice (which is fill pixels). You can also create vector masks by choosing Layer, Vector Mask, Reveal All or Layer, Vector Mask, Hide All.

Quick Mask Mode

Masks and selections are nearly one and the same. Sometimes you want to create a simple quick selection, and you can best do that by using one of Photoshop's many painting tools. That's where Quick Mask comes into play. Press the Q key on your keyboard to enter Quick Mask mode. You can tell you're in Quick Mask mode because it's indicated in the document's title bar.

When you're in Quick Mask mode, anything you paint or draw shows up in a transparent red color (demonstrated in Figure 6.29).

FIGURE 6.29
Use Quick Mask Mode to "paint" your selection, such as the leaf in this flower photograph.

Press Q again, and whatever was not red becomes your selection. This is extremely useful for creating selections that you will use in a layer mask. For example, imagine that you want a photo to fade into the layer under it. So you select the layer that the photo is on, press Q, select the Gradient tool, drag a gradient, and press Q again—your selection is now the gradient. Then you click the New Layer Mask button, and you're done.

Applying Transformations

Throughout the design process, you constantly need to make edits and changes to your artwork. Photoshop can help by enabling you to apply transformations to your layers and selections as you need them. These functions could be as simple and straightforward as moving an object from one side of the document to the other, or as complex as applying a warp distortion.

You can apply these transformations by choosing Edit, Transform. In Photoshop, when you choose a transform function with a selection already made, the transform applies only to your selection. If you choose a transform function with no selection, the transform applies to the entire layer (or group).

If you want to apply a quick transformation, you can also choose Free Transform, which enables you to move, rotate, scale, and apply perspective to a selection all in one step.

A unique transformation called Warp enables you to twist and distort your selection. When you've chosen to apply a warp, you are presented with a grid. By pulling the different parts of the grid, you can distort the pixels within it. Figure 6.30 demonstrates the setup of a warp effect before it is applied to a square.

FIGURE 6.30
Transformations, such as Warp, apply useful and interesting changes to your images.

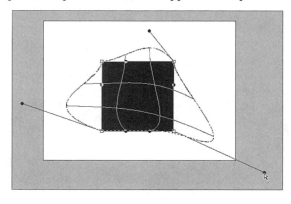

 The Warp transformation feature can be very useful for distorting artwork or images. You can make them appear as if they are wrapped around a bottle, displayed on a monitor or video screen, or on billboards or signs.

Smart Objects

As you learned in Chapter 2, "So Many Applications: Which One to Use?," pixel-based images are limited, in that their resolution determines how they can be transformed. Enlarging pixels reduces the final quality of an image. This limitation can make the design process more difficult because you might want to reduce a particular element in size, but you know that you won't be able to enlarge it later if you need to. As soon as you scale the element in size, the extra pixels are removed from the file, never to be seen again. This is especially true when placing content into Photoshop. For example, you might want to place some vector art from Illustrator into Photoshop. Although you can place the vector art at the size you need, they become pixels when you commit them and are then tied directly to the resolution of the file.

To address this issue, Photoshop has a feature called Smart Objects that enables you to scale artwork in Photoshop without losing any detail. Here's how it works. When you place an Illustrator file into Photoshop, a copy of the Illustrator file is embedded inside the Photoshop file. The artwork is placed onto a special kind of layer called a Smart Object, which displays the file in pixels, as a normal layer would. When you want to scale the Smart Object, Photoshop uses the embedded Illustrator file to regenerate the file at the higher resolution and simply updates the Smart Object layer.

In fact, you can even create Smart Objects from any raster file or Photoshop layer. Doing so enables you to scale your art smaller and back to the original size, with no loss of detail (scaling the artwork larger than the original won't help, though). Using Smart Objects, you can perform many edits in a nondestructive manner.

Did you Know?

You can create a Smart Object in Photoshop in several ways:

- ▶ Copy and paste artwork from Illustrator to Photoshop.

- ▶ Drag artwork from an Illustrator window directly into a Photoshop document.

- ▶ Place any file into a Photoshop document by choosing File, Place.

- ▶ Select a layer in your Photoshop document and choose Layer, Smart Objects, Convert to Smart Object, or choose Convert to Smart Object from the fly-out menu in the Layers panel, as seen in Figure 6.31.

FIGURE 6.31
You can easily convert an existing layer into a Smart Object.

You can tell that a layer is a Smart Object by the icon that appears in the thumbnail of the layer (a page with black and white boxes, as seen in Figure 6.32).

FIGURE 6.32
Smart Objects
are denoted by
a page icon
within their layer
thumbnail.

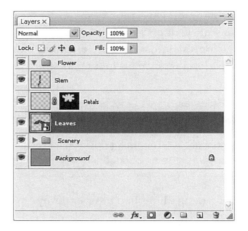

After you've created a Smart Object in Photoshop, you can apply transformations as
you would any layer. Additionally, you can perform certain functions with Smart
Objects to allow for further editing. If you've created a Smart Object from Illustrator
content, you can choose Layer, Smart Objects, Edit Contents. Alternatively, you can
double-click the Smart Object icon in the Layer thumbnail. This action launches
Illustrator and opens the Smart Object in Illustrator for editing. When you've made
your changes to the file, save it and close the file. Upon returning to Photoshop, the
Smart Object updates with the changes you made. Performing Edit Contents on a
Smart Object that was created from a Photoshop layer opens that Smart Object in a
new Photoshop file for editing.

By the Way

Remember that when you perform an Edit Contents function, you aren't editing the
original Illustrator or Photoshop file; Photoshop is creating a temporary file from
the embedded Smart Object.

Additionally, you can replace the contents of a Smart Object by choosing Layer,
Smart Objects, Replace Contents. This enables you to embed either an updated
Illustrator file or a totally new Illustrator file (similar to the Relink feature in
InDesign).

Digital Painting

Until now, we've been looking at Photoshop as a tool specifically for working with
existing images and photographs. In reality, there's a whole other side to Photoshop,
in which your screen is a canvas and your colors are paints and your mouse (or
pressure-sensitive tablet) is your paintbrush.

Choosing Colors

Photoshop enables you to choose colors in just about any way you desire. You can specify colors in RGB, CMYK, HSB, Lab, or Hexadecimal. Additionally, Photoshop ships with many different industry-standard custom color libraries such as Pantone and TOYO.

You can choose colors in Photoshop in any of several ways:

▶ **Click the Foreground or Background color proxy in the toolbox—** Photoshop presents you with the Color Picker (seen in Figure 6.33), where you can choose just about any color, including industry-standard spot colors (by clicking on the Color Libraries button).

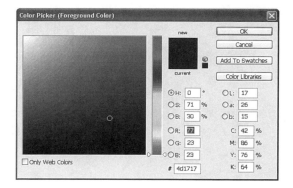

FIGURE 6.33
The Color Picker enables you to find and choose colors easily.

▶ **Click the Foreground or Background color proxy in the Color panel**—Photoshop, again, presents you with the Color Picker.

▶ **Click anywhere on the color ramp at the bottom of the Color panel**—This changes, depending on the color mode you have selected, and also provides quick shortcuts to black and white.

▶ **Adjust the color sliders in the Color panel**—You can choose to use the sliders to choose a color by eye, or you can enter values directly for a specific color (see Figure 6.34).

▶ **Choose a color from the Swatches panel**—You can store your own custom colors as well as access other color libraries from the Swatches panel flyout menu (see Figure 6.35).

FIGURE 6.34
Use the Color panel to quickly choose colors without opening the Color Picker.

FIGURE 6.35
Save and access commonly used colors in the Swatches panel.

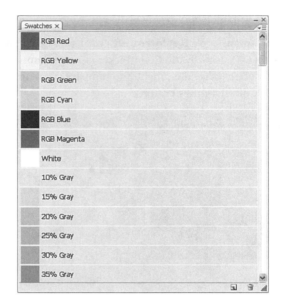

▶ **Use the eyedropper tool**—Sample a color from any area on your document or screen.

 To quickly fill an area with the Foreground color, press (Option-Delete) [Alt+Delete].

Gradients

Before soft drop shadows became the latest design fad, there were gradients: fills that fade gradually from one color to another, sometimes with multiple colors. Gradients can also fade from a color to transparent.

Creating gradients in Photoshop is quite easy, and there are basically two ways to accomplish the task. The first way is to add a Gradient Overlay layer style, as discussed earlier when talking about layer styles. The second—and far more popular—way is to use the Gradient tool.

With the Gradient tool selected, the Tool Options bar changes to reflect the different options you have for applying gradients. Click the pop-up arrow to get a list of pre-defined gradients (shown in Figure 6.36), and you can choose from any of five types of gradients: linear, radial, angle, reflected, and diamond.

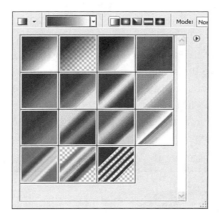

FIGURE 6.36
Choose from preset gradients or set your gradient type in the Tool Options bar.

To apply a linear gradient, with the Gradient tool selected, position your cursor at the point you want the leftmost color of the gradient to begin. Press and hold the mouse button while you drag to the place where you want the rightmost color of the gradient to end, as seen in Figure 6.37. When you release the mouse, Photoshop applies the gradient.

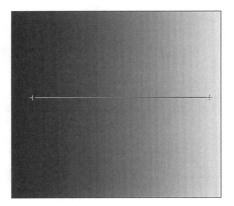

FIGURE 6.37
Click and drag to set your gradient endpoints.

If you don't have a selection made, using the Gradient tool results in a gradient that fills the entire layer.

By the Way

Did you Know?

You can drag your mouse outside of your selection, or even the document window, so that only a portion of the gradient is applied.

You can also create your own gradients by clicking on the gradient proxy in the Tool Options bar to open the Gradient Editor, seen in Figure 6.38. Click the New button to define a new gradient. Add a new color stop by clicking in an empty area under the gradient. You can edit the colors by double-clicking on the color-stop arrow. Arrows that appear above the gradient are *opacity stops,* and they let you define the transparency of the gradient at a specific point. You can have as many stops as you want in your gradient. The little diamonds that appear between the color stops are the midpoint of that section of the gradient; at that point, there's 50% of each color. You can adjust those points by dragging them left and right as well.

FIGURE 6.38
Use the Gradient Editor to create and save your own preset gradient designs.

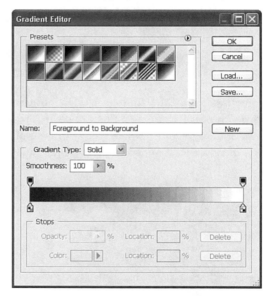

Did you Know?

Remember that using the Quick Mask feature along with the Gradient tool can help you create faded selections in the blink of an eye.

The Brush and Pencil Tools

To draw or paint with Photoshop, you can use either the Pencil tool or the Paintbrush tool. The Pencil tool is akin to the speedball inking pens of yesterday, enabling you to lay down solid pixels using different brush shapes. It's great for touching up small areas or for drawing lines and the like. The Paintbrush tool, on the other hand, has more of an organic feel to it, and you can even set it to act and feel like an airbrush using the Enable/Disable Airbrush Capabilities button to the right of the Brush and Pen controls in the Tool Options bar.

To paint with these tools, simply choose a brush shape from the pop-up menu in the Tool Options bar (demonstrated in Figure 6.39) and have fun painting!

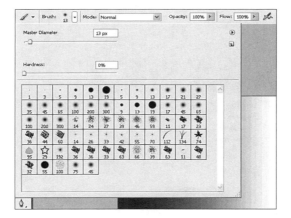

FIGURE 6.39
Use the pop-up menu in the Tool Options bar to change the shape of your painting tool.

Pressing the bracket keys ([ ]) on your keyboard is a quick way to increase or decrease your brush size.

Did you Know?

The power of the Brush tool comes from the brush engine inside Photoshop.

The Brush Engine

Historically, when it came to organic painterly drawing, Photoshop had always played second fiddle to another program, called Painter. But that changed when Adobe introduced the new brush engine back in Photoshop 7.

Let's take a closer look at the incredibly powerful brush features. Click once on the button that appears at the far right of the Tool Options bar when the Brush tool is selected, or choose Window, Brushes to open the Brushes panel, shown in Figure 6.40.

FIGURE 6.40
Choose and customize the capabilities of your brushes.

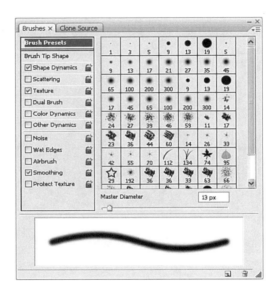

Along the left side of the panel are all the settings you can apply to a brush, the right side contains all the specific controls for each setting, and the bottom features a real-time preview of your brush.

Want more brushes? You can access hundreds of brushes from the Brushes panel fly-out menu.

Click each of the settings along the left to customize the behavior of your brush. With these settings, painters and illustrators can finally get the control they want and need right in Photoshop. For example, the Jitter attributes allow for a level of randomness that gives the brushes a real hand-drawn quality. When you're done finding the right settings for your brush, you can save them to use again later.

Defining Your Own Brush

Photoshop's brush engine lets you define your own custom brush shapes. Start with a grayscale image, and silhouette it. Then select it and choose Edit, Define Brush Preset. Give your custom brush shape a name, as seen in Figure 6.41, and when you choose the Brush tool, you'll see your custom shape appear in the Brush Tip Shape list.

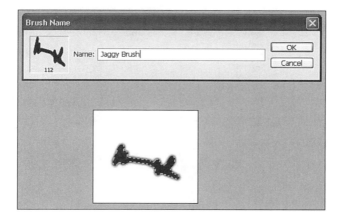

FIGURE 6.41
Create your own custom brushes!

History Brush

Adobe hasn't invented time travel just yet (I'm sure it will be in the next version, though), but there *is* a way to go back in time using Photoshop's History Brush.

The History Brush paints in your current file (or canvas) using pixels from a snapshot or a previous state of the file. For example, say that when you first opened your file, the sky in the photo was blue. Then you changed that blue color to orange. If you select the History Brush and indicate the source to be the original snapshot, painting with the History Brush will produce blue pixels as you paint on the sky. This is one way to get the popular "one splash of color in a black-and-white photo" effect.

Did you
Know?

Know Your History

Although Photoshop doesn't have multiple undos (as InDesign and Illustrator do, for example), it does have something called the History panel, which records each step you make as you work. You can step backward one step at a time, or you can jump to a previous step by clicking on the entries in the History panel (shown in Figure 6.42).

FIGURE 6.42
Navigate through changes using the History panel.

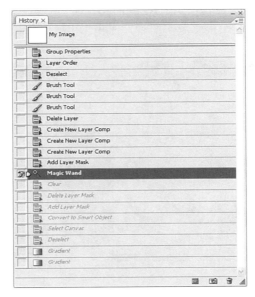

Clicking the Create New Snapshot button freezes the state of your document in time. This snapshot of your document can be used as a reference for other functions (such as the History Brush). Snapshots are stored near the top of the panel; the bottom part of the panel is a running history of the file itself (since the last time it was opened).

To use the brush, select the History Brush (the brush icon with the circle arrow behind it) from the toolbox and then open the History panel. To the left of each entry in the History panel is an empty square, and clicking there selects it as the source for the History Brush (indicated by an icon).

Art History Brush

A variation of the History Brush, the Art History Brush lets you paint pixels from a previous history state or snapshot, but with a twist. Instead of just copying the pixels exactly, you can paint with artistic brushes, giving a really creative look to your photos. With the Art History Brush's default settings, and using the same method as with the History Brush, the brush seems to produce very odd results. To best see the effect, you should create a new blank layer and fill it white. As you paint, you can easily see how the Art History Brush is re-creating the art that was in the snapshot, yet with a very stylized look (demonstrated in Figure 6.43).

FIGURE 6.43
The Art History Brush can create unique effects.

In the Tool Options bar, you can adjust any of several options for the Art History Brush. It's a good idea to decrease the brush size to 3–5 pixels so you can better see the effect. You'll also want to experiment with the options in the Style pop-up menu. Additionally, you can choose just about any brush shape and size via the Brushes panel.

Remember, if you ever get tool settings just right and you know you're going to want to use that combination of settings again in the future, you can save it as a tool preset.

Photoshop and the Web

The World Wide Web, as we know it today, supports several image formats. Actually, it isn't the Web itself that supports the formats, but the software—or browsers—that people use to view the Web. A web browser, such as Microsoft Internet Explorer,

Netscape Navigator, Firefox, or Apple's Safari, is a window in which you can view the content of the Web. These browsers support various image formats, mainly GIF and JPEG. Other formats are supported through the use of plug-ins—add-on software that you can download (usually free)—that add functionality to your browsers. Formats that are supported by plug-ins are PNG, SWF, and SVG, although the latter two are vector-based formats and don't apply to Photoshop. Most of today's modern browsers come installed with some of these plug-ins.

If you've ever surfed the Web, you know that speed is everything. Although DSL and cable modems are becoming more popular, many people still use 56K dial-up connections. Many others are also using wireless devices such as iPhones and other devices to access the Internet. That means that surfing the Web and viewing website pages filled with graphics and images could take a long time. A designer's challenge is to design web graphics that are small in file size, which would allow the pages to load faster. It's always a balance—you don't want a page that's filled only with text, yet you also don't want a page that contains so many images that users will skip to the next site because they have to wait too long for your page to load.

The image file formats that are supported in web browsers have many settings for such things as colors and compression, giving designers some degree of control over the final file size of each graphic. There is a direct correlation between the visual quality of a graphic and its file size. You can choose to make a file size smaller at the expense of how good the image looks. Likewise, a better-looking image will result in a larger file size.

Photoshop's Save for Web and Devices feature enables designers to make that decision easily by previewing an image in any of the supported web formats, along with all the color and compression settings. The Save for Web and Devices feature also lets you know what your final file size will be, giving you all the information you need to decide how you want to save your web graphic—all before you even save the file.

By the Way

> The Save for Web and Devices feature is such an integral feature for web designers that Adobe has included the entire Save for Web and Devices feature inside other CS3 applications as well. We cover that specifically within each chapter.

When you're ready to save your image for the Web, you choose File, Save for Web and Devices, which launches a larger-than-life dialog box that features tools, previews, and panels of its own, as shown in Figure 6.44. We cover these settings in detail in Chapter 7.

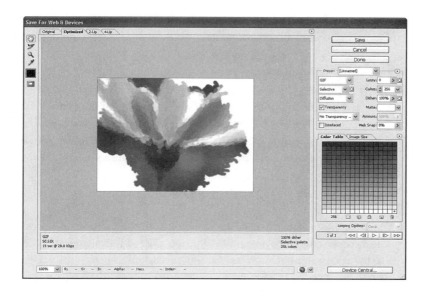

FIGURE 6.44
The Save for Web and Devices dialog box prepares an image for use on a website.

Slicing

In an effort to gain even more control over how images are displayed on the Web, a method called *slicing* was born. In simple terms, web slicing is the process of cutting a large image into several smaller images. This is desirable for various reasons.

First of all, there's perception. If you tried to load a web page that had one single large image on it, you would sit there impatiently waiting for it to download and appear on the page. But when an image is sliced into smaller parts, each smaller image loads faster, and it feels like the image is loading faster.

On that same note, you can apply different optimization settings to each image slice, which could save some valuable file size space, making for a faster-loading graphic overall. As you'll see later, these settings directly impact the final file size (read: download time) of your total image.

Slicing is also helpful if parts of a graphic need to be updated often. Instead of always creating larger images, you can update just a part of the image. Swapping out a slice or two can be more efficient than having to work with one large, bulky file all the time.

Because each slice is its own image, you can assign a link, or URL, to it, effectively making it a button. If someone clicks on a sliced part of an image, that person is linked to another web page. Of course, you can specify other functionality for such a button as well.

Finally, slices are necessary for creating rollovers, which enable you to specify that a graphic should change when the user interacts with it (such as rolling a mouse over it).

Slices Explained

So what exactly happens when you create a slice? In reality, Photoshop CS3 splits a single image into multiple images. An HTML table is created, with each cell of the table containing one of these slices, or pieces of the image. In this way, when you display the web page in a browser, all the sliced images appear together, almost like a puzzle. This is an important concept to keep in mind because you can create only rectangular slices.

Creating Slices

To create a slice in Photoshop, choose the Slice tool from the toolbox and click and drag in your document window, as seen in Figure 6.45. You'll notice that the Slice tool snaps to the edges of other slices, making it easy to use.

FIGURE 6.45
Click and drag
to create
slices in your
document.

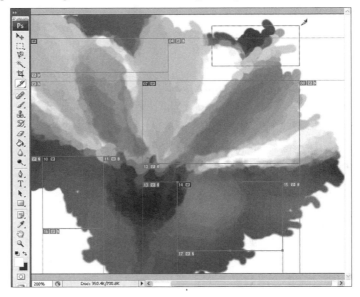

One thing to notice as you create slices is that when you draw a slice, other dimmed slices might appear automatically in the document. These are called *auto slices*. Slices that you create are called *user slices*. As you continue to create slices, Photoshop updates the auto slices accordingly.

If you want to convert an auto slice to a user slice, you can right-click the slice icon to the right of the slice number, and then choose Promote to User Slice.

It makes sense to create your slices after you've finished the design process because if your design changes after you draw your slices, you might need to readjust your slices. Photoshop does have the capability to create a slice that changes with your design—something called a *layer-based slice*. A layer-based slice is a slice that's automatically created to fit the contents of a layer. So, for example, if a layer had some text on it, defining that layer as a layer-based slice would create a slice the exact size of the text. If you changed the text at any point after that, the slice would update accordingly. To create a layer-based slice, highlight a layer in the Layers palette and choose Layer, New Layer Based Slice.

Slice Attributes

You can specify certain attributes for a slice. When saved for the Web, a slice is created as a cell in an HTML table. So, for example, a slice can have its own background color or URL link. Settings for each slice are specified via the Slice Options dialog, shown in Figure 6.46, which you can access by double-clicking a slice with the Slice Select tool.

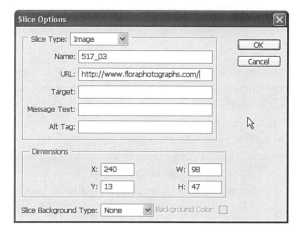

FIGURE 6.46
Set slice attributes to create additional functionality for the Web.

Creating Simple Web Animations

Although Flash provides most of the animation features you'll need, Photoshop can create frame-based animations in a pinch. You can use this to add simple motion to GIFs should the need arise.

Frame-based animation means that the illusion of movement is achieved by displaying image after image in succession. You have complete control in Photoshop over how many frames your animation will have, and you can also control timing, such as how long each frame is displayed in a browser. All the settings necessary to create animations are in the Animation panel, as seen in Figure 6.47.

FIGURE 6.47
Photoshop can be used to create simple animations. Here, a simple two frame animation is shown, but more complicated animations can be accomplished with tweening.

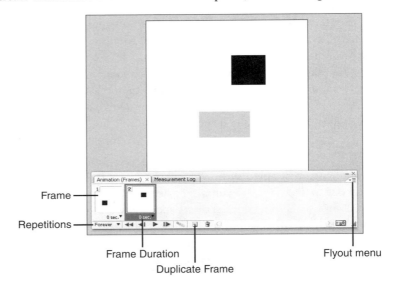

To add frames to a file, choose New Frame from the Animation panel fly-out menu, or click the Duplicate Current Frame button at the bottom of the panel. Photoshop also can help animate objects for you by using a process called *tweening*. The process of tweening, which comes from the word *between*, involves creating additional frames between two frames in an animation, changing them slightly. For example, if you had some text at the top of your image in one frame and then created a new frame and moved the text to the bottom of your image, tweening those two frames would produce an additional frame between the two, with the text in the middle of the image.

To tween frames in Photoshop CS3, select a frame and choose Tween from the Animation panel fly-out menu (or click the Tween button) to get the Tween dialog box, shown in Figure 6.48. You can then specify to tween with the previous frame or the first frame, as well as specify the number of frames you want to add to your animation. More frames produce a smoother-looking animation but result in a larger file size. You can also specify what parts of your image and what attributes should be tweened.

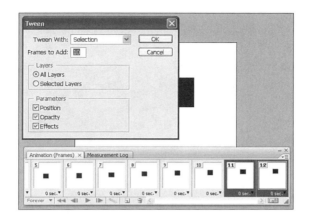

FIGURE 6.48
Use tweening to create animations without drawing all the frames manually.

You can use the controls at the bottom of the Animation panel to play the animation to see how it looks.

Under each frame in the animation is a pop-up menu that enables you to specify the duration of that frame. As an animation plays, you can specify pauses as desired to make the animation play as intended.

To save the animation as an animated GIF, choose File, Save for Web and Devices, and then make sure the GIF format is selected. You can also choose to play back the animation in the dialog box to get one last look at what you're going to get.

Setting Type

Although you might not need text features to color-correct your digital photos, you will most likely need them for doing any kind of web design. In fact, you never really know when you might need a little bit of text. Although you're better off using Illustrator or InDesign for most text needs, there will be plenty of times when it will make sense to add text in Photoshop.

To add text to your image, choose the Type tool and click in your document. You'll get a blinking insertion mark and you can begin typing. Notice that Photoshop automatically creates a new kind of layer for you—a type layer (seen in Figure 6.49).

FIGURE 6.49
A type layer is added when you add type to a document.

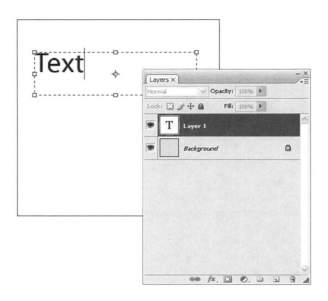

You can double-click the thumbnail of a type layer to select the text quickly and easily.

Use the Move tool to position the type layer in your document. You can also double-click the layer in the Layers panel to apply a layer style, just as you can with any normal layer. (Remember to click anywhere in the layer's entry except on the name of the layer itself.)

Styling Text

With the Type tool selected, you'll notice that the Tool Options bar, shown in Figure 6.50, updates to offer text-specific settings such as font, size, justification (left, centered, right), and color. You can also choose from several anti-aliasing options.

Anti-aliasing is a method used to make graphics appear smoother onscreen. With small text especially, anti-aliasing can make some words blurry or unreadable. Various algorithms are available for anti-aliasing, and Photoshop lets you choose from among them to get the best result. As you change algorithms, you'll see a live preview of your text.

FIGURE 6.50
Access common
type settings
from the Tool
Options bar.

Choose Window, Character to bring up the Character and Paragraph panels to access even more text controls (see Figure 6.51). The Character panel lets you specify kerning and tracking values (the spaces between letters), as well as leading (pronounced "ledding"), which is the amount of space between each line of text in a paragraph. The Paragraph panel, on the other hand, provides access to alignment, justification, and indent settings.

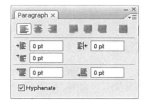

FIGURE 6.51
Access more
text settings
through the
Character panel.

Warping Text

To add cool effects, you can apply warps to text, as demonstrated in Figure 6.52.

FIGURE 6.52
Warp text for
interesting
effects.

To warp text, select some text and click the Create Warped Text button in the Tool Options bar to get the Warp Text dialog box. Here you can choose from 15 preset warp effects, as well as tweak the individual settings of each type of warp, as shown in Figure 6.53.

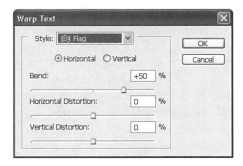

Adjusting Images

A day will come when a camera will be introduced that can compensate for every possible thing that could go wrong in the fraction of a second it takes to snap a photo. Like the sun going behind the clouds at just the wrong moment. Like the flash not going off for some reason. Like the bright yellow taxi that just drove by. Like the lights that just went out.

Until that day comes, photos will always need some kind of adjustments made to them so they reproduce and print how you want them. Above that, sometimes you want to purposefully embellish photos, such as give them a specific color cast or engulf them in shadows.

Photoshop contains a wealth of tools and functions that can help you turn less-than-ideal photos into perfect ones.

Auto Controls

For quick fix-me-ups, Photoshop has three auto controls that can make adjustments to files: Auto Levels, Auto Contrast, and Auto Color. All three can be found in the Image, Adjustments submenu. Depending on the photo, these controls can either be okay or useless. At times, you just want a quick edit, and that's fine, but for most other tasks, you'll want to read on....

Levels

A step above the auto controls is the Levels command. Press (Cmd-L) [Ctrl+L] to bring up the Levels dialog box. Notice that you are presented with a histogram that shows you the highlight, shadow, and midtone areas of your image, as seen in Figure 6.54. Drag the little triangle sliders to make adjustments.

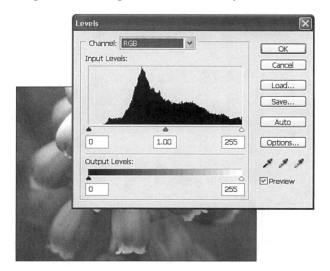

FIGURE 6.54
The Levels setting shows the levels within each channel of the image.

You can adjust the black-and-white points of your image by selecting the black eyedropper tool in the dialog box and then clicking on the darkest area of your photo. Repeat again with the white eyedropper, clicking on the lightest point in your image. The histogram then updates as Photoshop makes the adjustments.

I often use levels to "tint back," or lighten, images. Drag the black Output Level triangle (on the lower left) toward the right until you get what you need.

Did you Know?

What's great about the Levels dialog box is that you can apply these changes to the entire image overall, or you can make adjustments to specific color channels by choosing one from the pop-up menu at the top of the dialog box. When you're happy with the adjustments you've made, click OK.

Curves

Although the Levels feature is easy to use and pretty much straightforward, it's limited to applying linear adjustments only. For even more control over the tonal range and values of your images, choose Image, Adjustments, Curves. Here you also have the eyedroppers to choose black and white points, but you have more precision when it comes to making tonal adjustments.

The grid in the center, seen in Figure 6.55, is your image—the region at the upper right is where the highlights are, and the region at the lower left is where your shadows live. Midtones are smack in the middle.

FIGURE 6.55
The grid represents your image, with shadows in the lower left and highlights in the upper right.

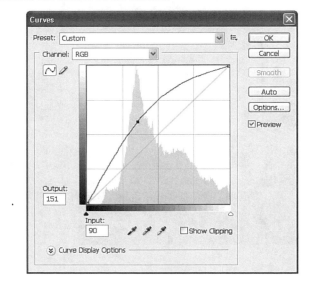

You can click in the grid to add a point and drag it to adjust the curve. The benefit here is that you can open up the shadows, but you can also add more points and adjust the curve to keep the highlights from getting blown out, as demonstrated in Figure 6.56.

FIGURE 6.56
Using curves provides fine-tuned control over your image.

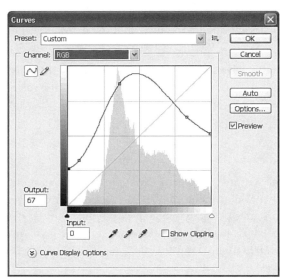

As you drag in your document, a circle appears on your curve indicating where that area falls on the curve. You'll see that as you click the lighter areas of your image, the circle appears closer to the top right of the grid, whereas darker areas fall lower and to the left.

Just as with levels, you can apply curves to the entire image as a whole or to individual channels using the Channel pop-up menu. When you've made your adjustments, click OK.

Shadow/Highlight

The Shadow/Highlight command automatically adjusts both the shadows *and* the highlights of a picture while using "smart" intelligence to ensure that the image doesn't lose any detail. In my humble opinion, this is probably the most valuable of all the adjustments in Photoshop.

The Shadow/Highlight command works on RGB, CMYK, and grayscale images.

To use this command, choose Image, Adjustments, Shadow/Highlight. Use the Shadows and Highlights sliders to make adjustments as necessary, and then click OK as seen in Figure 6.57.

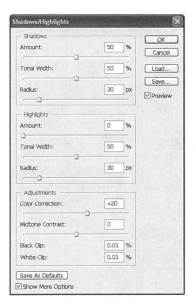

FIGURE 6.57
Choose your adjustments for shadows and highlights.

For even greater control, click the Show More Options check box at the bottom of the window. This provides the controls for shadow and highlight tonal width and radius, as well as color correction.

Adjustment Layers

All the adjustments we've spoken about are called destructive adjustments because after these adjustments are applied and saved, the actual pixels in the file are changed and there's no way to go back to the original version of the file.

Although sometimes you know that what you're doing is final (or you have the original backed up), there are plenty of times when you are required to make multiple adjustments (for example, each time you go back to visit the clients, they change their minds—although I'm *sure* that never happens to you).

So Adobe created something called an *adjustment layer* that enables you to keep certain adjustments "live" and editable—even long after you've saved and closed the file. This is accomplished by adding the adjustment itself as a special kind of layer. To add an adjustment layer for Levels, for instance, click the Adjustment Layer button (a black and white circle) at the bottom of the Layers panel and choose Levels, as seen in Figure 6.58. You'll see the normal Levels dialog box, as you've seen earlier, but when you click OK, you'll notice that a new layer has been added to your file. Any layer that falls below this adjustment layer will be affected by it.

FIGURE 6.58
An adjustment layer provides the same type of effects we've seen, but is non-destructive.

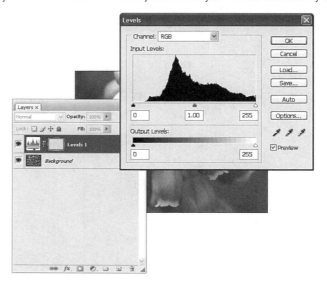

Adjustment layers are great when you want to make adjustments to only certain layers in your file. Any layers that appear above the adjustment layer aren't affected.

At any time, you can double-click an adjustment layer to edit it or make changes to it (double-click the adjustment thumbnail, not the name of the layer). Of course, you can also drag it to the Trash icon in the Layers panel if you want to get rid of it altogether.

> You can also have adjustment layers affect only a portion of a file by first making a selection and then adding the adjustment layer. In doing so, you create an adjustment layer with a layer mask.

Did you Know?

Match Color

It always ends up that the lighting and color are good in some photos from a photo shoot, but the person's expression and face are better in another. Using the Match Color feature, you can pull the color from one image and apply it to another one.

First, open both images—the one you want to change and the one that has the perfect color, which we'll call the source image (from where the color data will be coming). From the document that has the bad color, choose Image, Adjustments, Match Color to open the Match Color dialog box, shown in Figure 6.59. The first step is to look at the Image Statistics area and, from the Source pop-up menu, choose the source file. Now that you can see the new color applied, you can tweak the settings using the sliders in the Image Options section of the dialog box. When you're happy with the results, click OK.

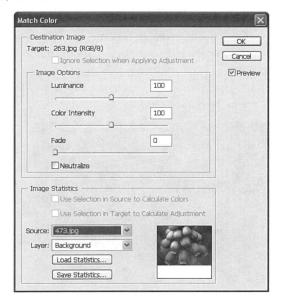

FIGURE 6.59
Match Color can be used to create consistent color across images.

Dodge and Burn Tools

If you've ever spent time in a traditional darkroom, you might know that *dodging* is underexposing film, making it lighter, whereas *burning* film is overexposing it, making the image darker. Photoshop has both Dodge and Burn tools that let you "paint on" these kinds of effects. Simply choose the Dodge or Burn tool, choose a brush size, and go to town. The Dodge tool looks like a black circle on a stick, and the Burn tool looks like a pinching hand, located by clicking and holding the Dodge tool icon.

Did you Know?

While using the Burn tool, you can hold down the (Option) [Alt] key to temporarily access the Dodge tool. The same applies in the reverse.

Retouching Images

Some people make their living doing one thing only: retouching photographs. Although some tasks are complicated and require masterful re-creations of elements in a photo, many retouching jobs simply require getting rid of a few scratches or a stain. Others require removing a person from a photo or restoring an aged and cracked photo to pristine quality. In either case, Photoshop has several tools you can use to assist in the task.

The Clone Stamp Tool

Probably the most popular retouching tool of all time, the Clone Stamp tool does what its name implies. You sample one area of your image and then paint with the tool elsewhere. As you paint, a clone of the area that you sampled is painted in the new location. For example, you could sample a single flower and then create many more of them in your photo (see Figure 6.60).

FIGURE 6.60
Sample a portion of your image, and then clone it!

To use the Clone Stamp tool, select it from the toolbox and hover the mouse cursor over the area you want to sample. Press the (Option) [Alt] key and click once to sample the area. Now move your mouse pointer to hover over the area you want to paint on, and click and drag the mouse to clone the area.

> You might want to work on a copied layer when doing retouching—this way you always have the original to go back to, if necessary. To duplicate a layer, drag the layer to the New Layer icon in the Layers panel.

Besides being used to duplicate objects, the Clone Stamp tool is very useful for fixing up blemishes and stains, or for repairing parts of a photo—such as removing a telephone wire or removing a mole from a person's face. Just sample a clean area and clone it over the blemished area.

The Healing Brush

I still remember the first time I saw a demonstration of the Healing Brush tool in action, and the only word to describe what it does is *magic*. One of the problems with using the Clone Stamp tool is that not every part of an image has the same underlying tonal values. For example, say you want to remove wrinkles on a person's face. Because of the lighting in the photo, the right side of the person's face is darker than the left side. If you take a sample with the Clone Stamp tool from one side of the face and try to clone the other side of the face, you'll see a visible change of tone and luminosity where you've painted.

> The Healing Brush icon looks like a BAND-AID without a spot. The BAND-AID with a spot is the Spot Healing Brush, which we'll look at next. The healing brushes make all of your boo-boos better. Click and hold on the Spot Healing Brush to access the Healing Brush.

You use the Healing Brush tool the same way you use the Clone Stamp tool. Find a nice clean area, (Option-click) [Alt+click], and then paint over the area you want to fix. At first, it appears to be painting it all wrong because you clearly see the brush marks. But when you let go, Photoshop examines the luminosity and tonal values of that area and compensates for them. This means you can clone from the dark side of a face to the light side of the face without worrying about the shading.

The Spot Healing Brush

As if the Healing Brush wasn't already easy enough to use, Photoshop includes a variation of the tool called the Spot Healing Brush. When you use the Spot Healing Brush, you don't have to sample a clean area. Instead, you just select the tool and start painting over blemished areas. As you use the brush, Photoshop looks for areas close to where you are clicking to find clean areas from which to sample.

The Patch Tool

Calling on the same underlying technology as the Healing Brush, the Patch tool (a patch icon, located in the same place as the healing tools) provides a different way to quickly clean up or repair parts of your image. You select the Patch tool and then draw a selection around the blemished area of your photo (just like with the Lasso tool). When you've selected the area, click inside the selected area and drag the selection to a clean area of your photo (see Figure 6.61).

FIGURE 6.61
The Patch tool is useful for quickly patching a bad area of a picture with a clean source area.

Note that you can use this tool in the reverse as well. Simply choose the Destination option in the Tool Options bar (rather than the default Source setting) and select a clean area of your photo. Then drag the selection on top of the blemished areas.

Red Eye Correction

Even though today's modern cameras promise to offer red eye–free images, we still see countless pictures that have red-eye issues. You can use any of Photoshop's many image-correction features to manually remove red eye, but you can fix images faster using Photoshop's Red Eye tool. After you've selected the tool (it's grouped with the Healing Brush), simply click on the red area, and you're done. Note that the Red Eye tool doesn't work in CMYK mode.

Optical Lens Correction

At times, photographs exhibit lens distortion, either from specialty lenses or from a variety of natural causes. Photoshop enables you to correct for this by choosing Filter, Distort, Lens Correction. When the Lens Correction dialog box opens, you can adjust for pincushioning (vertical or horizontal distortion that bends toward the center of the image), rotation, and even chromatic aberration (glow-like artifacts that sometimes appear around the edges of detail in digital photos). The configuration options can be seen in Figure 6.62.

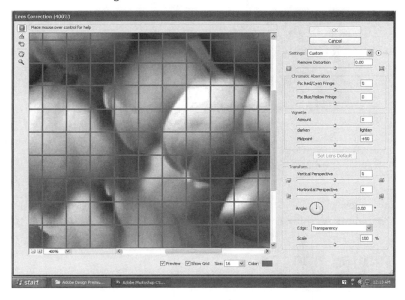

FIGURE 6.62
Apply the Lens Correction filter to clean up distortion in photographs.

Blurring Images

When excessive artifacts are in your image, you can try applying a Gaussian blur to soften the image and reduce the effect of the artifacts. Above that, the Gaussian Blur filter can be used for special effects, such as when you want part of an image to appear in soft focus or even completely out of focus.

Choose Filter, Blur, Gaussian Blur to bring up the dialog box, and experiment with different radius values until you achieve the effect for which you're looking (see Figure 6.63). This filter can also be helpful when you're trying to clear up moire[as] patterns (rippling lines that often distract from an image and that result from scanning photos from a magazine or newspaper).

FIGURE 6.63
The Blur filter softens images and can be used for effect or to clean up harsh edges and patterns.

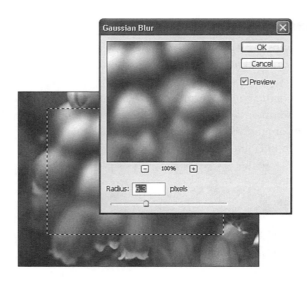

You can apply plenty of other blur effects to achieve special effects, such as Motion, Radial, and Lens blurs.

To blur just a few pixels at a time, you can use the Blur tool (a water droplet). I find the tool incredibly useful to soften up edges after I've silhouetted an image.

Sharpening Images

For images that are blurry or out of focus, you can try to sharpen them by choosing Filter, Sharpen, Unsharp Mask. I find that almost every photo that I scan or import requires some level of sharpening—especially images that I will be uploading for viewing on the Web. Sharpening a photo enhances the edges or borders of color, giving a clearer image that seems to have more life to it. You want to be careful not to oversharpen an image, though, because this will introduce visible artifacts, as shown in Figure 6.64.

Did you Know?
I was always taught to consider the line screen at which the image will be printed to best determine the radius setting for Unsharp Mask. For a 133-line screen, set your radius to 1.3 pixels. A 200-line screen would get a 2.0 radius setting, and so on. Of course, line screens apply only to images that will be used for print purposes.

Alternatively, you can use the Sharpen tool (a cone, grouped with the Blur tool) to touch up small parts of your image interactively.

FIGURE 6.64
Oversharpening can lead to artifacts in your images.

I've found that many times, sharpening will enhance not only the faces of people and objects in the photo, but also dust and scratches in the photo, making them visible. After sharpening, you might need to apply the Dust and Scratches filter to clear up those artifacts.

Did you Know?

Getting Rid of Dust and Scratches

Usually when scanning from photo prints, you'll notice dust or scratches in your scanned image. Sometimes it's because the glass on your scanner is dirty (I clean my scanner glass daily), whereas other times it's because the photo itself has scratches on it. In those cases you can choose Filter, Noise, Dust and Scratches to clear them up (see Figure 6.65). Be careful not to use too high of a setting because doing so might blur out parts of your image that should remain sharp.

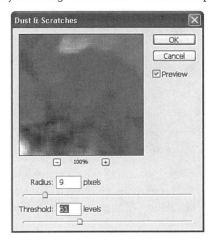

FIGURE 6.65
The Dust and Scratches Filter can clean up flaws in your original source photos.

> Instead of applying the Dust and Scratches filter to an entire image, I use the following technique to save time and take advantage of the Dust and Scratches filter while retaining the sharp parts of my image:
>
> Apply the Dust and Scratches filter, and use a setting that is just a bit more than you would ordinarily use. Then click the Create New Snapshot icon in the History panel to create a snapshot of the blurred image. Press (Cmd-Z) [Ctrl+Z] to undo the Dust and Scratches filter. You now have your original file. Select the History Brush, and in the History panel, click the box to the left of the snapshot you just took. This sets the History Brush to paint from that snapshot. Now paint over the scratched-up areas on the photo (use a big enough soft-edged brush). This enables you to easily and selectively apply the Dust and Scratches filter.

Other Filters

As you've learned by using the photo-retouching filters, one of Photoshop's trademarks is the capability to quickly change the appearance of a photograph or an image. Not only does Photoshop ship with a laundry list of filters for this purpose, but you also can buy other third-party filters for even more specialized purposes. Here we'll cover a few more filters that might be useful to you beyond basic photo-retouching.

> If you notice that a Photoshop filter's name is grayed out in the Filter menu, there's a good chance your document is set to grayscale or CMYK. A handful of Photoshop's filters work only in RGB documents. This is specifically because those filters use calculations that can be applied only in RGB. If you need to use one of these filters in a CMYK document, choose Image, Mode, RGB to switch color modes, apply the filter, and then choose Image, Mode, CMYK to go back to your original color space. Be aware that color shift might (and most likely will) occur.

Vanishing Point

Every so often, a feature comes along that is so amazing, it just blows your mind. The Vanishing Point filter is one of those features.

The Vanishing Point filter (Filter, Vanishing Point) enables you to perform a variety of Photoshop functions in perspective. By defining a series of vanishing points, you can easily establish what Photoshop calls planes, which determine how your edits are applied to your image.

It's always best to create a new empty layer before using Vanishing Point. In this way, your results are always put into the blank layer, keeping your original image intact.

When the Vanishing Point dialog box is open, you begin by first defining a plane. Using the Create Plane tool, click four corners to define the plane with which you want to work.

You can press the X key on your keyboard to temporarily zoom in while you're defining your plane to make it easier to align it correctly. After you've clicked to select the fourth corner, Photoshop creates a plane that can be used for editing (see Figure 6.66).

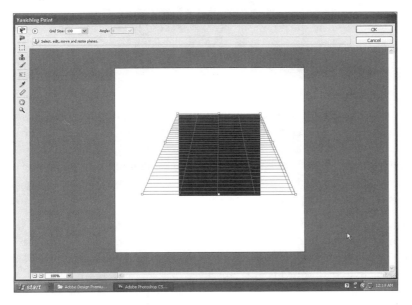

FIGURE 6.66
After setting your points, the plane is created.

If you copied some art onto the Clipboard before opening Vanishing Point, you can paste it right into the dialog box. As you drag the pasted image or art onto the plane, Vanishing Point automatically adjusts it to the correct perspective (see Figure 6.67). Pretty cool, eh?

FIGURE 6.67
Your image is
automatically
adjusted to the
perspective
you defined.

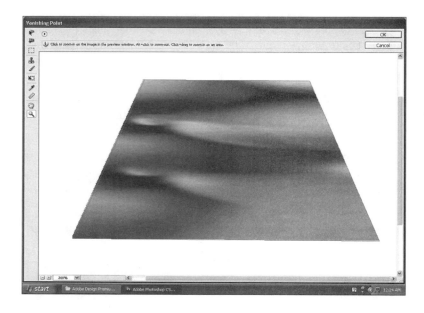

It gets better. With Vanishing Point, you aren't limited to just one plane. You can extend planes to create a complete world of perspective and use tools such as the Clone Stamp tool to perform cloning in perspective. Start by opening an image and creating a new layer. Then open Vanishing Point and set up your first plane. When you have a plane created, press the (Cmd) [Ctrl] key and drag out a new plane from the edge of your existing plane. Adjust the plane so it is in the correct perspective.

You can drag out additional planes as necessary. When you drag one plane from another, it keeps the planes all in perspective to each other. You can then use any of the editing tools listed along the left side of the Vanishing Point dialog box, shown in Figure 6.68, to perform edits in perspective.

Filter Gallery

Besides being able to retouch just about any image in Photoshop, you can stylize or adjust a photo to give it a certain look. For example, Photoshop can apply a filter to a standard photograph to make it appear as if it was painted with watercolor or drawn with chalk and charcoal.

Photoshop's Filter menu is filled with a plethora of these types of effects, but unless you know exactly what you're looking for, it can be quite time-consuming having to go through them all and see how your selected image will look with a filter applied. So it's with good reason that Photoshop has a feature called Filter Gallery that

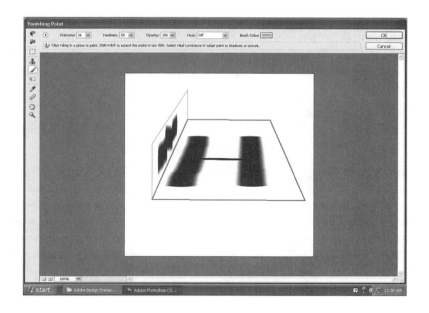

FIGURE 6.68
Using the Vanishing Point tools, you can edit your image in the defined perspectives.

enables you to visually preview any of the many artistic and stylistic filters—and even combine them—in a single dialog box.

Choose Filter, Filter Gallery, and you're presented with a full-screen dialog box, seen in Figure 6.69, that consists of four sections.

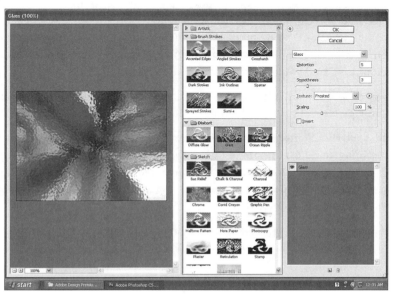

FIGURE 6.69
Experiment with filters to find a combination you like!

The far-left area gives you a preview of your image, and the middle section is where you choose the kind of filter you want to apply. The upper-right section enables you to tweak the individual settings of the filter that's chosen in the center panel, and the lower-right panel allows you to control multiple filters and how they are applied to your image.

Using Filter Gallery is not only easy and useful, but it's also addictive and fun. The possibilities are endless. Why settle for a standard stock photo for that brochure when you can create an entire stylized look by applying filters?

What makes this feature so powerful is how it enables you to experiment and apply multiple filters to your image. In the lower-right section of the dialog box, use the New Effect Layer button to add another effect (as many as you like), and choose a different filter from the middle panel. Stacking order is important, so you can also drag the filters up and down to see how the appearance changes depending on which filter is applied last. You can also disable an effect by clicking on the eye icon to the immediate left of the effect listing, just as you would with layers.

You can also apply filter effects to gradients or patterns that you've created to make interesting and unique backgrounds.

Extract

When we talked about selections way back in the beginning of this chapter, we mentioned that you can use tools such as the Magic Wand and the Magnetic Lasso to help make selections. Many times what you're trying to do is remove the background from a photograph (called *silhouetting*). Depending on the image, this could be a tedious task, and you might want to try using the Extract filter.

When you choose Filter, Extract, you're presented with another large dialog box with a large preview of your image in the center, as demonstrated in Figure 6.70.

Select the Edge Highlighter tool to trace over the edge of the shape you're trying to silhouette. You can adjust the size of the brush; the goal here is to have the actual edge you're tracing fall into the highlighted area. Make the brush big enough that you can easily trace the edge, but at the same time, don't make it so big that other elements are being highlighted as well.

When you've highlighted the edge, switch to the Fill tool and click the part of the image you want to keep, as demonstrated in Figure 6.71.

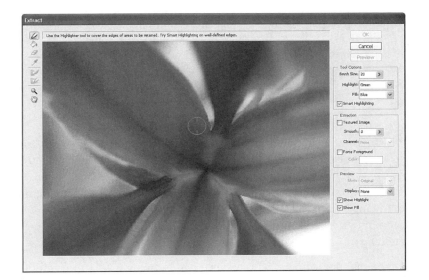

FIGURE 6.70
Use the Extract Filter to help silhouette a portion of your image.

FIGURE 6.71
Trace and fill your image.

The Extract filter removes whatever is not highlighted in your file. Click the Preview button to see what the results will look like. Click OK when you're happy with the results.

> In my experience, I've found that at times you want to manually silhouette an image (rather than use the Extract filter) because either the actual shape isn't good or you want to enhance it. For example, if a person's hair is blowing in the wind and a few strands are flying in odd directions, you'll want to get rid of those strands, not keep them.

Liquify

Thinking back, one of the highlights of kindergarten for me was finger painting (hey, it wasn't *that* long ago, was it?). The cool squishy paint, the smell, and, most of all, the ability to mush around and mix the colors to create art worthy of nothing less than my mother's refrigerator door. Although Photoshop can't create bright orange handprints on your classmate's dress, the Liquify feature can come pretty close to adding fun to your day (and Mom will still hang it on the fridge).

Seriously, though, the Liquify filter (demonstrated in Figure 6.72) can be quite useful by enabling you to smudge, pull, and distort your photos. Begin by choosing Filter, Liquify, and once again your entire screen is filled with a dialog box.

FIGURE 6.72
Create liquid-like effects using the Liquify filter.

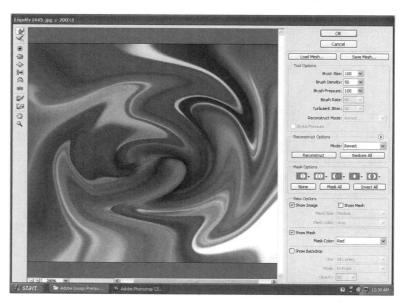

Choose any of the Liquify tools along the left of the dialog box, and change the brush size by using the bracket keys on your keyboard. Other options are available in the Tool Options section on the right side of the dialog box, and there's an option to use your pressure-sensitive tablet as well.

What's so great about this filter is that you can apply distortions to your file, but you can also reconstruct your image to reverse the effect of your distortions by using the Reconstruct tool. You can also use the Freeze Mask tool to highlight areas that you don't want affected by the distortion tools. If you use the Liquify filter on a low-resolution image, you'll see real-time performance and you'll have a fun time distorting your image. But you won't be having as much fun on high-resolution images because applying distortions to them takes a lot of computing power.

If you've used Illustrator before, you might be familiar with something called a mesh. Used for gradients and envelopes, a *mesh* is a matrix of points used to describe a distortion (in its most basic form). Photoshop incorporated this mesh concept behind the scenes with the Liquify filter; as you use the tools to create your distortions, Photoshop saves all the information as a mesh. At home, you're thinking, "Um, glad to hear that—let's get on with the lesson already," but this enables you to save your distortion mesh from Photoshop and apply it to other files.

Let's apply the concept to a real-world example. You are working with a low-resolution file in your comps, and then when you get client approval, you'll replace all of your files with high-resolution ones. You can save the mesh from your low-res file and then apply it to your high-res one. To save a mesh, click the Save Mesh button in the Liquify dialog box, and use the Load Mesh button to load one.

Noise

In physics, the word *noise* is defined as "a disturbance, especially a random and persistent disturbance, that obscures or reduces the clarity of a signal." But as with most things in life, you can take something that appears to be negative and turn it around, making it into a positive—something you can use. Sometimes you might have distortion in certain parts of an image, and adding some noise to that area might improve the overall appearance. Here are two examples:

▶ Most digital cameras save pictures in JPEG format, and the pictures can sometimes contain artifacts (random pixels and anomalies, and so forth). Many times these artifacts appear because of distortion in the Blue channel. Applying some noise to just the Blue channel might result in a smoother and cleaner image overall.

▶ Gradients that span large areas (entire pages, spreads, or large documents, such as movie posters) can print with banding—visible shifts or steps of color. This is especially evident with light colors, such as yellow. Adding a bit of noise can visually break up these steps and produce a smoother-looking gradient (although more grainy in appearance).

Adding noise is also a great way to create background textures and special effects.

To add noise to a selection (or, if nothing is selected, an entire image), choose Filter, Noise, Add Noise. The dialog box shown in Figure 6.73 appears. Use the Amount slider to control how much noise is added, and choose Uniform or Gaussian distribution.

FIGURE 6.73
Noise can be used to smooth over rough transitions.

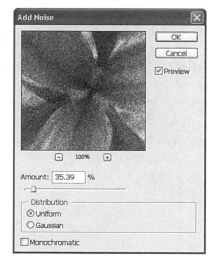

I find that when you're adding smaller doses of noise, Gaussian looks best, but Uniform gives a better appearance when you're adding large amounts of noise. The Monochromatic option adds only black noise (very useful for mezzotint-like effects).

Of course, sometimes you'll want to remove noise from an image. Digital images or scans can have artifacts that take away from the overall look of the image. Choose Filter, Noise, Reduce Noise to make this adjustment.

Smart Filters

As you've learned, filters are a great way to apply an enormous number of effects to your documents. They are, however, destructive—after you apply a filter and save the document, there is no way to get the original graphic back. In Photoshop CS3, this is no longer the case!

Photoshop CS3 provides a very simple way to apply filters in a non-destructive way—through the use of Smart Filters. Best of all, you don't need to learn any new or complicated process to use this feature!

To apply a Smart Filter, you must first convert the layer that you're working with to a Smart Object. The easiest way to do this is to simply choose Convert for Smart Filters from the Filter menu. This turns your active layer into a Smart Object.

After you've completed the conversion, simply apply a filter as you normally would. Although nothing appears to be different in the results, you'll notice that the Layers panel looks a bit different, as seen in Figure 6.74.

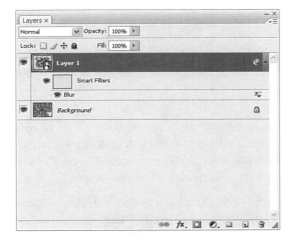

FIGURE 6.74
Smart Filters are non-destructive and can be removed or reordered.

Here you can see multiple different filters that have been applied to a layer. To get rid of a filter, simply drag it from the Layers panel to the Trash icon. You can also drag filters into different orders for a different combination of effects.

As you can see, this simple addition adds powerful new capabilities to your Photoshop toolset.

Although the vast majority of filters can be applied as Smart Filters, some cannot. The filters that are excluded are Extract, Liquify, Pattern Maker, and Vanishing Point.

By the Way

Automating Tasks

We've all made the following statement at some point in our lives: "For the price I paid for this computer, it should be making my coffee, too." Well, that might be asking too much, but it isn't too much to ask your computer to do repetitive tasks for you while you're busy refilling your mug with your favorite brew.

You'll be happy to know that Photoshop has best-in-class support for scripting and automation. You'll also find plenty of scripts and features ready to go right out of the box.

Actions

So you're probably thinking, "Sure, automation is great and everything, but I don't know—or even want to know—how to write in scripting language," right? Have no fear because Photoshop has something called actions—which require no knowledge of programming languages or any math, for that matter (I'm not a big fan of math).

The way it works is quite simple. You basically perform a set of operations once to show Photoshop what you want to do, and you save that sequence of events as an action. Then whenever you want to perform that sequence of events again, you play the script and Photoshop performs all the steps for you.

For example, say you have a CD that you use often, which is filled with RGB stock photos. You can't use the photos as is, so each time you want to use one of these stock photos, you open the file, convert it to CMYK, change the resolution, and then save it as a TIFF. So you open the Actions panel and click the Create New Action button, name the action, and click the Record button. Then you open a file, convert it to CMYK, change the resolution, and save the file as a TIFF, all as you would normally do. When you are finished, you click the Stop Recording button in the Actions panel. And you're done.

The next time you need to use a photo from that CD, you can use the action you recorded to do the conversion for you automatically. Now this might sound nice and all, saving you a few keystrokes, but it gets even better. You can apply an action to an entire group of files at once, called batch processing. In this way, you can apply conversions to all the images on your CD automatically—all while you go and grab some lunch.

To apply a batch action, choose File, Automate, Batch. Then specify the action and choose a source location (where the files are being opened from) and a destination location (where you want the adjusted files to be saved). This being Adobe

Photoshop, of course, you also have many options on how to name new files and how to deal with dialog boxes and warnings, as seen in Figure 6.75.

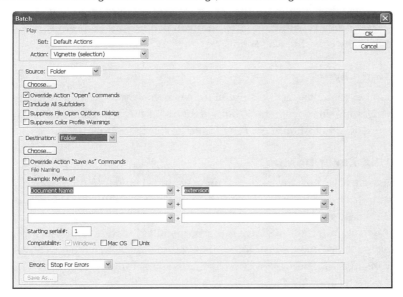

FIGURE 6.75
Choose the options for how Photoshop will handle files during batch operations.

Scripts

Photoshop has built-in support for both AppleScript (used on Macintosh computers) and Visual Basic Script (used on Windows computers). If you are familiar with either of these scripting languages, you can tell Photoshop to do just about anything.

> Scripts and actions differ in that actions are simply a recording of specific key-strokes and interface selections. Scripts can contain logic and perform functions based on different conditions. For example, in the actions example mentioned earlier, a script could check what color mode the document is in and perform different functions depending on what the setting is. Scripts can also allow Photoshop to "talk" with other applications. For example, you could have a script do the file conversions, and then launch InDesign, place the photos into InDesign, and print a catalog of images. Actions are limited to functions within the application.

By the Way

If you're like me and can write a script as well as you can write a thesis on the advances of brain surgery in the twenty-first century, you're thinking that this scripting stuff won't be of much help in your everyday life.

Don't despair. Nowhere is it stated that to use a script, you have to write it yourself. Plenty of people write them and post them to the Web, sell them, or even make themselves available to write custom scripts for people. More important, Adobe includes several scripts with Photoshop that you can use right out of the box. You can find these by choosing File, Scripts.

Exporting Layers

The Export Layers to Files script is useful for when you want to create a separate file for each layer in your document. What's great about this script is that it can generate files in JPEG, Photoshop, TIFF, PDF, Targa, and BMP formats.

Exporting Layer Comps

We discussed earlier how layer comps can assist in keeping tabs on multiple design ideas within a single Photoshop document. To extend that functionality even further, Photoshop includes three scripts specifically designed for the layer comps feature. You can automatically generate separate files for each of your comps, create a multiple-page PDF file that contains all of your designs, or create a web photo gallery (WPG) of your designs (which we discuss momentarily)—all with a single command.

Photomerge

Some cameras are designed to shoot photos in panoramic mode, giving you a very wide view of such things as a landscape or a stadium. There's also a technique of using a regular camera to shoot a panoramic view in multiple photographs, which you can then "stitch" together in Photoshop. Photomerge is an automatic feature that attempts to create one single large file from a range of specified files by analyzing the edges of each of the pictures and aligning them where they match. Photomerge actually does a very impressive job, and, of course, you can touch up the final file as necessary, using Photoshop's other retouching tools.

Choose File, Automate, Photomerge to get the Photomerge dialog box. When you've chosen the source files, click OK and watch as Photoshop does all the work, demonstrated in Figure 6.76.

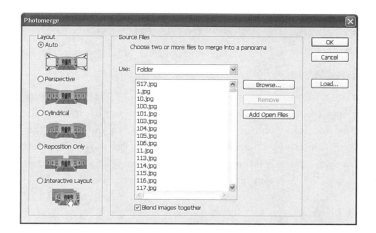

FIGURE 6.76
Use Photomerge
to automatically
stitch your
images
together.

Crop and Straighten Photos

Scripts are cool, and watching scripts work right before your eyes is even cooler. One of the problems with scanning images on a flatbed scanner is that it's a pain to make sure that each photo is perfectly straight. It's also time-consuming to have to scan one picture at a time.

The Crop and Straighten Photos feature solves all of that by enabling you to cram several photos on your scanner at once and scan it as one large image. You also don't need to fret about whether the images are perfectly straight. Scan your photos and choose File, Automate, Crop and Straighten Photos. Then watch as Photoshop magically detects each photo, rotates it perfectly, and then puts each one into its own file.

Spot Colors

We discussed RGB colors and CMYK inks before, but there is an additional "color space" called spot colors. A *spot color* is a specified ink color that printers can use to reproduce a color exactly. There are different ways of specifying colors, and one of the most popular in the United States is the Pantone Matching System. Pantone publishes a guide of specific named colors. When you specify a Pantone color, your printer knows exactly what color you want because he uses the same Pantone guide to know what ink to put on the press.

Spot colors play a very specific role in Photoshop (they play a much larger role in applications such as InDesign and Illustrator). Photoshop can create spot channels, in which a channel is specified as a spot color. Additionally, spot colors are used when you are creating photos that will print entirely in one or several custom colors—most commonly, duotones.

Spot Channels

Just as there are channels in your document for RGB or CMYK plates, you can have channels for spot color plates. You can add a spot channel by opening the Channels panel and choosing New Spot Channel from the panel fly-out menu. The benefit here is that you can specify an exact color so you can get a better preview onscreen. From the New Spot Channel dialog box, seen in Figure 6.77, click the color proxy to open the Color Picker. You can then choose from any of several standard spot color libraries.

FIGURE 6.77
Configure
your new
spot channel.

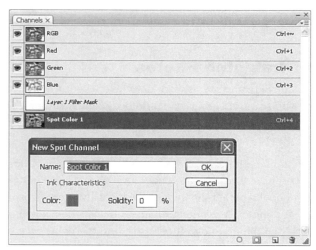

Anything that appears on a spot channel will separate on its own spot color plate when printed from an application such as InDesign.

Monotones, Duotones, Tritones, and Quadtones

By far, the most common use of spot color in Photoshop is related to multitone files, which include monotones, or images that are entirely one spot color; duotones, or images that consist of two spot colors; tritones, or images containing three spot colors; and quadtones, which are images that contain—you guessed it—four spot colors.

Duotones are mainly used to add color or style to print jobs that are printing in only two spot colors. Multitone files can also be used to add tonal depth to an image—

reason enough that some photographers and printers will print black-and-white photos as duotones made up of black and gray.

To create a multitone file, you must first make sure that your file is in Grayscale mode. If it isn't already, choose Image, Mode, Grayscale. You can then choose Image, Mode, Duotone to open the Duotone Options dialog box, shown in Figure 6.78. From the Type pop-up menu at the top of the dialog box, choose one of the four options.

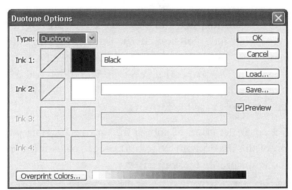

FIGURE 6.78
Set your duo-tone options.

For most applications to print duotones correctly, they must be saved as Photoshop EPS files. Illustrator and InDesign will also accept duotones saved as Photoshop PDF files.

Three settings exist for each ink:

- ▶ **Curves**—Click the Curves box to edit the duotone curve values for each ink color (the same way you adjusted curves earlier in the chapter).

- ▶ **Ink Color**—Click the ink color proxy to choose the ink color.

- ▶ **Ink Name**—Enter the name for the ink. If you choose a color from the Color Picker, a name is automatically added for you.

The ink name is extremely important in spot color workflows. To avoid having multiple plates separate for the same spot color, make sure that the spot color name in Photoshop and the spot color name in your page-layout application are the same.

If fooling around with duotone ink curves isn't your thing, you can use one of several settings that the folks at Adobe were kind enough to include with Photoshop.

Click the Load button in the Duotone Options dialog box and navigate to the Adobe Photoshop CS3, Presets, Duotones folder, where you can choose from duotones, tritones, and quadtones. Don't worry about the colors that are in these presets—you can easily change the colors yourself—but the valuable parts of these files are the curve settings. Experiment with different presets to find one that suits your needs.

Saving and Printing Files

When you're done with your file, you can either save it or print it in any of several formats. When saving your files, you can choose from many of Photoshop's supported formats, including JPEG, Photoshop PDF, Photoshop EPS, PNG, TIFF, or even Targa files (used for video workflows). Depending on your workflow, you might require different file formats or save directly to a Version Cue server. In Part III, "The Projects," we dive deeper into many of these file formats.

To print your file, choose File, Print, as shown in Figure 6.79. Here you can scale and control the position of the art on your page and choose color-management options, such as specifying a color profile for your printer.

FIGURE 6.79
The Photoshop Print dialog box gives you many controls over the output.

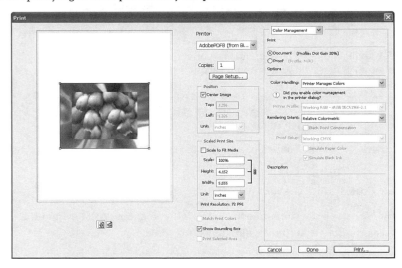

Summary

Adobe Photoshop is the defacto standard for desktop graphics applications. Exploring and familiarizing yourself with Photoshop will give you an edge when it comes to everything from animation in Flash, to print publications, and web design.

In this chapter you learned about many of the features available in Photoshop, including layers, channels, selection methods, transparency, basic animation tools, color, and much much more! You'll find that even the most seasoned Photoshop users discover new tips and tricks as they use the application, so the best way to get comfortable with the software is to play! Since you're not paying for paints and canvas, it doesn't matter if you don't get the hang of things immediately—just keep practicing with the tools and you'll quickly see how Photoshop can improve any projects that feature graphical elements.

CHAPTER 7

Using Adobe Illustrator CS3

Illustrator is a program that seems to have an identity crisis. By that, I mean it's a tool that can do many of the things that InDesign can (such as page layout), and it can also do many of the things that Photoshop can (such as web design). Of course, there are also plenty of things that Illustrator alone can do (such as edit PDF files or create 3D graphics). As you'll see in this chapter, one thing is certain: Illustrator is a very deep program, with a wide range of features and uses.

What's New in Illustrator CS3?

Here's a quick overview of what's new in the CS3 version of Illustrator: a refined user interface that better matches the rest of the CS3 suite, an improved organization of features and functions, enhanced color control, better integration with Flash, and, of course, much more.

Illustrator is such a huge application that we won't get to all of its features, but we will look at the most important and get you comfortable with the interface so you can explore on your own.

Introduction to Illustrator CS3

When you first launch Illustrator, you're greeted with the Illustrator CS3 welcome screen (see Figure 7.1). The welcome screen is split into four sections. The top two areas offer quick links to open recent files and access common functions, such as creating a new file. The bottom portion of the window provides links to How-to documents and online resources. If you'd prefer to avoid this screen altogether, you can do so by clicking the "Don't Show Again" check box.

FIGURE 7.1
The Illustrator
CS3 welcome
screen.

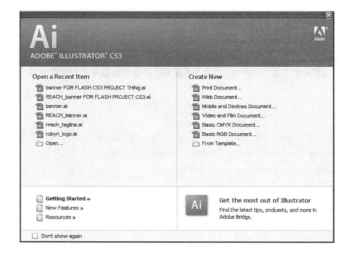

Taking a look at the screen when you first start Illustrator (see Figure 7.2), you have the standard menu bar across the top of the screen and, directly beneath it, Illustrator's context-sensitive Control panel. Along the left side of the screen is the toolbox, which contains all of Illustrator's tools, as well as several other functions. The color proxy indicates the fill and stroke colors (you can also choose colors by double-clicking on them); the two icons above the proxy enable you to set the colors to the default white fill and black stroke, and to swap the fill and stroke colors. Directly below the proxy icons are three buttons that can be used to quickly apply three kinds of colors: a white fill, a black-to-white gradient, and none. Under those are the different view modes, Standard, Full Screen with Menu Bar, and Full Screen (just as in Photoshop). You can toggle through the view modes by repeatedly pressing the F key on your keyboard (the letter *F*, not the Function key).

Some useful keyboard shortcuts to remember and get used to are the X key to toggle focus between the fill and the stroke, Shift+X to swap the two colors, and the D key to set the colors to their default settings.

Along the right side of your screen are some of Illustrator's panels. We discuss what each of them does and how to use them as we go through this chapter.

Finally, the document window is where you work on your file. The black outline is your document size, or *artboard*. Illustrator lists the filename, the view percentage, and the color mode right in the title bar of each file. Along the bottom left of the window, you'll find a zoom indicator as well as the status bar.

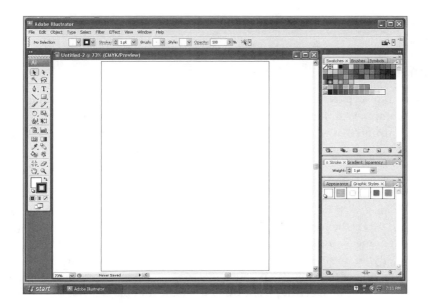

FIGURE 7.2
The Illustrator
CS3 workspace.

By default, the status bar displays the tool you currently have selected or the Version Cue status. You can display some other items instead by clicking on the status bar. To see an Illustrator Easter Egg, press and hold the (Option) [Alt] key when clicking on the status bar. (Yes, that's my home phone number listed in the status bar!)

Did you Know?

Illustrator's Control panel has several cool features built into it that make it extremely powerful and easy to use (see Figure 7.3). On the left of the Control panel, Illustrator indicates the targeted selection (in this case, a path). You'll also notice that some of the words in the panel are underlined and are colored blue, just like links in a web browser. When you click on these words, Illustrator opens the panel for that feature, giving you access to all of the necessary functions. For example, you can easily specify the width for a stroke in the Control panel, but you can also click on the word *Stroke* to open the Stroke panel and specify additional settings. At the far right of the Control panel is the Go to Bridge button and a flyout menu that enables to you show or hide different functions in the Control panel itself.

FIGURE 7.3
The Control
panel in
Illustrator
CS3.

Creating and Opening Files

In a program such as Photoshop, you usually start with a scanned image or a digital photograph. With Illustrator, though, you'll most likely be creating new documents more often, as well as creating new documents based on predefined templates. Of course, Illustrator can also open existing documents.

Creating a New File

To start from scratch and create a new file, choose File, New, or press (Cmd-N) [Ctrl+N] to access the New Document dialog box (see Figure 7.4). Here you can give your file a name (you can do this later when you actually save the file, too), choose a profile for your document, and specify your artboard size and orientation. You can choose from any of Illustrator's supported measurement systems: points, picas, inches, millimeters, centimeters, or pixels. Using the Templates button, you can jump to a directory containing dozens of templates ranging from event planning to DVD labels to give you a jumpstart on your document design.

For even greater control, click the Advanced button to choose a preview mode, color mode, and the PPI in which raster effects will be rendered.

FIGURE 7.4
The New
Document
dialog box.

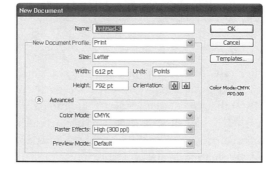

Illustrator lets you create files in one of two color modes, and it's important to know which one to choose. Although you can change color modes later, such changes will cause color shifts. Each color mode has a *gamut*, or range of colors that can be produced. Some gamuts are wider, or can contain more colors, than others. For example, certain colors can be displayed in RGB that simply can't be reproduced in CMYK (for example, bright greens, oranges, or pastel colors). So converting an RGB file to CMYK might cause some colors to become dull or change the colors altogether because those colors don't exist in CMYK. Let's take a look at each of the supported color models:

▶ **RGB Color**—RGB (red, green, blue) is a color method used to display color on televisions, computer monitors, and video screens. In RGB, you start with black (when your TV is off, the screen is black), and adding equal values of red, green, and blue results in white. When you're working on files that will be used in video, for broadcast, on the Web, or for onscreen presentations, RGB is the format you should use.

▶ **CMYK Color**—CMYK is a color method used to print color on paper. Unlike RGB, in the CMYK color space, if you mix all the colors together, you get black, but if none of the colors is present, you get white. Anything you see in print uses CMYK (a blank piece of paper is white), so obviously, when you're designing content that will be printed in color, CMYK is the color model of choice. CMYK stands for cyan (a shade of blue), magenta (a shade of red), yellow, and key (black).

As I mentioned earlier, the CMYK gamut isn't nearly as wide as most designers would like, so designers use spot colors (for example, Pantone colors) that allow them to pick a specific color ink (including metallic inks, bright colors, pastels, and so on). We cover spot colors in detail later in "Solid Colors."

By the Way

After you've specified your new document settings, you can click the OK button to create a new Illustrator file.

Creating a New File from a Template

An Illustrator template file is a special kind of Illustrator file, sporting an .ait file extension instead of the usual .ai reserved for Illustrator files. Templates are used for designs that are used repeatedly, and they can contain anything a normal Illustrator file can contain, including layers, paragraph styles, symbols, page size— even artwork itself. When you open an Illustrator template, the file opens a copy of the template as an untitled document (as if you had created a new file). This prevents you from accidentally overwriting the template file.

Illustrator ships with many professionally designed royalty-free templates you can use. When you choose File, New from Template, or click the Templates button in the New dialog, Illustrator automatically navigates to the folder where these templates are installed. Using the Adobe file dialog, you can choose Thumbnails from the View pop-up menu at the far right of the window. This automatically shows a preview of each template file as you browse, as seen in Figure 7.5. You can also use Bridge to browse through the templates if you prefer its interface.

FIGURE 7.5
Opening an
Illustrator
template file.

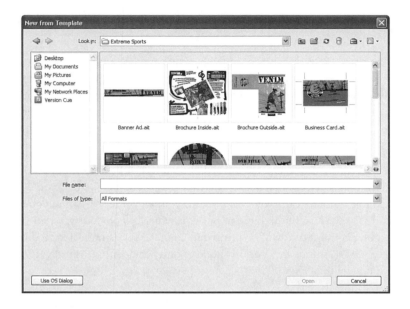

For those who feel that using prerendered content is beneath them, Illustrator also ships with a full collection of blank templates. These can be quite useful for nearly any user.

 By the Way

> Illustrator installs all templates by default; they can be found in the Cool Extras folder inside your Illustrator CS3 application folder.

Opening Files

As with just about any computer program, you can open a file by choosing File, Open or pressing (Cmd-O) [Ctrl+O] to open a file. By default, this invokes the Adobe File dialog box which features file content previews and direct access to Version Cue. If you're more comfortable with your default operating system dialog, click the OS Dialog button. After you've located the file you want to open, click on the Open button to open the file. Keep in mind that you can always use Adobe Bridge to browse for the right file you need.

Illustrator does more than just open Illustrator files. You can open a wide range of files in Illustrator, including PDF, EPS, JPEG, PSD, GIF, PNG, and more. Illustrator can also open native CorelDRAW and FreeHand files (versions 8, 9, and 10 officially, although other versions might work with varying success). In many ways, both Photoshop and Illustrator can be used as utilities to open just about any kind of graphics file.

If you need to edit PDF files, you can open them in Illustrator, but you'll have to remember a few limitations. Illustrator can open only one page of a PDF file at a time (as seen in Figure 7.6), form data might be removed, and structured text (tagged text) will be lost.

FIGURE 7.6
When you're attempting to open a multi-page PDF file, Illustrator asks you which page you want to open.

Drawing Basic Vector Objects

Back in Chapter 2, "So Many Applications: Which One to Use?" we discussed the underlying basics of vector graphics. Now you'll learn how to draw them. We begin with drawing closed paths, and then we move on to drawing open paths. Finally, we discuss how to edit existing vector paths and objects.

Drawing Closed Vectors: Shapes

Illustrator can draw primitive shapes quite easily, and several shape tools enable you to create rectangles, ellipses (circles and ovals), polygons (multisided shapes), and stars. We go through each of these tools and how they are used, but, of course, the best way to get to know them is to launch Illustrator and try them for yourself.

One thing you'll notice, though, as you read through the remainder of this chapter, is that there are usually several ways to accomplish the same task. This is true for most of the functionality you'll find in Illustrator and throughout the CS3 suite. As you become more familiar with Illustrator, you'll get a better feel for which method makes the most sense for a specific purpose or is best suited to your personal workflow.

Finally, as you'll see, most of Illustrator's shape drawing tools, shown in Figure 7.7, are dynamic, in that you can press certain keys on your keyboard to change certain aspects of the shape as you are drawing it.

FIGURE 7.7
Choose your
drawing tools.

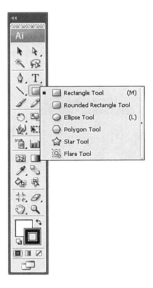

The Rectangle Tool

To draw a rectangle, choose the Rectangle tool and click and drag the mouse on the artboard. Before you release the mouse, you can utilize any of the following functions that will affect the shape you are drawing:

- ▶ Press the Shift key to constrain your shape to be a perfect square.

- ▶ Press the (Option) [Alt] key to draw your shape from the center outward.

- ▶ Press the spacebar to "freeze" your shape and position it elsewhere on your artboard.

- ▶ Press the tilde (~) key to create numerous copies of your shape.

To draw a rectangle numerically, choose the Rectangle tool and click once on your artboard to get the Rectangle dialog box (see Figure 7.8). Enter a value for the width and height, and click OK. To draw a rectangle numerically from its center, press and hold the (Option) [Alt] key while you click once on the artboard.

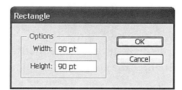

The Rounded Rectangle Tool

To draw a rounded rectangle (in which the corners of the rectangle are rounded), choose the Rounded Rectangle tool and click and drag the mouse on the artboard. Before you release the mouse, you can utilize any of the following functions that will affect the shape you are drawing:

▶ Press the Shift key to constrain your shape to be a perfect square with rounded corners.

▶ Press the (Option) [Alt] key to draw your shape from the center outward.

▶ Press the spacebar to "freeze" your shape and position it elsewhere on your artboard.

▶ Press the tilde (~) key to create numerous copies of your shape.

To draw a rounded rectangle numerically, choose the Rounded Rectangle tool and click once on your artboard to get the Rounded Rectangle dialog box (see Figure 7.9). Enter a value for the width, height, and corner radius, and click OK. To draw a rounded rectangle numerically from its center, press and hold the (Option) [Alt] key while you click once on the artboard.

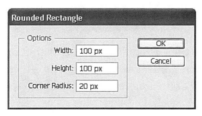

FIGURE 7.9
The Rounded
Rectangle
dialog box.

You can use the Rounded Corners live effect to apply rounded corners to any vector object, with an added benefit that you can make adjustments to the Corner Radius setting at any time. We cover this live effect later in "Live Effects."

Did you
Know?

The Ellipse Tool

To draw an ellipse (also called an oval), choose the Ellipse tool and click and drag the mouse on the artboard. Before you release the mouse, you can utilize any of the following functions that will affect the shape you are drawing:

▶ Press the Shift key to constrain your shape to be a perfect circle.

▶ Press the (Option) [Alt] key to draw your shape from the center outward.

▶ Press the spacebar to "freeze" your shape and position it elsewhere on your artboard.

▶ Press the tilde (~) key to create numerous copies of your shape.

To draw an ellipse numerically, choose the Ellipse tool and click once on your artboard to get the Ellipse dialog box (see Figure 7.10). Enter a value for the width and height, and click OK. To draw an ellipse numerically from its center, press and hold the (Option) [Alt] key while you click once on the artboard.

FIGURE 7.10
The Ellipse
dialog box.

The Polygon Tool

The Polygon tool in Illustrator is a bit disconcerting. A real polygon is simply a closed shape with at least three sides. In Illustrator, the Polygon tool can create only closed shapes with three or more sides, but in which all the sides are equal in length.

To draw a polygon, choose the Polygon tool, and click and drag the mouse on the artboard. A polygon is always drawn outward from its center. Before you release the mouse, you can utilize any of the following functions that will affect the shape you are drawing:

▶ Move your mouse in a circular motion to rotate the shape.

▶ Press the Shift key to constrain your shape straight to the baseline (or whatever your constrain angle is set to in General Preferences).

▶ Press the up arrow key on your keyboard to add sides to your shape.

▶ Press the down arrow key on your keyboard to remove sides from your shape.

▶ Press the spacebar to "freeze" your shape and position it elsewhere on your artboard.

▶ Press the tilde (~) key to create numerous copies of your shape.

To draw a polygon numerically, choose the Polygon tool and click once on your artboard to get the Polygon dialog box (see Figure 7.11). Enter a value for the radius and the number of sides, and click OK.

FIGURE 7.11
The Polygon dialog box.

Need to draw a quick triangle? You can use the Polygon tool to create an equilateral triangle in an instant.

Did you Know?

The Star Tool

The Star tool in Illustrator can be quite useful for creating starbursts to call out specific items in a design.

To draw a star, choose the Star tool and click and drag the mouse on your artboard. A star is always drawn out from its center. Before you release the mouse, you can utilize any of the following functions that will affect the shape you are drawing:

▶ Move your mouse in a circular motion to rotate the shape.

▶ Press the Shift key to constrain your shape straight to the baseline (or whatever your constrain angle is set to in General Preferences).

▶ Press the up arrow key on your keyboard to add points to your shape.

▶ Press the down arrow key on your keyboard to remove points from your shape.

▶ Press the (Option) [Alt] key to align the shoulders of your star (forcing lines on opposite sides of the star to share the same baseline).

▶ Press the (Cmd) [Ctrl] key to adjust the inner radius of the star. Dragging toward the center of the star decreases the radius, and dragging away from the center of the star increases it.

▶ Press the spacebar to "freeze" your shape and position it elsewhere on your artboard.

▶ Press the tilde (~) key to create numerous copies of your shape.

To draw a star numerically, choose the Star tool and click once on your artboard to get the Star dialog box (see Figure 7.12). Enter a value for Radius 1 and Radius 2, enter the number of points, and click OK.

FIGURE 7.12
The Star
dialog box.

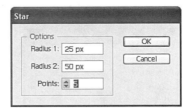

The Flare Tool

Illustrator CS3 introduces the Flare tool. Unlike the other shapes we've looked at, flares are a bit more complex. The Flare tool is used to generate the lens flare effect—a series of concentric circles, rays, and staggered halos, similar to what you might see when light shines through a lens. To get the best effect from the Flare tool, you should use it on top of existing artwork, much as you'd see one in a photograph.

To draw a flare, choose the Flare tool, and then click and drag the mouse to set a size. The main flare shape will be drawn. Next, move the mouse and click and drag to set the secondary halos for the flare. You can use the mouse to adjust their location in relation to the primary shape. Before you release the mouse, you can utilize any of the following functions that will affect the shape you are drawing:

▶ Press the Shift key to constrain the angle of the rays in the flare straight to the baseline (or whatever your constrain angle is set to in General Preferences).

▶ Press the up arrow key on your keyboard to add rays to your flare.

▶ Press the down arrow key on your keyboard to remove rays from your flare.

▶ Press the (Cmd) [Ctrl] key to keep the center of the flare from moving as you draw.

▶ Press the tilde (~) key to create numerous copies of your shape.

To draw a flare numerically, choose the Flare tool and click once on your artboard to get the Flare Tool Options dialog box (see Figure 7.13). Enter values for the center, rings, halo, and rays, and click OK.

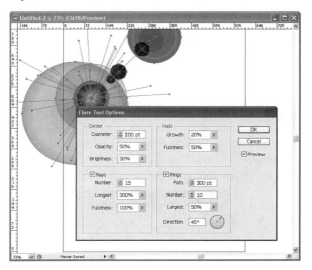

FIGURE 7.13
The Flare Tool Options dialog box.

Drawing Open Vectors: Paths

Although drawing complete shapes is something just about everyone needs to do inside of Illustrator, it's equally important to create open-ended paths. Illustrator has several tools for creating these kinds of paths (seen in Figure 7.14) and, as you'll see, different ways to edit them as well.

FIGURE 7.14
Choose your path drawing tools.

The Line Tool

To draw a straight line, choose the Line Segment tool and click and drag the mouse on the artboard. Before you release the mouse, you can utilize any of the following functions that will affect the path you are drawing:

▶ Press the Shift key to constrain your path to increments of 45º.

▶ Press the spacebar to "freeze" your path and position it elsewhere on your artboard.

▶ Press the tilde (~) key to create numerous copies of your path.

To draw a line numerically, choose the Line tool and click once on your artboard to get the Line Segment Tool Options dialog box, shown in Figure 7.15. Enter a value for the length and the angle, and click OK.

FIGURE 7.15
The Line
Segment Tool
Options
dialog box.

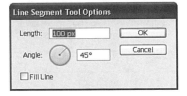

The Arc Tool

To draw an arc, choose the Arc tool and click and drag the mouse on the artboard. Before you release the mouse, you can utilize any of the following functions that will affect the path you are drawing:

▶ Press the Shift key to constrain your path so that the length of the x- and y-axes are the same (thus creating a perfect quarter-circle).

▶ Press the (Option) [Alt] key to draw your path from the center outward.

▶ Press the up arrow key on your keyboard to make the slope of the path more convex.

▶ Press the down arrow key on your keyboard to make the slope of the path more concave.

▶ Press the C key to draw the arc as a closed-path shape.

▶ Press the F key to flip the path along its axis.

▶ Press the spacebar to "freeze" your path and position it elsewhere on your artboard.

▶ Press the tilde (~) key to create numerous copies of your path.

To draw an arc numerically, choose the Arc tool and click once on your artboard to get the Arc Segment Tool Options dialog box (see Figure 7.16). Enter values for the length of the x-axis and the y-axis, and for the slope. Choose also to draw an open or closed path and an axis on which to base the path, and click OK.

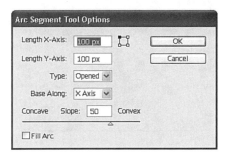

The Spiral Tool

Illustrator has a cool tool for drawing spirals, and the best part is that you don't get dizzy drawing them!

To draw a spiral, choose the Spiral tool and click and drag the mouse on the artboard. A spiral is always drawn outward from its center. Before you release the mouse, you can utilize any of the following functions that will affect the path you are drawing:

▶ Move your mouse in a circular motion to rotate the path.

▶ Press the Shift key to constrain the path to increments of 45º.

▶ Press the up arrow key on your keyboard to add segments (or winds) to your path.

▶ Press the down arrow key on your keyboard to remove segments (or winds) from your path.

▶ Press the (Option) [Alt] key to adjust the length of the path.

▶ Press the (Cmd) [Ctrl] key to adjust the decay of the path. The decay setting controls how close the winds of the spiral are to each other.

▶ Press the spacebar to "freeze" your path and position it elsewhere on your artboard.

▶ Press the tilde (~) key to create numerous copies of your path.

To draw a spiral numerically, choose the Spiral tool and click once on your artboard to get the Spiral dialog box (see Figure 7.17). Enter values for the radius, the decay, and the number of segments; then choose a style and click OK.

FIGURE 7.17
The Spiral
dialog box.

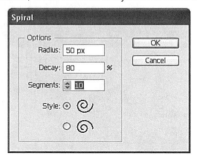

The Rectangular Grid Tool

Although it's not necessarily a path tool, the Rectangular Grid tool enables you to easily construct a grid using both paths and a single rectangle.

To draw a rectangular grid, choose the Rectangular Grid tool and click and drag the mouse on the artboard. Before you release the mouse, you can utilize any of the following functions that will affect the grid you are drawing:

- ▶ Press the Shift key to constrain your grid to a perfect square.

- ▶ Press the (Option) [Alt] key to draw your grid out from its center.

- ▶ Press the up arrow key on your keyboard to add rows to your grid.

- ▶ Press the down arrow key on your keyboard to remove rows from your grid.

- ▶ Press the right arrow key on your keyboard to add columns to your grid.

- ▶ Press the left arrow key on your keyboard to remove columns from your grid.

- ▶ Press the X and C keys to skew your columns to the left and right.

- ▶ Press the V and F keys to skew your rows to the top and bottom.

- ▶ Press the spacebar to "freeze" your grid and position it elsewhere on your artboard.

- ▶ Press the tilde (~) key to create numerous copies of your grid.

To draw a rectangular grid numerically, choose the Rectangular Grid tool and click once on your artboard to get the Rectangular Grid Tool Options dialog box (see Figure 7.18). Enter the appropriate values and click OK.

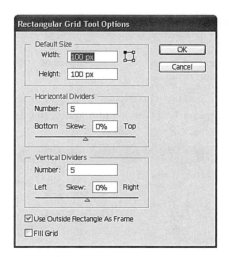

FIGURE 7.18
The Rectangular Grid Tool Options dialog box.

The Polar Grid Tool

Similar to the Rectangular Grid tool, the Polar Grid tool creates grids that are circular in form.

To draw a polar grid, choose the Polar Grid tool, and click and drag the mouse on the artboard. Before you release the mouse, you can utilize any of the following functions that will affect the grid you are drawing:

- Press the Shift key to constrain your grid to a perfect circle.
- Press the (Option) [Alt] key to draw your grid out from its center.
- Press the up arrow key on your keyboard to add concentric dividers to your grid.
- Press the down arrow key on your keyboard to remove concentric dividers from your grid.
- Press the right arrow key on your keyboard to add radial dividers to your grid.
- Press the left arrow key on your keyboard to remove radial dividers from your grid.
- Press the X and C keys to skew your concentric dividers closer to or farther from the center.
- Press the V and F keys to skew your radial dividers to the left and right.

▶ Press the spacebar to "freeze" your grid and position it elsewhere on your artboard.

▶ Press the tilde (~) key to create numerous copies of your grid.

To draw a polar grid numerically, choose the Polar Grid tool and click once on your artboard to get the Polar Grid Tool Options dialog box (see Figure 7.19). Enter the appropriate values and click OK.

FIGURE 7.19
The Polar Grid Tool Options dialog box.

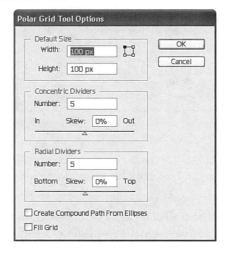

The Pencil Tool

For drawing freestyle on your artboard, use the Pencil tool. This tool can be especially useful for sketching if you have a tablet. If you hold down the (Option) [Alt] key as you draw, Illustrator closes the path for you when you release the mouse.

There are several settings for the Pencil tool, which you can access by double-clicking on the Pencil tool itself in the toolbox. The Pencil Tool Preferences dialog box (see Figure 7.20) enables you to edit the Fidelity and Smoothness settings, which affect how clean and smooth your drawn lines will be. The Keep Selected option keeps the last path you've drawn with the Pencil tool selected, and the Edit Selected Paths option enables you to simply draw over an existing path to adjust it. Finally, the Fill New Pencil Strokes applies a fill to your pencil strokes after you draw them.

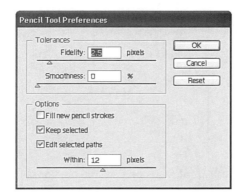

FIGURE 7.20
The Pencil Tool
Preferences
dialog box.

Béziers and the Pen Tool

One of the most common tools you'll use in Illustrator is a Bézier path. Let's learn what these paths look like and how they work inside Illustrator.

The first type of Bézier path is a straight line; it contains two anchor points with a straight line connecting them (see Figure 7.21). This type is the simplest Bézier path and requires the least amount of memory to store and print—you just need the coordinates of the first and second points.

FIGURE 7.21
A straight Bézier
path with the
anchor points
visible.

The second type of Bézier path is the curve, and here the description gets complicated. A curve consists of two anchor points, with a curved line connecting them. The curve is determined by control handles, which are attached to each anchor point. The control handles define exactly how the curved line is drawn between the two anchor points (see Figure 7.22).

FIGURE 7.22
A curved Bézier
path, with the
anchor points
and control
handles visible.

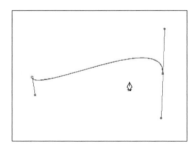

Of course, when the paths print, you don't see the anchor points or the handles. They just appear onscreen so you can edit the paths.

Until now, you've been creating Bézier paths without even knowing it. The shapes and paths you've created are all made up of Bézier paths. You were doing fine until now, so why bring up all of this complicated anchor-point and control-handle information? The answer is, sure, you could perform several tasks in Illustrator without knowing what Bézier paths are, but you lose out on all the power that Illustrator offers. Additionally, both Photoshop and InDesign have the Pen tool and enable you to draw and edit Bézier paths.

The Anchor Points

Illustrator has three kinds of anchor points: the straight corner point, the smooth point, and the combination point. Each kind of anchor point has its specific attributes, and each is used to create different types of paths. A Bézier object can be made up of any of the three kinds of anchor points and can contain any combination of them as well. For example, a square is made up of four straight-corner anchor points, whereas a circle is made up of four smooth anchor points. A shape such as a pie wedge contains both straight-corner and combination anchor points.

The Straight-Corner Anchor Point

The straight corner is the simplest form of the anchor point, and it is primarily used to connect straight lines (see Figure 7.23). To draw straight lines, press P to switch to the Pen tool and click once on your screen to define the first point in your line. Now click where you want the second point to appear (don't drag from the first point—just click and release). Each time you click in a different place, Illustrator draws a line connecting the anchor points. To create a closed shape, click on the first anchor point (the Pen tool icon appears with a little O next to it when you're about to close a path).

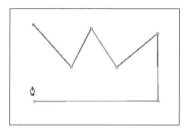

FIGURE 7.23
The straight-corner anchor point.

The Smooth Anchor Point

The smooth anchor point contains two control handles (see Figure 7.24). By adjusting the control handles, you determine the slope and sharpness of the curve on either side of the point. Because the path continues through the point without a sharp change in direction, it is called a smooth anchor point.

To draw curved lines, click and drag the mouse with the Pen tool to create your first point. Notice that as you drag, you're pulling control handles out from the point. Release the mouse button and then click and drag again at a different place on your artboard. As you drag, you'll see control handles being created for the second point, and a curved line will appear between the two points.

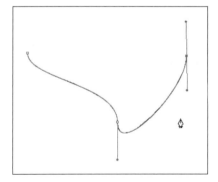

FIGURE 7.24
The smooth anchor point.

The Combination Anchor Point

The combination anchor point is a combination of the straight anchor point and the smooth anchor point (see Figure 7.25), so using these types of points can get a bit confusing. To draw a path using a combination point, click and drag with the Pen tool to create a smooth point. Then just click elsewhere on the screen to create a corner point. Then click and drag again elsewhere to create yet another smooth point.

FIGURE 7.25
The combination
anchor point.

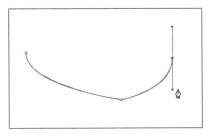

You'll notice that the point in the middle has no control handles, yet it has curved paths connected to it. In reality, the combination point has two sides to it: a straight side (from the single click) and a curved side (from the click and drag).

In its documentation, Adobe uses different terms for what I call control handles and control lines; it sometimes calls them direction points and direction lines. Also, you won't find a combination anchor point mentioned anywhere in the Adobe Illustrator manual. I use my own terms here because I feel that my terminology is easier to understand. I wanted to bring this to your attention in case you reference the Illustrator manual and happen upon those terms.

Editing Shapes and Paths

After you draw a path, you might want to change the shape or style of the points, adjusting the curve of the path or making a corner point into a smooth point. Several tools enable you to modify a path by changing, adding, or deleting a point.

The Direct Selection Tool

Perhaps the simplest method of editing a path is to use the Direct Selection (hollow arrow) tool. By selecting only one anchor point, you can reposition it (see Figure 7.26). By selecting a path and then dragging on a control point, you can change the shape of the curve for that path.

The Add Anchor Point Tool

Simple in concept, the Add Anchor Point tool—which looks just like the Pen tool with a little + (plus sign) next to it—enables you to place additional anchor points on an existing path (see Figure 7.27). Each new point takes on the attributes of the path on which you click. If you add a point to a straight path, the new anchor point is a straight anchor point, and clicking a curved path results in a new smooth anchor point.

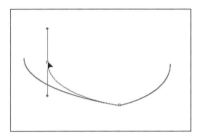

FIGURE 7.26
Repositioning a
single point on
a path with the
Direct Selection
tool.

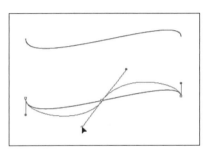

FIGURE 7.27
Before and after
adding an
anchor point to
an existing path
with the Add
Anchor Point
tool.

The Delete Anchor Point Tool

The Delete Anchor Point tool simply deletes existing anchor points. It also looks just like the Pen tool, except that it has a minus sign (–) next to it. If you click an anchor point with the Delete Anchor Point tool (see Figure 7.28), the point is removed, and Illustrator automatically joins the preceding anchor point with the next point on the path. If you were to select an anchor point and press the Delete key on your keyboard, the anchor point would be deleted, but the path would be broken at that point.

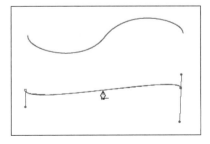

FIGURE 7.28
Before and after
removing an
anchor point
from an existing
path with the
Delete Anchor
Point tool.

Did you
Know?

Illustrator has a preference setting that automatically causes the Pen tool to change to the Add Anchor Point tool any time you mouse over an existing path. Likewise, the Pen tool automatically changes to the Delete Anchor Point tool when you mouse over an existing anchor point. This preference is turned on by default. Although this behavior is desirable at times, it can also get in the way. To turn it off, check the Disable Auto Add/Delete option in the General panel of the Preferences dialog box (see Figure 7.29).

FIGURE 7.29
The Disable Auto Add/Delete option in the General panel of the Preferences dialog box.

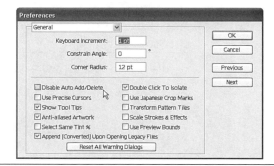

The Convert Anchor Point Tool

What do you do when you already have an anchor point, but you need to change it from one type of point to another? You use the Convert Anchor Point tool. You can easily access this, the last tool from the Pen tool quartet, by pressing (Option) [Alt] when any of the Pen tools is active. Notice that the cursor changes to an inverted V shape.

This tool works the same way as the Pen tool; clicking a point converts it to a straight anchor point. Clicking and dragging on a point makes that point a smooth anchor point. To make a smooth point into a combination point, click and drag on a control handle (see Figure 7.30).

FIGURE 7.30
Converting a smooth anchor point into a combination anchor point, using the Convert Anchor Point tool.

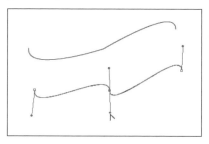

> If you want to convert a straight anchor point to a combination anchor point, you must first make the point a smooth anchor point and then click and drag on the control handle.

The Smooth Tool

When you create paths, they aren't always as clean or as smooth as you might like, especially when using the Pencil tool and drawing with a mouse. The Smooth tool (grouped with the Pencil tool) enables you to "get the kinks out" and get a smooth vector path. Use the tool to draw over any part of a selected path to smooth out that section of the path.

Simplifying Paths

Sometimes a shape has many extra anchor points (as a result of autotracing, or an autotrace program such as Adobe Streamline). Sometimes entire paths need to be smoothed out as well. Although you can use the Smooth tool for certain applications, as mentioned previously, sometimes you want to apply those effects on a larger scale.

With any path or object selected, you can choose Object, Path, Simplify to remove extra anchor points and smooth out vector paths. You can specify that only straight lines be used (no curves), and you can also choose to show a preview of the original path, to compare how close the new simplified path will be to the original (see Figure 7.31). Making adjustments to the Curve Precision and Angle Threshold sliders will control how many anchor points are removed and how smooth the result will be.

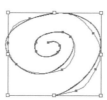

FIGURE 7.31
The Simplify feature gives you the option to compare the original path with the proposed simplified one.

The Erase Tool

The Erase tool doesn't erase the fill of an object, nor does it work the way the Eraser tool does in Photoshop or other paint programs by erasing pixels. The Erase tool can be used only on a selected path. Any part of a path that you draw over with the Erase tool will be deleted from that path.

Using Simple Shapes to Create Complex Shapes

No doubt you had more fun drawing the simple shapes discussed earlier than you did trying to make sense of the likes of the Pen tool. When it comes to creating more complex shapes, however, you can still use the primitive shape tools that are easy to use, along with a powerful collection of functions called Pathfinder. In fact, these functions are so useful that they have their own panel.

The idea behind the Pathfinder functions is that you can use several simple shapes to create a single, more complex shape. The Pathfinder panel is split into two rows of functions. The buttons on the top row are called Shape Modes, and they enable you to add, subtract, intersect, and exclude shapes. The buttons on the bottom row are referred to as Pathfinders, and they enable you to divide, trim, merge, crop, outline, and apply a Minus Back function (see Figure 7.32).

FIGURE 7.32
The Pathfinder panel, with the Shape Mode functions on the top row and the Pathfinders on the bottom row.

If you've used older versions of Illustrator, you might be wondering what happened to the Unite Pathfinder command. That function has been replaced by the Add shape mode.

Shape Modes

The shape modes are used primarily to create complex shapes from two or more other paths. To use these functions, you simply select the shapes you want to affect and click on the appropriate shape mode. There are four shape modes in Illustrator CS3:

▶ **Add**—The most commonly used command, the Add shape mode combines all the selected objects into one object (see Figure 7.33).

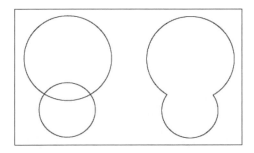

FIGURE 7.33
Two objects, before and after the Add shape mode is applied.

▶ **Subtract**—The Subtract shape mode subtracts the frontmost object in your selection from the shape behind it, leaving a hole cut out of it (see Figure 7.34).

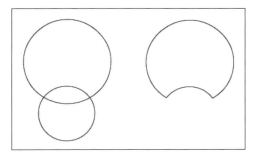

FIGURE 7.34
Two objects, before and after the Subtract shape mode is applied.

▶ **Intersect**—The Intersect shape mode is used on two or more objects that overlap each other. When it's applied, only the area where the objects overlap remains. The other parts of the objects are not visible (see Figure 7.35).

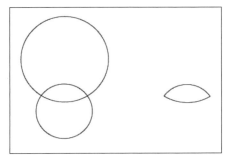

FIGURE 7.35
Two objects, before and after the Intersect shape mode is applied.

▶ **Exclude**—The Exclude shape mode is the exact opposite of the Intersect shape mode. When it's applied to overlapping objects, only the parts that don't overlap remain visible (see Figure 7.36).

FIGURE 7.36
Two objects, before and after the Exclude shape mode is applied.

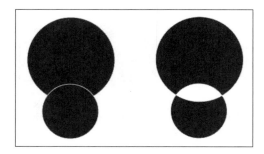

Shape modes are nondestructive, meaning that you can continue to edit the primitive shapes after you've applied a shape mode. Objects that have shape modes applied to them are called *compound shapes*. You can use the Direct Selection tool to select parts of a compound shape to edit them (see Figure 7.37).

FIGURE 7.37
Editing individual elements of a compound shape after the shapes have been combined.

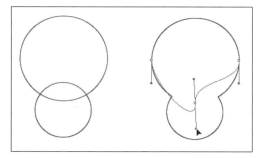

If at any time you want to "flatten" a compound shape so that the individual primitive shapes are no longer accessible, select the compound shape and click on the Expand button in the Pathfinder panel (see Figure 7.38). Alternatively, if you want to create a flattened object to begin with, you can press and hold the (Option) [Alt] key while applying any of the shape modes.

FIGURE 7.38
Expanding a
compound
shape.

Illustrator's compound shapes are similar to Photoshop's shape layers (vector masks). In fact, you can copy an Illustrator compound shape and paste it into Photoshop as a vector shape layer. Likewise, you can copy a vector shape layer from Photoshop and paste it into Illustrator as a compound shape (see Figure 7.39).

Did you Know?

FIGURE 7.39
When you're pasting a vector shape layer from Photoshop, Illustrator asks whether you want to paste the art as a compound shape.

Pathfinders

The Pathfinder functions are primarily used for splitting objects into parts or deleting unwanted parts of objects. There are several kinds, each with a different purpose:

▶ **Divide**—The Divide Pathfinder cuts up any overlapping shapes into separate shapes wherever they overlap (see Figure 7.40). An invaluable tool, Divide enables you to split up objects quickly. Divide looks at each object and divides each overlap individually, so it makes no difference whether you're dividing compound paths, groups, or whatever—they all become individual shapes. After Divide is applied, all the resulting objects are grouped together. You have to ungroup them if you want to work with each piece separately (or use the Direct Selection tool).

▶ **Trim**—The Trim function removes the parts of the back object that are behind front objects. It also removes the stroke (see Figure 7.41).

FIGURE 7.40
Two objects, before and after the Divide Pathfinder is applied.

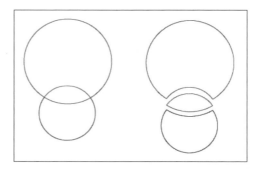

FIGURE 7.41
Two objects, before and after the Trim Pathfinder is applied.

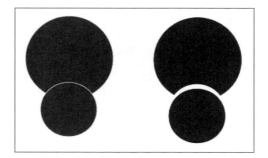

▶ **Merge**—The Merge function operates differently, depending on the fills of the selected objects. If the fills are all the same, the result is similar to what's achieved with the Add shape mode, making the objects form one single (flattened) object. If the fills are all different, Merge works like the Trim function. If some of the objects are filled the same, the like objects are united and the rest are trimmed (see Figure 7.42) .

FIGURE 7.42
Three objects, two of them with the same fill, before and after the Merge Pathfinder is applied.

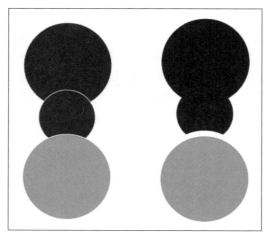

▶ **Crop**—The Crop function removes any parts of selected objects that are not directly under the frontmost object (see Figure 7.43). The final result of the Crop function is similar to what you would see if you created a mask. The only difference is that the Crop function actually deletes the art that is not visible, unlike a mask, which just covers it up. Be careful before you run this command because you cannot retrieve the artwork that is cropped out.

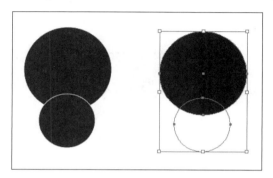

FIGURE 7.43
Two objects, before and after the Crop Pathfinder is applied.

▶ **Outline**—Choosing the Outline function converts all shapes to outlines and also divides the lines where they intersect, similar to a Divide function for strokes (see Figure 7.44).

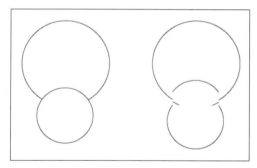

FIGURE 7.44
Two objects, before and after the Outline Pathfinder is applied.

▶ **Minus Back**—The reverse of the Subtract shape mode, Minus Back subtracts a part of an object based on what's behind it (instead of what's in front of it). This function is also not a shape mode, so the final result is a single flattened object (see Figure 7.45).

FIGURE 7.45
Two objects, before and after the Minus Back Pathfinder is applied.

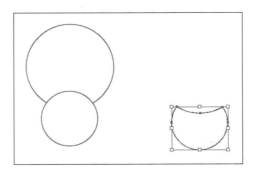

Working with Selections

In typical paint programs, you use selection tools to select pixels. In Illustrator, things are a bit different—rather than pixels, we're primarily interested in objects. Illustrator has several selection tools and selection methods, so let's take a look at them.

The Selection Tool

The Selection tool (or the black arrow, as I like to call it because of its appearance) is used to select entire objects. You select an object simply by clicking on it. When an object is selected, you can move it by dragging the object.

You can select multiple objects by holding down the Shift key as you click on other objects.

The Shift key technique can really save time when you're making certain selections, such as when you want to select all objects in your file except for one of them. In this case, you can simply select all and then Shift+click the one you want to deselect, and you're done.

Another method of selecting objects with the Selection tool is called *marquee selecting*, in which you click on a blank area and then drag the mouse while holding down the mouse button. As you drag the mouse, a box appears. Any objects that fall within the marquee box become selected when you release the mouse button (see Figure 7.46). It's almost like catching fish with a net.

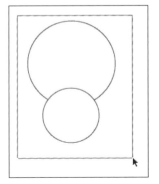

FIGURE 7.46
Selecting two objects using the marquee selection method.

By default, you can click anywhere inside a filled object to select it. However, if you turn on the Object Selection by Path Only option in the Selection and Anchor Display Preferences (see Figure 7.47), you are able to select a path only by clicking on its path or outline. I find it useful to turn on this preference when I'm working in very complex illustrations because this option makes it more difficult to accidentally select unwanted objects.

Did you Know?

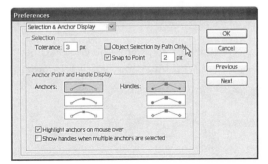

FIGURE 7.47
The Object Selection by Path Only option in the Selection and Anchor Display Preferences dialog box.

The Direct Selection Tool

The Direct Selection tool (or as I like to call it, the white arrow) is the selection tool used the most in Illustrator. In a few moments, you will see why. As you just learned, the Selection tool is used to select entire objects. The Direct Selection tool, on the other hand, is used to select parts of an object. If you click on a path and drag, only that path moves. The same applies when you click on an anchor point—only that anchor point moves (see Figure 7.48).

FIGURE 7.48
Moving a single
anchor point
using the Direct
Selection tool.

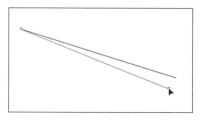

FIGURE 7.48
Moving a single
anchor point
using the Direct
Selection tool.

You can use either the Shift+click method or the marquee method to select multiple anchor points and move them at the same time.

Grouping Objects

Illustrator enables you to group several objects to make it easier to organize your artwork. However, the benefits of grouping objects go far beyond having art that is "neat" or organized. First, when you use the Selection tool to select one object in a group, the entire group is selected. This makes it easier to move objects around. Second, a group itself can have certain attributes or effects applied to it. Finally, groups can be nested. That means you can have a group inside another group (and so on).

To make a group, select the objects you want to group, and choose Object, Group (see Figure 7.49). To release a group, select it and choose Object, Ungroup.

FIGURE 7.49
Choosing
the Group
command.

Groups are extremely helpful when you are working in complex documents, and grouping items as you create them is always a good idea. After you create a logo, for instance, group it. This way, you can move it around easily, and, more important, you won't accidentally lose parts by trying to select each piece every time (inevitably, you'll miss one or two parts).

When you double-click on any object in a group using the Selection tool, a gray box appears at the top of the window (see Figure 7.50). This gray box indicates that you're in group isolation mode, and any new shape that you now draw automatically becomes part of the group. To get out of group isolation mode, click the arrow in the box. We talk more about group isolation mode when we cover Live Paint, later in "Live Paint Groups."

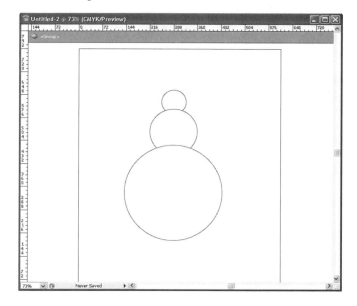

FIGURE 7.50
The gray border indicates that you're in group isolation mode.

The Group Selection Tool

The Group Selection tool is a variation of the Direct Selection tool. It is grouped with the Direct Selection tool and can be found by pressing and holding the mouse button on the Direct Selection tool in the toolbox. In complex illustrations, you might have nested groups that contain many groups. The Group Selection tool makes working with these groups easy.

Each time you click with the Group Selection tool, it selects the next higher group, giving you easy access to any group with a nested group.

As mentioned earlier, the Direct Selection tool is the most-used selection tool in Illustrator. If you switch back to the Direct Selection tool and press and hold the (Option) [Alt] key, you'll notice that the cursor for the Direct Selection tool on your screen turns into the Group Selection tool. Releasing the (Option) [Alt] key returns you to the Direct Selection tool.

Now you have the power to select parts of an object, or, by simply holding down the (Option) [Alt] key, you can select an entire object or entire groups of objects. For 90% of your work, you never have to go back to the Selection tool (black arrow).

The Lasso Tool

Using the marquee method for making selections with the Selection and the Direct Selection tools can be useful, but only if you're okay with selecting objects that fall into a rectangular marquee area. The Lasso tool enables you to draw irregularly shaped marquees to select objects or parts of objects.

The Lasso tool works much like the Direct Selection tool, in that if an object falls completely within the boundaries of the marquee, the entire object becomes selected. But if only a portion of the object falls into that marquee area, only that portion of the object becomes selected (see Figure 7.51).

FIGURE 7.51
Selecting only a portion of an object with the Lasso tool results in only those parts of the object falling within the marquee being selected.

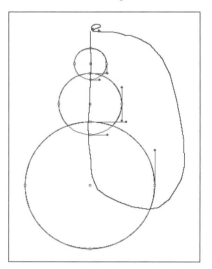

To use the Lasso tool, choose it from the toolbox and draw a marquee area. You don't have to complete the marquee by drawing back to the point you started from because the Lasso tool completes the marquee selection area after you release the mouse.

The Magic Wand Tool

Photoshop has a Magic Wand tool that's used to select pixels of similar color. Likewise, in Illustrator the Magic Wand tool is used to select objects of similar attributes. Double-clicking on the Magic Wand tool in the toolbox opens the Magic Wand panel, where you can specify a Tolerance setting and specify to which attributes the Magic Wand is sensitive (see Figure 7.52).

FIGURE 7.52
The Magic Wand panel, with all options displayed.

Fills and Strokes

Illustrator wouldn't be incredibly useful if it were capable of creating only shapes with white fills and black strokes. It's time to splash a bit of color on the topic of applying fills and strokes to objects in Illustrator.

You can specify colors for selected objects in Illustrator by using the Color panel. When expanded fully, the Color panel contains a fill and stroke indicator, color sliders, and a color ramp (see Figure 7.53). To specify a color for the fill of an object, you have to click on the fill indicator first. Likewise, to specify a color for the stroke of an object, click on the stroke indicator.

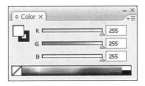

FIGURE 7.53
The fully expanded Color panel.

The keyboard shortcut to change the focus between the fill and the stroke is the X key. Learning this shortcut will save you many trips to the Color panel. A fill and stroke indicator also appears in the toolbox.

Did you Know?

The Color panel can define colors in Grayscale, RGB, HSB, CMYK, and Web-safe RGB color modes. To switch among these color modes in the Color panel, choose from the list in the panel flyout menu (see Figure 7.54). Alternatively, you can Shift+click on the color ramp to cycle through the different supported color modes.

FIGURE 7.54
Switching
between color
modes in
Illustrator.

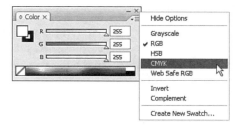

> **By the Way**
>
> Even though you can specify colors in any of several color modes, those colors are converted to the document-specified color space after they are applied to objects in your document. So it usually makes sense to specify colors using the document's color space.

You can store saved colors in the Swatches panel (see Figure 7.55). To create a swatch, simply drag a color from the stroke indicator or the fill indicator in the Color panel into the Swatches panel. Illustrator also ships with numerous swatch collections, which you can access by choosing Open Swatch Library from the Swatches panel flyout menu.

FIGURE 7.55
The Swatches
panel.

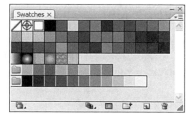

You can create basically three kinds of swatches inside Illustrator: solid colors, gradients, and patterns.

Solid Colors

Solid colors are simple and are really prerequisites for the other types of swatches. You can define a solid color just as mentioned previously, by specifying a color in the Color panel. However, you need to be aware of really *two* types of solid colors: process colors and spot colors.

Process Colors

A *process color*, by definition, is a color made up of a mix of colors. In the print world, a process color is one made up of different values of CMYK. In the Web arena, Illustrator would also consider an RGB color a process color.

You specify a process color for jobs you'd be printing in four-color process or publishing on the Web.

A variation of the process color, called a *global process color* (see Figure 7.56), enables you to easily track and update colors throughout your document.

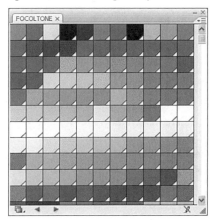

Spot Colors

A *spot color* is a predefined ink color that you can either specify on your own or choose from a list such as Pantone, Focoltone, or Toyo. Spot colors also are referred to as *custom colors*. They are standard colors that have been designated to ensure color accuracy.

Spot colors have a single value, or a *tint value*, that determines the strength at which the ink will be printed. Spot colors are usually specified when you want to print a specialized ink (a metallic color, for example) or when you want to save money by printing a two- or three-color job (instead of having to print a full process–color job).

Illustrator ships with many standard custom color libraries, all of which you can load by choosing Open Swatch Library from the Swatches panel flyout menu.

Gradients

Gradients are a powerful feature in Illustrator, enabling you to specify a fill of different colors blending with each other. Illustrator can create a gradient between just 2 colors or up to 32 colors. Gradients can be used to achieve cool shading effects or to add dimension to objects (see Figure 7.57).

FIGURE 7.57
Using gradient
fills to achieve
cool effects.

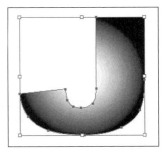

FIGURE 7.57
Using gradient
fills to achieve
cool effects.

You can apply a gradient to a selected object simply by selecting a gradient swatch from the Swatches panel. To create or edit a gradient, however, you need to open the Gradient panel. With the panel expanded fully, you will find a gradient swatch, an option to make the gradient linear or radial, fields for Angle and Location, and a gradient slider (see Figure 7.58).

FIGURE 7.58
The fully
expanded
Gradient panel.

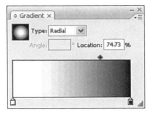

Defining a Gradient

You create a gradient in much the same way you create a color. Click on the Gradient swatch in the Gradient panel. Notice that under the gradient slider are icons that look like little houses. They are *color stops*, indicating the points at which a color is used in the gradient. To create a new color stop, click anywhere beneath the gradient slider. When a new color stop appears, you can drag it to the left or right. You can also drag any color from the Swatches or Color panel onto the gradient slider to create a color stop in that color. To change an existing color stop, either drag a new color directly on top of it, or click the color stop icon to select it and choose a new color in the Swatches or Color panel.

To delete a color stop from a gradient, simply drag the color stop off the bottom of the Gradient panel and it disappears.

Notice also that little diamond-shape icons appear on top of the gradient slider. These indicate the location of the midpoint of the gradation. In other words, wherever the icon is, that's the place where 50% of each color appears. You can drag the *midpoint indicator* left or right to adjust where the midpoint should be (see Figure 7.59).

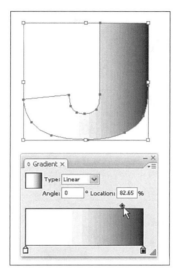

FIGURE 7.59
Dragging the midpoint indicator of a gradient.

After you've created the perfect gradient, click the New Swatch icon in the Swatches panel. After you create the new swatch, you should double-click it and give it a name. Illustrator gives your creations the names New Gradient Swatch 1, New Gradient Swatch 2, and so on, which don't really offer any insight into what they are.

Using the Gradient Tool

The Gradient tool in Illustrator is used to control the direction and placement of a gradient in an object or over several objects. After you fill an object with a gradient, select the Gradient tool and, with the object still selected, click and drag across the object in the direction you want the gradient to go (see Figure 7.60). The place where you begin dragging is the position where the gradient starts, and the place where you let go is the position where the gradient ends. If you stop dragging before you get to the end of the object, Illustrator continues to fill the object with the color at the end of the gradient.

FIGURE 7.60
Using the
Gradient tool
to draw a
directional
gradient across
an object.

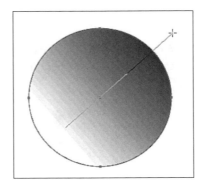

Patterns

Patterns can be real time savers. A pattern is a defined piece of art, or tile, created in
Illustrator that, as a fill attribute, is repeated over and over again, much like wallpaper (see Figure 7.61).

FIGURE 7.61
An object filled
with a pattern.

Defining a Pattern

Defining a pattern is a little different from defining gradients or colors. Instead of
clicking the New Swatch icon, you drag your objects directly into the Swatches panel
from the artboard. After you create a pattern swatch, remember to give it a unique
name so you can identify it quickly when you need it.

If you want to edit a pattern that is already defined, simply drag the swatch itself
out from the Swatches panel into your artboard, and Illustrator places the art that
was used to create the pattern.

When you're creating a pattern design, remember that your object will be repeated
over and over again, so be careful how you set it up. If you need extra space around

your art (which is usually the case), create a rectangle and send it to the back of your artwork. Then select your art, along with the empty box in the background, and define the pattern. Illustrator treats a rectangle that's at the bottom of the stacking order as a boundary for the repeat area of the pattern.

In truth, you could probably write an entire book on creating patterns. Designing repeats is an art form in itself, and practicing how to define and apply patterns in Illustrator is the best way to master these features.

By the Way

Strokes

A *stroke* is the line that's drawn around an object, and you can specify solid colors, gradients, or patterns to color a stroke. The Stroke panel is where you can control the actual settings for how a stroke appears (see Figure 7.62).

FIGURE 7.62
The fully expanded Stroke panel.

The most-used option in the Stroke panel is Weight. It determines how thick or thin the stroke is. Illustrator's default is 1 point. For hairline rules, most people use 0.25 point (anything thinner probably won't show up on an offset printing press).

The Miter Limit option determines how far the stroke protrudes on a sharp corner. A thick line, for example, needs more room to complete a sharp point than a thin one does (see Figure 7.63).

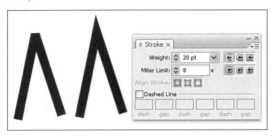

FIGURE 7.63
An acute angle combined with a thick stroke needs a higher miter limit to draw the complete point.

Line Caps and Joins

Line caps determine the appearance of the ends of a stroked path (see Figure 7.64). This setting in the Stroke panel is used only for open-ended paths. By choosing different caps, you can make the ends either flat or rounded, or have the stroke width enclose the end of the path as well.

FIGURE 7.64
The three types of line caps (top to bottom): Butt, Round, and Projecting.

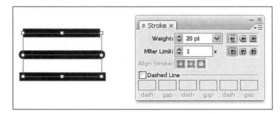

Line joins control how the stroke appears at each corner of the path (see Figure 7.65). You can choose from Mitered, Round, and Beveled options.

FIGURE 7.65
The three types of line joins (top to bottom): Mitered, Round, and Beveled.

Align Stroke

By default, Illustrator draws the weight of a stroke on the center of a path. That means a 20-point stroke results in 10 points applied to the inside of the path and 10 points to the outside of the path. However, you can use the Align Stroke buttons in the Stroke panel to specify that the weight of the stroke be applied entirely inside the path or entirely outside the path (see Figure 7.66).

Dashed Strokes

The last option in the Stroke panel, Dashed Line, can be one of the most powerful. Here you can specify dashed or dotted lines. Depending on what settings you have set for weight, line caps, and line joins, you can create a stitched line, a skip line, or almost anything. You control the dash and gap (the space between each dash) by entering numbers into the Dash and Gap fields at the bottom of the panel. If you're using only one sequence, you can enter just the first two fields. Alternatively, you can enter up to three Dash and Gap settings to achieve complex dash patterns (see Figure 7.67).

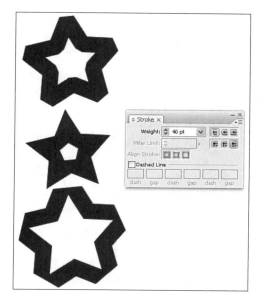

FIGURE 7.66
A shape with a 20-point stroke applied to it. You can choose to align the stroke to the center, inside, or outside of the vector path.

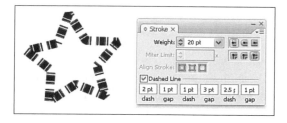

FIGURE 7.67
Create complex dash patterns using multiple Dash and Gap settings.

Offset Path and Outline Path

For outlining and special effects, Offset Path is a great function. Offset Path creates an object that perfectly outlines, or traces, a selected path at an offset that you specify. To use it, select one or more objects and choose Object, Path, Offset Path. The Offset Path dialog box then appears. Enter an amount for the offset (you can use positive or negative numbers) and click OK. Note that Offset Path always makes a copy of your selection and does not affect the original.

Outline Path is another great feature that converts strokes into filled objects. Found in the same location as the Offset Path command, Outline Path works by creating a filled shape the size of the stroke width.

The Outline Path command doesn't outline dash information. To outline a dashed stroke, choose Object, Flatten Transparency, and click OK.

Live Paint Groups

We've discussed groups, but Illustrator also has a special kind of group called a Live Paint group. Ordinarily, coloring objects in Illustrator requires the careful creation of closed vector shapes. For example, if you were to draw a tic-tac-toe board using four straight lines (see Figure 7.68), there would be no easy way to fill the middle section with a color, even though it appears to be a closed area. With Live Paint however, you can do so.

FIGURE 7.68
Drawing four intersecting paths.

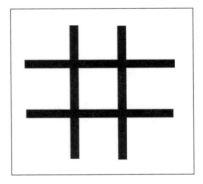

With the four lines selected, you could select the Live Paint Bucket tool (a paint bucket pouring into a small square) and then click on any of the paths to convert them to a Live Paint group. In a Live Paint group, any area on your screen that looks like a closed shape acts like one. You can then choose a color from the Swatches panel and click on the center region of the art with the Live Paint Bucket tool to fill the area. As you move the Live Paint Bucket tool, areas that can be filled with color are highlighted (see Figure 7.69).

Live Paint groups are also easier to use when making edits. You can switch to the Selection tool and double-click on the group to enter group isolation mode. Then you can use the Line tool to draw a new line through the middle of the group. Using the Selection tool, double-click outside the group to exit group isolation mode. You can use the Live Paint Bucket tool to apply color to the dissected regions.

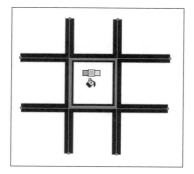

FIGURE 7.69
Areas that can be filled with color are highlighted when the Live Paint Bucket tool is passed over them.

You can click and drag with the Live Paint Bucket tool to color multiple regions simultaneously.

The Live Paint Selection tool enables you to select regions or segments of paths and even delete them.

When creating freestyle art, there are sometimes gaps between the paths because not every path lines up perfectly. You might want to fill a region with color even if the region isn't visibly closed. With a Live Paint group selected, you can choose Object, Live Paint, Gap Options, to specify that gaps of a certain size (which you define) will automatically close when creating filled areas (see Figure 7.70).

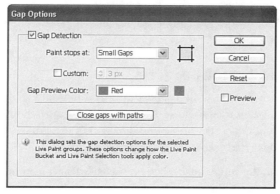

FIGURE 7.70
The Gap Options dialog box.

At any time, you can also expand a Live Paint group by selecting the group and choosing Object, Live Paint, Expand. This returns the objects to normal Illustrator vector objects.

Brushes

Illustrator includes four kinds of brushes, all applied in the same way. The traditional way to apply a brush in Illustrator is to use the Paintbrush tool, which works similarly to the Pencil tool. Instead of just drawing a plain stroked path, the Paintbrush tool applies one of the four kinds of brushes.

Brushes are stored in the Brushes panel (see Figure 7.71), and the truth is that you don't need to use the Paintbrush tool to apply a brush at all. That's because you can select an existing object and click on any brush in the Brushes panel to apply that brush stroke to the selected path. Of course, the Brush tool makes it easier to create more artistic brush strokes, but as you'll soon see, certain kinds of brushes don't require that kind of artistic touch.

FIGURE 7.71
The Brushes panel.

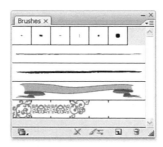

Did you Know?

Illustrator CS3 ships with predefined brushes that you can use. From the Brushes panel flyout menu, choose Open Brush Library to see a list of brush libraries.

Calligraphic Brushes

The first kind of brush is the Calligraphic brush. A calligraphy pen has an angled tip, or nib, which, when used to draw or write, creates a tapered line that gets thicker or thinner, depending on the angle and direction of the stroke. The Calligraphic brush simulates this effect (see Figure 7.72).

To create a new Calligraphic brush, click on the New Brush icon in the Brushes panel and choose New Calligraphic Brush to get the Calligraphic Brush Options dialog box (see Figure 7.73).

FIGURE 7.72
An example of
strokes created
with the calli-
graphic brush.

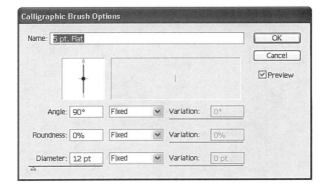

FIGURE 7.73
The Calligraphic
Brush Options
dialog box.

In the Calligraphic Brush Options dialog box, you can specify the following settings:

▶ At the top of the box, you can specify a name for the brush.

▶ Directly under the name is a white box with a picture of an ellipse with an arrow going through it and two black dots on either side. This is the Brush Shape Editor. Simply click and drag on the arrow to rotate the brush shape and adjust its angle. Click and drag inward on the black dots to adjust the roundness of the brush shape.

▶ To the immediate right of the Brush Shape Editor is an area that shows you a preview of your brush shape. Notice the three shapes, of which the outer two are grayed out and the center one is black. If you have variations set (see the next bullet item), the gray shapes illustrate the minimum and maximum values for the brush shape.

▶ You can specify values for angle, roundness, and diameter numerically at the bottom of the dialog box. Each option can have one of three variation attributes: Random, in which Illustrator randomly changes the setting; Pressure, which enables you to determine brush shape by how hard you press with a pressure-sensitive pen and tablet; and Fixed, which assigns a constant value that you define.

Scatter Brushes

The Scatter brush distributes predefined art along the path you draw with the Paintbrush tool (see Figure 7.74). To define a new Scatter brush, you have to start with a piece of art. When you've created the art you want to use for the brush, select the art and drag it into the Brushes panel. When the New Brush dialog box appears asking what kind of brush you want to create, choose New Scatter brush and click OK.

FIGURE 7.74
An example of the kind of stroke the Scatter brush can create.

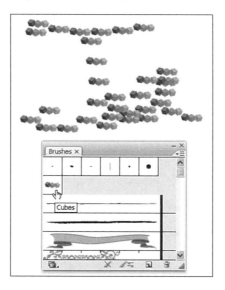

Illustrator then opens the Scatter Brush Options dialog box, where you can specify the behavior of the new Scatter brush (see Figure 7.75).

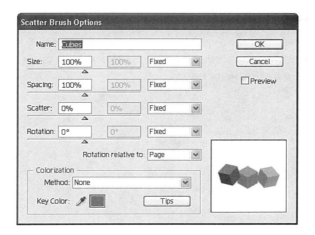

FIGURE 7.75
The Scatter
Brush Options
dialog box.

In the Scatter Brush Options dialog box, you can specify the following settings:

▶ At the top of the box, you can specify a name for the brush.

▶ Directly under the name are four options for which you can enter numerical values to specify the size of the art when it's drawn on the path; the spacing between the art as it appears on the path; the scatter, which defines how far from the path the art can stray; and, finally, the rotation, which specifies the rotation of each individual piece of art on the path. You can set the rotation to be relative to the page or to the actual path itself. For each of these four settings, you can specify Fixed, Random, or Pressure, just as you could for the Calligraphic brushes. The Pressure option works only if you are using a pressure-sensitive tablet, such as a Wacom tablet.

▶ The final option for the Scatter brush is Colorization. This option enables you to specify color changes to the art that appears on your painted strokes. Choosing None keeps the color consistent with the original color defined with the brush you have selected. To use the Hue Shift option, click the Eyedropper box, and click to choose a color from the art that appears in the box to the right. This procedure works on colored objects only, not black-and-white objects. Clicking the Tips button can help you see how the color changes are applied.

If you're thinking that the Scatter brush seems similar to the brushes you created in Photoshop, you're absolutely right. As you'll see in "The Symbolism Tools," there's a more powerful feature in Illustrator, the Symbol Sprayer tool, that can create art that looks similar to the Scatter brush.

Art Brushes

The Art brush differs from the Scatter brush in that the Art brush stretches a single piece of predefined art along a path (see Figure 7.76), whereas the Scatter brush litters the path with many copies of the art.

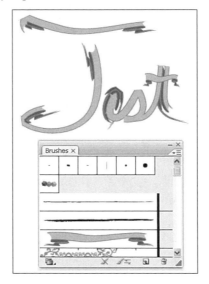

To define a new Art brush, you have to start with a piece of art. After you've created the art you want to use for the brush, select the art and drag it into the Brushes panel. When the New Brush dialog box appears asking what kind of brush you want to create, choose New Art Brush and click OK.

Illustrator then opens the Art Brush Options dialog box, where you can specify the behavior of the new Art brush (see Figure 7.77).

In the Art Brush Options dialog box, you can specify the following settings:

- ▶ At the top of the box, you can specify a name for the brush.

- ▶ Directly under the name is a white box with the art in it. Notice that an arrow goes through the art. This arrow indicates the direction the art is drawn on the path; you can edit it by clicking any of the arrows that appear to the right of the white box.

- ▶ Below the Direction option is the Size option, in which you can specify what size the art appears on the painted path. If you select the Proportional option, the artwork retains is height-to-width relationship for the length of the stroke. You can also specify whether the art should be flipped along or across the painted path.

▶ The final option for the Art brush is Colorization, which functions exactly like the Scatter brush does, as described earlier.

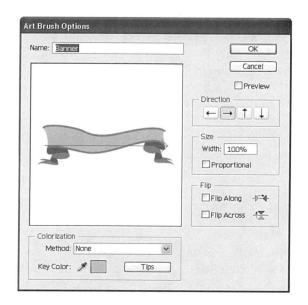

FIGURE 7.77
The Art Brush Options dialog box.

Pattern Brushes

Apparently, three kinds of brushes in Illustrator just weren't enough for the engineers over at Adobe, so they added a fourth—arguably the most powerful of the bunch. The Pattern brush applies patterns across a painted path (see Figure 7.78). What makes this different from any brush until this point is that you can define patterns with different attributes for corners and ends. We covered how to create patterns earlier in the chapter; when you have your patterns listed in your Swatches panel, you can define a Pattern brush by clicking on the New Brush icon in the Brushes panel and choosing New Pattern Brush.

FIGURE 7.78
An example of
the kind of
stroke the
Pattern brush
can create.

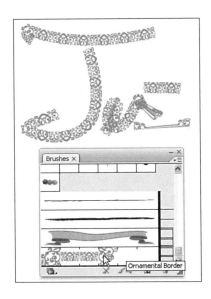

Illustrator then opens the Pattern Brush Options dialog box, where you can specify
the behavior of the new brush (see Figure 7.79).

FIGURE 7.79
The Pattern
Brush Options
cialog box.

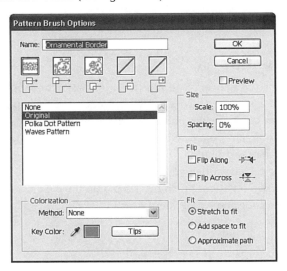

In the Pattern Brush Options dialog box, you can specify the following settings:

▶ At the top of the box, you can specify a name for the brush.

▶ Directly under the name are five boxes, each representing a different tile of the pattern: Side, Outer Corner, Inner Corner, Start, and End. You do not need to define all five parts, and Illustrator uses the parts only when necessary. With a tile section selected, choose a pattern from the list that appears directly under the tiles.

▶ As with the previous brushes, you can specify Scale and Spacing, as well as specify whether the pattern should be flipped along or across the path.

▶ With the Pattern brush, you can decide how Illustrator fits the pattern to the path. Obviously, not every pattern will fit every path length perfectly. If you select Stretch to Fit, Illustrator stretches the pattern tiles to make the pattern fit seamlessly across the entire painted path. If you select Add Space to Fit, Illustrator does not adjust the size of the pattern tiles, but spaces them evenly across the painted stroke. Finally, the Approximate Path option adjusts the size of the path itself to fit the size of the pattern tiles.

▶ The final option for the Pattern brush is Colorization, which functions exactly as it does for the Scatter and Art brushes, as described earlier.

In closing, if you find it hard to identify each brush type just by looking at the Brushes panel, you can opt to view the brushes by name. Choose List View from the Brushes panel flyout menu, and an icon on the far right of each brush listing indicates the brush type (see Figure 7.80).

FIGURE 7.80
Viewing the list of brushes by name. The icons on the far right of each listing indicate the brush type.

Organizing Your Files Using Layers

Using layers in Illustrator enables you to better organize the objects in your file. Although it might not make much sense to spend time creating and working with layers to work on a simple logo, it certainly makes sense for illustrations or designs that are more complex.

The Layers Panel

Illustrator's layers are specified in the Layers panel. When you start working in a new document, all artwork is automatically placed on a layer called Layer 1 (see Figure 7.81). To open the Layers panel, choose Layers from the Window menu. The order in which layers appear in the Layers panel is important: Layers that appear closer to the top of the panel appear above (or in front of) other objects that might appear on layers that are closer to the bottom of the Layers panel.

FIGURE 7.81
The Layers panel, with the default Layer 1 showing.

Some artists prefer to create several layers before they begin working, adding art to each layer as they progress. Others prefer to add or delete layers as necessary as they work on a project. Still others like to create the entire piece and then chop it into different layers afterward. As you'll soon see, there are certainly some benefits to working with layers during the design process (instead of after the fact).

To create a new layer, click on the New Layer button at the bottom of the Layers panel. Illustrator creates the layer and assigns it a name. You can double-click on the layer to rename it, or instead you can (Option-click) [Alt+click] on the New Layers button to create a new layer and name it in one step. In either case, it's a good idea to name your layers because trying to identify layers that are named Layer 1, Layer 2, Layer 3, and so on is difficult (to say the least).

Did you Know?

> When you click the New Layer button, a new layer is added just above the currently selected layer. If you hold down the (Cmd) [Ctrl] key while clicking the New Layer icon, a new layer is added to the top of your Layers panel.

To delete a layer, either click the layer in the Layers panel to highlight it and then click on the Trash icon at the bottom of the panel, or drag the layer itself onto the Trash icon. If you try to delete a layer that contains artwork on it, a warning dialog box appears, alerting you about the situation; Illustrator deletes the layer and its contents only with your permission.

You can duplicate a layer—and all the contents of that layer along with it—by click-ing and dragging an existing layer onto the New Layer icon in the Layers panel.

Using Layers in the Design Process

As I mentioned earlier, there are certainly benefits to working with the Layers panel as you design your art. Let's take a closer look at the Layers panel to better under-stand these benefits.

Each layer in the Layers panel has several icons, which enable you to perform cer-tain functions (see Figure 7.82). We discuss these functions beginning on the far left of a layer listing.

FIGURE 7.82
The different icons within each layer in the Layers panel.

On the far left, each layer has an icon that looks like an eye. Clicking on the eye toggles the visibility of that layer. Pressing the (Option) [Alt] key while clicking on the eye hides/shows all other layers at once.

The next icon to the right of the eye is a lock indicator. Click in the box to toggle the layer to be locked or unlocked. Pressing the (Option) [Alt] key while clicking on the lock locks/unlocks all other layers at once.

The next icon to the right of the lock is a disclosure triangle. Click on the triangle to reveal the contents of the layer. If there isn't a triangle on a layer, there are no objects on that layer.

> Take note that layers are shaded with a gray background. However, objects them-selves (which appear inside of layers) appear in the Layers panel with a white background (refer to Figure 7.82). People often are confused by Illustrator's behav-ior of "automatically creating all of these layers each time I create something," but in reality, each time you create a new object, Illustrator isn't creating a new layer at all.

By the Way

To the right of the disclosure triangle is a thumbnail icon that gives a graphical pre-view of the objects on that layer. Be aware that for documents with many layers, thumbnails can slow the performance of Illustrator because it has to draw each and every thumbnail.

To the right of the thumbnail is the layer name.

To the right of the layer name is a little circle. This is the target icon. For an effect or attribute to be applied to an object in Illustrator, that object (or group or layer) has to be targeted. Illustrator actually employs something called *smart targeting* that automatically does the targeting for you; however, sometimes you want to specifically target something yourself. To target a layer or an object, click once on the circle icon, which then appears with a circle outlined around it. Layers or objects that have an appearance applied to them display the circle as a shaded 3D sphere (which the Adobe engineers refer to as the "meatball").

Finally, if you click on the far right of the layer, it selects all the objects in that layer. Selections are indicated by a colored square. This square can appear in two sizes. If all the objects on the layer are selected, you will see a large square, but if only some of the objects on a layer are selected, a smaller square displays. You can move artwork from one layer to another simply by dragging the colored square to a different layer. You can press the (Option) [Alt] key while dragging the square to copy the selected art to a different layer.

Illustrator layers can be used for more than just organizing artwork inside Illustrator. When saving files as Scalable Vector Graphics (SVG) or for certain web applications, you can have Illustrator convert layers to CSS layers. You can also export an Illustrator file as a Photoshop file with layers intact. Finally, you can save a PDF file out of Illustrator that's compatible with Acrobat 6 or later, enabling you to view Illustrator's layers in Adobe Reader and Acrobat Professional.

The Appearance Panel

Ask me what I think the key is to getting a real grasp on using Illustrator, and I'll tell you it's the Appearance panel. That's because the Appearance panel gives you the information you need to know about your targeted selections. For example, if you select a rectangle, the Appearance panel tells you that a path is targeted and indicates what the fill and stroke of that object are. More important, the Appearance panel tells you whether transparency settings or live effects have been applied to the object (see Figure 7.83). Later in "Live Effects" we cover exactly what live effects are, but examples are a soft drop shadow and a warp effect.

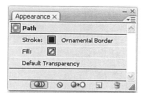

FIGURE 7.83
The Appearance panel helps identify the appearance of an object.

The Appearance panel also enables you to add multiple strokes or multiple fills to an object, a group, or a layer. To do so, simply choose Add New Fill or Add New Stroke from the Appearance panel flyout menu.

We're going to be looking at the Appearance panel a bit more closely in "Live Effects," but I wanted to point out that, just as with the Layers panel, items that appear in the Appearance panel represent the stacking order for those items. By default, an object's stroke appears above the fill, but you can actually change that in the Appearance panel by dragging the fill to appear at the top of the stacking order. Following the same line of thinking, you can click on just the fill to highlight it and then apply an opacity setting that will be applied only to the fill, not to the stroke of that object (see Figure 7.84).

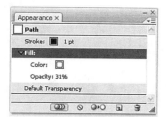

FIGURE 7.84
An opacity setting applied specifically to the fill of an object.

Masking Objects

A mask conceals, or covers, parts of an object behind it, yet it reveals parts of the object behind it as well. For example, a mask that you wear to a masquerade party might cover parts of your face, yet some parts might not be covered. A mask in Illustrator works in much the same way: You can use just about any shape or object in Illustrator to mask other elements in your design. After a mask is applied, you can edit the art behind the mask or the mask itself, independently of each other.

You can apply basically three types of masks in Illustrator: a clipping mask, a layer clipping mask, and an opacity mask. Each of these masks has its own specific uses and capabilities.

Clipping Masks

The clipping mask, the simplest kind of mask in Illustrator, can be made of any vector shape. A clipping mask works in this way: You have a shape that sits on top of your objects. When the mask is created, any objects that fall within the boundary of the top shape (the mask) are visible, but anything that falls outside that boundary is hidden. It's important to realize that the hidden art is not deleted—it's still there, but it's hidden from view.

To create a clipping mask, draw a shape for your mask and bring it to the front of the stacking order. Position your mask over the art you want the mask to affect and select both the art objects and the mask shape above it (see Figure 7.85). Then choose Object, Clipping Mask, Make to create the mask (see Figure 7.86). When the mask is applied, both the objects and the mask above it are grouped together; however, you can use the Group Selection tool to select just the mask or just the objects to make edits. This is useful when you want to reposition the mask to reveal a different part of the objects below it.

FIGURE 7.85
The objects selected, with the object that will be the mask on top.

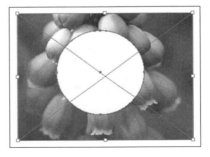

FIGURE 7.86
The masked art.

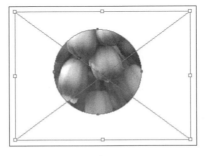

To release a mask (and have all the objects below the mask revealed again), select the group of the mask and objects, and choose Object, Clipping Mask, Release.

Layer Clipping Masks

Layer clipping masks are very similar in concept to clipping masks, except that they are applied in the Layers panel and affect all items on a specific layer. To create a layer clipping mask, simply create a shape that's on the same layer as the art you want to mask, and click on the layer listing in the Layers panel to highlight it. Then click the Make/Release Clipping Mask button at the bottom of the Layers panel (see Figure 7.87).

FIGURE 7.87
Creating a layer clipping mask.

Any object you add to that layer automatically becomes masked as well. Likewise, any object you pull out of that layer no longer is masked. A mask object is indicated by a listing in the Layers panel with an underline. To release a layer clipping mask, highlight the layer in the Layers panel and click the Make/Release Clipping Mask button.

Opacity Masks

As Emeril Lagasse says, let's kick it up a notch! Opacity masks are like clipping masks on steroids. First of all, you can use just about anything as an opacity mask—even gradients and photographs.

> Because opacity masks use the luminosity values of the mask itself, you can actually create a photograph or a vector object that truly fades to transparent. Simply use a black-to-white gradient as your opacity mask.

Did you Know?

The same basic rules for clipping masks apply to opacity masks, in that you place the mask at the top of the stacking order and then select both the mask and objects under it before applying the mask.

When you have the objects selected, open the Transparency panel and expand the panel so you can see all the options. You'll see a thumbnail of your selection on the left side of the panel. From the Transparency panel flyout menu, choose Make Opacity Mask. You'll now see that a second thumbnail appears in the Transparency panel beside the original one, which is the mask itself (see Figure 7.88).

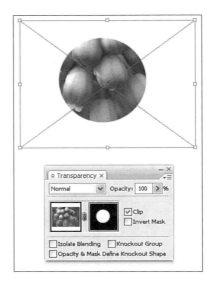

The thumbnail icons in Illustrator's Transparency panel function exactly the same way as layer mask icons work in Photoshop. For example, if you Shift+click on the mask thumbnail, the mask is disabled.

After an opacity mask is applied, you have several options in the Transparency panel:

- ▶ To edit the art, click on the left thumbnail. You can tell that the thumbnail is highlighted if you see a black outline around it. Any edits you make on the artboard will affect the art objects themselves, and there's no way for you to access or edit the mask object itself.

- ▶ To edit the mask object itself, click on the right thumbnail. There are two ways you can tell that you're editing the mask itself and not the art under it. The mask thumbnail is highlighted with a black outline, and the Layers panel changes to display only a single item—the opacity mask itself (see Figure 7.89). While you're editing an opacity mask, you cannot make any edits to other art in your file.

▶ Between the two thumbnails, there is a link icon (on by default). When the art and the mask are linked, they will be transformed together. So if you move the art, the mask will move with it as well (so that the appearance will be the same). You can click on the link icon to disable the link, at which time you can move the mask and the art independently.

▶ The Clip option uses the shape of the mask to also clip the art under it (basically giving the same effect as a clipping mask in addition to the opacity levels).

▶ The Invert Mask option enables you to reverse the luminosity values of the mask object. In simple terms, when you toggle this option, anything that was previously visible through the mask becomes hidden, and everything that was hidden becomes visible.

An object with an opacity mask applied to it is indicated in the Layers panel with a dashed underline. To release an opacity mask, select the masked object and choose Release Opacity Mask from the Transparency panel flyout menu.

Applying Transformations

Illustrator has five basic transformation functions: Move, Rotate, Scale, Reflect, and Shear. Illustrator also has a Free Transform tool and a feature called Transform Each that enables you to apply transformations to multiple objects with one click. You can also use the Transform panel, which makes for quick and precise transformations. I know it sounds confusing, but hang in there because this will all be second nature before you know it.

Before we talk about transformations, I want to point out one particular keyboard shortcut that is a real time saver. Holding down the (Cmd) [Ctrl] key at any time activates the most recent arrow selection tool you've used. For example, if you last used the Selection tool, pressing this keyboard shortcut while using any of Illustrator's other tools temporarily activates the Selection tool. If the Direct Select or Group Select tool is active, you get the Selection tool; if the Selection tool is active, you get the Direct Selection tool.

When it comes to transformations specifically, you are always selecting objects and making minor changes to the art. Having to switch back and forth between the transformation tools and the selection tools is a pain. With the (Cmd) [Ctrl] key, the Selection tool is always just a keystroke away.

Moving Objects

Although not necessarily a transformation, in that the actual object is changed, moving an object is considered a transformation because the coordinates of the object are being changed (we talk more about coordinates shortly, when we discuss the Transform panel).

You already learned one way to move an object: by clicking and dragging a selection. Illustrator also lets you move things more precisely. If you click and drag a selection and then hold down the Shift key, you can drag your selection only along a constrained axis in increments of 45°.

Want to get even more precise? After you make a selection, you can use your keyboard's arrow keys (up, down, left, and right) to "nudge" your selection incrementally. You can control how much each nudge is in the General Preferences panel by pressing (Cmd-K) [Ctrl+K] and changing the keyboard increment (see Figure 7.90).

FIGURE 7.90
Specifying the keyboard increment in the General Preferences panel.

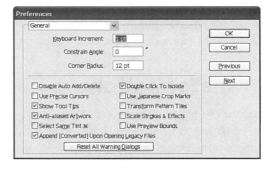

Still not precise enough for you? If you want to move objects numerically, make your selection and then double-click on the Selection tool in the toolbox (the black arrow). In the resulting dialog box, seen in Figure 7.91, you can specify an exact amount to four decimal places. Entering negative numbers moves the object down or to the left. In this dialog box, you can also choose to move a copy of your object—and there's a Preview button that enables you to view the results of the move before clicking OK.

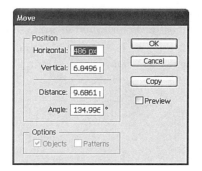

FIGURE 7.91
The Move dialog box.

There's yet another way to move something: Illustrator's Transform panel, which we'll get to soon.

Rotate, Scale, Reflect, and Shear

The four transformation tools—Rotate, Scale, Reflect, and Shear—are very similar. As you should know by now, before making any transformations, you must first make a selection.

The Bounding Box

With Illustrator's default setting, when you make a selection, the object is highlighted with a rectangular shape that has hollow squares at the corners and the centers of each line (see Figure 7.92). This is called the *bounding box*, and it enables you to make certain transformations to the selection without having to select a different tool.

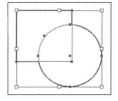

FIGURE 7.92
A selected object, with the bounding box shown.

You can turn off the bounding box by choosing View, Hide Bounding Box, or you can use the keyboard shortcut (Cmd-Shift-B) [Ctrl+Shift+B].

Did you Know?

Clicking and dragging on any of the hollow squares enables you to scale the selection in that direction. Pressing the Shift key while dragging one of the hollow squares constrains the proportions of your selection. Pressing the (Option) [Alt] key when dragging scales the selection from its center.

If you position your cursor just outside any of the corner hollow squares, you'll notice that your cursor changes from a straight arrow to a bent arrow. If you click and drag outside the object while the bent-arrow cursor is showing, you can rotate your selection around its center (see Figure 7.93). Pressing the Shift key while dragging constrains your rotations to increments of 45º.

FIGURE 7.93
Rotating an object using the bounding box.

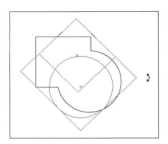

Using the Transformation Tools

I'm not a big fan of the bounding box myself. For one, it was added to Illustrator a few versions back to appeal to users who had used other illustration tools, such as CorelDRAW, that featured this kind of functionality. Second, as you're about to find out, there are specific scale and rotate tools in Illustrator that offer more powerful options. Finally—and most important, in my opinion—you can't perform certain transformations when the bounding box is turned on. For example, say you want to drag an object by its corner to move it (I'll explain in a moment why you would want to do that). With the bounding box turned on, if you drag from a corner, the object will scale rather than move. Illustrator has a snap-to-point feature that enables you to easily align objects as you position them. So you might want to grab a rectangle by its corner and move it to the edge of the page where the corner would snap to the edge of the page, making it easy to move objects with precision.

Anyway, I digress. The bottom line is that you're now going to learn the most powerful way to perform scale, rotate, reflect, and shear transformations in Illustrator. The bounding box was really created for anyone who doesn't plan to read this book. Although you can certainly keep the bounding box option turned on when using the other transformation tools, I'm going to suggest that you turn it off for now because it will be easier to learn the new tools that way. You can toggle the bounding box by pressing (Cmd-Shift-B) [Ctrl+Shift+B].

Rotate

To apply a rotation, make a selection and press the R key on your keyboard. Right away, you'll notice a new icon in the center of your selection, which is called your *origin point*. The origin point is the place from where your transformation begins. As you'll soon see, all the transformation tools use an origin point, but specifically with the Rotation tool, your origin point dictates the center of your rotation.

If you want to rotate your selection around a point other than its center, you can redefine the origin point simply by dragging it to a new location, as seen in Figure 7.94.

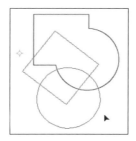

FIGURE 7.94
Rotating an object using the Rotate tool after moving the origin point.

You can set the origin point to just about any arbitrary point on your artboard. You'll see why this is so useful as we progress with the transformation tools.

To rotate a selection, position your cursor a fair distance away from the origin point and click and drag with the mouse. You don't necessarily grab the object itself (although you can), but if you click too close to the origin point, it will be difficult to accurately apply your rotation.

Pressing the Shift key while you drag constrains the rotation to increments of 45º. Pressing the (Option) [Alt] key while dragging rotates a copy of your selection.

Scale

Probably the most frequently used transformation tool, the Scale tool enables you to change the size of your selected objects. You apply a scale transformation in much the same way as you do a rotate transformation. Make a selection and press the S key on your keyboard. If you want, you can move the origin point to a location other than the center of the selected objects.

To scale a selection, position your cursor a fair distance away from the origin point, and click and drag with the mouse. As you drag away from the origin point, your objects will scale larger. As you drag toward the origin point, your objects will scale smaller.

Pressing the Shift key while you drag constrains your objects to scale proportionally. Pressing the (Option) [Alt] key while dragging scales a copy of your selection.

Scale Stroke and Effects

Specifically with the Scale tool, Illustrator gives you the option to specify whether you want to scale any strokes or effects that are applied to your selection in addition to the object itself.

In a simple example, say you have a rectangle with a one-point stroke applied to it. By default, when you scale that rectangle, the stroke will remain at one point even though the rectangle is now a different size. If you double-click on the Scale tool in the toolbox, you're presented with the Scale dialog box, where you can check the Scale Strokes and Effects box to have the stroke setting change size as well (see Figure 7.95). In a more complex example, if you have an effect such as a drop shadow applied to your selection, that effect's settings will change size only if this option is turned on.

FIGURE 7.95
The Scale Strokes and Effects option in the Scale dialog box.

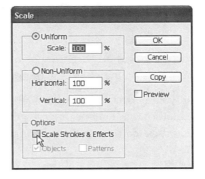

Reflect

The Reflect tool enables you to flip or mirror your selected objects. This tool is most useful for creating symmetrical artwork. When you create one side of your art, simply flip a copy of it to complete the design (see Figure 7.96). Make a selection and press the O key on your keyboard (you can remember O for "opposite"). If you want, you can move the origin point to a location other than the center of the selected objects, which is common with the Reflect function because rarely will you reflect an object from its center.

To reflect a selection, position your cursor a fair distance away from the origin point, and click and drag with the mouse. As you drag, you will reflect your artwork.

Pressing the Shift key while you drag constrains your objects to reflect in increments of 45°. Pressing the (Option) [Alt] key while dragging reflects a copy of your selection.

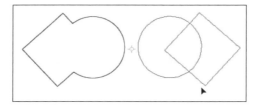

FIGURE 7.96
Creating a
reflection of a
design.

Shear

The Shear tool enables you to skew your selected objects. You apply a shear transformation in much the same way as you apply the other transform functions. Make a selection and switch to the Shear tool (it's found grouped with the Scale tool in the toolbox). There's no keyboard shortcut assigned to this tool (although if you find yourself using this tool often, you can assign one to it). If you want, you can move the origin point to a location other than the center of the selected objects.

To shear a selection, position your cursor a fair distance away from the origin point and click and drag with the mouse. As you drag away from the origin point, your selection skews (see Figure 7.97).

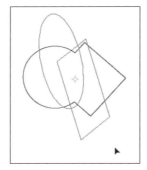

FIGURE 7.97
Shearing a
selected object.

Pressing the Shift key while you drag constrains your selection, and pressing the (Option) [Alt] key while dragging shears a copy of your selection.

Going by the Numbers

Sometimes you need to make a precise transformation, such as rotating something 38°, or scaling something 221%. In those cases, you can apply transformations numerically by making your selection and then double-clicking on the transformation tool you need to use. A dialog box appears where you can enter specific values and choose to apply the transformation to your selection or to a copy of your selection.

When you double-click on a tool to apply a transformation numerically, the origin point for that transformation is always the center of the selection. If you want to apply a transformation numerically and you also want to specify an origin point, make your selection, choose the appropriate transformation tool, and click where you want the origin point to be while holding down the (Option) [Alt] key.

Do You See a Pattern Here?

If your selection has a pattern fill applied to it, you can choose to transform both the object and the pattern, just the object, or just the pattern (see Figure 7.98). By default, Illustrator scales just the object, not the fill pattern. When you're applying transformations via any of the transform dialog boxes (see the preceding subsection, "Going by the Numbers"), there's a check box where you can specify whether pattern fills are transformed. Alternatively, you can press and hold the tilde (~) key (usually near the Escape key) as you're dragging with any of the transform tools. This works even when you're dragging with the Selection tool to move something.

FIGURE 7.98
From left to right, the original object, the object rotated with the Pattern option turned off , and, finally, the object rotated with the Pattern option on.

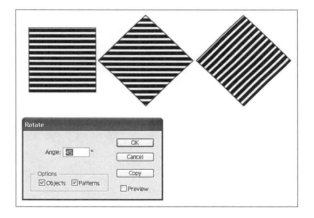

The Free Transform Tool

Admittedly, I was a bit unkind to the bounding box feature in Illustrator earlier in this chapter. The truth is, there's a tool that offers similar functionality to the bounding box in Illustrator—yet is far more powerful—called the Free Transform tool.

The Free Transform tool originally appeared in Photoshop. At that time, a simple transformation such as a rotate or a scale could take several minutes to calculate and apply, and if you had to apply both a scale and a rotate, it meant applying one transformation, waiting, and then applying the second one. The Free Transform tool enabled you to specify several kinds of transformations all in one step. The tool was added to Illustrator shortly thereafter, although the benefits aren't as revolutionary in Illustrator.

To use the Free Transform tool, make a selection and press the E key on your keyboard, or choose the Free Transform tool from the toolbox. Unlike with the other transformation tools, you can't change the origin point when using the Free Transform tool.

The Free Transform tool enables you to perform a plethora of functions, which I've conveniently listed for you here:

▶ Click inside the bounding box and drag to move the selection.

▶ Click outside the bounding box and drag to rotate the selection.

▶ Click and drag on any of the four corner handles to scale the selection. Press the Shift key to constrain proportion. Press the (Option) [Alt] key to simultaneously scale the opposite side of the selection.

▶ Click and drag on any of the middle four handles to scale horizontally or vertically. Press the Shift key to constrain proportion. Press the (Option) [Alt] key to simultaneously scale the opposite side of the selection.

▶ Click and drag on any of the four corner handles and press the (Cmd) [Ctrl] key to distort your selection. Press the (Option) [Alt] key to simultaneously distort the opposite side of the selection. Make sure you click on the handle first and then press the (Cmd) [Ctrl] key.

▶ Click and drag on any of the four middle handles, and press the (Cmd) [Ctrl] key to skew your selection. Press the (Option) [Alt] key to simultaneously skew the opposite side of the selection. Make sure you click on the handle first and then press the (Cmd) [Ctrl] key.

To apply a transformation with the Free Transform tool, simply deselect your objects, and you're done.

Transform Each

The Transform Each function offers two excellent benefits: the capability to perform scale, move, rotate, and reflect transformations simultaneously, and the capability to transform each object in a selection independently of the others. Let's take a closer look.

First, making multiple transformations is a snap when you use Transform Each. Make a selection and choose Object, Transform, Transform Each to bring up the Transform Each dialog box (see Figure 7.99). Here, you can specify measurements for scaling, moving, rotating, and reflecting your selection. A Preview box enables you to view your transformation in real time. You'll see in a minute how the Transform Each feature is more powerful than you might think.

FIGURE 7.99
The Transform
Each dialog box.

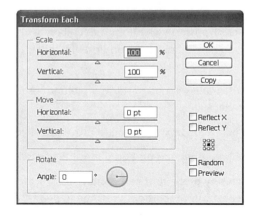

The second benefit I mentioned was the capability to transform multiple objects individually. To demonstrate, I've created a grid of squares (see Figure 7.100). If you select all the squares and use the Rotate tool to rotate the selection 45°, the entire selection rotates as one—sharing a single origin point (see Figure 7.101). However, if you apply the Transform Each function to the same selection and specify a 45° rotation, each square rotates individually—each with its own origin point (see Figure 7.102).

FIGURE 7.100
A grid of
squares.

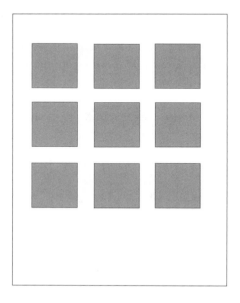

FIGURE 7.101
The grid of squares, rotated 45° with the Rotate tool.

FIGURE 7.102
The grid of squares, rotated 45° with the Transform Each command.

Although you can't set an exact origin point with the Transform Each function, you can use the proxy inside the dialog box to choose from one of nine origin-point locations (the default is set to center).

By the Way

The Random button in the Transform Each dialog box transforms each object a little differently, making for an irregular, almost hand-drawn look. If you have the Preview box checked, you can see how the objects will be affected. Unchecking and then checking the Random option gives different results each time (it truly is random!).

The Transform Panel

Simply because there aren't already enough panels in Illustrator, you can also apply transformations via the Transform panel (see Figure 7.103). In truth, this panel is quite valuable because it enables you to precisely position artwork on your page, using x, y coordinates. No other transform function in Illustrator offers that capability. On the left side of the panel is a proxy you can use to specify an origin point, and to the right is a lock icon that enables you to automatically scale objects proportionally. The Transform panel is also accessible via the Control panel (click on the *X* or *Y* next to the coordinate fields).

FIGURE 7.103
The Transform panel.

Transform Again

The Transform Again command enables you to repeat the last-applied transformation. To learn how this feature works, try creating tick marks in the shape of a circle—like what you'd find on a clock or a compass.

1. Begin by drawing a single tick mark.

2. Press the R key to choose the Rotate tool, and (Option-click) [Alt+click] below the mark to specify a numeric rotation while setting a custom origin point (see Figure 7.104).

FIGURE 7.104
Positioning the cursor to (Option-click) [Alt+click] to define a custom origin point and bring up the Rotate dialog box, all in one step.

3. Enter a value of 30° for the rotation and click the Copy button.

4. Press (Cmd-D) [Ctrl+D] repeatedly until all the tick marks have been created (see Figure 7.105).

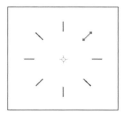

FIGURE 7.105
The completed
illustration.

Take what you've learned until now about transformations, and you'll quickly see how powerful this feature can be. You can use Transform Again after you've applied a transformation using the Transform Each command, so you can even use this command to repeat multiple transformations at once.

Aligning Objects

While we're talking about moving artwork around, I should mention that there are plenty of times when you need to align objects—either to each other or to the artboard itself. The Align panel (see Figure 7.106) is perfect for this task and for distributing objects as well. You can find the Align panel in the Window menu (by default, it's clustered with the Pathfinder and Transform panels).

FIGURE 7.106
The Align panel.

The icons in the top row in the panel are alignment functions. Simply select multiple objects and click on the icons to align them as specified. If you're trying to align an object to the artboard (for example, centering an item on the page), you can choose the Align to Artboard option by clicking the Artboard pop-up menu in the lower-right corner of the panel. This function is actually a toggle, so your objects will align to the artboard until you go back to the panel and disable the feature.

The Align panel recognizes groups, which makes it easier to align art made up of several objects. When you align a grouped item, the Align panel treats that group as a single object.

The buttons in the second row of the panel are distribution functions. After you select a range of objects, clicking on these buttons evenly distributes them, using the objects on the extreme ends as anchors. The objects that fall in the middle magically spread evenly between the two anchors (see Figure 7.107).

FIGURE 7.107
Several objects, before and after the distribute commands have been applied.

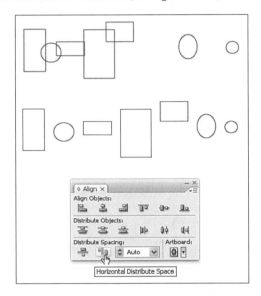

Using the horizontal and vertical spacing buttons in the bottom row of the panel, along with the spacing field, you can specify to distribute objects a set distance from one another.

Defining a Key Object

You'll notice that when you're aligning several objects, they all shift when they are aligned. However, sometimes you might want to align several objects to a specific object. In other words, you want to have one object remain stationary and all other objects align to that one object.

You can accomplish this task in Illustrator by defining a *key object*. When you've selected all the objects you want to align, click on the object to which you want all the other objects to align. Then align your objects as you would normally with the buttons on the Align panel. After you've defined a key object, you can choose a different one simply by clicking on a different object. You can also choose Cancel Key Object from the Align panel flyout menu.

Using Symbols

One of the most powerful features added to Illustrator over the years is symbols. A *symbol* is a saved set of objects that can be referenced within a document. That probably sounds vague, so I'll give you an example. Say you create a company logo, which is made up of several objects. You can define that completed logo as a symbol, which you can then reuse as many times as your heart desires within your document. Each *instance* of the symbol is a reference or alias of the original art that you defined. If you ever update or modify the symbol, all the instances automatically update as well.

Illustrator also uses symbols for the artwork mapping 3D feature, which is covered later in "The 3D Effects."

By the Way

Defining a symbol is easy. Simply create your art and then drag it into the Symbols panel (which you can find in the Windows menu). After you've defined a symbol (see Figure 7.108), you can delete the art you created because you can always access that art again later. Double-click on a symbol in the Symbols panel to rename it.

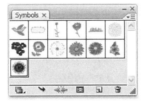

FIGURE 7.108
The Symbols panel, with several symbols defined.

To define a symbol and place an instance of it at the same time, press and hold the (Cmd-Shift) [Ctrl+Shift] keys while dragging the art into the Symbols panel to define the symbol.

Did you Know?

To place a symbol instance, drag it from the Symbols panel onto your artboard. You can apply any transformation to a symbol instance, and you can also apply settings from the Transparency panel. You'll always be able to tell a symbol instance from actual art because an instance has a square bounding box when you select it with the Direct Selection tool (see Figure 7.109).

FIGURE 7.109
A symbol
instance
appears with a
square bound-
ing box when
selected.

Did you Know?

Illustrator ships with hundreds of royalty-free symbols you can use to your heart's content. Choose Open Symbol Library from the Symbols panel flyout menu to find them.

If you want to edit a symbol, you can drag it onto your artboard and then click on the Break Link to Symbol button (a broken chain icon) at the bottom of the Symbols panel. Doing so disassociates the art from the symbol, and you'll have access to the art objects themselves. You can then make any changes or modifications to the art.

If you want to redefine a symbol, you can first edit it, as mentioned previously, and then select the art. Then, in the Symbols panel, click on the symbol you want to redefine. You'll know that the symbol is selected when you see a black outline around it. Then choose Redefine Symbol from the Symbols panel flyout menu.

Did you Know?

Symbols save file size space. PDF, SVG, and SWF are three formats that can take advantage of symbols to save precious disk space (and file download time from the Web).

To save your own library of symbols, create a document and define a collection of symbols. When you're done, choose Save Symbol Library from the Symbols panel flyout menu and give your collection a name. The next time you launch Illustrator, your symbol library appears in the list of libraries you can access from the Open Symbol Library option in the Symbols panel flyout menu.

The Symbolism Tools

Before you learn about this next feature, I just want to say that this feature comes with a disclaimer attached to it. It's *extremely* fun and addictive. If you were intrigued by the use of symbols, this will blow your socks off. Okay, enough talking the talk—let's get to walking the walk.

The symbolism tools are a collection of tools that enable you to exploit the power of symbols in a very graphical and natural way. There are eight symbolism tools in all (see Figure 7.110). The first one, the Symbol Sprayer tool, enables you to add symbols to your page, and the remaining seven tools are used to adjust symbols that are already placed on your page.

FIGURE 7.110
The symbolism tools.

The symbolism tools are pressure sensitive, so if you have a graphics tablet, you'll want to be sure to give it a try.

Did you Know?

To use the Symbol Sprayer tool, select the tool from the toolbox and then open your Symbols panel. Select a symbol (which will be indicated by an outline), and then click and drag your mouse on the artboard to start flooding your screen with symbols (see Figure 7.111). Notice that when you're using the Symbol Sprayer tool, rather than having multiple instances of symbols placed on your page, a single *symbol set* is created. A symbol set acts as one single object (which you can clearly see if you change your view to Outline mode). If you click and drag the mouse again with the symbol set selected, more symbols will be added to your symbol set. Press and hold the (Option) [Alt] key while dragging to remove symbols, if you've added too many.

FIGURE 7.111
Creating a
symbol set by
spraying sym-
bols onto the
artboard.

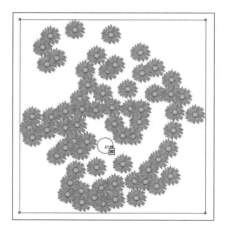

The remaining seven symbolism tools enable you to adjust and edit the symbols
inside a symbol set:

▶ **Symbol Shifter**—This tool enables you to move symbols in a very organic
fashion. It's almost like your cursor is a magnet, and as you click and drag,
you can push symbols in a specified direction (see Figure 7.112). Pressing and
holding the Shift key while using this tool changes the stacking order of the
symbols.

FIGURE 7.112
Moving symbols
with the Symbol
Shifter tool.

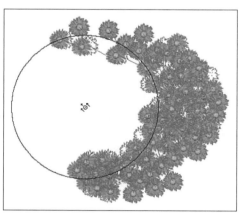

▶ **Symbol Scruncher**—This tool enables you to make the symbols sit closer to
each other, making the overall result more dense. Pressing and holding the
(Option) [Alt] key while using this tool reverses the effect and pushes symbols
farther away from each other.

▶ **Symbol Sizer**—This tool enables you to enlarge the symbols as you click and drag over them. Pressing and holding the (Option) [Alt] key while using this tool reverses the effect and scales symbols to be smaller.

▶ **Symbol Spinner**—This tool enables you to rotate the symbols as you click and drag over them. As you drag, you'll see arrows appear indicating the direction the symbols will spin.

▶ **Symbol Stainer**—This tool enables you to colorize the symbols as you click and drag over them. With the Symbol Stainer tool selected, choose a color from the Color panel or the Swatches panel. Then click and drag within your symbol set. You can change colors as often as you like.

▶ **Symbol Screener**—This tool enables you to reduce the opacity level of the symbols as you click and drag over them (making them transparent). Pressing and holding the (Option) [Alt] key while using this tool reverses the effect and increases the opacity level of the symbols.

▶ **Symbol Styler**—This tool enables you to apply graphic styles to symbols as you click and drag over them. It works similarly to the Symbol Stainer tool. With the Symbol Styler tool selected, choose a style from the Graphic Styles panel and then click and drag within your symbol set.

When you're continually switching between the different symbolism tools, it can be tiring traveling back to the toolbox each time just to select a different tool. With any of the symbolism tools already selected, try this instead: (Option+right-click) [Alt+right-click]. When the circle of tools appears (see Figure 7.113), simply move your mouse over the tool to which you want to switch and let go.

By the Way

FIGURE 7.113
A special contextual menu enables you to switch among the different symbolism tools.

As you can see, these tools are not only easy and fun to use, but quite useful as well. Try using a range of different symbols to achieve natural and organic effects. The Hair and Fur and the Nature symbol libraries that Illustrator ships with contain some great symbols to use.

It's no coincidence that the name of each of the symbolism tools begins with the letter S. Chalk that up to good old-fashioned "attention to detail" on Adobe's part.

Working with Type

Illustrator has many of the text features you will also find in InDesign. Illustrator can create two kinds of text objects. The first is called *point text*, which is the simpler of the two. You create point text by selecting the Type tool and clicking on a blank area on your artboard. You're presented with a blinking cursor, and you can begin to enter text immediately. Illustrator calls this point text because your text is aligned by the point that was created when you clicked with the Type tool (see Figure 7.114). Point text does not reflow, meaning that as you continue to enter text, the line grows longer and longer, and doesn't break to a second line (unless you press Return or Enter).

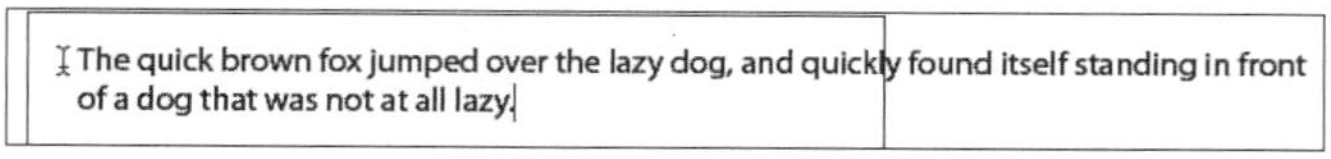

FIGURE 7.114
A sample of point text in Illustrator.

The quick brown fox jumped over the lazy dog, and quickly found itself standing in front of a dog that was not at all lazy.

The second kind of type object that Illustrator can create is called *area text*. There are two basic ways to create area text in Illustrator: either select the Type tool and click and drag with the tool to draw a box, or select the Type tool and click inside any existing closed vector path. Again, you're presented with a blinking cursor, where you can begin entering text. The difference here is that when your text gets to the boundary of the shape, the text flows to the next line automatically (see Figure 7.115).

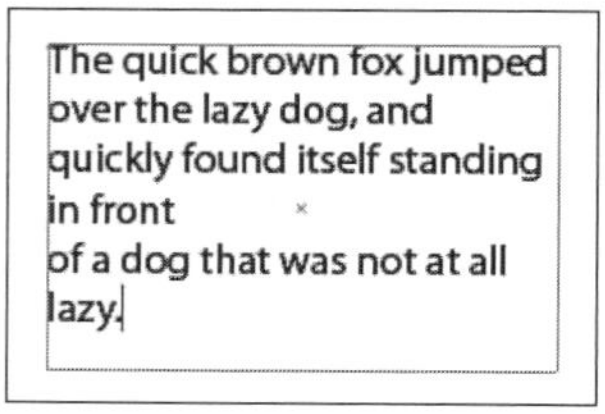

FIGURE 7.115
Text flows from line to line in an area text box.

The quick brown fox jumped over the lazy dog, and quickly found itself standing in front of a dog that was not at all lazy.

Area text also has specific functionality that point text does not, and you can access some of those functions by selecting a text area object and choosing Type, Area Type Options (or by double-clicking the Type tool icon) to bring up the dialog box (see Figure 7.116).

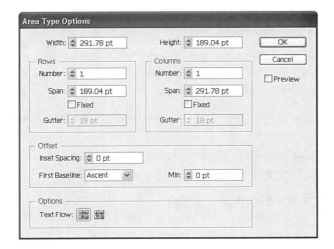

FIGURE 7.116
The Area Type Options dialog box.

Area text can also be threaded, meaning that you can link several area text objects so that the text flows from one to the next. Every area text object has an in-port box and an out-port box. Just as in InDesign, if your area text object isn't large enough to display all of your text, the out-port box is colored red with a plus sign, indicating that there's more text (see Figure 7.117). You can either enlarge the area text object or use the Selection tool to click on the out-port box and then click on another object, to make the overflow text continue into that object.

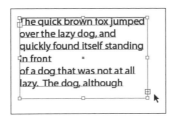

FIGURE 7.117
The overflow indicator, alerting you that there's more text.

To see how text threading links among multiple area text objects, choose View, Show Text Threads.

By the Way

Text on a Path

There's a third kind of text object in Illustrator: type on a path—although in reality, it's a kind of area type object. To create text that follows along the outline of a vector path, select the Type on a Path tool and click on any path (it can be open or closed). You'll get a blinking cursor, where you can begin typing.

You can adjust three distinct functions when setting type on a path (see Figure 7.118):

- ▶ **In- and out-port boxes**—As with area text, Type on a Path objects can also flow from one path to the next.

- ▶ **Start and end points**—You can determine where text begins and ends on a path by dragging these vertical bars with the Direct Selection tool.

- ▶ **Center point**—Type can flow along either side of a path, and you can choose which side by using this point. Click and drag the point to the side of the path you want the text to flow along. This point also enables you to position the center of the text.

FIGURE 7.118
Position your text along a path.

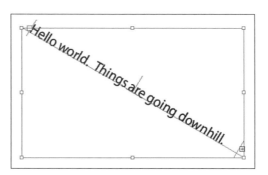

Formatting Text

Of course, it wouldn't be much fun if you were forced to use 12-point Myriad Pro for every text object in your document, so it's nice to know that Illustrator's text-formatting capabilities are on par with those found in InDesign. Because much of the functionality between Illustrator and InDesign is consistent, I discuss these features briefly here; you can refer to Chapter 8, "Using Adobe InDesign CS3," for more detailed information.

The Character Panel

Open the Character panel by choosing Window, Type, Character. Here you can specify font information (see Figure 7.119), type size, leading (pronounced *ledding*, which is the amount of space between lines), kerning, underline, and more.

FIGURE 7.119
The fully expanded Character panel.

The Paragraph Panel

Open the Paragraph panel (see Figure 7.120) by choosing Window, Type, Paragraph. Here you can specify paragraph information such as alignment, justification, composition method, indents, spacing, and more.

FIGURE 7.120
The fully expanded Paragraph panel.

The OpenType Panel

OpenType is a new font standard that really takes typography to a whole new level. Illustrator ships with more than 100 OpenType fonts, so you have a head start on getting to use them. Type 1 fonts (PostScript) have a limit of 256 glyphs per font. This is why Type 1 fonts always had these Expert font collections—there was simply no way to store all of those extra glyphs in a single font file. OpenType fonts, on the other hand, have a limit of 65,000 glyphs per font file (yes, 65,000—that's not a typo). This gives type designers the freedom to add all of these cool variations of letters, swashes, ligatures, fractions, and the like to their type designs. Probably the most important aspects of OpenType fonts are that they are stored in a single file (instead of separate files for screen fonts and printer fonts) and they are cross-platform compatible (so a single file can be used for either Mac or Windows).

Illustrator has full support for OpenType fonts and also has added functionality that enables you to take advantage of the special features OpenType offers. You can access these features through the OpenType panel (which you can find in the

Windows, Type submenu). To use it, simply select a range of text and click on the buttons at the bottom of the panel (see Figure 7.121). If the font you're using contains swash characters, for example, those characters automatically appear. The same applies for fractions, ordinals, and other special type treatments.

FIGURE 7.121
The OpenType panel lets you easily access standard ligatures, contextual alternates, discretionary ligatures, swash, stylistic alternates, titling alternates, ordinals, and fractions.

Finding Special Characters

If you want to find a specific glyph character in a font, you don't have to try pressing every character combination on your keyboard to find it. Choose Type, Glyphs to open the Glyphs panel (see Figure 7.122). From the pop-up menu at the bottom of the panel, choose a typeface; every glyph present in that font displays in the panel's window. If you have a blinking text cursor anywhere in your document, double-clicking on any glyph in the Glyphs panel places that glyph in your text string.

FIGURE 7.122
The Glyphs panel in Illustrator.

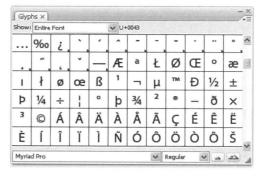

Paragraph and Character Styles

Paragraph and character styles enable you to easily style and format type. It's also a way to consistently manage and update text formatting across your entire document. You can find the Paragraph Styles panel by choosing Window, Type, Paragraph Styles. The Character Styles panel appears in the same submenu. Refer to Chapter 8 for information on how to define and use paragraph and character styles.

Converting Text into Vector Shapes

Sometimes you want to edit actual character shapes in Illustrator. For example, you might start off designing a logo with some text, and then you want to make adjustments or modifications to the shapes of the letters themselves. To convert text to editable vector paths, select your type with the Selection tool (not the Type tool) and choose Type, Create Outlines (see Figure 7.123). You can convert only an entire point text object or an entire area text object to outlines—there's no way to convert just a few characters in a text string.

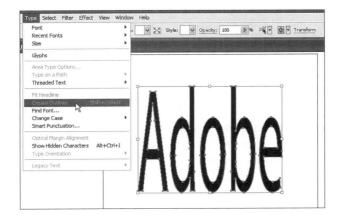

FIGURE 7.123
Text that is converted to outlines can be modified and edited as Bézier paths.

Live Effects

Effects are a wide range of options you can apply to your objects. For example, you can apply soft drop shadows, 3D extrudes, warping, Gaussian blurs, feathering, and more. What makes these effects so unique is the way they are applied in Illustrator. Effects are applied to objects as *appearances*, leaving the original objects intact. For example, you might draw a plain rectangle and apply a warp effect to it. The rectangle will appear as being warped, but behind the scenes, it's still a rectangle (see Figure 7.124). If you edit the rectangle, the effect that was applied to it simply updates to reflect the change. This also means that at any time, you can remove the effect completely and be left with the rectangle you created. For this reason, effects in Illustrator are referred to as live effects.

FIGURE 7.124
A rectangle with a Warp effect applied to it. Although you can see that the rectangle is selected, its appearance is quite different.

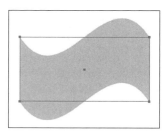

By the Way You might wonder why many of the items listed in the Effect menu are also present in the Filter menu. Items that appear in the Filter menu are applied to an object and then cannot be reversed. They are sometimes referred to as dead effects for this reason.

As mentioned before, effects are applied as appearances, so when you apply an effect to an object, that effect shows up in the Appearance panel when that object is selected (see Figure 7.125). As you'll soon see, you will be applying a new effect to an object by choosing it from the Effect menu. However, when you want to edit an effect that you've already applied, you have to double-click on the effect item that appears in the Appearance panel.

FIGURE 7.125
After an effect is applied to an object, you can see the effect listed in the Appearance panel.

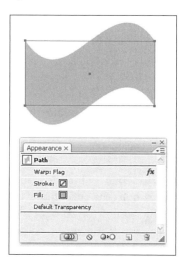

Live effects can be applied to objects, but they can also be applied to groups or layers. To apply an effect to a group or a layer, you have to specifically target the group or layer in the Layers panel, which we discussed earlier in "The Layers Panel." If a layer has an effect applied to it, for example, any object you add to that layer automatically takes on that effect attribute.

There's a wide variety of effects in Illustrator, and some of them (Gaussian Blur, for example) are raster effects. Some effects (such as Drop Shadow) can also be applied to placed images. In fact, effects can also be applied to text without having to convert the text to outlines. Let's take a look at some of the more popular live effects found in Illustrator.

The 3D Effects

The capability to create 3D graphics is not only exciting, but it's also fun (and extremely addictive). I should emphasize that the 3D you're about to learn isn't just some cute effect, but real 3D rendering, including extrusions, bevels, revolves, and something called artwork mapping. If these terms sound foreign to you, don't worry—you've been doing great so far, and I'm sure you'll catch on to this as well.

To start off, 2D graphics have two coordinates, referred to as *x* and *y* values, usually indicating width and height. In addition to the x, y coordinate, 3D graphics have a third, referred to as the *z* value, which indicates depth. When describing 3D graphics, the x, y, and z values are usually referred to as axes rather than values. From now on, when talking about 3D, we'll refer to these settings as the *x-axis*, the *y-axis*, and the *z-axis*.

Because Illustrator is rendering real 3D, performance is something to keep in mind. Complex art can take time to render, especially on an older or less capable machine. For those lucky enough to have an Intel Core 2 Duo-based machine, the performance should be excellent.

By the Way

3D Extrude and Bevel

The 3D Extrude effect adds dimension to your selected object. To apply the effect, make a selection and choose Effect, 3D, Extrude and Bevel. In the 3D Extrude and Bevel Options dialog box, click on the Preview button so you can see what your selected art will look like with the effect applied (see Figure 7.126).

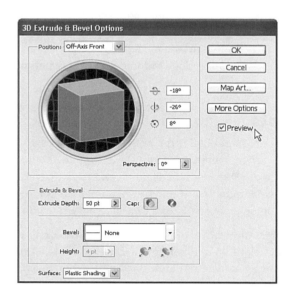

> **By the Way**
>
> The 3D effect in Illustrator is very deep, meaning that there are many different settings, but don't get frustrated with all the settings. You don't have to know what every setting is to produce great 3D art. Familiarity with all the functions will come over time.

At the top of the dialog box is the *track cube*, which you can use to rotate your object in 3D space. To use it, click and drag anywhere on the cube, and you'll see a wireframe (outline) of your object on your screen update as you drag with the mouse. If you move your mouse over any of the edges of the track cube, you'll notice that the edges highlight in red, green, or blue (see Figure 7.127). Clicking and dragging on these highlighted lines constrains the track cube to rotate the shape only along the x-, y-, or z-axis. Right above the track cube is a pop-up menu that contains several predefined views for your object.

The Perspective slider controls lens distortion. If you press and hold the Shift key while you drag the slider, you will see your art update in real time.

The Extrude Depth setting determines how far back in space your object will extend. Here also, you can press the Shift key while adjusting the slider to see real-time feedback. Press the Cap buttons to add and remove end caps on the front and back of your extruded object.

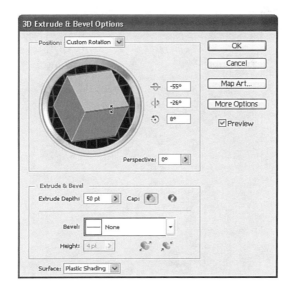

Illustrator draws 3D graphics differently based on whether an object has a stroke applied to it. If an object has a fill and a stroke applied, the fill color will be used for the face of the object, and the stroke color will be used for the extruded part of the object. If no fill is specified on the object, the extrude color will be the same as the fill color.

By the Way

A bevel is a chiseled edge you can apply to your 3D object. Bevels are added only to the front surface and the back surface. To apply a bevel, choose one from the Bevel pop-up menu (see Figure 7.128). Illustrator ships with several predefined bevels, although you can create your own if you dare (instructions for how to do so can be found in the Bevels.ai file found in the Illustrator Plugins folder). After you've applied a bevel from the pop-up menu, you can specify a height for the bevel as well. To remove a bevel that you've already applied, choose None from the Bevel pop-up menu.

Illustrator's 3D effect also lets you choose a surface type for your object from the Surface pop-up list (see Figure 7.129). By default, the Plastic Shading option is chosen, which gives your shape a glossy, reflective look. Choose Diffuse Shading for a surface that is matte in appearance. You can also choose to not shade your object at all by choosing No Shading. Finally, you can specify to have your 3D object display as a wireframe.

FIGURE 7.128
Choosing from a
list of bevels.

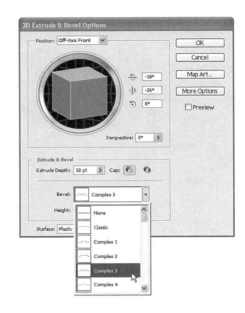

FIGURE 7.129
Choosing a sur-
face property
for your object.

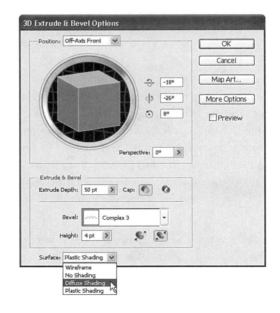

Remember that if you want to edit a 3D effect after it has been applied, don't choose 3D from the Effect menu; double-click on the 3D effect in the Appearance panel.

Extended 3D Functionality

In an effort to make the 3D feature as easy to use as possible, Adobe created the 3D Options dialog box in two parts. If you click on the button marked More Options, you'll see some additional 3D features from which to choose (see Figure 7.130).

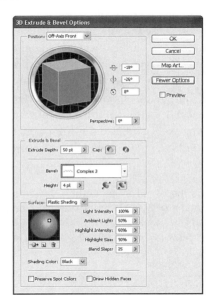

FIGURE 7.130
The additional features in the expanded 3D dialog box.

To create realistic shading and highlights on a 3D object, Illustrator utilizes lighting effects. The sphere that appears in the lower left of the dialog box is a representation of your graphic, and you can position a light to shine and illuminate your object from any direction. Making adjustments to the lighting of your object can change its appearance dramatically. To adjust the position of the light, click and drag on the light and move it around to different parts of the sphere. Pressing and holding the Shift key while you drag the light enables you to see a preview of the result in real time.

You can also add multiple lights by clicking on the New Light button under the sphere (see Figure 7.131). To delete a light, select it on the sphere and click on the Trash button.

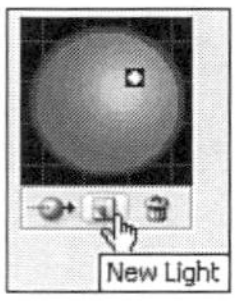

FIGURE 7.131
Adding and
positioning
multiple lights.

If you're working with spot colors, you can check the Preserve Spot Colors option, which uses black as a shade color and sets that black color to overprint. You need to have the Overprint Preview mode turned on to see the correct results on your screen.

Ordinarily, Illustrator draws only the parts of a 3D object that are visible to you. For example, if the back of a box isn't visible in the view you've specified with the track cube, it won't be drawn (unless you change the view again, of course). Illustrator does this to save render time. However, you can force Illustrator to draw these hidden sides by checking the Draw Hidden Faces option. This option is useful when you're creating 3D objects that are transparent (and you want to see through the front of the object to the back). It's also useful when you want to break apart the different sides of the object after you've applied the effect (something called Expand Appearance, which we cover later in "Expanding an Appearance").

A very important setting is the Blend Steps setting, which is set to 25 by default. Illustrator creates the shading of 3D objects by drawing blends. For printing high-quality jobs, you might want to use a value of 100 blend steps, or even higher. Note that higher numbers slow performance, so you might want to leave it at a low setting when working on concepts and proofs, but change it to a higher setting when sending out the final job.

3D Revolve

The 3D Revolve feature revolves the profile of an object you draw in Illustrator around an axis to produce a 3D shape. For example, you might draw the profile of a vase and then use the 3D Revolve effect to create a realistic vase (see Figure 7.132).

To apply this effect, select the profile you've drawn, and then choose Effect, 3D, Revolve. When the 3D Revolve Options dialog box appears, check the Preview button so you can see how your object will look with the Revolve effect applied (see Figure 7.133).

FIGURE 7.132
The profile and revolved profile of a vase.

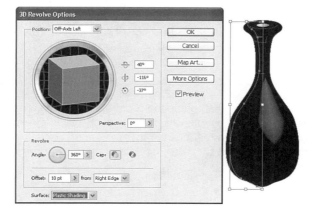

FIGURE 7.133
The 3D Revolve Options dialog box.

You can rotate your object in 3D space the same way we discussed when talking about the 3D Extrude effect. Use the track cube to position your artwork to your liking, and use the Perspective setting to apply lens distortion.

The Angle setting determines how far Illustrator will apply the Revolve effect around the axis. By default, this is set to 360° (a full, complete revolve); however, you can adjust this number to be lower, in which case you'll see a part of your shape removed, or "cut out" (see Figure 7.134).

FIGURE 7.134
The same vase as before, except that this one has an angle setting of 220 instead of 360.

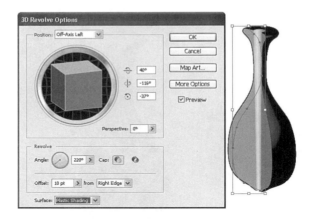

We've mentioned that the Revolve effect uses an axis, almost as an origin point, which the profile is revolved around. By default, the axis is set to the leftmost part of the object. However, you can choose to specify the rightmost part of the object as your axis. Additionally, you can specify an offset, meaning that you can choose to move the axis a specified amount from the edge of your object. This is useful if you want to create a hole that goes through the center of your object.

> At any time, either in the 3D Revolve Options dialog box or the 3D Extrude and Bevel Options dialog box, you can press the (Option) [Alt] button, and the Cancel button changes to the Reset button, which resets all the settings of the dialog box to the way they were when you first opened it.

3D Rotate

The 3D Rotate effect enables you to rotate your object in a 3D space, but without adding any depth (extrusion) to it. You can apply this effect by making a selection and choosing Effect, 3D, Rotate. The settings in the 3D Rotate Options dialog box are a subset of what appears in the 3D Extrude and Bevel Options dialog box.

Artwork Mapping

What sets Illustrator's 3D feature apart from any of its competitors is something called *artwork mapping*, which is the capability to wrap 2D art around a 3D object. For example, you might want to use the 3D Revolve effect to create a vase, and with artwork mapping, you could also place a label onto the surface of that vase (see Figure 7.135).

FIGURE 7.135
A 3D object with artwork mapped onto its surface.

The first step in using the artwork mapping feature in Illustrator is to define a symbol. Illustrator uses symbols to map art onto a 3D surface, so if you want to place a label onto a 3D rendering of a bottle, you first have to define your label as a symbol. Earlier in "Using Symbols," we discussed how to define and modify symbols.

When you're creating 3D art that will have artwork mapping applied, it's best to use shapes that are not stroked. This is because Illustrator sees each stroke as a side that can contain a mapped symbol, and this could result in a 3D shape with many more sides than necessary.

Did you Know?

After you've defined a symbol, create your 3D object by using either the 3D Extrude and Bevel effect or the 3D Revolve effect. In the 3D options dialog box, click on the Map Art button (it's right under the Cancel button); you're presented with the Map Art dialog box (see Figure 7.136). Check the Preview button to see the results onscreen as you apply effects.

When you create a 3D object, there are several sides to the object (for example, a cube has six sides). When you want to map art in Illustrator, you first have to indicate on which side of the object you want the art to appear. Use the arrows at the top of the dialog box to cycle among the different sides of an object. In the window area of the dialog box, you'll see the shapes of the different sides. Shaded areas indicate the parts of the objects that are hidden from view (for example, the back side of a cube). Illustrator also draws a red outline on the artboard to indicate the side of the object that is chosen.

FIGURE 7.136
The Map Art
dialog box.

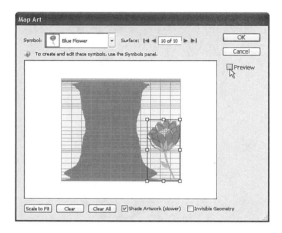

If you see a large number of sides on your shape, you most likely have a stroke on your object, or you've applied a bevel to an extruded object.

When you've found the side of the object you want, choose a symbol from the Symbol pop-up menu. If you defined a symbol earlier, it will appear in this list.

You can then position the art by dragging it or by using the bounding box handles to scale or rotate it. The Scale to Fit button reduces or enlarges the symbol to fit the entire surface that is selected. A single symbol cannot be wrapped around multiple surfaces—each surface is basically on its own. You can then switch to another surface and apply a symbol, and so forth.

The Shade Artwork option also applies lighting and shading effects to your artwork. The Invisible Geometry option actually hides the 3D shape itself, showing only the mapped art, which can be used to create some interesting effects.

When you're happy with the settings, click OK to apply the Map Art settings, and then click OK to apply the 3D settings. Because Illustrator uses symbols for artwork mapping, if you were to modify the symbol that you used, it would automatically update on the 3D object (you don't have to reapply the mapped art).

The Rasterize Effect

To rasterize vector artwork using an effect, choose Effect, Rasterize. The Rasterize effect (see Figure 7.137) enables you to convert a vector into a raster as an effect, which is pretty cool when you think about it. The underlying shape is still a vector shape, but the result is a raster. You can specify the resolution for the raster as well as other settings, such as antialiasing.

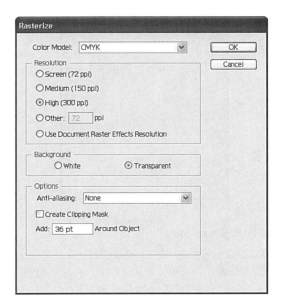

FIGURE 7.137
The options available for the Rasterize effect.

The Rasterize effect is also very useful for rasterizing rasters. By that, I mean you can place a full-color photo but apply a rasterize effect and change the color mode to grayscale. The original image is still intact, but it appears in grayscale.

Did you Know?

The Stylize Effects

The live effects you will utilize most often are found in the Effect, Stylize submenu. Things such as arrowheads, soft drop shadows, and rounded corners are all found here.

Adding Arrowheads

To add arrowheads at the ends of a selected path, choose Effect, Stylize, Add Arrowheads. In the resulting dialog box (see Figure 7.138), you can specify a wide variety of arrowheads to appear at the start, the end, or both parts of a vector path. You can also choose to scale the arrowhead to be bigger or smaller, to your preference, by using the Scale value.

FIGURE 7.138
The Add
Arrowheads
dialog box.

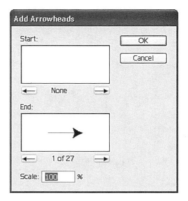

Adding a Soft Drop Shadow

To add a soft drop shadow to a targeted selection (text and images included), choose Effect, Stylize, Drop Shadow. In the dialog box (see Figure 7.139), choose an X Offset value and a Y Offset value (how far the shadow falls from the object) and a Blur value (how soft the shadow is). You can choose a color for the drop shadow as well (including spot colors) by clicking on the Color box.

FIGURE 7.139
The Drop
Shadow dialog
box.

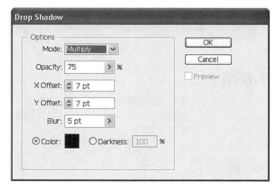

Feathering Vector Objects

To apply a feathered edge to a selected vector object (see Figure 7.140), choose Effect, Stylize, Feather, and specify a value for the feather (higher numbers result in softer edges). Remember that to edit a feather, you double-click on the feather item in the Appearance panel.

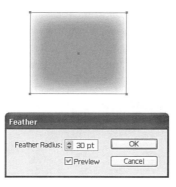

FIGURE 7.140
A vector object
with a feathered
edge applied.

Applying Rounded Corners

If you want to round off the corners of a selected vector shape, choose Effect, Stylize, Rounded Corners and specify a radius value. This effect works on any vector shape that has a corner anchor point in it.

Using the Scribble Effect

The Scribble effect is one of those effects that look straightforward, but when you take a closer look, you begin to realize that it's far more powerful than you original-ly imagined. On a very basic level, the effect gives a hand-drawn appearance to your selection (see Figure 7.141). However, if you think about how effects can be used and how multiple effects can be applied to a single selection, you can easily create interesting hatch effects and textures.

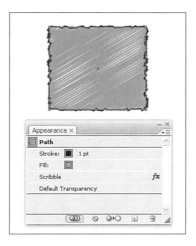

FIGURE 7.141
A simple
Scribble effect
applied.

To apply this effect, make a selection and choose Effect, Stylize, Scribble. It might be easier to grasp the plethora of settings if you understand what Illustrator is really doing with the Scribble effect, which is basically converting the fill (or stroke) of the object into one long stroke. Let's start simple by taking a look at the Scribble Options dialog box (see Figure 7.142).

FIGURE 7.142
The Scribble Options dialog box.

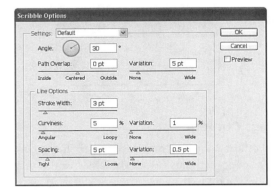

In the Scribble Options dialog box, you can specify the following settings:

▶ The **Settings** pop-up menu enables you to choose from several presets that Adobe ships with. Unfortunately, you can't save your own presets here (although you can always save a graphic style after you've applied the effect). Adobe included these presets to quickly show how you can achieve very different results by adjusting the settings of this effect.

▶ The **Angle** setting determines the angle at which the scribble is drawn.

▶ The **Path Overlap** determines how far the scribble draws "out of the lines." A setting of 0 causes the scribble to come just to the edge of the boundaries of the objects. A positive setting makes the scribble extend past the boundaries of the object, whereas a negative value forces the scribble to stay farther inside the boundaries of the shape. This setting also has a Variation slider, which varies the length of each scribble to make the effect look more random and hand-drawn.

▶ The **Stroke Width** setting enables you to specify how thick or thin your scribble stroke will be.

▶ The **Curviness** setting controls how straight or curved the scribble path will be. This setting also has a Variation slider, which varies the Curviness setting to make the effect look more random and hand-drawn.

▶ The **Spacing** setting controls how much spacing there will be between the strokes as they are drawn across the entire shape. A low setting results in very tight lines with little whitespace between them, whereas a higher setting produces more whitespace in the scribble. This setting also has a Variation slider, which varies the spacing to make the effect look more random and hand-drawn.

The Scribble effect can be applied to vector objects and to text. It can't be applied to a raster image, but it can certainly be used as an opacity mask for a photograph. You can also specify several different fills for a single object, each with a different scribble setting, to achieve spectacular effects, such as hatching (see Figure 7.143).

FIGURE 7.143
An object with several fills applied to it, each with a different Scribble effect setting, results in a hatchlike effect.

Warp

Sometimes you want to stretch or distort a graphic, and the Warp effect is perfect for those kinds of tasks. To apply a warp to a selected object, choose Effect, Warp, and pick one of the 15 kinds of warps Illustrator supports. Note that it really isn't important which one you choose because in the Warp Options dialog box that will appear, you can switch among the warps easily (see Figure 7.144).

In the Warp Options dialog box, specify settings for how much bend you want to apply and whether you want distortion applied as well. Check the Preview box to see your effect before it's applied.

FIGURE 7.144
Choosing a
warp type from
the Warp
Options
dialog box.

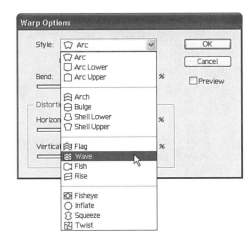

Global Live Effects Settings

It's important to realize that some effects employ techniques that involve raster
data. For example, the soft drop shadow effect draws its drop shadows as a raster
image. The 3D effect rasterizes gradients and images that are used for artwork mapping. If you're creating art that will be used for high-quality printing, you'll want to
be sure your effects are set to render at a high resolution (such as 300dpi).

You can adjust this setting by choosing Effect, Document Raster Effects Settings (see
Figure 7.145). Note that the settings in this dialog box apply to all live effects in
your document, so you can't have some live effects using one resolution setting and
some using another.

FIGURE 7.145
Choosing to edit
the document's
raster effects
settings.

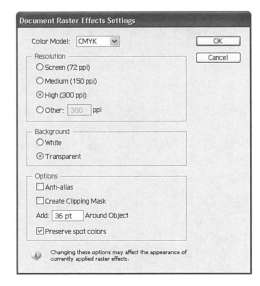

The thing to watch out for is that some effects, mainly the ones that fall in the lower half of the menu (what I call "below the line"), base their appearance on the resolution chosen. For example, the Pixelate effect bases its results on how many pixels there are. In that case, changing the document raster effects settings could change the appearance of any objects that have that effect applied. So it's important to make any necessary adjustments to the Document Raster Effects Settings dialog box *before* you begin working on your design.

Expanding an Appearance

When you apply an effect, you can't physically select it or work with it because it's simply an appearance that's applied to your object. However, sometimes you want to "break apart" an appearance so you can make adjustments or edits that the effect itself might not support. To do so, select the object with the effect applied to it, and choose Object, Expand Appearance.

After this function is applied, the effect no longer is live, and you can edit the actual final appearance of the object. If the object has several different effects applied or has multiple fills or strokes, the Expand Appearance function might create several overlapping objects.

Distortion with Envelopes

Sometimes you want to distort an object using a specific shape. For example, you might want to squeeze some art into the shape of a circle. Although the Warp effect provides some simple distortion tools, it's limited in that you can't customize the distortions themselves. That's where envelope distortion comes in. Almost similar to the way a mask works, you create a vector shape that will be the envelope. Then you place your art inside the envelope, but the result is that the art stretches or squeezes itself to conform to the shape (see Figure 7.146).

FIGURE 7.146
An envelope in
Illustrator.

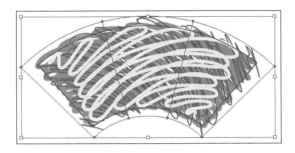

Illustrator can place any kind of art into an envelope, even raster image files. There are three ways to create envelopes in Illustrator:

▶ **Make with Warp**—Select the object you want to distort and choose Object, Envelope Distort, Make with Warp. You're presented with a dialog box that looks similar in functionality to the Warp effect, except that when you click OK, you'll notice that an envelope shape was created for you in the shape of the warp you specified (see Figure 7.147). You can use the Direct Selection tool to move each of those points individually. You can also use the Mesh tool to add more points for better control.

FIGURE 7.147
The envelope
shape, created
in the shape
of the warp
specified.

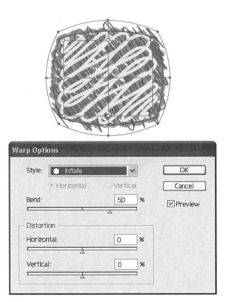

▶ **Make with Mesh**—Select the object you want to distort and choose Object, Envelope Distort, Make with Mesh. Specify how many rows and columns you want for your mesh (although you can always add more later with the Mesh tool) and click OK. Again, you can use the Direct Selection tool to move the mesh points, which distorts the art inside the envelope.

▶ **Make with Top Object**—Draw or select a shape you'd like to use as the envelope. Bring the shape to the front of the stacking order. Then add the art you want to distort to your selection, and choose Object, Envelope Distort, Make with Top Object.

As mentioned before, working with envelopes is similar in many ways to working with opacity masks. After you apply an envelope, you can access only the envelope itself, not the art that's inside it. If you need to make a change to the art inside the envelope, select the envelope, and choose Object, Envelope Distort, Edit Contents (see Figure 7.148). You then can make changes to the art itself. When you're done, remember to choose Object, Envelope Distort, Edit Envelope so you can work with the envelope again.

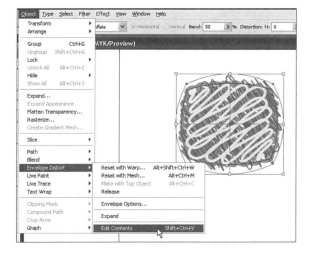

FIGURE 7.148
Choosing to edit the contents of a selected envelope.

Blends

Illustrator has the capability to take two vector objects and create a blend between them. If the shapes are different, Illustrator morphs one shape into the other, which can produce some cool effects (see Figure 7.149). Blending can be used to create airbrushlike effects. Blends can also be used to help create steps or frames for animations, which can then be saved as Flash animations.

FIGURE 7.149
A blend
between two
vector objects.

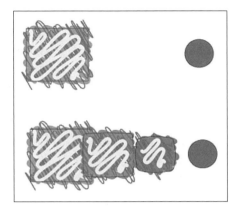

To create a blend, select two vector shapes and choose Object, Blend, Make. To
change the options of a blend, select the blend and choose Object, Blend, Blend
Options. You can specify a smooth colored blend, which automatically calculates
how many steps are created in the blend, or you can choose to specify the exact
number of steps you want to create (see Figure 7.150).

FIGURE 7.150
The Blend
Options dialog
box.

A blend follows along a straight path that is automatically drawn between the two
objects (it doesn't print), which is called the spine of the blend. If you want the
blend to follow a specific curve (see Figure 7.151), select both the blend and the
curve, and choose Object, Blend, Replace Spine.

A blend in Illustrator is live, meaning that if you make changes to the two outer
shapes, the blend updates accordingly. If you want to break a blend into its individual parts, choose Object, Blend, Expand.

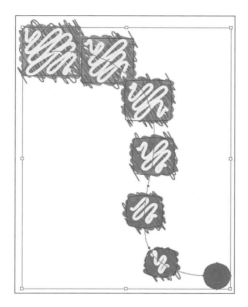

FIGURE 7.151
Replacing the
straight spine
with a curved
one.

Working with Raster Images

You can place raster images into Illustrator to perform various tasks, including applying transformations (rotating, scaling, and so on), as well as using images in a mask.

Images in Illustrator can be either linked or embedded. Linking a file involves placing a reference to that file into your Illustrator file, but the image remains a separate file. If you want to make an edit to that image, you open the original file and change it. Upon saving the file, you return to using Illustrator. Because Illustrator maintains a link to that image, Illustrator knows that you've updated the image and asks whether you want the image to be updated in your layout. However, if you were to delete that linked image from your computer, Illustrator would not be capable of printing the file correctly.

Embedding an image is the process of permanently adding the image to the Illustrator file. Any changes you make to the original image will not be updated in your Illustrator layout. Embedding a file also increases the file size of your Illustrator document—significantly, if you're embedding large high-resolution images.

You can choose to either link or embed your placed image at the time you place it. The Place dialog box contains a check box marked Link (which is on by default).

When you're placing PDF or EPS duotone images in Illustrator, always use the Link option. If you embed a duotone image, the image could be converted to the document color space (CMYK or RGB).

You can track and manage the use of linked images in your Illustrator documents by using the Links panel (found in the Window menu). If you want to edit a linked image, select the image in the Links panel (see Figure 7.152) and click on the Edit Original button at the lower right of the panel. Additionally, you can double-click on any of the items in the Links panel to get more information about that link.

FIGURE 7.152
The Links panel.

If you place a Photoshop file that has layer comps into an Illustrator file (or if you choose to open a Photoshop file from Illustrator's Open dialog box), you can specify which layer comp you want to appear when the image is placed. For more information on layer comps, refer to Chapter 6, "Using Adobe Photoshop CS3."

Vector Tracing

Sometimes you want to convert raster images into vector objects. Whether you want to digitize a logo, draw a sketch by hand and then scan it, or turn a photo into something artistic, the Live Trace feature in Illustrator can make it easy to do.

Start by placing any raster-based file into your Illustrator document. When you've selected it, choose Object, Live Trace, Make or click Live Trace in the Control panel at the top of your window.

By default, Illustrator uses a simple black-and-white setting for tracing, but you can choose from Objects, Live Trace, Tracing Options or use the Tracing Options pop-up menu in the center of the Control panel to change the color (see Figure 7.153).

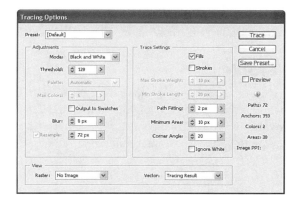

FIGURE 7.153
The Tracing
Options dialog
box.

Live Trace objects maintain a link between the original raster image and the final traced vector result. You can always change between the Live Trace presets, or you can choose Object, Live Trace, Tracing Options to specify exact settings. Illustrator's Live Trace feature actually performs some conditioning to the raster image before it traces it, allowing for better results. The left side of the Tracing Options dialog box contains settings for the raster conditioning. The right side of the dialog box contains settings that affect how the vector art is created.

To edit the actual vector paths of a traced object, you have to expand the Live Trace object first. With the Live Trace object selected, click on the Expand button in the Control panel. Alternatively, you can click on the Live Paint button to expand the traced art and convert it to a Live Paint group in one step, enabling you to easily fill the traced art with color using the Live Paint Bucket tool. When a Live Trace object is expanded, you can no longer change its trace settings.

If you know you want to trace and expand your artwork immediately, you can (Option-click) [Alt+click] on the Live Trace button in the Control panel to trace and expand in a single step.

Did you Know?

Charts and Graphs

The advantage of using Illustrator instead of a dedicated graph program to create graphs is that when you create a graph in Illustrator, it is made up of vector objects. Therefore, you can edit the graph just as you would any illustration, giving you complete control over the appearance of your graph or chart. If necessary, you can also export the graph in any of Illustrator's many export formats, including the Save for Microsoft Office feature.

Illustrator can draw any of nine types of graphs: Column, Stacked Column, Bar, Stacked Bar, Line, Area, Scatter, Pie, and Radar.

Creating a Graph

To create a graph, choose one of the graph tools from the toolbox (see Figure 7.154). You start by first defining the area or size for your graph, and you specify this in much the same way that you do to create a rectangle. Either click and drag with the mouse, or click once on the artboard to enter a numeric value.

FIGURE 7.154
Choosing from one of Illustrator's nine graph tools.

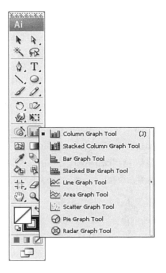

The next step is to give Illustrator the facts—the actual values that will be used to make the graph mean something. After it creates the bounding box for your graph, Illustrator presents you with the Graph Data panel. If you've ever used Microsoft Excel, this panel will look familiar to you. It is filled with rows and columns in which you enter the graph data (see Figure 7.155).

In reality, the Graph Data panel acts more like a dialog box than a panel. For one thing, you have to click the Apply button to update values. Second, you can't perform certain functions until you close the window. Finally, there's no collapsible panel tab that panels usually exhibit.

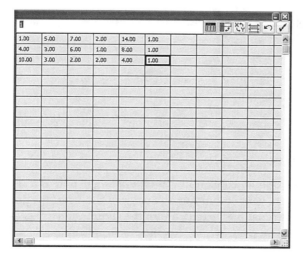

FIGURE 7.155
The Graph Data panel.

Adding Graph Data

Across the top of the Graph Data panel are several items. The first is an area where you input your values. Select a cell (cells are the boxes that actually contain the data), and then type your value. Pressing Tab takes you to the next column; pressing Enter takes you to the next row.

Cells can also be navigated using the arrow keys. Additionally, unlike with most data-entry programs, Shift+Tab does not move to the previous cell; instead, it is used to select multiple cells. Both Shift+Tab and (Shift-Return) [Shift+Enter] can be used to highlight multiple contiguous cells for such purposes as copy and pasting.

Did you Know?

You can either enter data manually or import data from Excel or any tab-delimited text file. Notice that in the upper-right corner of the Graph Data panel are six buttons. The following describes these buttons from left to right:

▶ **Import Data**—Imports data from an external file.

▶ **Transpose**—Switches columns and rows of data, no matter what the graph type is.

▶ **Switch X/Y**—Swaps the values of the x- and y-axes on a scatter graph only.

▶ **Cell Style**—Sets the parameters for a selected cell. You can set the number of decimal places as well as the column width.

> **Did you Know?**
> You can also change the column width manually by grabbing a vertical line and dragging it to the left or right.

▶ **Revert**—Sets the data in the graph back to the way it was before you last clicked the Apply button.

▶ **Apply**—Accepts and applies your changes to the graph.

Editing Graph Data

What makes the graph function in Illustrator even more powerful is the capability to update the data in your graph. At any time, you can select the graph and choose Object, Graph, Data. You are presented with the Graph Data panel again, where you can update the numbers. When you click the Apply button in the Graph Data panel, the graph is automatically updated with the new information.

Graph Options

After you create your graph, you can edit it to perfection. Choose Object, Graph, Type, and you are presented with the Graph Type dialog box (see Figure 7.156). You are first presented with Graph Options. Here you can change the type of graph, even though you selected another type from the toolbox. You can also choose where you place the value axis.

FIGURE 7.156
The Graph Type dialog box.

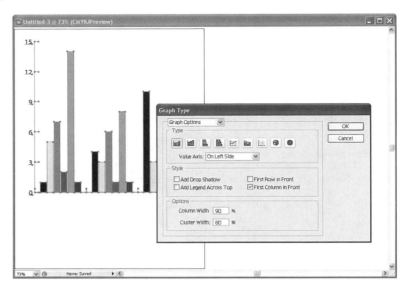

In addition to the options to add drop shadows or add a legend across the top, you can set the column width and cluster width here. These settings control the width and spacing of the bars or columns in a graph. Specifying a value greater than 100% causes the columns to overlap and can produce very unusual results.

In the Graph Type dialog box, you can also specify settings for the Value Axis and Category Axis. Select them from the pop-up menu at the top of the dialog box. In the Value Axis screen, you can set the length of tick marks, which are the lines along the side of the graph that help indicate the position of data. Setting tick marks at full length causes them to be drawn as lines throughout the entire graph. You can also specify tick marks for the Category Axis.

Ungrouping Your Graph

A graph is actually a special kind of group. You can ungroup a graph at any time—but be aware that when you do, the art loses its reference as a graph, and you can no longer make changes to it through the Graph Data panel and Graph Type dialog box. This process is similar to converting text to outlines: After you change it, it becomes a different kind of object. If you need to ungroup a graph, save a copy of the original grouped graph so you can go back to that stage, if needed.

> For some interesting graph ideas, try applying a 3D Extrude effect to a pie chart, or a Scribble effect to a bar graph. Because they are live effects, you can still update the data of the graph at any time.

Did you Know?

Web Graphics

Illustrator is a great tool for designing web graphics. Be it an entire site design, a navigation design, or a single graphic, the object-based properties of Illustrator graphics make it easy to create, design, and edit them. Additionally, because the graphics in Illustrator are resolution independent, you won't need to re-create them at a higher resolution if you ever need to use the graphics for print purposes (something you might need to do if you use Photoshop).

Pixel Preview

When you're designing for print, rarely are you ever concerned about pixels themselves. This is because image setters print at very high resolutions, such as 2400dpi or 3600dpi, and edges are always razor sharp. Even when you're printing to lower-resolution devices, such as a 600dpi laser printer, the dots themselves are barely noticeable.

Web graphics are different, though, because images are rendered at the resolution of a computer monitor, which, in most cases, is 72 pixels per inch. To make graphics look prettier and smoother onscreen, a computer uses a method called *antialiasing* to slightly blur the contrasting edges of colors. The result is an image that looks clean and smooth instead of hard-edged and jagged (see Figure 7.157).

FIGURE 7.157
The line on the right is antialiased.

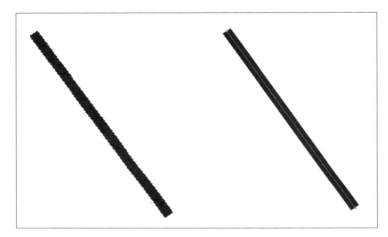

When you save or convert your graphic in a raster format, you can specify that Illustrator should apply antialiasing. However, when you're viewing your graphic in Illustrator on the artboard, you also want to see what your graphic will look like with antialiasing applied. For that reason, Illustrator has a special preview mode called *Pixel Preview*, which you can find under the View menu. In Pixel Preview mode, your graphics display on your artboard as they would when viewed in a web browser. You can work and edit graphics in Pixel Preview mode, and you should do so when designing graphics for the Web.

Now, I know you're probably thinking, "Why should I care what my image looks like when it's antialiased?" The answer is that although antialiasing is generally a good thing, sometimes it can work against you. The side effect of blurring edges of color is that it sometimes makes your graphics illegible. This is especially true when your design contains small text or thin lines. Using Pixel Preview will help you see these issues before you export these graphics.

Disabling Antialiasing on a Per-Object Basis

If you want to disable antialiasing for a single object, you can use the Rasterize live effect to do so. Make your selection and choose Effect, Rasterize. Choose 72ppi for the Resolution setting, choose None for the Antialiasing setting, and click OK. With Pixel Preview turned on, you can clearly see the difference.

Object-Based Slicing

As with many of the other applications in the CS3 suite, Illustrator has a Slice tool and a Slice Select tool for creating and selecting web slices, although it's a bit different in Illustrator.

When you draw a slice with the Slice tool, Illustrator is really drawing a rectangle with no fill and no stroke, and making it a slice. When you want to edit the slice, you can use the Slice Select tool to change the boundaries of the slice.

However, Illustrator also has a different kind of slice. Instead of creating graphics and drawing slices over them, you can apply a slice as an attribute to a selection—something that Illustrator calls an *object-based slice*. To apply this kind of slice, make a selection and then choose Object, Slice, Make. Using this method, if you make an edit to your graphic, the slice updates automatically along with it.

> If you want to hide all the little squares and numbers that indicate slices on your screen, you can do so by choosing View, Hide Slices.

Did you Know?

After a slice is applied, you can choose Object, Slice, Slice Options to specify settings such as URL and ALT text. When you specify text as an object-based slice, you can also set the slice to be an HTML slice (rather than an image slice). In that case, Illustrator exports the text as editable HTML text instead of a graphic.

> HTML text slices might not format exactly as you see them in Illustrator. Although bold or character attributes are preserved, exact fonts and sizing depend on the browser used. Other text features, such as kerning and baseline shift, are ignored.

By the Way

Save for Web and Devices

Illustrator allows you to prepare your finished artwork for deployment on the Web using the Save for Web and Devices option, which is virtually identical to the similarly named feature in Photoshop (see Chapter 6).

You can use Illustrator's Save for Web feature to preview up to four optimized settings at once to help you choose the perfect web image, and you can find it by choosing File, Save for Web and Devices. You can also set different optimizations for your web slices and export graphics in GIF, JPEG, PNG, and WBMP formats.

Illustrator's Save for Web and Devices feature does have two additional capabilities you won't find in Photoshop, however: the capability to save in web vector formats and support for CSS layers.

Vector Formats Support

Illustrator is a vector graphics application, so it only makes sense that Illustrator would support the vector graphics formats that are supported on the Web. Although the most popular graphics formats for Web use are raster based (GIF, JPEG, and PNG), two formats have become the Web standard for displaying vector-based graphics (see Figure 7.158): the Flash format (SWF) and the Scalable Vector Graphics format (SVG).

FIGURE 7.158
Choosing a vector web format from the file format pop-up in the Save for Web and Devices dialog box.

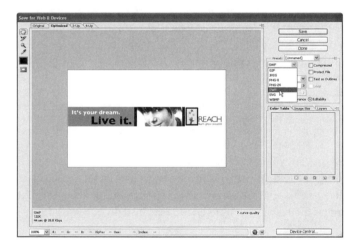

Flash (SWF)

The Flash format has taken the Web by storm and has become the standard for creating interactive content—and even full websites—for the Web. The benefits of Flash are that you can animate content, add interactivity, add sound, and even script it with logic. To view SWF files in your web browser, you need to have a plug-in installed (a free download from Adobe's website). Just about every web browser these days already comes with the Flash plug-in preinstalled.

For animation, the Flash format uses a frame-based model. Much like movies are made, each step of the animation is a separate frame. As each frame plays back, it gives the appearance of motion. For Illustrator specifically, you can use top-level layers as frames of an animation. The Save for Web and Devices dialog box gives you two options when saving a file in SWF format: AI File to SWF File, which saves your art as one static SWF file, and Layers to SWF Frames, in which your layers are converted to frames at export time and your SWF plays as an animation in a web browser or any Flash-capable browser.

You can also choose a frame rate (higher numbers make your animation play back faster, lower numbers make your animation play back slower). Setting your animation to loop makes it replay over and over again in your browser. Otherwise, it plays once and then stops.

If you have repeating objects in your design, you should define and use symbols because the Flash format supports the use of symbols to save file size. Remember that you can blend between symbols in Illustrator as well. Illustrations that are drawn using the symbolism tools are also exported to SWF as symbols. In fact, if you save your file in the SWF file format and then open that file in Flash, any symbols in your file become editable symbols in Flash as well.

Scalable Vector Graphics (SVG)

The SVG format isn't as widely used as the Flash format, but it has specific features that make it a better choice for certain kinds of graphics. SVG is an open standard file format based on XML and JavaScript. It supports animation, interactivity, and scripting. There's no direct support for sound inside SVG, but you can use the SMIL standard to add sound to SVG graphics.

Because SVG is based on XML, which is also an open standard, SVG files are really just text files, meaning that they can be edited or changed very easily at any time. That opens SVG to a high level of customization functionality, including interaction with a database. For this reason, back-end developers and programmers lean toward SVG because it empowers them to use quality graphics but control and customize those graphics very easily. Many of the new cell phones that are available on the market today use SVG to display their graphics onscreen. SVG files that are created for display on cell phones usually conform to the SVG-Tiny standard. Other wireless devices, such as PDAs, utilize the SVG-Basic standard. Illustrator supports the export of both these formats.

In contrast, the Flash format is a binary file, and it can't be opened or edited other than in the Adobe Flash application itself.

Animation in SVG is timeline based. That means you specify an object to travel a set distance over a set amount of time (most video-based applications such as Adobe's Premiere and After Effects and Apple's Final Cut Pro use this method). Illustrator itself does not have a timeline, and there's no way to specify SVG animation from within Illustrator. Most people who use Illustrator to create SVG graphics hand-code animation into their files after they have exported the file from Illustrator as an SVG file, or they use a third-party application.

SVG does support image slicing, as well as image maps that you can define using the Attributes panel. Any URLs you specify for an object inside Illustrator will export correctly in an SVG file.

Finally, Illustrator also provides variable support inside SVG files. We mentioned earlier that SVG is an open text-based file, allowing SVG to update graphics on the fly. Illustrator's Variables panel (see Figure 7.159) enables you to define XML-based variables for text, linked images, and graphs, and to control visibility.

FIGURE 7.159
The Variables panel in Illustrator.

CSS Layer Support

Increasingly, web designers and developers are seeing the benefits of using CSS layers in their web designs. Cascading Style Sheets (CSS) are a way to define how objects lay out on a web page. CSS enables designers to position graphics precisely, as well as overlap graphics. Developers also like CSS because of how efficient it can be when they're creating large sites with many pages; it's easy to make global changes using Cascading Style Sheets.

In Illustrator, you can export graphics from the Save for Web and Devices dialog box with CSS layers by clicking on the Layers tab and specifying which top-level layers you want to export (see Figure 7.160). You can also choose to export a layer as visible or hidden.

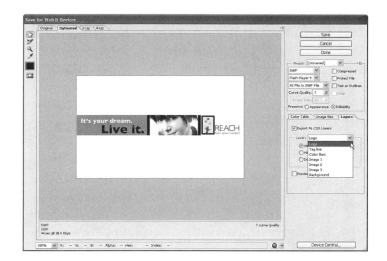

FIGURE 7.160
Choosing to
export CSS lay-
ers from the
Save for Web
and Devices
dialog box.

Saving/Exporting Files

Illustrator can save files in various formats, each suited for different uses. Illustrator
can also export files in a wide range of formats, which is one of the reasons some
people consider Illustrator a valuable utility—even if they never actually draw anything with it.

Save

Generally, Illustrator uses the Save command to save files that are "round-trip-
pable," meaning that those files can be reopened in Illustrator with no loss of
editability. To save a file, choose File, Save; then from the pop-up menu, choose a
format to save your file in (see Figure 7.161). If you want to save an existing file
with different options, choose File, Save As.

Adobe Illustrator Document (.ai)

In reality, Illustrator's native file format is PDF—when you save a file as a native
Illustrator file, you can open and view that file in Adobe Acrobat or in the Adobe
Reader. This is also how InDesign is capable of placing native Illustrator files—
because it reads the file as a PDF file.

FIGURE 7.161
Choosing a format to save your file in.

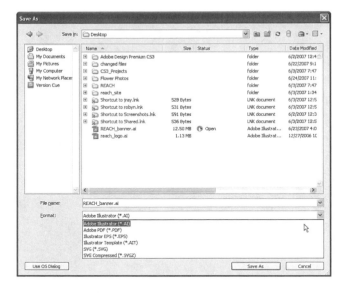

FIGURE 7.162
The Illustrator Options dialog box.

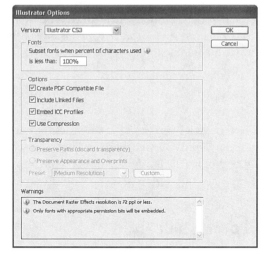

You can choose from several options when saving an Illustrator file (see Figure 7.162):

▶ **Create PDF Compatible File**—As mentioned earlier, you can view a native Illustrator file in Adobe Acrobat because the Illustrator file is really a PDF file. However, this is true only when the Create PDF Compatible File option is checked when you save your file (it's on by default). To significantly save file size, you could turn off this option, but be aware that other applications won't be able to open the file correctly. For example, you won't be able to place the file into InDesign. Uncheck this option only if you know that you will be only opening the file again in (and printing it from) Illustrator CS3 (the file won't open in older versions of Illustrator, either).

▶ **Include Linked Files**—Check this option to include linked images inside the Illustrator file itself. This adds to your final file size but could allow Illustrator to print linked images if the link is broken or lost. To reopen the file in Illustrator, you'll still need the linked images. If you have no linked images in your document, this option is grayed out.

▶ **Embed ICC Profiles**—If you have placed images that contain ICC color profiles into Illustrator, you can choose to embed those profiles using this option. If you have no images with ICC profiles in your document, this option is grayed out.

▶ **Use Compression**—Check this option (it's on by default) to allow compression in the file to create a smaller file size.

You should save in the Illustrator format for the following:

▶ Files that will be opened again in Illustrator CS3

▶ Files that will be placed into InDesign 2.0 or later

▶ Files that will be imported into an After Effects composition

Illustrator EPS (.eps)

EPS, which stands for Encapsulated PostScript, has been an industry-standard format since the industry of desktop publishing was created. The printing of EPS files requires a PostScript printer (or one that has a PostScript emulator). Because the EPS format has been around for so long, most applications that enable you to place art support the popular file format.

You can choose from several options when saving an Illustrator EPS file (see Figure 7.163) :

▶ **Preview**—A PostScript file itself can't be displayed on your screen (unless your computer screen understands PostScript), so a raster preview is included in the file as well. Macintosh previews (PICT files) won't show up on a Windows computer, so if you're planning to use your EPS on a Windows machine, choose a TIFF preview instead.

FIGURE 7.163
The Illustrator
EPS Options
dialog box.

▶ **Transparency**—You have the option to either preserve or discard your overprint settings when saving an EPS file (some RIPs or trapping software prefer to handle overprint settings themselves). Additionally, if your document contains transparency, it requires flattening (PostScript doesn't support transparency), and you can choose a transparency flattener style to use for that process.

▶ **Adobe PostScript**—If you're printing to a PostScript Language Level 2 or 3 device, you can specify that here. By default, Language Level 2 is chosen, but you can change that to Language Level 3 if you have a printer that supports it, to take advantage of such things as smooth shading (which prevents banding in gradients).

You should save in the EPS format for the following:

▶ Files that will be placed into QuarkXPress

▶ Files that will be placed into various other applications that support the EPS format (video applications, 3D rendering programs, and so on)

Illustrator Template (.ait)

Saving a file as an Illustrator template enables you to use that file as a document template on which to base other files. We discussed templates at the beginning of this chapter. There are no specific settings for saving a template file.

You should save files in the Illustrator template format if you want to use them as a template for future Illustrator documents.

Adobe PDF (.pdf)

One of the most popular formats chosen for saving files out of Illustrator is PDF. The PDF has become universally accepted around the world for viewing high-quality, graphically rich documents.

You can specify many different settings when saving a PDF file (see Figure 7.164):

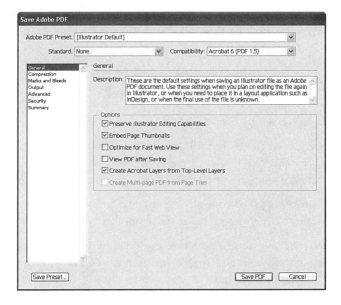

FIGURE 7.164
The Save Adobe PDF dialog box.

▶ **Compatibility**—There are several versions of PDF to choose from in Illustrator. PDF 1.3 is the version of PDF that Acrobat 4 uses, and it does not support transparency (and requires flattening). PDF 1.4 is the version of PDF that Acrobat 5 uses, and it does support transparency (no flattening is required). PDF 1.5 is the version of PDF that Acrobat 6 uses, and it supports both transparency features and PDF layers. PDF 1.6 is the version of PDF that Acrobat 7 uses.

▶ **Preserve Illustrator Editing Capabilities**—This option (on by default) includes extra information in the file that allows Illustrator CS3 to reopen the PDF file and retain full editability. Turning off this option results in a significantly smaller PDF file, but it can result in lost information when the file is reopened in Illustrator. If you plan to turn off this option, I suggest keeping a copy of your original file for future editing.

▶ **Embed Page Thumbnails**—On by default, this option embeds raster thumbnails into the file, which some programs use to display PDF page previews.

▶ **Optimize for Fast Web View**—This option enables the PDF to start loading in a web browser as soon as it begins downloading, allowing viewers to see some contents of the PDF as they load rather than having to wait until the entire PDF is downloaded. This is similar in concept to interlacing.

▶ **View PDF After Saving**—If you're sending your file to a client or a printer, you might want to open the file in Acrobat just to review it and make sure that it's correct. Checking this option automatically opens the newly created PDF file in Acrobat as soon as you save it.

▶ **Create Acrobat Layers from Top-Level Layers**—When using the Acrobat 6 or Acrobat 8 compatibility setting, you can choose to export your top-level Illustrator layers as PDF layers (which can be viewed in either Acrobat 6 and higher or in the Adobe Reader).

▶ **Compression**—The PDF has full support for compression, and you can specify settings for different kinds of images. You can also specify the downsampling of images to create smaller PDF files (for onscreen viewing).

▶ **Marks and Bleeds**—If your file is going to a printer, you want to make sure that your final PDF has both bleed space and trim marks specified.

▶ **Security**—PDF files can be password protected on two levels. You can choose from these settings and also specify whether files can be printed at high resolution—or even printed at all.

Did you Know?

> You can use the Save Preset button at the bottom of the Adobe PDF Options dialog box to save frequently used settings for PDF files. Saved PDF presets show up in the Preset pop-up menu at the top of the Adobe PDF Options dialog box.

More detailed information on specific PDF settings can be found in Chapter 11, "Using Adobe Acrobat 8 Professional." You should save in the PDF format for the following:

▶ Files that will be opened in Adobe Acrobat or Adobe Reader

▶ Files that will be sent to a client for review

▶ Files that will be submitted to a printer for final processing

▶ Files that will be submitted as ads for publications

SVG (.svg)

As discussed earlier, SVG files are XML-based graphics files. Although you can export SVG files from the Save for Web and Devices feature, you can also save SVG files, which, by default, contain round-trip information to allow the files to be reopened in Illustrator with no loss in editability.

You can specify several settings when saving an SVG file (see Figure 7.165).

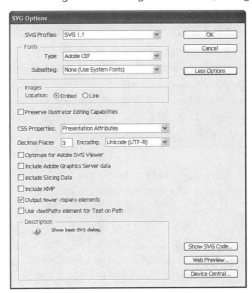

FIGURE 7.165
The SVG Options dialog box.

The Preserve Illustrator Editing Capabilities option (on by default) includes extra information in the file that allows Illustrator CS3 to reopen the SVG file and retain full editability. Turning off this option results in a significantly smaller SVG file, but it can result in lost information when the file is reopened in Illustrator. If you plan to turn off this option, I suggest keeping a copy of your original file for future editing.

SVGZ is a compressed SVG format that exhibits the same settings as SVG. You should save in the SVG format for the following:

▶ Files that will be uploaded to a web page or wireless device

▶ Files that will be used as templates for the Adobe Graphics Server

▶ Files that will be sent to a web or back-end developer

Export

When you export a file from Illustrator, you can expect to lose some editability if you want to reopen that exported file in Illustrator. To export a file, choose File, Export, and then choose a format in which to save your file from the pop-up menu.

Whenever you are exporting files from Illustrator, you always should save and keep a version of your file in case you need to make edits later.

PNG (.png) and JPEG (.jpg)

The PNG (pronounced *ping*) format is a raster-based format. You might remember that you can export this format from the Save for Web and Devices function in Illustrator. However, the PNG format can also be used for non-Web applications. For example, you can place PNG files into Microsoft Word (which the Export for Microsoft Office feature uses). Using the PNG export feature enables you to export high-resolution files and specify certain features, such as interlacing and support for transparency.

By the same token, you can also save high-resolution JPEG images in RGB, CMYK, or Grayscale color modes via the Export feature in Illustrator.

Photoshop (.psd)

Most people aren't aware that you can actually save a Photoshop file from Illustrator. Instead of copying and pasting data from Illustrator to Photoshop, you can retain a lot more information by writing a Photoshop (.psd) file right from Illustrator. Features that are retained using this method are layers, layer names, nested layers, transparency blending modes, opacity levels, clipping masks, opacity masks, compound shapes, text, web slices, slice optimization settings, and image maps.

TIFF

When you simply want to rasterize your entire Illustrator file, you can export a TIFF file using the TIFF export option.

Save for Microsoft Office

One of the challenges a designer faces is when a client asks for an image that he or she can place into a Microsoft Office application. With Illustrator CS3, you can use a feature called Save for Microsoft Office that creates a PNG file with one click of a button. Although PNG files are raster-based images, they are saved with a high enough resolution to look great both onscreen and on a printout.

If you require specific PNG settings, you can always use the PNG export option mentioned earlier.

To save a file for use in Microsoft Word, Excel, or PowerPoint, choose File, Save for Microsoft Office. When the file is created, you should use the Insert from File command in the Office application of choice to place the file.

Printing

To print a file, choose File, Print; you're presented with the Print dialog box (see Figure 7.166). Along the left side of the dialog box is a list of different groups of options. The dialog box was designed so that most users don't really have to go beyond the first group of options, though. Near the bottom of the dialog box is a Fit to Page option, which enables you to automatically enlarge or reduce your art to fill the paper size that's chosen.

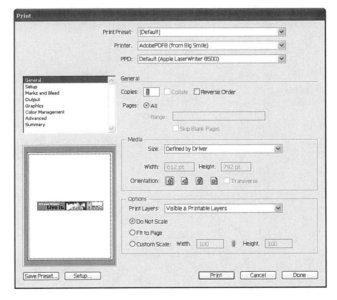

FIGURE 7.166
The Illustrator Print dialog box.

The lower left of the dialog box also contains a print preview window, which gives you a real-time representation of what your file will look like when it's printed. You can click on the preview and drag it to reposition the art on the page, if you like.

Illustrator also lets you save all the Print dialog box's settings as a print preset, which then appears for reuse in the Preset pop-up menu at the top of the dialog box.

Summary

If you're like me, your head starts to hurt when you think about everything you can do in Illustrator. From drawing to text layout to charting and 3D rendering... this program can do it all. This chapter introduced you to many of the key features of Illustrator, but there is still more to learn! Be sure to take advantage of Bridge Home and the built-in help features of Illustrator to find out even more.

CHAPTER 8

Using Adobe InDesign CS3

Now that you know how to use Illustrator, learning InDesign is easy. That's because Illustrator and InDesign are like identical twins. Many of the tools, panels, and features are the same between the two, and they work on the same conceptual level. If you're coming to InDesign from another page-layout application, such as QuarkXPress, PageMaker, or Publisher, three main things will be very different from your past experiences: the capability to place native files from other Adobe applications into layouts directly (no need for flattened EPS or TIFF files), direct import and export of PDF files, and the use of transparency. As you read through this chapter, you'll understand why InDesign has quickly become the most popular page-layout application on the market.

> **What's New in InDesign CS3**
>
> If you've used InDesign before, here's a quick overview of what's new in the CS3 version of InDesign: a more customizable and consistent user interface, an improved capability to work with long documents, a plethora of effects that can be applied in a way very similar to Photoshop, and styles that can be applied directly to tables and cells. InDesign can now export directly to XHTML, meaning that you can easily take your documents and move them to Dreamweaver, Adobe GoLive, or whatever your web development application of choice may be.

Introduction to InDesign CS3

When you first launch InDesign, you're greeted with the InDesign CS3 welcome screen, as seen in Figure 8.1. The welcome screen is split into several sections. The top half enables you to quickly create a new file, create a new file based on a template, or open an existing file. The bottom half offers quick links to learn about new features, find helpful tutorials, and find out about some of the extras that come with InDesign.

FIGURE 8.1
Welcome to
InDesign!

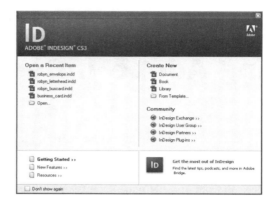

Creating a New File

To start from scratch and create a new file, choose File, New or press (Cmd-N)
[Ctrl+N] to access the New Document dialog box (seen in Figure 8.2). Here you can
specify the settings for your document.

FIGURE 8.2
Create a new
InDesign
document.

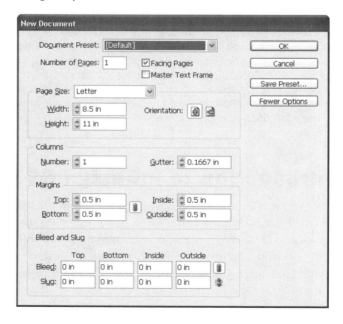

Although you change just about any of these settings after you've already created
your document, this is the only time all of these settings appear in a single, convenient dialog box.

Here's an explanation of the items that appear in the New Document dialog box:

- ▶ **Document Preset**—All the settings found in the New Document dialog box can be saved as a document preset by clicking on the Save Preset button. Creating presets of often-used document sizes and specifications can save time. Document presets appear in this pop-up menu after they have been saved.

- ▶ **Number of Pages**—This setting determines the number of pages your document will have. Don't worry if you don't know—there are plenty of ways to add and remove pages from your document at any time.

- ▶ **Facing Pages**—A document that has facing pages will specify all pages as either a left page or a right page. If you turn off this option, all pages will be identical. You would use facing pages when designing a document such as a book or magazine, when you have layouts that might be different depending on the side of the page on which they appear.

- ▶ **Master Text Frame**—If you know you'll be using master pages in your document, and if text will automatically flow from one page to another, using the Master Text Frame option will make life easier for you by automatically creating linked text frames on your master pages.

- ▶ **Page Size**—The page size is the actual size of your final page (also called trim size).

- ▶ **Columns**—Columns are vertical guides that divide a page. When you specify columns, you define how many you'd like and the amount of space that appears between each column, which is called the *gutter*.

- ▶ **Margins**—Margins are a defined area that encloses the content on your page (also called a safe area). Although you can always add content outside your defined margins, this setting helps you align objects and make pages appear consistent. It's also used (along with the Columns setting) to define the width of text frames when automatically flowing text into a document.

- ▶ **Bleed**—Available when you click on the More Options button in the New Document dialog box, the Bleed setting defines a guide that extends past the page size. This helps you create your bleed and also defines an area that InDesign can use later in the workflow. The screen preview, Print dialog box, and PDF Export dialog box all contain an option to either include or exclude bleed. This makes it easy to create your file with bleed from the start, and then decide when to show the bleed and when to hide it later in the process. If you aren't familiar with the term, *bleed* means the artwork extends beyond the edges of a page so that the art comes right up to the edge of the page after it has been printed and trimmed to size.

▶ **Slug**—This feature is also visible when you click on the More Options button. Sometimes people put information at the bottom or side of a file that describes the particular job or client. The information is called a *slug*, and internally, you want to print it, but externally, you usually don't want others seeing it. By defining a slug area, you can specify an area off the page where you can add any kind of information. Like the bleed setting, you can control whether the slug will print or export to PDF.

After you've specified your new document settings, you can click the OK button to create a new InDesign file.

Creating a New File from a Template

An InDesign template file is a special kind of InDesign file, sporting an .indt file extension instead of the usual .indd usually reserved for InDesign files. Templates are used for designs that are used repeatedly, and they can contain anything a normal InDesign file can contain, including layers, styles, page size—even artwork itself. When you open an InDesign template, the file opens as an untitled document (as if you had created a new file). This prevents you from accidentally overwriting the template file.

If you want to open a template file to edit it, you can choose the Open Original option (instead of Open Normal) when you open the file through the Open dialog box.

InDesign ships with many professionally designed royalty-free templates you can use. When you choose the New from Template button in the Welcome screen, InDesign automatically launches Bridge and navigates to the folder where these templates are installed.

The Open Dialog Box

As with just about any computer program, you can open a file by choosing File, Open or pressing (Cmd-O) [Ctrl+O] to bring up the Open dialog box. After you've located the file you want to open, click on the Open button to open the file. There are two file dialog boxes, the standard OS dialog box and an Adobe dialog. If you don't recognize what you're seeing, click the button in the lower-left corner (Use OS Dialog or Use Adobe Dialog) to switch between the two dialog boxes.

If you want to choose a file from a Version Cue project, you'll need the Adobe dialog box. Of course, you can always use Adobe Bridge to browse for the right file you need.

The InDesign Workspace

Taking a look at the screen when you first start InDesign, you have the standard menu bar across the top of the screen and, directly beneath it, a context-sensitive Control panel. Along the left side of the screen is the toolbox, which contains all of InDesign's tools as well as several other functions. The color proxy indicates the fill and stroke colors (you can choose new colors by double-clicking on them), and the two icons surrounding the proxy enable you to set the colors to the default white fill and black stroke and to swap the fill and stroke colors. Directly below the proxy icons are two icons to toggle attributes between the container and text, and three buttons that can be used to quickly apply three kinds of fills: a black fill, a black-to-white gradient, and none. Under those are buttons to toggle between different view modes: Normal, Preview, Bleed, and Slug. These controls can be seen in Figure 8.3.

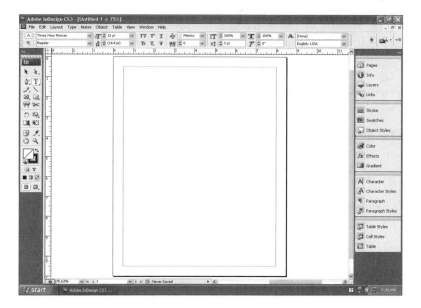

FIGURE 8.3
Introducing the InDesign workspace.

Some useful keyboard shortcuts to remember and get used to are the / key to fill with None, and the W key to switch between Normal and Preview view modes.

Did you Know?

Along the right side of your screen are some of InDesign's panels. We discuss what each of them does and how to use them as we go through this chapter.

Finally, the document window is where you work on your file. The black outline is your document size. InDesign lists the filename and the view percentage right in the title bar of each file. Along the bottom left of the window, you'll find a button to toggle the Structure pane, zoom and page controls, and a Version Cue status bar.

High-Resolution Preview

Adobe products use a graphics engine called Adobe Graphics Manager (AGM) to draw art to the screen. This technology gives you the capability to see pixel-perfect images in Photoshop and clean smooth vectors in Illustrator. When working in page-layout applications, people are used to seeing low-resolution previews for placed images, but InDesign can also use AGM to display high-quality previews of your layouts.

InDesign actually has three settings for how art is drawn to the screen, which you can choose from the View, Display Performance submenu. The Fast Display setting grays out all graphics for the speediest redraw, the Typical Display setting—InDesign's default—draws low-resolution graphics to the screen, and the High Quality Display setting displays graphics at their full resolution. Using the High Quality Display setting slows redraw performance, but placed art and graphics files will appear just as they would in Illustrator or Photoshop.

Rulers and Guides

By default, InDesign documents have rulers showing, which appear horizontally across the top and vertically down the left side of the document window. You can toggle the view of rulers by choosing View, Show/Hide Rulers. You can right-click on either of the rulers to change their measurement method, as seen in Figure 8.4.

FIGURE 8.4
Change your measurements as needed.

InDesign allows both rulers to use different measurement systems (which some workflows require). You can change the ruler *zero point* (the point from which distances are measured) by dragging the intersection of the horizontal and vertical rulers to any location within your document window, and you can reset the zero point by double-clicking on it.

Guides are horizontal and vertical lines that you can use to help align objects and create consistent layouts. Guides act like magnets when drawing and moving objects, making it easy to position items precisely. You can click on a ruler and drag a new guide onto your artboard. Guides act much like regular objects do, and you'll notice that after you've created a guide, you can click on it to select it. Shift-click multiple guides to select more than one and move them all simultaneously. You can delete a guide simply by selecting it and pressing the Delete key. When you select a guide, the Control panel shows the coordinates for that guide, and you can specify an exact numerical location for the guide through the Control panel as well. You can even use the Align buttons in the Control panel to quickly distribute guides evenly.

InDesign is pretty smart, in that you can use the marquee-selection method to select guides. But if your marquee area has an actual object inside of it, the object will become selected, not the guides. You can't move objects and guides simultaneously.

Making Selections and Applying Transformations

You select objects in InDesign the exact same way that you do in Illustrator. The Transform tools also work identically between the two applications. If you're a QuarkXPress user, the two selection tools might be confusing at first, but you'll get used to it. You'll learn about when to use each of the different selection tools to perform different tasks as you read through this chapter.

Placing Content

As we discussed extensively in Part I, "The Suite," InDesign is built to incorporate content from multiple sources into a single layout. Overall, you'll be placing two main categories of content into your layouts: text and graphics. Let's explore how this works.

To Frame or Not to Frame?

All content on an InDesign page must reside within a frame, which is a container for the content. Think of this frame as a plate for your food. You don't place food directly on your table (which would be rather messy); you first put a plate (the container) on your table and then place your food on the plate. Whether your "food" is a block of text or some kind of graphic, it must reside within a frame. InDesign has basically three types of frames: one that holds text, one that holds graphics, and one that is unassigned, as seen in Figure 8.5 This last type is actually just a regular vector shape. In fact, try not to even focus too much on what kind of frame something is because all that InDesign cares about is that you have some kind of frame, which, under the hood, is simply a vector object. Any shape can be a frame for content. You can copy and paste a shape from Illustrator, and it can be a frame in an InDesign layout.

FIGURE 8.5
Frames hold your content.

The reason I say not to focus on the frame type is that an InDesign frame is like a chameleon: It changes to match its environment. If you select the Type tool and click on an existing graphic frame, InDesign automatically switches the frame to a text frame so you place text in it. Because InDesign just needs an underlying vector frame to hold content, it can change the type of frame to whatever it needs. If you think about it, InDesign is simply helping you by dynamically changing things as you work, keeping you from having to manually convert a frame from one type to another. The danger in this, of course, is that, at all times, InDesign assumes you know what you're doing.

Rather than be forced to create frames every time you want to place text or a graphic, InDesign can sometimes create the frame for you so you don't have to. Instead of trying to explain it, let's explore how you actually place content into an InDesign document, and everything will become clear.

Placing Text

Placing text is basically a two-step process. You start by first choosing File, Place and picking the file you want to place. Then you specify where and how the text should appear in your document. When you've chosen a file to place from the Place dialog box, InDesign shows you a loaded cursor, indicating that text is ready to be placed, as seen in Figure 8.6.

FIGURE 8.6
Text is loaded and ready to be placed.

At the bottom of the Place dialog box is an option called Show Import Options. With the option turned on, InDesign looks at the file type and presents additional options that you can apply to the text before you actually import it. For example, if the file that you're placing is a Microsoft Word or Excel file, InDesign has specific filters that enable you to strip formatting out of the files or even to map Word styles to InDesign styles (so that text is styled to your specifications automatically as it is imported).

> Instead of checking the Show Import Options button when placing files, you can have InDesign display the Import Options dialog box by pressing the Shift key while clicking on the Open button.

Did you Know?

Next, you specify how and where the text will appear in your document, using any of the following techniques:

▶ Click on any empty area in your document window. This places your text into a text frame that InDesign automatically creates for you. The width of the frame matches the width of your column.

▶ Click and drag in any empty area in your document window to draw a text frame. When you release the mouse button, InDesign immediately places your text into the frame.

▶ Click on an existing text frame or any empty frame (graphic or unassigned).

If you have a text frame already selected when you choose File, Place, InDesign automatically fills that selected frame with your text as soon as you click the Open button.

Text Threading

InDesign attempts to place all of your text into a frame, but if the frame isn't big enough to hold all of the text, you'll see an icon with a red plus sign on the lower right of the text frame, which indicates text overflow. You can either enlarge your text frame or have the overflow text spill into another text frame. Having text flow from one frame to another is called *threading*, and InDesign makes it quite simple to do.

When you click on a text frame with the Selection tool, you see eight handles that enable you to scale the frame, but you also see a larger box on the upper left and lower right of the frame. These boxes are called the in-port and out-port, respectively. Text flows into a frame through the in-port and flows out via the out-port. An empty in-port indicates the beginning of a story, and an empty out-port indicates the end of a story. As we mentioned earlier, a red plus sign in the out-port of a text frame indicates overflow text, meaning that there is more text in the story that isn't currently visible (see Figure 8.7).

FIGURE 8.7
The out-port is used to direct overflow text.

When you click on an out-port, your icon changes to the loaded text icon, and you can use any of the three techniques listed earlier to create a thread across text frames. A text thread is indicated by a blue arrow that appears in the in- or out-ports. If you choose View, Show Text Threads, InDesign shows a visible line connecting the ports, making it easier to identify how a thread of text flows, which can be especially helpful if you have several different text threads on a single page (demonstrated in Figure 8.8), as in a newsletter or newspaper layout.

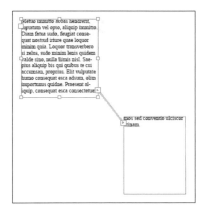

FIGURE 8.8
Text threading is
represented by
lines connecting
the ports within
the text frames.

Later in "The Power of Typography," we talk about editing the text inside of the
frames. Next, we explore how to place images into your layout.

> You can save a lot of time when placing text by either Shift+clicking or (Option-
> clicking) [Alt+clicking]. Shift+clicking places all incoming text at once, flowing from
> one column or page to the next until all the text is placed. If necessary, InDesign
> will even add pages to your document to make room for all the text. (Option-click-
> ing) [Alt+clicking] places the text into the current column (just like clicking without
> a modifier key held down), but it loads any overflow text back into the cursor for
> further placement, saving you the step of clicking on the overflow indicator.

Did you
Know?

Placing Images

InDesign can place many different kinds of image formats, including EPS, TIFF, and
JPEG. However, because you're using InDesign as a part of Adobe Creative Suite, you
also have the capability to place native Photoshop (.psd), native Illustrator (.ai), and
PDF files. InDesign offers rich import options and features to support these native
files.

As with text, placing images is basically a two-step process. You start by first choosing File, Place and picking the file you want to place; then you specify where and
how the image should appear in your document. When you've chosen a file to place
from the Place dialog box, InDesign shows you a loaded cursor, indicating that a
graphic is ready to be placed (see Figure 8.9).

FIGURE 8.9
Place a graphic
within the
design.

At the bottom of the Place dialog box is an option called Show Import Options. With the option turned on, InDesign looks at the file type and presents additional options that you can apply to the graphic before you actually import it. For example, if the file that you're placing is a PDF file, InDesign's PDF filter enables you to specify which page you want to place, or even to place all the pages in the PDF file at once, demonstrated in Figure 8.10.

FIGURE 8.10
Additional
options are
available in the
Import Options.

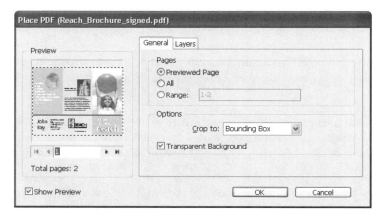

> **By the Way**
>
> When placing native Illustrator files, you'll notice that using Show Import Options brings up the Place PDF dialog box. That's because native Illustrator files are actually PDF files.

Next, you'll specify how and where the graphic will appear in your document, using any of the following techniques:

▶ Click on any empty area in your document window. This places your graphic into a frame that InDesign automatically creates for you. The size of the frame matches the size of the graphic.

▶ Click and drag in any empty area in your document window to draw a graphic frame. When you release the mouse button, InDesign immediately places your graphic into the frame. The graphic might be cropped (not fully visible) if the frame that you created isn't large enough to display the entire graphic. Don't worry, though; you can correct this later (see "Cropping and Scaling Images," later in this chapter).

▶ Click on an existing empty graphic or unassigned frame.

If you have an empty graphic frame already selected when you choose File, Place, InDesign automatically fills that selected frame with your graphic as soon as you click the Place button.	**Did you Know?**

By default, InDesign has the Replace Selected Item option turned on in the Place dialog box, which enables you to select and fill a frame that already has a graphic in it. To prevent this from happening, you can uncheck this option, which will remain off until you turn it back on again.	**By the Way**

Cropping and Scaling Images

I'm sure you're breezing along, telling yourself how easy this InDesign thing is. But in my experience, what you're about to learn is the one thing that most people struggle with initially: cropping and scaling images. If you were able to grasp the concept of the two selection tools in Illustrator (the Selection tool and the Direct Selection tool), this will be easier to digest, but in any case, with a little bit of practice, you'll do just fine.

From a conceptual point of view, a graphic that has been placed into an InDesign document is composed of two things: the image itself—which we'll call the content— and the frame that holds the image—which we'll call the container. When working with images, you must always be aware of when you want to make adjustments to the content individually, the container individually, or both the content and the container simultaneously. That's where the two selection tools come into play. For the most part, when you want to edit the container, you'll be using the Selection tool. When you want to edit the content, you'll be using the Direct Selection tool. Let's take a closer look.

When you click on a placed graphic with the Selection tool, you'll see a blue outline and the eight scale handles. What you currently have selected is actually the container, not the content. If you drag on any of the scale handles, you'll notice that the size of the container changes, but the content inside the frame does not. If you resize the container to be smaller than the image inside of it, you effectively crop the image because you will be able to see only a portion of the image, as shown in Figure 8.11.

FIGURE 8.11
Shrinking the
container crops
the image.

Switch to the Direct Selection tool and click on the graphic (don't click on the path of the frame—click on the image itself). You'll notice that the blue outline is gone and is now replaced with a red outline, with handles of the same scale. Depending on the size of the frame, the red outline might be smaller or larger than the actual frame. This red outline is the content of the frame. Click and drag on any of the scale handles to resize the image, and you'll see that the image is being scaled, but the container is not changing size at all. When the content is selected, you can change the size of only the actual placed graphic. If you click and wait a second before you start dragging the mouse to scale, you'll see a ghost image appear that will make it easier for you to resize your image, demonstrated in Figure 8.12. If you place your cursor within the frame, the cursor changes to the hand tool, and you can click and drag to position the content inside the container. Again, waiting a second before dragging enables InDesign to generate a preview to view the entire image.

FIGURE 8.12
Use the ghost
image to help
position your
content.

When you select an image with the Selection tool, the size information in the Control panel or Transform panel reflects the size of the container. If you want to see how much an image was scaled, you have to first click on the image with the Direct Selection tool. The panels will then show the size information for the content of the frame.

InDesign sports a few additions to the Control panel that make this process a bit easier to manage. When you have an image selected, there are buttons that allow for the resizing of content within a container (or resizing the container to match the size of the content); for toggling between selecting the container and the content; and for rotating, scaling, and other common manipulation functions, as seen in Figure 8.13.

FIGURE 8.13
Use the Control panel to help manage the sizing of your containers and content.

Managing Placed Content

All placed content is tracked in the Links panel. When you place an image, a new listing appears in the Links panel, seen in Figure 8.14. This listing contains information about the placed image, such as file type, color space, and, most important, the actual location of the original file (which could be somewhere on your computer, on a CD or DVD, on a server, and so on). You can view this information by double-clicking on the filename in the Links panel.

FIGURE 8.14
Use the Links panel to track all your placed content.

InDesign can generate high-resolution previews when it can find the original of a linked file and when the High Quality view setting is used; otherwise InDesign stores a low-resolution preview in the InDesign document.

> If you're using Adobe's text-editing application, InCopy, you'll see that linked stories also appear in the Links panel. If you turn on the Create Links When Placing Text and Spreadsheet Files option in the Type panel of Preferences, the Links panel will also display placed Word and Excel files.

By the Way

Several buttons along the bottom of the Links panel offer extended functionality for working with placed content. Relink enables you to either update a missing link or replace a current file with a completely different one (perfect for replacing low-resolution images with final high-resolution files). The Go To Link button navigates to the selected linked image in your file, which is helpful especially in larger publications or in files that were created by others. The Update Link button enables you to update linked files that have been modified outside of InDesign.

The last button at the lower right of the panel, Edit Original, is probably the most important. If you need to make modifications to a placed file, choosing Edit Original opens the linked file in the application that created the file so you can edit it. After you've made the required changes, you can save and close the file; upon returning to InDesign, the file will be updated automatically to reflect the changes you made.

Did you Know?

You can (Option-double-click) [Alt+double-click] on a placed graphic in your layout to invoke the Edit Original function more efficiently.

From the Links panel flyout menu, you can choose Link File Info to view the metadata of the linked file; if you're using Adobe Stock Photos compositions (comps) in your layout, you can choose Purchase This Image to access your shopping cart to buy the high-resolution version of the comp image.

Layers in Placed Photoshop Files

If you place layered Photoshop (PSD) files into an InDesign document, you can actually choose which layers of that file are visible in your layout. Select the graphic frame with the PSD and choose Object, Object Layer Options. You can then choose which layers you want to be visible and which ones you want to be hidden, as seen in Figure 8.15. You can also choose from different layer comps if the Photoshop file was saved with layer comps in it.

FIGURE 8.15
Access layers within your Photoshop files.

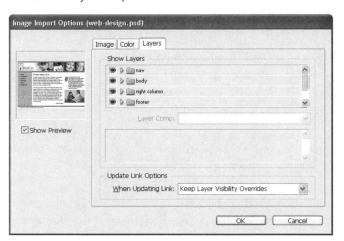

The Power of Typography

Take away all the fancy features of InDesign, and you expose the core of what really makes InDesign so special: typography. In fact, with a simple glance at a few columns of text in a newspaper or magazine, you can usually tell whether InDesign was used to lay out the page. My first real job (when I say "real," I mean "paying") was as a typesetter, and I used a sophisticated system in which I typed in codes to change typefaces. Then I had to wait until I developed the output from the image-setter in a darkroom to see what my page actually looked like. Although that may sound archaic (and I assure you, it was), the result was perfectly kerned type, clear spacing, and immaculate columns.

At the time, PageMaker and QuarkXPress were touting how desktop publishing was going to change the world (which it did), but as a type professional, I simply could-n't get the same beautiful typography that the "archaic" systems offered. You could buy a CD of 10,000 fonts for $20, but the quality you got in return wasn't close to what you were used to seeing from a high-end typesetter. To many, the fine art of typography was lost. But our story has a happy ending—InDesign is the hero that saves the day.

Features such as optical kerning, optical margin alignment, the Paragraph Composer, and OpenType support bring professional-level typesetting into the hands of any designer. And through the use of paragraph and character styles for text, you can have InDesign set perfect text without skipping a beat.

Fonts and OpenType Support

Before we get into the text features themselves, let's talk about fonts. InDesign has full support for OpenType fonts, so you can take advantage of the extended technology such as Unicode and cross-platform compatibility that we discussed back in Chapter 7, "Using Adobe Illustrator CS3." You can access OpenType options from the Character panel flyout menu (Window, Type and Tables, Character), shown in Figure 8.16. Additionally, you can specify OpenType functionality when defining both paragraph and character styles.

FIGURE 8.16
Access OpenType options from the Character panel.

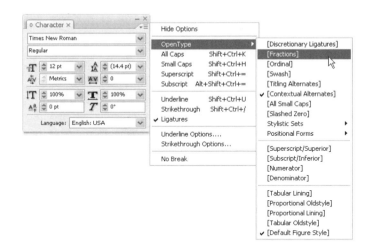

The Glyphs panel

The Glyphs panel lets you view all glyphs in a typeface, which is extremely helpful when you're looking for a specific glyph, such as the inch mark (which is hard to get because InDesign, in its infinite wisdom, tries to sell you on curly quotes instead). The Glyphs panel also becomes your best friend when using OpenType Pro fonts, which contain thousands of different glyphs, including alternate characters, as seen in Figure 8.17. To view the Glyphs panel, choose Window, Type and Tables, Glyphs. To insert a glyph into your text, just double-click the desired glyph.

FIGURE 8.17
The Glyphs panel can be used to explore a font.

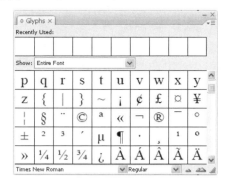

Find Font

I used to have a poster on my wall that read "Whoever dies with the most fonts, wins." I know some people who take that saying to heart, and files from those people contain an abundance of fonts. Sometimes you need to reduce the number of fonts they've used in a file.

The Find Font command lets you make global font changes to your document. This is especially useful if you open a document for which you don't have the correct fonts, or if you have several versions of a font and need to replace one version of say, Helvetica, with another.

To replace fonts in your document, choose Type, Find Font. This displays the Find Font dialog box with a list of all fonts used in the document, demonstrated in Figure 8.18. Select a font from the list and then choose a replacement font from the pop-up menus at the bottom of the dialog box. After you have specified the source and replacement fonts, you can either find and replace specific instances of a font with the Find and Change buttons, or do a global replacement with the Change All button.

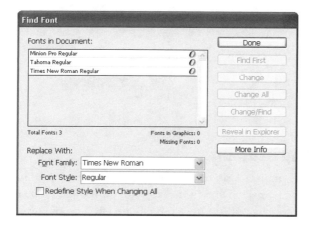

FIGURE 8.18
Replace fonts using the Find Font option.

WYSIWYG Font Menu

If you have trouble remembering what your fonts look like, InDesign offers a font preview in the Font menu. You can control this preview through the Font Preview Size setting in the Type preferences panel. The icons that appear to the left of each typeface indicate whether a font is TrueType, PostScript, OpenType, or Multiple Master.

Character Formatting

InDesign has a full range of character-formatting capabilities, from simple stuff such as font and size to very precise control over kerning (space between pairs of characters), tracking (space between a range of characters), scaling (resizing), and baseline shift (vertical position of characters relative to the baseline).

Character formatting can be accomplished using either the Control panel or the Character panel (Window, Type and Tables, Character). The Control panel actually has more functionality than the Character panel because it also includes controls for applying character styles. Two very useful but often-missed dialog boxes can be found in the panel menu (for both the Control and the Character panels): Underline Options and Strikethrough Options, which give you total control of your underlines and strikethroughs, seen in Figure 8.19.

FIGURE 8.19
Access the underlines and strikethroughs from the panel flyout menus.

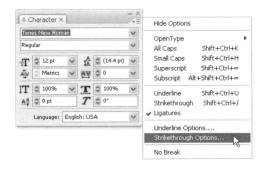

Kerning and Tracking

InDesign's kerning and tracking controls are particularly useful for making headlines and body text look good and fit the way you want them to. Both kerning and tracking work very subtly but can have a profound effect on the overall aesthetic of the page.

To kern a letter pair, position the insertion point between the two letters and use the kerning controls in the Character panel until the two letters are positioned as desired. Kerning is usually used to reduce whitespace between letter pairs, but it can be used to increase it as well.

To change the tracking for a block of text, start by selecting the entire block. Use the tracking controls in the Character panel to adjust the spacing of the text.

Virtually all fonts have instructions (called metrics) that specify adjustments to kerning for certain letter pairs. InDesign, however, has a really slick feature called optical kerning that adjusts the space between letters based on what the letters actually look like together. It's a subtle difference, but I always recommend checking out optical kerning (the first option in the Kerning pop-up menu) anytime you are adjusting letter pairs.

Paragraph Formatting

The difference between character and paragraph formatting is subtle yet significant: Whereas character formatting affects as little as a single character at a time, paragraph formatting automatically affects the entire paragraph. Keeping this in mind makes it simple to remember into what type of formatting category a certain control falls. For instance, alignment (flush left, center, justified, and so on) is paragraph based because you always affect an entire paragraph with a change to that option.

Paragraph-formatting controls are located primarily in the Paragraph panel, accessed by choosing Window, Type and Tables, Paragraph. Other paragraph-specific options are Paragraph Styles and Paragraph Rules (see the following text for more details on each).

Adobe Paragraph Composer

One incredibly useful but totally invisible technology in InDesign is the Adobe Paragraph Composer, the type engine that controls character placement within InDesign. The Adobe Paragraph Composer is on by default, and it helps create better spacing, hyphenations, and the overall "color" of type. It is especially helpful in justified text.

If you want to use the Single Line Composer instead of the Paragraph Composer, you can switch between the two in the Paragraph panel flyout menu (see Figure 8.20).

FIGURE 8.20
Switch between the Single Line and Paragraph Composers.

Drop Caps

The term *drop cap* refers to the first character of a paragraph that has been enlarged downward to span more than one line (think books of fairy tales and nursery rhymes). Creating drop caps is almost ridiculously easy in InDesign. All you have to do is click in the desired paragraph and then use the Drop Cap controls in the Paragraph panel to set the height of the drop cap (see Figure 8.21).

FIGURE 8.21
Use the
controls in
the paragraph
panel to set
drop cap height.

Paragraph Rules

A rule is a horizontal line above or below a paragraph of text. It looks like an object but acts like text, and it moves with the paragraph if text reflow causes the paragraph to move. Although they are usually simple lines, InDesign rules can be one of many types and can be any color or width.

To create a rule, select a paragraph and then access the Paragraph Rules command from the flyout panel menu on the Paragraph panel or Control panel (in paragraph mode). Select Rule Above or Rule Below from the pop-up menu at the top of the dialog box, and click the Rule On check box.

Did you Know?

To create rules both above and below a paragraph, select Rule Above or Rule Below, click Rule On, choose your desired rule formatting options, repeat the process to create the other rule, and then exit the dialog box.

Styles

Styles are, without a doubt, the most powerful and flexible formatting feature of InDesign. A style is a collection of formatting instructions that can be applied to paragraphs or to characters. With styles you can ensure consistent formatting of all text in your document, and you can reformat vast amounts of text in just a few seconds. Both paragraph styles and character styles can be accessed in the same panel group (choose Window, Type and Tables, Character Styles or Window, Type and Tables, Paragraph Styles).

Paragraph Styles

Paragraph styles are applied to entire paragraphs and contain both paragraph-level formatting, such as alignment, line spacing, and tab stops, and character-level formatting, such as font and font size.

To create a paragraph style, select a paragraph of text and format it as desired. With the paragraph still selected, click the Create New Style button at the bottom of the Paragraph Styles panel. A new paragraph style (titled Paragraph Style 1) appears in the list of styles. Double-click this new style to open the Paragraph Style Options dialog box, shown in Figure 8.22. From here you can type in a new name for the style and set additional formatting options, if desired.

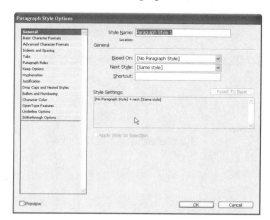

FIGURE 8.22
Define commonly used styles.

To apply a paragraph style to text, select the desired text and click on the name of the style you want to apply to that text. The paragraph will be reformatted to match the selected style.

If you change a style (by changing any of the formatting settings within the Paragraph Style Options dialog box), all paragraphs that have that style applied to them are instantly updated to reflect the changes. This is a huge timesaver and ensures a consistency that you could never achieve if you had to go back and reformat the text manually.

Character Styles

As you might suspect, character styles are styles that are applied to characters, not full paragraphs. Character styles are created, applied, and modified exactly the same way paragraph styles are, but to smaller blocks of text—words, characters, and sentences, for example.

Nested Styles

The term *nested styles* refers to character styles that are embedded inside paragraph styles. By setting up a paragraph style with nested character styles, you can apply complex formatting with one click of a button. For example, if you want to create a numbered list in which the number is bold and colored red, a word is bold and set to small caps, but the rest of the text on the line is normal weight and black, a nested style could apply all those settings at once.

To create a nested style, you first create the character styles you need. In the previous example, you would create a character style for text that is bold and colored red. Then you would create a new paragraph style and specify a nested style in which the first character of every paragraph has the bold and red character style applied to it, as seen in Figure 8.23.

FIGURE 8.23
Nested styles embed multiple character styles inside a paragraph style.

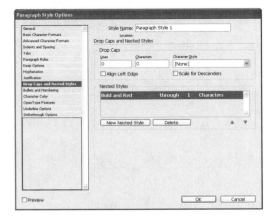

Did you Know?

You can apply styles quickly while working in text using InDesign's QuickApply feature. At any point, you can press (Cmd-Return) [Ctrl+Enter] to bring up a pop-up box with all of your defined styles, demonstrated in Figure 8.24. You can use your arrow keys to navigate to the style you want to apply, or you can type in the first few letters of the name of the style for which you are looking. Press (Cmd-Return) [Ctrl+Enter] to apply the style and close the pop-up box.

FIGURE 8.24
A quick keyboard shortcut can display all your styles.

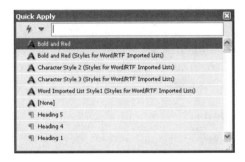

Setting Tab Stops

Tabs are variable-width spacer characters that you insert into your text by pressing the Tab key on your keyboard. *Tab stops* are paragraph-formatting instructions that determine how far a tab travels before it stops. Tab stops are created, modified, and deleted in the Tabs panel, which can be displayed by choosing Type, Tabs (see Figure 8.25).

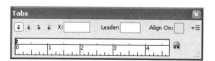

FIGURE 8.25
Tab stops are modified in the Tabs panel.

To set a tab stop, click on the type of tab stop you want (left-aligned, centered, right-aligned, or character-aligned), and then either click in the narrow strip above the dialog box ruler at the desired location or simply enter a location measurement in the X field.

If you want this tab stop to have a tab leader (a set of characters leading up to the tab stop), enter the character in the Leader field. If you are creating a character-aligned tab stop, the Align On field becomes active and you can enter a character other than a decimal point (the default) into this field.

To move an existing tab stop, just drag it to a new location. To delete a tab stop, drag it down off the tab ruler.

It is easiest to set up tab stops when the Tabs dialog box is positioned directly over the selected paragraph(s). Click the Position panel's Above Text Frame button (a magnet) in the lower-right corner of the Tabs dialog box to snap it over the selected paragraph(s).

Did you Know?

Change Case

InDesign has four handy commands for changing text case: UPPERCASE, lowercase, Title Case, and Sentence case. All are available from the Type, Change Case submenu.

Converting Text to Outlines

Converting text to outlines transforms normal text to drawn objects. After being converted, text can no longer be edited as text, but it can be manipulated as a graphic object. This is perfect for creating logos, labels, or other textual graphic treatments. It also lets you use text as a frame within which you can place other graphics.

To convert text to outlines, select the desired text and choose Type, Create Outlines.

The Story Editor

The Story Editor is InDesign's built-in text editor, which looks and feels very much like your standard word processor. The idea of the Story Editor is that you can edit text without worrying about how it looks in your layout. The text appears consistent in the Story Editor, so you don't have to zoom in to read small point sizes or scroll between pages to make edits.

To activate the Story Editor, select a text frame and choose Edit, Edit in Story Editor (see Figure 8.26). Choose Edit, Edit in Layout to return to the normal view.

FIGURE 8.26
The Story Editor behaves like a built-in word processor.

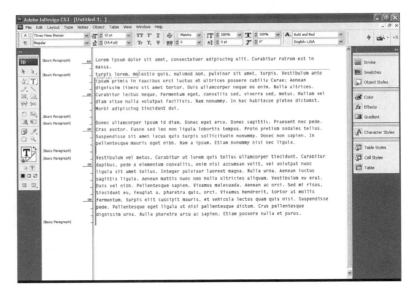

Some useful ideas for using the Story Editor include when you need to edit text in multiple-page layouts. If an article starts on page 2 but then finishes on page 24, you can still see the entire text in the Story Editor window. The Story Editor is also great for editing small type that you might have in your document (such as captions or legal speak) so that you can avoid having to continuously zoom in and out.

You can use the Story Editor Display panel in Preferences to control how text appears in the Story Editor.

Checking Spelling

InDesign has the capability to check the accuracy of your spelling in your document as you type. Just like you might see in a certain popular word processor, misspelled words appear with cute red squiggles under them. To turn on this feature, check Enable Dynamic Spelling in the Spelling panel of Preferences. Additionally, you can check the Enable Autocorrect box in the Autocorrect Preferences panel to have InDesign correct misspelled words as you type. A shortcut for activating both of these features can be found under the Edit, Spelling submenu.

To perform a traditional spell-check, choose Edit, Spelling, Check Spelling. The Check Spelling dialog box appears, as shown in Figure 8.27; just click the Start button, and InDesign will find all the words that aren't in the InDesign dictionary (it's interesting to note that *InDesign* is in the dictionary, but *QuarkXPress* is not). You can customize a few options for which words get flagged in the Spelling panel of the Preferences dialog box (and, no, there's no option for "don't flag competing products").

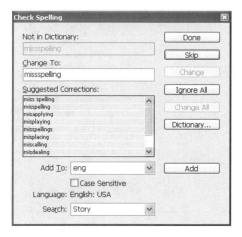

FIGURE 8.27
Check your spelling using the built-in tools.

Using the Dictionary

As you're checking your spelling, you might run across a word that you know is spelled right but InDesign doesn't recognize it, such as *qoph* (a favorite "legal" word of Scrabble players everywhere). Click the Add button in the Check Spelling dialog box to add the word to your custom dictionary. From that point on, *qoph* won't be flagged as being spelled incorrectly (which is nice because it wasn't spelled wrong in the first place).

Search and Replace

InDesign's search-and-replace feature is deceptively powerful. In addition to the standard options for finding and changing text, pop-up menus to the right of the Find and Change fields in the Find/Change dialog box contain a very thorough list of special characters that you can search for and replace (see Figure 8.28). You can also search for and replace text or special characters in all open documents with a single command. For those with extremely complex search and replacement needs, a GREP (regular expression) search is available. GREP searches are based on patterns (called "regular expressions") rather than specific text or characters. A regular expression might be written, for example, to match telephone numbers or email addresses.

FIGURE 8.28
Find and change words, characters, and patterns in your document.

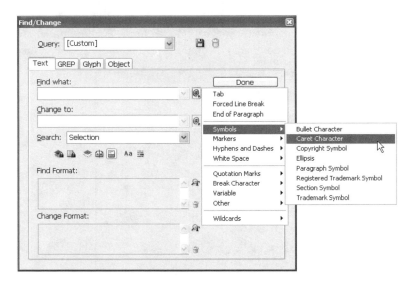

The Find/Change dialog box can be accessed by choosing Edit, Find/Change.

Text Frame Options

Each text frame has several options for displaying the text within it. These include multiple columns within a single frame, inset spacing (similar to page margins, but applied to the frame), baseline offset (the vertical distance above or below the imaginary line the text sits on), and vertical justification (the vertical placement of the text in its text box). To change any of these options, select a text frame and choose Object, Text Frame Options, as shown in Figure 8.29.

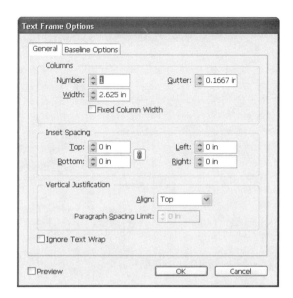

FIGURE 8.29
Customize your
text frame
options.

Working with Objects

Most of the drawing tools found in InDesign come straight from Illustrator and work
in the same way. We don't cover tools such as the Pen or Rectangle tools here, but
rather, we talk about some of the things that InDesign enables you to do with
objects in your layout.

Grouping Objects

Any objects you create (paths, text objects, or images) can be grouped so that they
stay with each other when they're moved or otherwise manipulated. You can even
group groups to keep things more organized.

To group objects, select the objects and choose Object, Group. When objects are
grouped, clicking on any one of the objects in a group selects the entire group. You
can still use the Direct Selection tool to select a single object or point, however, or
ungroup using Object, Ungroup.

The Pathfinder and Align Panels

The Pathfinder panel is used to control the way shapes interact with each other. For
instance, you can use the Pathfinder Add button to merge three circles to form a
snowman (see Figure 8.30). Access the Pathfinder panel from the Object and Layout
submenu of the Window menu.

FIGURE 8.30
The Pathfinder
panel can be
used to define
how objects
interact with
one another.

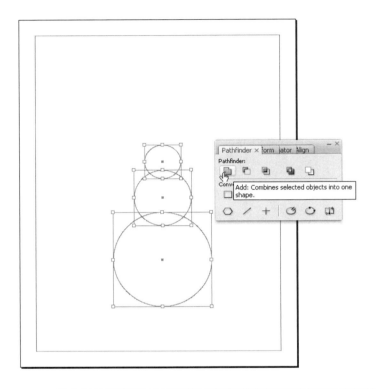

> **By the Way**
>
> The Pathfinder functions in InDesign aren't "live" the way they are in Illustrator, so the original objects are gone after you click the button, leaving the resulting shape(s) only.

To use any of the Pathfinder functions, select the paths you want to affect and then click the button. Here are the different buttons and what they do:

- Add merges two or more paths into a single path.
- Subtract removes the area of the frontmost objects from the backmost object.
- Intersect leaves only the overlapping area of the selected objects.
- Exclude Overlap removes the overlapping area of the selected objects.
- Minus Back removes the area of the backmost object from the frontmost objects (pretty much the opposite of Subtract).

Additionally, you can use any of the Convert to Shape buttons to change the shape of an existing frame.

Aligning and Distributing Objects

InDesign has the capability to quickly align and distribute several objects at once. This is done through the Align panel, accessed by choosing Window, Object and Layout, Align. You can align and distribute objects in the exact same way as you do in Illustrator, by clicking on the different icons in the panels.

Unfortunately, InDesign doesn't have the capability to "lock" the position of one object by defining a key object, like Illustrator can. If you want to align several objects relative to a particular object, you can lock the position of that object by choosing Object, Lock Position. Then select the objects and perform the Align function.

Coloring Objects

You can change the color of any selected object by either choosing a color from the Color panel or clicking on a swatch in the Swatches panel. Both panels are accessed directly under the Window menu.

Fills and Strokes

As with Illustrator, objects in InDesign can have both their fill (the color, gradient, or pattern inside an object) and their stroke (the actual lines or borders that define the object) changed. The fill/stroke proxy in the toolbox, the Color panel, and the Swatch panel controls what is being changed. The solid square represents fill, whereas the hollow square represents stroke. Whichever of these is in front controls what is in focus. To make the stroke active when the fill is in front, click the stroke proxy. To make the fill active when the stroke is in front, click the fill proxy.

The Stroke panel lets you change the weight (thickness), corner, and ends of a stroke (if the selected path is closed and has no ends, the start and end options do nothing). You can also choose to align a stroke to the center line, inside, or outside of a path, as seen in Figure 8.31.

Working with Swatches

Swatches are a way for you to keep track of which colors are being used in your document. They also help you keep those colors consistent so that all your light blues match each other (because they're applied to your objects with the same swatch).

To create a new swatch, click the New Swatch button at the bottom of the Swatches panel. Double-click the new switch, adjust the sliders until the color looks just right, and then click the OK button. A new swatch is created. To apply a color to an object, select the object and click on the swatch.

FIGURE 8.31
Manage stroke
properties,
including align-
ment, from the
Stroke panel.

Spot Colors

Two types of colors exist when it comes to printing: process colors and spot colors.
Process colors are made by combining various percentages of cyan, magenta, yellow, and black (the four standard colors used in color printing). Spot colors are
made by using a single ink that is a specific color. If you're creating a design that is
black and green, you'll probably want to use a spot color for the green. A popular
system for specifying spot colors is the Pantone Color system, and you can define
Pantone colors as spot color swatches as well. When you choose to create a spot
color from the Color Type pop-up menu in the Swatch Options dialog box, choose a
Pantone library from the Color Mode pop-up menu (see Figure 8.32).

FIGURE 8.32
Access Pantone
library colors.

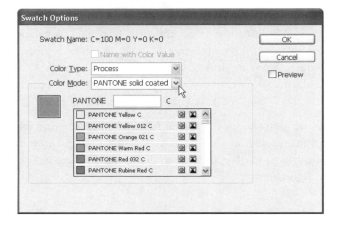

Although you can use any number of spot colors in a document, doing so will
result in your printer having to use a different ink for each color, which can cost
significantly more than using process colors.

Corner Options

Corner effects can be used on any corner of any path (the corners on a rectangle, a star, or any path you've drawn with the Pen tool) to give the corners a little more visual interest than a standard corner. Access these settings by choosing Object, Corner Options.

Transparency Effects

Most objects in InDesign can be made transparent, which is really to say that you can make them less opaque so that objects below can be viewed through them. Of course, InDesign provides more than just basic opacity controls, but that's what you'll be using the most.

To see transparency on objects more clearly, choose View, Grids and Guides, Show Document Grid. This puts the grid behind all objects in the document and shows you the difference between tinted objects and partially opaque ones.

Did you Know?

In the Effects panel (Window, Effects), you control both opacity (via the Opacity slider) and blending mode (via the pop-up menu). Slide the Opacity slider to the left (toward 0%) to make the selected object more transparent. Experiment with the different blending modes to see the results. You can also access these same settings (albeit through a slightly different interface) by choosing Object, Effects, Transparency.

Soft Drop Shadows and Feathers

You can apply drop shadows to any object. To do so, select the object and choose Object, Effects, Drop Shadow. Although most of the options are self-explanatory, as seen in Figure 8.33, one isn't: The Size field controls how fuzzy the edges of the drop shadow are. Increase the size to make the shadow edges fuzzier (the fuzziness is transparent). You can also add noise to a drop shadow to prevent banding. Remember that drop shadows are object attributes, so you can apply a shadow only to an entire text frame, not individual words.

FIGURE 8.33
Applying drop
shadows to
objects is very
straightforward.

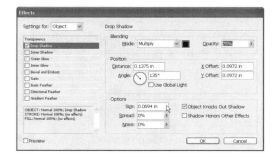

Feathering makes the edges of an object gradually fade transparently into the background. To feather an object, select it and choose Object, Effects, Basic Feather.

Other Effects

As you've seen in Photoshop, effects can be applied to create visual interest within a design. InDesign now sports many of the same effects as Photoshop. To add an effect, choose from Object, Effects. You'll notice that the Effects dialog box is very similar to Photoshop. You can use the selections along the left side of the dialog box to activate and configure multiple effects on an object. Chapter 6, "Using Adobe Photoshop CS3," has additional information on the effects available in InDesign.

Object Styles

InDesign has the capability to define object styles, which enable you to quickly apply object attributes consistently across an entire document. To define an object style, open the Object Styles panel by choosing Window, Object Styles. Then choose New Object Style from the panel menu.

The New Object Style dialog box, shown in Figure 8.34, lets you specify different attributes, or you can select an already-styled object to have InDesign create a new style from that existing object. Object styles can also be applied using the QuickApply feature mentioned in the "Nested Styles" section.

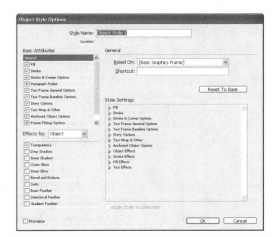

FIGURE 8.34
Create object styles to easily apply attributes to multiple objects across your document.

Layout Techniques

Working in InDesign isn't limited to just creating frames and filling them with content. You can also spend time arranging objects within your layout. Let's explore some of the techniques that are used to manipulate page layouts in InDesign.

Snippets

As you're working in InDesign, you can drag objects from your layout into Bridge. Doing so creates an InDesign *snippet*, which is like a miniature InDesign file. You can then drag snippets back into any InDesign layout as you need them. These snippets are actually saved in an XML-based InDesign format (.inds) and can even be copied to servers or emailed to others as well. Snippets can contain styles and maintain all formatting of objects.

Creating a Text Wrap

A text wrap specifies an object to repel text. Whenever the text of a document encounters an object with a text wrap, the text runs around the edges of the object. This is accomplished quite easily in InDesign with the Text Wrap panel.

To apply text wrap to an image, follow these steps:

1. Select the object with which you want to work.

2. Choose Window, Text Wrap to display the Text Wrap panel.

3. In the Text Wrap panel, select the type of text wrap and the offset between the text and the object, as seen in Figure 8.35.

FIGURE 8.35
Text wrap forces
text to run
around the
edges of an
object.

The third option in the panel, Wrap Around Object Shape, enables you to specify a text wrap that follows the contour of an object's shape. If you are wrapping text around a Photoshop image, you can even choose to have InDesign use an embedded Photoshop path or channel to define the contour of the object. Otherwise, you can have InDesign attempt to detect the edges of the object on its own.

The Pages Panel

The Pages panel, seen in Figure 8.36, is used to navigate within your document, rearrange pages, insert pages, duplicate or delete spreads, create master pages, and apply master pages to document pages.

FIGURE 8.36
Manage the
organization of
your document
with the Pages
panel.

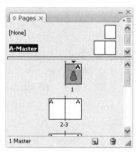

You can jump to a page simply by double-clicking it, rearrange pages by dragging them within the Pages panel, and insert new pages by clicking the Create New Page button at the bottom of the Pages panel.

Spreads

A spread is a collection of pages designed to be viewed together. The simplest type of spread is a two-page spread, such as the one that you are viewing right now as you read this book.

To duplicate or delete a spread, select the spread in the Pages panel and choose Duplicate Spread or Delete Spread from the panel flyout menu.

> Spreads that appear with a checkerboard pattern in the Pages panel are those that contain live transparency effects that require flattening at print or export time.

By the Way

Master Pages

Master pages serve as templates for the pages within your document. If a master page has two text boxes and a placeholder for a page number in one corner, and you apply that master page to a regular page in your document, that regular page will have two text boxes and the correct page number in the corner. Master pages help ensure consistency from page to page.

To create a new master page, select the New Master command from the Pages panel flyout menu. Double-click on the new master page to view it, and then just create elements on the page as you normally would.

To apply a master page to a document page, simply drag the master page icon onto the desired document page.

To rename a master page or change other options, select the master page and then choose the Master Options command from the Pages panel flyout menu.

Layers

Like Photoshop and Illustrator, InDesign supports document layers. In InDesign, the best use of these layers is to separate different elements of your layout, such as text from graphics, or background objects from foreground objects, or different versions of a layout (say, for client approval). All documents have a default layer that contains everything unless you create your own layers. Layer actions are carried out through the Layers panel, seen in Figure 8.37.

FIGURE 8.37
Layers can be used to separate different elements of your page layout.

The three most common layer-related actions are adding layers, rearranging layers, and deleting layers:

- ▶ To add a layer to a document, click the New Layer button at the bottom of the Layers panel.

- ▶ To rearrange layers (moving one above or below another), simply drag the layer up or down in the list of layers.

- ▶ To delete a layer (which deletes everything on the layer), drag it to the Trash button at the bottom of the Layers panel.

Double-clicking a layer lets you rename it or set layer options, and the two boxes to the left of the layer name let you set layer visibility (the eye icon) and lock a layer to prevent any changes to it (the lock icon).

Working with Large Documents

The longer your document is, the more structure and navigational aids you need to give your reader. InDesign makes it easy to add page numbers, tables of contents, and indexes. It also lets you group document files into books to keep them organized.

Page Numbering

One universal requirement of both large and small documents is page numbers. InDesign makes it very easy to add page numbers to your documents:

1. Double-click on the Master Page icon in the Pages panel.

2. Create a text frame on the master page where you want the page number to appear.

3. Choose Type, Insert Special Character, Markers, Current Page Number.

   If your document layout includes facing pages, repeat this process for the second master page.

You can also easily change the format or starting number for the page numbers in different sections of your document using the Numbering and Sections Options dialog box, found under the Layout menu, as seen in Figure 8.38.

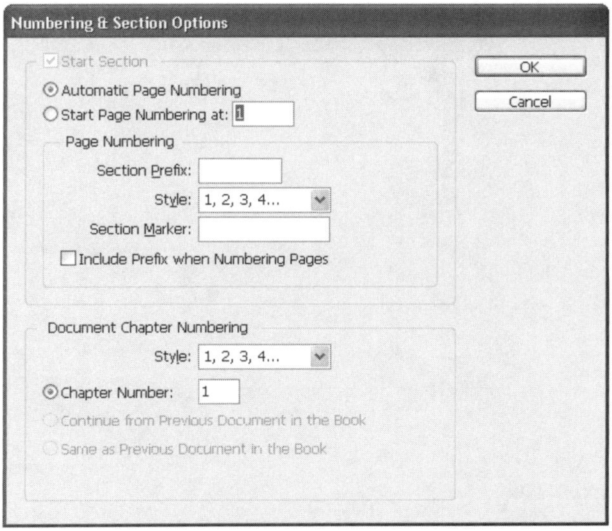

FIGURE 8.38
Configure your numbering options.

Creating a Book

A book in real life is a collection of related pages, all bound together. A book in InDesign is a collection of related documents, also bound together. Collecting document files into a book makes it easier to access and organize documents, sequentially number chapters, and create tables of contents and indexes that span multiple documents.

To create a book, follow these steps:

1. Choose File, New, Book.

2. Enter a name for the book. The Book panel appears.

3. Click the Add Documents button at the lower-right corner of the Book panel.

4. Browse to the document you want to add and click the Open button.

   Continue adding files until the book is complete. Drag filenames up or down in the list to change the order in which the documents appear in the book, as shown in Figure 8.39.

FIGURE 8.39
Create books
by combining
multiple files.

Table of Contents

The Table of Contents (TOC) feature in InDesign is very deep and powerful, enabling you to create any variation of TOC imaginable. To start creating a TOC, you must first define TOC styles (Layout, Table of Contents Styles). Create a new style (click the New button), and choose which paragraph style is associated with that style. Repeat for each level of heading that you want to appear in the TOC.

To generate the TOC, choose Layout, Table of Contents; click OK; and then place the TOC in your document. You'll need to replace the TOC each time you make an update to your document that might affect the TOC.

Indexing

InDesign takes all the pain out of indexing: The process of tracking words and what pages they occur on is automatic and straightforward. All you have to do is provide the entries for the index, set up the basic structure, and apply any formatting to the index. In many ways, indexes and TOCs are alike—they track where certain words (indexes) or styles (TOCs) are located within your document.

To create an index, start by selecting an entry (any word in your document) and then displaying the Index panel (Window, Type and Tables, Index). Click the New Index Entry button (at the bottom of the panel), and then click OK in the dialog box that follows. You've created your first entry!

When you've created all your index entries, you'll notice that the Index panel gives you a preview of your index. To create the real thing, choose Generate Index from the Index panel submenu, and place the text as you would any story. The Index text is *not* live or linked to the index panel, so if you make changes to your document, you'll need to generate a new index and place it again.

Creating and Using Tables

One very useful feature of InDesign is how easy it is to create attractive and functional tables. InDesign tables support borders, fill colors, paragraph formatting, and table headers and footers. Tables also flow between text frames just like regular text.

To create a table, place the insertion point inside a text frame and choose Table, Insert Table. In the Insert Table dialog box, seen in Figure 8.40, specify how many rows and columns you want. You can also specify header and footer rows (see "Table Headers and Footers," a little later in the chapter). Click OK when done.

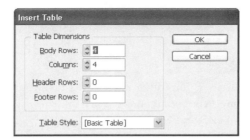

FIGURE 8.40
Add tables to
your text areas.

To convert tabbed text to a table, select the text and choose Table, Convert Text to Table. In the Convert Text to Table dialog box, specify which characters to use as column separators (usually tabs) and row separators (usually paragraphs). Click OK when done.

After your table is created, you can enter data into it by clicking in a cell, typing your data, and pressing the Tab key to move to the next cell (or Shift+Tab to move to the previous cell). A tab character can be inserted into a cell with (Option-Tab) [Alt+Tab].

Modifying Tables

After tables are created, they can be easily modified. Typical changes include adding or deleting rows or columns, changing row height or column width, and merging cells.

Basic table modification in InDesign is a simple matter of adding, deleting, and adjusting rows and columns and merging cells:

▶ To add rows or columns, select the same number of rows or columns that you want to add at the location where you want the new rows or columns inserted, and then choose Table, Insert, Row/Column.

▶ To delete rows or columns, select the rows or columns you want to remove, and choose Table, Delete, Row/Column.

▶ To adjust row height or column width, drag the bottom edge of the row or the right edge of the column. Hold down the Shift key while dragging to prevent rows below or columns to the right from moving.

▶ Hold down the Shift key and drag the bottom or right edge of the entire table to change the height of all rows or the width of all columns.

▶ To merge cells, select the desired cells and choose Table, Merge Cells.

▶ To split a cell into two, select it, and then choose Table, Split Cells.

Styling Tables

InDesign has a wide variety of formatting options to make your tables attractive and easy to read. The most common options are column/row strokes (cell borders), table borders, and fills. Before applying any formatting, though, you need to select the columns, rows, or individual cells with which you want to work:

▶ To select multiple cells, drag across them with the text cursor.

▶ To select entire rows, position the cursor on the left side of the table until the cursor changes to a right-pointing arrow and then click or click and drag.

▶ To select entire columns, position the cursor at the top of the table until the cursor changes to a down-pointing arrow, and then click or click and drag.

After cells are selected, you can format them by choosing Table, Cell Options, Strokes and Fills (choose Table, Table Options, Table Setup for stroke and fill options for the entire table). This dialog box contains controls for changing the weight, color, and type of stroke, as well as the fill color. The only tricky thing about this dialog box is the cell border proxy. This is a fake cell (or group of cells, if you have multiple cells selected) with blue borders (see Figure 8.41). Any border that is blue will be affected by your changes. Clicking a proxy toggles it between blue (selected) and gray (unselected).

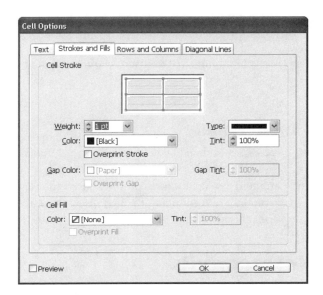

FIGURE 8.41
Table formatting
can be applied
to single cells,
rows, columns,
or groups of
cells.

Table Styles

Much as you can create styles for characters and paragraphs, you can use the Table
Styles panel to create consistent table styles across all of your table objects. To create
a new table style, open the Table Styles panel by choosing Window, Type and Tables,
Table Styles. When the panel appears, click the new style icon (in the lower-right
corner). Double-click the style to open the Table Style window and customize the
style appropriately.

Table Headers and Footers

Conceptually, table headers and footers are very similar to traditional document
headers and footers. The main difference is that, with document headers and footers, you have no control over the "units" of document data that they enclose—they
always appear at the top and bottom of the page. With InDesign's table headers
and footers, though, you can have them appear once per page, once per frame, or
every text column. Table headers and footers can also consist of as many rows as
you want.

To set up table headers and footers, follow these steps:

1. Choose Table, Table Options, Headers and Footers.

2. Specify how many rows to use for your header and footer.

3. Specify how often your table header will appear and how often your table footer will appear.

4. You can also choose to skip the first or last appearance of your table header or footer.

Using the Table Panel

After your table is created, the Table panel (Window, Type and Tables, Table) can be a quick way to perform such common table functions as changing the number of rows and columns, changing row height or column width, changing the vertical text alignment or the text rotation, and changing the text inset. The Table panel cannot be used to insert rows or columns, merge cells, or add borders and shading.

Adding Interactivity

InDesign can add many of the same interactivity features you will find in Acrobat, such as hyperlinks, bookmarks, buttons, and embedded sound and movie files. These features let a viewer of a PDF version of your document click on things to jump to new locations or otherwise interact with the document. Obviously, if you are not going to be creating a PDF version of your document, you won't be using any of these features. This section focuses on the two most common interactivity features, hyperlinks and bookmarks. Although you can add other types of interactivity in InDesign, it is much easier to open the PDF file in Acrobat and add the features there (especially because interactivity features cannot be previewed in InDesign anyway).

Movies

You can place movie and Flash files right into your InDesign layout as you would static images, like Photoshop files. Simply choose File, Place and navigate to a movie file. After you place a movie in your document, you can double-click on it to specify options such as poster frames, when you want the movie to play, and whether the movie will play just once or will loop repeatedly, as seen in Figure 8.42.

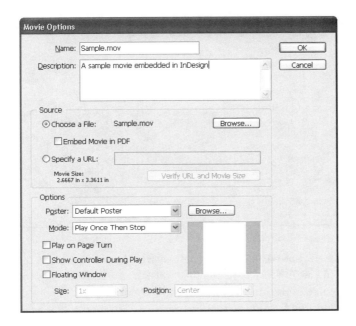

FIGURE 8.42
Believe it or
not, you can
add movies to
your InDesign
document!

Hyperlinks

A hyperlink is a section of text that, when clicked, sends the viewer to a new location. This location can be either a page in another document or a URL that points to a web page or a file. All hyperlinks have two parts: a source and a destination. The source is the text that sends the viewer to a new location, and the destination is the location itself.

To create a hyperlink to a web page, do the following:

1. Select the text you want to use as the source.

2. Choose Window, Interactive, Hyperlinks.

3. Click the Create New Hyperlink button at the bottom right of the Hyperlinks panel.

4. In the New Hyperlink dialog box, select URL from the Type pop-up menu, as seen in Figure 8.43.

5. Enter the full URL in the URL field.

6. Click the OK button.

FIGURE 8.43
Use the
Hyperlink panel
to add links into
your document.

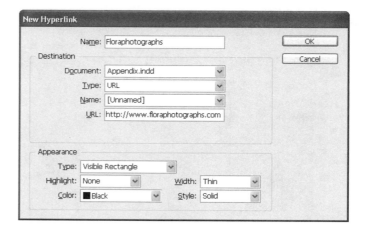

You can set the appearance of the link here as well, but you won't be able to see what it looks like until you export the file to PDF, and none of the options really creates an acceptable appearance. I recommend instead that you choose the Invisible Rectangle option and format the text yourself in a way that lets the viewer know that it is a clickable item (such as blue underlined text).

Bookmarks

Bookmarks are a feature of Acrobat that let you create a navigational structure for viewers that they can use to quickly move between pages or entire sections of a document. Unlike hyperlinks, bookmarks don't appear within the document itself; they appear as a separate pane within the PDF document window.

Using and editing bookmarks is covered in detail in Chapter 11, "Using Adobe Acrobat 8 Professional," but basically there are two types of bookmarks: page and text. Page bookmarks take you to a specific page, whereas text bookmarks take you to a specific block of text. Creating bookmarks can be done just as easily in InDesign as in Acrobat.

To create a bookmark, follow these steps:

1. Choose Window, Interactive, Bookmark.

2. Either navigate to the page that you want the bookmark to point to (for a page bookmark) or select a block of text (for a text bookmark).

3. Click the New Bookmark button at the bottom of the Bookmarks panel.

4. Rename the bookmark, if necessary.

Saving, Printing, and Prepress

To save your InDesign file, choose File, Save. It's that easy. If you want to save your file to be compatible with InDesign CS, you can save it in the InDesign Exchange format (INX).

Exporting Files

InDesign files can be exported to a few different file types. In some cases, such as PDF, the result matches (at least visually) exactly what was in the original document. However, in all cases, the native InDesign information is lost, meaning that InDesign functionality tied to the document, such as layers and object definitions, is gone when the file is exported. For that reason, be sure to always save a copy of the original InDesign file in addition to the exported version.

Exporting PDF

To export to PDF directly from InDesign, choose File, Export, and then choose Adobe PDF. You can choose from many different options, including compression and security settings. You can also choose to create a PDF file that conforms to the PDF/X standard.

Because there are so many different ways to create PDF files these days, and because there's really no control over what a PDF can or cannot contain, leaders in the print community created a standard called PDF/X as a subset of the PDF spec that is tailored for CMYK and spot-color printing workflows. For example, a PDF/X-1a file has all transparency flattened, has no RGB content, and has all fonts embedded in the file.

Exporting EPS

If you need to export single pages in the EPS format (this can be useful for opening InDesign files in Adobe Illustrator or Photoshop), you can do so through the Export dialog box (File, Export). Choose EPS as your file type (which changes the extension to .eps), and click the Save button.

The Export EPS dialog box appears with a myriad of options. If you'll be exporting for use in Photoshop or Illustrator, there's no need to mess with most of the options unless you have placed images in your document. If you have placed images, you should review and adjust options as appropriate in the Advanced panel of the Export EPS dialog box. The important thing to pay attention to is the Flattener Preset setting, which should be set to High Resolution if you have transparency in your file.

Separations Preview

You can view individual spot or process color plates onscreen in your document at any time. This is accomplished through the Separations Preview panel (accessed by choosing Window, Output, Separations Preview). In this panel, you can view each of the plates individually, or in any combination with other colors, by clicking the eyeballs on the left (see Figure 8.44). Note that when you are down to any one color, it always appears onscreen as black.

FIGURE 8.44
View individual spot or process color plates with the Separations Preview panel.

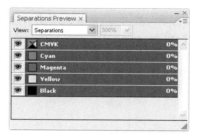

Additionally, you can choose Ink Limit from the View pop-up menu to have InDesign highlight the areas in your document that exceed the ink coverage percentage that you specify in the panel.

The Ink Manager

When printing color separations, you might want to specify certain settings for each ink, such as dot type and screen angle. You can access these settings by choosing Ink Manager from the Separation Preview panel flyout menu. The Ink Manager, shown in Figure 8.45, also enables you to specify ink aliases, which can be extremely helpful when working in a document that contains several spot colors.

FIGURE 8.45
Use the Ink Manager to set options for each ink.

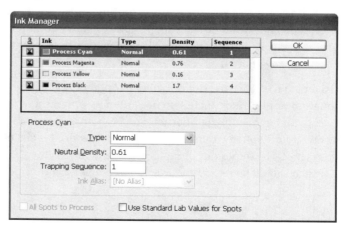

If you have two versions of the same Pantone color in your document, you can specify one as an ink alias of the other, effectively combining both colors to separate to the same plate. The Ink Manager also contains a single button that you can use to convert all spot colors to process.

Preflight

Preflighting in InDesign is the process of ensuring that all files and fonts are intact and current, and that all colors and print settings are correct. InDesign makes this process straightforward by providing a Preflight dialog box, accessed by choosing File, Preflight. Clicking on each of the items in the list on the left of the box (Summary, Fonts, Links and Images, Color and Inks, Print Settings, External Plug-ins) displays detailed information about those areas (see Figure 8.46).

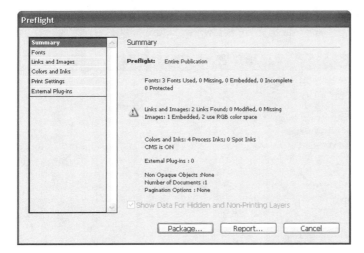

FIGURE 8.46
Run a preflight check to ensure that your design resources are available and intact.

Package

The Package command (File, Package) provides a quick method for placing your InDesign file, all linked files, and any fonts used in the document into a single location (the same lists you saw when you chose File, Preflight, as described previously). You can then easily drag these files into an email or burn them onto a CD, confident that the recipient will have all the files needed to open, edit, and print your document.

Cross-Media Export

The Cross-Media Export command (File, Cross-Media Export) packages the components of your document (text blocks, imagery, and so on) into a form (XHTML) that Dreamweaver (or other web tools) can use to create a web page (or series of pages) from your InDesign document content. You can also use the cross-media export feature to export to Adobe Digital Editions—an ebook format with a free reader available from Adobe.

Printing

Because InDesign is an aggregation application, you'll find yourself needing to print from it more than all the other applications in the Adobe Creative Suite combined. To that end, the printing capabilities in InDesign (most of which are mimicked in Illustrator) are phenomenal. The following lists some of the more commonly used functions in the Print dialog box (shown in Figure 8.47).

FIGURE 8.47
Configure your
output settings.

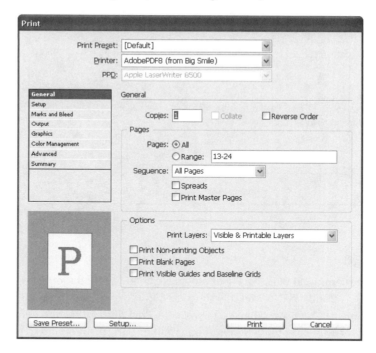

Print Dialog Options

Although InDesign supplies all sorts of detailed options at print time, most people use only a handful, such as copies and page ranges.

Enter the number of copies you'd like in the Copies text box. Check the Collate button if (when printing more than one copy) you'd like the pages to come out in sets in order, as 1/2/3, 1/2/3, 1/2/3, instead of 1/1/1, 2/2/2, 3/3/3.

To print a subset of the pages in your document, choose the Range radio button and type in the pages you want to print. For contiguous pages, use a hyphen (for example, 2-4). For individual pages, use commas (for example, 1, 4, 7).

Print Presets

If you're a tweaker when it comes to the Print dialog box, you'll find the Print Presets invaluable. They enable you to store *all* the Print dialog box settings (save them by clicking the Save Preset button at the bottom of the dialog box) and retrieve them simply by choosing them from the Print Preset pop-up menu at the top of the Print dialog box.

Marks and Bleed Settings

If you click the Marks and Bleed item in the list at the left in the Print dialog box, you're presented with an array of options for how various printer's marks appear and how to handle bleeding (which is how far past the edge of the defined page ink should appear).

Clicking the All Printers Marks check box and then printing a test document is a great way to see what all these things look like and where they will appear on your document.

Printing Separations

Separations are necessary for printing presses to reproduce color documents. Instead of one sheet being printed with all the colors on it, a separate sheet is printed for each color. Typically, you won't be choosing this option unless you're printing directly to plate or negatives (which are used to make plates for a printing press). To print separations, choose Output from the list on the left, and then choose Separations from the Color pop-up menu (see Figure 8.48).

Transparency Flattening

When printing files with transparency, flattening must occur to have the file print correctly. In the Advanced panel of the Print dialog box, you can specify a flattener preset that controls this flattening process, as demonstrated in Figure 8.49. The High Resolution setting results in the best quality output, but longer print times. For standard proofing, Medium Resolution is fine.

FIGURE 8.48
Use the output settings to print separations.

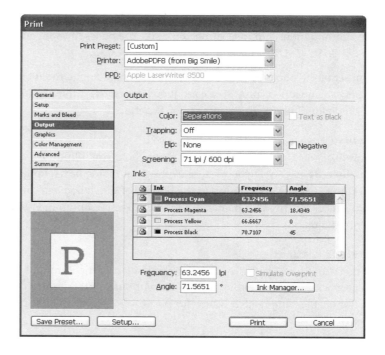

FIGURE 8.49
Set your flattening options to optimize your output quality.

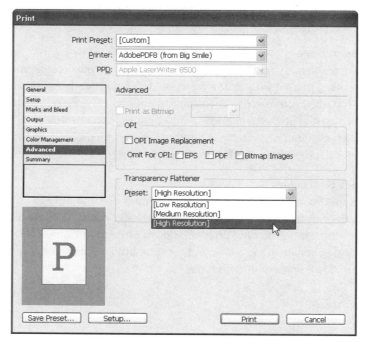

Summary

As you've probably gathered throughout this chapter, InDesign can be used to create almost any page layout that you can imagine. We'll put that to the test later in the book with several projects that make heavy use of InDesign.

One important thing to take away from your reading is the consistency of the tools across the CS3 suite. Adobe has gone a long way towards standardizing the terminology, appearance, and functionality of tools across all of CS3. As you spend more time using each application, you'll actually be learning skills that can be applied across the entire suite! Sweet!

CHAPTER 9
Using Adobe Flash CS3

Flash is everywhere. It is used for animated ads, online applications, and recently has become very popular for video. *Time* magazine named you Person of the Year for 2006 because individuals, rather than corporations, are starting to control content. YouTube, which is powered by Flash, has pioneered this concept.

In this chapter, we look at Flash CS3 and see how it can be used for everything from traditional animation to interactive applications. Flash is an exciting development environment that can be learned and used by everyone from casual designers to hardcore developers.

What's New in Flash CS3

As with the other Macromedia applications that Adobe acquired, Flash has taken on an appearance to match the other software in the CS3 suite. The drawing tools have also been updated to better match those of the Illustrator CS3 graphics package, and file importing from Illustrator and Photoshop are virtually seamless.

In addition, Flash CS3 incorporates a new scripting language, ActionScript 3.0, which provides advanced features for advanced users.

Getting Started with Flash

Flash, like the other CS3 applications, greets you with a welcome screen that gives you quick access to creating new documents and opening a range of template files. These features are also accessible directly from the File, New submenu.

By default, you are given the choice of creating everything from a Flash File (ActionScript 3.0) to a Flash Project (which is a collection of Flash and media files). Perhaps counterintuitively, you should always start with a Flash File (ActionScript 2.0) until you are fully familiar with the application and its advanced features. ActionScript 2.0 gives the best balance of features and functionality. Going with the newer ActionScript 3.0 format locks you out of features such as behaviors, which are very helpful for beginners.

If you're targeting a specific device, or know you want to make a specific type of Flash application, you might want to check out the templates, shown in Figure 9.1.

FIGURE 9.1
Templates can
help target spe-
cific devices.

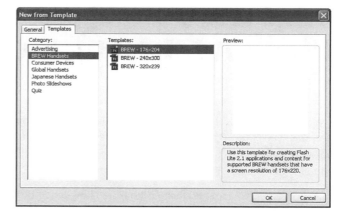

With many handsets now supporting Flash, you can actually choose a template for
and build an application that runs on someone's cell phone! For the purposes of this
chapter, however, we'll just assume that you've chosen a default Flash File
(ActionScript 2.0) and not a template.

Navigating the Flash Interface

The key to understanding Flash is always knowing where you are. You're given the
power to edit everything: static graphics, animations, buttons, and more. It's easy to
become disoriented about exactly on which element you're working. Let's start by
taking a tour of the primary elements of the Flash workspace:

▶ **The stage** —The visual workspace. Any graphics placed in this area are visible to the user.

▶ **Tools panel**—Contains all the many drawing tools in Flash, including those
you can add later (by selecting Edit, Customize Tools Panel).

▶ **Timeline panel**—Contains the sequence of images that make an animation.
The Timeline can also include many layers of animations. This way, certain
graphics can appear above or below others, and you can have several animations playing simultaneously.

▶ **Properties panel**—The Properties panel, as you've learned in other CS3
applications, gives you the controls over any selected object.

▶ **Library panel**—The Library panel contains assets that you can store and
reuse in your animations.

The Stage

The white rectangle in the center of Flash's workspace is called the stage. Text, graphics, photos—anything the user sees—goes on the stage, seen in Figure 9.2. The elements you add are the "actors," and the stage is where they will perform!

Timeline panel

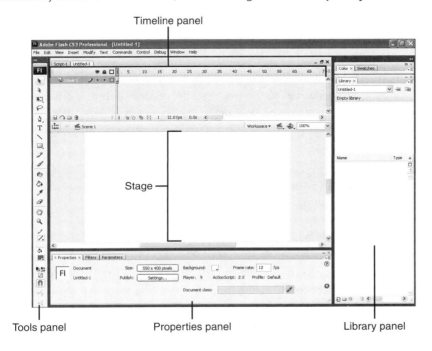

FIGURE 9.2
The stage is the large white box in the center. All the visual components of an animation are placed on the stage.

Tools panel   Properties panel   Library panel

Stage

Think of the stage as the canvas on which a painter paints or the frame in which a photographer composes pictures. Sometimes you'll want a graphic to begin outside the stage and then animate onto the stage. The gray area around the outside of the white area is off the stage. You can see the off-stage area only when the View menu shows a check mark next to Pasteboard. (Selecting this option toggles between checked and unchecked.) The default setting (Pasteboard checked) is preferable because it means you can position graphics off the stage.

The stage is quite simple. It is your visual workspace and where most of your animation work takes place. However, two important concepts are worth covering now: stage size and zoom level. By default, the stage is a rectangle that is 550 pixels wide by 400 pixels tall. Later you'll see how to change the width and height of a movie. However, the specific dimensions in pixels are less important than the resulting shape of the stage (called the *aspect ratio*). The pixel numbers are unimportant because, when you deliver a Flash movie to the Web, you can specify that Flash scale to any pixel dimension while maintaining a crisp appearance.

Aspect ratio is the ratio of height to width. Any square or rectangular viewing area has an aspect ratio. For example, television has a 4:3 aspect ratio—that is, no matter how big a standard TV screen is, it's always three units tall and four units wide. 35mm film has an aspect ratio of 3:2 (such as a 4"×6" print), and high-definition television (HDTV) uses a 16:9 ratio. Most computer screen resolutions have an aspect ratio of 4:3 (640x480, 800x600, and 1024x768). You can use any ratio you want in a web page; just remember that the portion of the screen you don't use will be left blank. A wide-screen ratio (as wide as 3:1, like film) has a much different aesthetic effect than something with a square ratio (1:1).

A Flash movie retains its aspect ratio when it scales, instead of getting distorted. For example, you could specify that a Flash movie in a web page scale to 100% of the user's browser window size. You could also scale a movie with the dimensions 100×100 to 400×400.

Not only can you deliver a Flash movie in any size (because Flash scales well), but while working in Flash, you can also zoom in on certain portions of the stage to take a closer look without having any effect on the actual stage size.

Stage View Controls

The Zoom control is located at the top right of the stage below the Timeline. This control provides one way to change the current view setting. Other ways include selecting View, Magnification and using the Zoom tool (the magnifying glass button in the Tools panel).

If the entire stage is not visible, you can view the other parts of the stage in one of two ways: by using the standard window scrollbars on the right and bottom or by using the Hand tool. The Hand tool is best accessed by simply holding down the spacebar. Go ahead and hold down the spacebar; then click and drag. You're *panning* to other parts of the stage without actually moving anything. It's important to understand that the Hand tool only changes your view port onto the whole stage. The best thing about using the spacebar to select the Hand tool is that it's spring loaded—that is, the Hand tool is active only while you hold down the spacebar.

Grids and Guides

Additional interesting tools are available from the View menu, including grids, guides, and snap settings. Select View, Grid, Show Grid. Behind all the graphics onstage, you see a grid (which the user won't see in production). The grid can help you line up graphics perfectly. Notice that you can also select View, Grid, Edit Grid to edit the color and spacing of the grid.

Guides are just like the grid, except you drag them into place where you want them. First, select View, Rulers. Now you can click either ruler and drag toward the stage to create and put into place a single guide. You make vertical guides by dragging from the left ruler, and you make horizontal guides by dragging from the top ruler. To remove the guides, drag them back to the ruler. As with the grid, you find the option to edit the guide settings—as well as a way to lock the guides in place—by selecting View, Guides, Edit Guides. Figure 9.3 shows the stage with a grid, rulers, and several guides active.

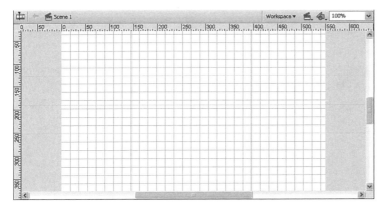

FIGURE 9.3
Use the grid, guides, and rulers to help with positioning.

The Tools Panel

The Tools panel is the panel with which you will likely become most familiar. Any time you create or edit anything on the stage, you need to have one tool selected from the Tools panel. By default, the Tools panel is a vertical column located on the left of your screen.

Although the Tools panel is used primarily to draw on the stage, it's also used to edit what you've already drawn. Shown in Figure 9.4, the Tools panel provides controls for editing, selecting, and coloring your content.

The Tools section enables you to create graphics and text (via the Line, Shape, and Text tool), edit graphics (via the Eraser tool and Paint Bucket tool), and simply select graphics (via the Selection tool, Subselection tool, and Lasso tool). The color selector near the bottom gives you control over the color of objects drawn. At the very bottom of the panel are context-sensitive options that modify how certain tools work. Depending on which tool is selected, you might not see anything in the Options section.

FIGURE 9.4
The Tools panel has tools for drawing, editing, and viewing, plus options that vary, depending on the currently selected tool.

We'll look more closely at some of these tools later, but there is no harm in selecting and trying them out now!

The Timeline Panel

The Timeline contains the sequence of individual images that make up an animation. When the user watches your animation, he sees the images on Frame 1 followed by Frame 2, and so on. It's as if you took the actual film from a conventional movie and laid it horizontally across the screen, with the beginning on the left and the end toward the right.

Like many other windows, the Timeline can be moved around so it floats just about anywhere on your screen (use the panel menu in the upper-right corner of the Timeline). If you want, you can dock the Timeline under the stage—or nearly anywhere else you want. People who have the hardware to support two monitors have even greater flexibility in the way they organize their workspace. If you completely close the Timeline to make more space (which is possible only when it's floating), you can always get it back by selecting Window, Timeline.

When you start to create animations, the Timeline includes many visual clues to help you. For example, you can quickly see the length of an animation simply by looking at the Timeline. Also, Flash uses a few subtle icons and color codes in the Timeline; this way, you can see how the animation will play.

> To collapse or show the Timeline panel, click the Timeline button (a filmstrip with a vertical line through it) at the top of the stage.

The Current Frame

In the Timeline, a red marker indicates which frame is currently being viewed. This red current-frame marker can be in only one frame at a time—the frame you're currently editing. Initially, you'll find that you can't move the current-frame marker past Frame 1 unless your file has more frames. You'll have plenty of opportunity to do this later; for now, just realize that the red marker indicates the current frame. If it helps, imagine a time machine. You can visit any moment in time, but you can visit only one moment at a time.

Layers

In addition to frames, the Timeline lets you have as many layers as you want in animations. As is the case with other drawing programs, objects drawn in one layer appear above or below objects in other layers. Each layer can contain a separate animation. This way, multiple animations can occur at the same time. By using layer names and special effects, you can create complex animations. Figure 9.5 shows the Timeline and layers of a finished movie.

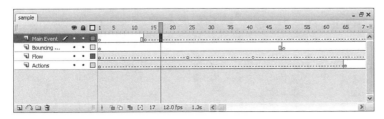

FIGURE 9.5
Most animations involve many layers. Each layer is independent of the others.

One important concept is that you can be in only one layer at a time. That is, if you draw or paste graphics, they are added to the currently active layer. The current layer is the layer with the pencil icon, as shown in Figure 9.5. You can just single-click another layer to make it the active layer (notice that the pencil moves to the layer you click). The key here is to always pay attention to what layer you're currently editing. For example, if the current layer is locked, you won't be able to affect it at all. Since the Flash Layers panel is virtually identical to that of Photoshop (and Illustrator/InDesign), please refer to Chapter 6, "Using Adobe Photoshop CS3."

The Properties Panel

As in the other CS3 applications, the Properties panel displays properties of the currently selected object so you can make adjustments. For example, when you select a block of text, the Properties panel lets you view and change the font face and size. When you select a filled shape, you can adjust the fill color of that shape.

> If nothing is selected, you can still make changes to the Properties panel. Although this seems to have no effect, you're actually specifying what will happen the next time you create an object. For example, if you first select the Text tool and (before clicking to type) you make a change to the font in the Properties panel, you'll see that font change in text you create later.

For example, in a new file, you can select the Text tool, click the stage, and then type a few words. At the bottom of the screen you'll see the attributes for the text within the Properties panel, as shown in Figure 9.6.

FIGURE 9.6
The Properties panel sets attributes for the active object.

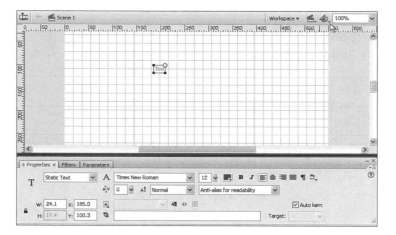

The Library Panel and Symbols

The Library is the best storage facility for all the media elements used in a Flash file. Media placed in the Library can be used repeatedly within a file, and—regardless of how many times you use those media—it doesn't significantly add to the file size! For example, if you put a drawing of a cloud in the Library, you can then drag 100 copies of the cloud onto the stage (making a whole sky full of clouds), but deep inside the Flash file, only one cloud exists. Using the Library is one way you can keep Flash movies small.

In practice, the Library is used in two basic ways: for editing and for maintaining (or accessing) the Library's contents. You might need to edit the contents of one Library item (called a symbol), and when you do, you are editing the contents of the Library. You might also need to access the Library to simply organize all the contents or to drag instances of the symbols into a movie. In such a case, you are maintaining the Library (as opposed to editing its contents).

A *symbol* is the name for anything—usually something visual, such as a graphic shape—you create and place in a file's Library. Although different types of symbols exist, the idea is that by creating a symbol, you're storing the graphic once in the Library. After it is in the Library, the symbol can be used several times throughout a movie without having a significant impact on file size.

An *instance* is one copy of a symbol used in a movie. Every time you drag a symbol from the Library, you create another instance. It's not a copy in the traditional sense of the word because there's only one master and each instance has negligible impact on file size. Think of the original negative of a photograph as the symbol and each print as another instance. You'll see that, like photographic prints, instances can vary widely (in their sizes, for example).

Other Panels

Let's review the other panels and what they contain. You've already seen the primary tools you'll be using for your work, but there are other useful features as well. Keep in mind that you *can* rearrange panels—so if your system doesn't match exactly, someone has probably been customizing things a bit. You can return to the default workspace by choosing Window, Workspace, Default from the menu.

Many panels are hidden initially. If you don't see one of the groups listed here, look under the Window menu. Following are the other panels you might find useful:

- ▶ **Color**—Used to set line and fill colors and styles for objects created in the stage.

- ▶ **Swatches**—A collection of reusable colors and color palettes. You can add your favorite colors here.

- ▶ **Filters**—Special effects that you can add to movie clips, text, and other objects within the stage. These are similar to (but not as varied as) filters within Photoshop and other graphics applications.

- ▶ **Parameters**—Similar to the Properties panel, but used to set the attributes of the screen during playback.

▶ **Info**—Just like the Info panel in Photoshop, this panel shows the position of the cursor, the size of the current selection, and the color located under the cursor.

▶ **Transform**—Gives quick access to tools for stretching, skewing, and rotating objects in the stage.

▶ **Components**—Used to access user interface elements (buttons, progress bars, and so on) for use within Flash applications.

▶ **Components Inspector**—Similar to the Properties panel, but for user interface components. It enables you to set attributes for the selected component.

▶ **Accessibility**—Set common accessibility attributes for a given object to make it accessible to the visually impaired.

▶ **History**—If you've used History to fix some boo-boos in Photoshop, you'll recognize the History panel immediately. The History panel contains a list of all the changes you've made to the document. You can immediately back up to any state that the document has been in since it was last saved. The History panel can hold 100 changes by default. You can reset this value (Undo Levels) in the General section of the Flash preferences, accessed by choosing Edit, Preferences or pressing Command-U/Control-U.

▶ **Scene**—A way to create unique animations with individual timelines within a single Flash file. Just like a feature length movie might be divided into scenes, you can divide an animation into scenes. The name of the current scene is always shown at the top of the stage.

▶ **Strings**—Can be used to store strings that are used in an application. Multiple language strings, for example, could be stored here and accessed to create a multilingual presentation in a single file.

▶ **Web Services**—Define web service URLs that can be accessed by your Flash applications. Web services are applications that provide specific information back to a calling program, such as returning weather data.

▶ **Actions**—Used to attach and edit ActionScript (the programming language behind Flash) to objects and animation frames.

▶ **Behaviors**—A library of prewritten ActionScripts that can be immediately used to apply complex behaviors to your onscreen objects.

▶ **Common Libraries (Buttons, Classes, Learning Interactions)**—Libraries of commonly used components that can be added and used in your documents. Unlike Components, these are prestyled, ready-to-go elements.

▶ **Debug Panels (Debug Console, Variables)**—Used to find errors in your Flash ActionScript code and monitor the value of variables during execution of the program.

Now that you know where things are, let's learn a bit about the graphics tools available in Flash. We'll then review the terminology of animation, and then get started making a simple animation.

Drawing in Flash

Most everything you do in Flash starts with a drawing on the stage. Sometimes, you'll want a graphic to start off the stage and then animate into view. Drawing off the stage requires that you have the Pasteboard selected with a check mark in the View menu. I recommend you leave this setting checked, but you should realize that the gray area around the outside of the stage is offstage and does not appear in your finished movie. The stage is the white rectangular area.

Tools

Your drawing tools should appear, by default, on the left side of the screen, as shown in Figure 9.7. If the tools aren't visible, you can access them by selecting Window, Tools.

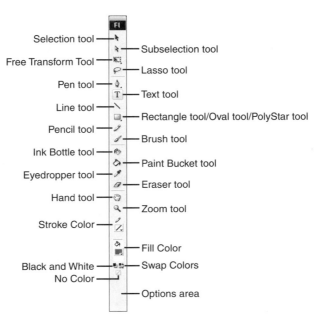

FIGURE 9.7
Flash's drawing toolbar might look simple, but because most tools have additional options, there's more than meets the eye.

The following sections look at how to draw with these tools. Keep in mind that whereas some tools (such as the Pencil and Brush tools) let you create artwork, others (such as the Selection and Zoom tools) simply help you modify or view your artwork. If you've used Illustrator, you'll feel at home here.

Viewing and Modification Tools

Both View tools—Hand and Zoom—have no effect on artwork. You simply use them to help you see your artwork.

To zoom in to critically inspect or change the artwork in the stage, click to select the Zoom tool (it's the one that looks like a magnifying glass). Notice that, as with many other tools, when you select the Zoom tool, additional buttons appear in the Options section of the toolbar. You should see two more magnifying glasses appear in the Options area: Enlarge (+) and Reduce (–).

To zoom in or out, just select the appropriate option, and then click the stage. Another way to zoom is to click and drag. You see a rectangle as you drag, and when you let go, that rectangle defines the viewable portion of the stage.

You always see the current zoom level displayed in the pop-up menu at the top right of the stage. If you click the Zoom control pop-up menu, you can return to 100%. Another quick way to return to 100% is to double-click the Zoom tool (not the Enlarge or Reduce option, but the main Zoom tool's magnifier).

The Hand tool is another non-modifying view tool that helps you navigate the stage without using the scrollbars. To use the Hand tool, simply select it, and then click and drag within the stage area to move your current viewing location.

Creation Tools

Although the View tools prove very useful, they can't change a file. To create artwork in Flash, you have to add to an image, change something you've already drawn, or remove some or all of what you've drawn. In the following sections, you'll see how to add to your artwork. This naturally gives you something to change or remove later. Let's go through each tool individually and then analyze how they can all be used together.

Drawing Lines

Two tools are available for just drawing lines: the Line tool and the Pencil tool. (To be fair, the Oval and Rectangle tools draw lines, but they also draw fills, as you'll see in the "Painting Fills" section later.) Lines can be given a stroke color, stroke width, and stroke style.

To draw a line, select the Line tool, which draws straight lines. When your cursor is on the stage, it changes to crosshairs. Click and drag to create a line. You might notice a dark ring that sometimes appears while you drag. This is Flash's way of assisting you while drawing by letting you know when your line is at a 45 degree increment or you're approaching an intersection with another object. In the case of the line, you'll find drawing perfectly horizontal and vertical lines to be easy when the Snap to Objects option is selected from the View menu.

To set the stroke width or stroke color of lines before you draw them, make changes in the Properties panel when the Line tool is selected. If you want to change the stroke attributes of a line you've already drawn, first select the Selection tool and then click once to select the line. When the line is selected, you can use the Properties panel to affect its attributes.

Another way to draw is with the Pencil tool. As you'd expect, the Pencil works like a pencil! Click and drag in the stage area and a line is drawn as you drag.

Three useful options for the pencil tool are

- ▶ **Straighten**—The Straighten option attempts to straighten what you draw using, well, straight lines. If you're trying to draw a polygonal shape, this is the mode you want.

- ▶ **Smooth**—The Smooth option can come in handy if you find that your hand-drawn images look too jagged. It automatically smoothes out images that you draw.

- ▶ **Ink**—Finally, the Ink Pencil Mode setting draws *almost* exactly what you draw. Flash adjusts what you draw to reduce the file size.

The Properties panel affects lines drawn with the Pencil tool in the same way it affects those drawn with the Line tool.

One attribute in the Properties panel you might want to experiment with is the stroke style. The pop-up menu shows a visual representation of each style. Solid (the default) is similar to Hairline, but Hairline effectively sets the stroke height to the lowest number possible.

When the Pencil or Line tool is selected, the Custom button on the Properties panel provides a way for you to create your own custom stroke styles. The dialog box that appears after you click the Custom button lets you control several attributes of your own custom stroke styles.

Painting Fills

In Flash, there are two components to any shape you draw: lines and fills. Some shapes are just lines (as you saw in the previous section), but some shapes are just fills (as you're about to see), and some shapes contain both.

A line has no thickness—only applied stroke attributes. A fill, on the other hand, has a left side, right side, top, and bottom. You can think of lines as the candy coating on an M&M and fills as the chocolate center (if that helps).

The two tools to create fills are the Brush tool and the Paint Bucket tool. To see how these work, it's easiest to just try them out.

First, let's look at the Paint Bucket tool. Create a few freehand circles using the Pencil tool—make sure they are complete circles without any gaps.

Next, select the Paint Bucket tool. Notice that the Options section has buttons for Gap Size and Lock Fill.

If you click with the Paint Bucket tool in an empty part of the stage, nothing happens. The Paint Bucket tool fills closed shapes with the selected fill color (the swatch next to the small paint bucket in the Colors section of the toolbox). It also changes the fill color of any fill already created. Change the Gap Size option to Close Large Gaps. Adjusting the Gap Size option should enable you to fill all your circles—even if they were not totally closed.

Now let's look at the Brush tool. Select it and try drawing a line. Because you've used the Brush tool, it's really a fill (not a line), despite the fact that it might look like a line.

To change the fill color of a brush stroke, use the color swatch in the Properties panel, or just click in the stroke with the Paint Bucket tool to replace the fill.

The Brush tool's Options area is definitely one you'll want to explore. The two pop-up menus that appear to be the same are actually quite different. The Brush Size option controls the brush's tip size. On the other hand, the Brush Shape option controls the brush's tip shape. For example, you can have a calligraphy look with the angled tip, as shown in Figure 9.8.

Brush Mode, another option, is very interesting and worth investigating. Depending on the mode type, the brush can be limited to only painting within or behind other shapes. It can even be constrained to affect only the current selection.

FIGURE 9.8
The Brush Shape option affects the style of a drawing. Here's a calligraphy effect using the angled Brush Shape option.

Drawing and Modifying Shapes Using Lines and Fills

When or the Rectangle tool, you create a shape using both a line and a fill. These shapes have a fill and a stroke, with all the attributes set in the Properties panel. You can actually draw an oval or a rectangle that has no fill by changing the fill to no color (the white square with a red line through it).

Similarly, you can create a shape without a stroke by changing the stroke color to no color. These tools are pretty self-explanatory. One tool option to take note of is the Round Rectangle Radius setting. If this setting is selected before you draw, it makes all rectangles you draw have rounded corners.

There are two fundamental components to the shapes you create—lines (or *strokes*) and fills—and each has a different set of tools. The Oval tool and Rectangle tool can create both strokes and fills at the same time. To create a new fill or affect one that's onscreen, you use the Brush tool or Paint Bucket tool. You can create lines using the Pencil tool or the Line tool, and you can change their characteristics using the Ink Bottle tool.

The Pen tool is primarily used to draw lines, but anytime you use it to draw a closed shape, the shape is filled automatically.

By simply clicking with the Pen tool, you can add sharp anchor points on straight lines. An anchor point is a point on a line or path that "ties" the object to the artboard. The Pen tool can also draw curves. Instead of just clicking to create a point, you can click and drag to create a curve. The direction in which you drag creates what will become a tangent to your curve. The distance you drag determines how gradual or extreme the curve will be—this is a Bé]zier curve and is one of your primary tools in Illustrator. I'd recommend practicing drawing with the Illustrator tools to become more familiar with the art tools in Flash.

Creating Text

To create text, you simply select the Text tool, click, and start typing. You can modify the font, color, and style of what you've typed after you create it. Modifying your text after it's typed, although counterintuitive, is usually your best approach because it enables you to fine-tune the appearance within your artwork.

Creating text in Flash is both easy and more sophisticated. Let's try a few of the tools and see how they work.

Select the Text tool, click the stage, and then type a few words. This click-and-type technique expands the margin for the block of text to the exact width of whatever you type. A circle that appears at the upper-right corner of the text block indicates that the margin will automatically adjust in this way (see Figure 9.9).

FIGURE 9.9
Creating text is easy. The subtle circle that appears is used to set the margins.

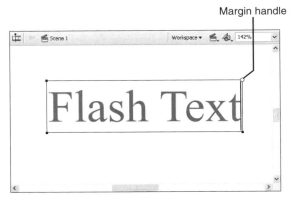

Margin handle

To adjust margins, click and drag the circle. It changes into a square to indicate that the margins are fixed. You can double-click the square margin control to restore the automatic margin adjustment (that is, to make it a circle again).

Now that you have some text in the block and have set the margins, let's review some attributes that can be modified. Click the Selection tool to stop editing the text. Your text block should become selected. (If it isn't, just click it once, and a rectangle appears around it.)

With the block selected, use the Properties panel to make modifications, as shown in Figure 9.10. You'll find these options easy to understand and use. They are very similar to most word processing tools.

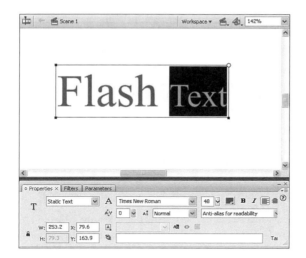

FIGURE 9.10
The Properties panel enables you to change text attributes such as font size and color.

Properties are applied to the entire block of text (if it is selected), or, if you prefer, just select individual words or sentences to have finer grained control over the text's appearance.

Selecting and Transforming Objects

Now that you've seen how to create lines, fills, shapes (with both lines and fills), and text, it's time to explore how to modify them. The process is simple. You select the object you want to modify using the Selection tool and then you modify it. Selecting exactly what you want to modify is actually the most challenging part.

Selection Tools

The two basic selection tools are the Selection tool and Lasso tool. The Subselection tool (the white arrow) is for selecting and editing individual anchor points (in the same way the Pen tool created them). Again, if you've used Illustrator, this should be very familiar to you.

The Selection tool is used to select an object by clicking it once. The key to the Selection tool is that the cursor changes to tell you what will happen when you click, such as resizing, moving, and reshaping. You can try this tool by adding objects to your document and then moving the cursor around the perimeter of the objects.

Another way to select an object is to *marquee* it. With the Selection tool selected, click outside the object and drag until you've drawn an imaginary rectangle that surrounds it entirely. When you let go, anything within the rectangle (presumably your object) becomes selected.

Sometimes the arrangement of other shapes onscreen makes the marquee technique difficult or impossible. Another tool you can use to make selections is the Lasso tool. Select the Lasso tool and then click and drag around a shape to select it. The Polygon Mode option for the Lasso tool makes the tool act almost like the Pen tool. Select the Polygon Mode option, and click and let go. Then click and release in a new location to extend the selection. Continue to extend the selection and then double-click when you're done.

Finally, you can decide to select just a portion of a shape. Suppose you want to chop off the top of the circle. You can use either the Lasso tool or the marquee technique with the Selection tool to select the portion desired.

You use the Selection tool to employ the marquee technique. If you click and drag an object, it moves or bends. However, when you click the stage where there are no objects, you see a rectangle appear while you drag (this is the marquee). You can draw that rectangle around other objects, and they will be selected when you let go. Using this marquee technique to select objects is often easier than clicking to select objects.

The Eyedropper Tool

One what you've drawn is to simply change the color. For example, the Paint Bucket tool can change a fill's color, and the Ink Bottle tool can change a stroke (its color and other attributes). This works fine when you make the effort to first select the fill color, for example, and then select the Paint Bucket tool and click a fill to change it. Sometimes, however, you want one fill to match the color of another. The Eyedropper tool enables you to sample a color from an object that is already onscreen.

Transforming Scale, Rotation, Envelope, and Distortion

The Free Transform tool is your key to advanced modifications. Basically, you just have to select an object with the Free Transform tool active. Four options appear any time you use the Free Transform tool and have an object selected. You can also find these options by selecting Modify, Transform.

Here's an example:

1. Use the Rectangle tool to draw a square. Select the Free Transform tool and double-click the center of the square to select it entirely.

2. At this point, none of the four options at the bottom of the Tools panel should be selected (see Figure 9.11). This means you're in Free Transform mode, and if you have a steady hand, you can rotate, scale, or distort the shape.

FIGURE 9.11
When an object is selected, you can use the Free Transform tool to alter its size and orientation.

3. Explore the possibilities by rolling your cursor over the square handles at the corners and sides of the shape—but don't click yet. Depending on where you move your mouse, the cursor changes to indicate its action. A line with two arrows for Scale, a circular arrow for Rotate and two parallel lines for Skew. Additionally, if you hold down Ctrl, the corners make the cursor change to the Distort option.

Free Transform mode can be really touchy, so let's access the options individually using the option buttons at the bottom of the Tools panel. Select your object, then select the Scale option.

The selected object shows square handles in the corners and on the sides. The cursor changes when you roll over these handles. The corner handles enable you to scale both width and height equally and at the same time. The side handles let you change just width or just height. Click and drag a handle to change the scale. Notice that this version of Scale (compared to Scale in Free Transform mode) can maintain your shape's proportions (horizontally and vertically).

Next, make sure the square is still selected and select the Rotate and Skew option in the Tools panel. Now the corner handles rotate; side handles skew. Roll your cursor over the handles to see the cursor change.

Click and drag a corner handle and notice that you can rotate the square. Actually, if the default Snap to Objects option is selected (that is, if the magnet button is pressed in), the object snaps into place at 45° angles.

For our next trick, choose the Distort option. Drag the shape by the handles on the corners to distort. It turns out that the Selection tool can create the same effect as Distort, but only when the shape itself has a corner to grab. Without this Distort option, making a distorted ellipse would be nearly impossible. Finally, try holding down the Shift key when you distort (by dragging a corner handle). This way, you can distort two sides evenly.

Finally, the wildest of transformation options is Envelope. To best understand this option, draw a new square, select the Free Transform tool, and click the Envelope button. When your shape is selected, you see many handles. Move the square handles to "influence" the shape. It's as though the shape tries to touch all the squares, even if they're pulled out to one side. The circle handles are like the tangents created when you draw using the Pen tool. They control the rate at which a shape bends to reach the square handles.

> The Transform options can also be accessed from the dedicated Transform panel.

Smoothing and Straightening Shapes

After you draw a shape, you can at any time smooth or straighten what you've drawn. The Smooth and Straighten options are available when the Selection tool is selected. The process is quite simple: You select a shape and click either Smooth or Straighten. Clicking repeatedly continues to smooth or straighten whatever is selected.

Using Snap to Objects to Connect Shapes

By selecting View, Snapping, Snap to Objects (or clicking the magnet button in the Tools panel when the Arrow or Free Transform tool is active), you can draw perfectly round circles, perfectly horizontal or vertical lines, and much more. The visual clue that Snap to Objects is helping you is the dark ring that often appears next to your cursor while you drag. When you see that ring, you know Flash is trying to help you draw.

You might already know from using other software that holding the Shift key constrains your cursor similarly to Snap to Objects. But Snap to Objects can do much more. In addition to helping you draw perfect shapes, Snap to Objects also enables you to connect two shapes. It's much more than simply making two shapes touch— they actually become bonded. In Flash, unless two shapes have been snapped together, they might look connected when they actually aren't.

Animation Basics and Terminology

If you start using Flash without understanding the basics of animation, you might be a bit overwhelmed. To get a better grasp of how Flash tools work, you'll need to get a few definitions under your belt.

Frames and Frame Rate

At its most basic, animation is a series of still images. Each image is called a *frame*. In movies, frames are the individual pictures on the film itself. In Flash, frames are the little rectangular cells in the Timeline. They're numbered at the top of the Timeline, and every fifth frame is gray; the rest of the frames are white with a gray outline. The Timeline displays all the frames, but normally you can look at the contents of one frame at a time. (Later you'll see how the Onion Skin option can help you view multiple frames.) The red current-frame marker can be in only one place at a time—the frame you're currently viewing. You don't draw into a frame on the Timeline—you draw onto the stage. The current-frame marker indicates the frame whose contents are currently onscreen. Figure 9.12 shows the Timeline in its initial state. Until this movie's duration is extended, you can't move the red current-frame marker past Frame 1, and only Frame 1 is enclosed by a solid white box with a hollow circle.

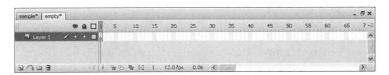

FIGURE 9.12
The Timeline, with its many cells, is initially only one frame long.

By default, a Timeline is initially one frame long. The current-frame marker is unmovable at that point because it can be placed only in a frame of an animation, and so far the animation has only one frame. When a longer animation is loaded (or created!), the timeline extends. The current-frame marker moves to where you click; be sure to click in the numbered area toward the top of the Timeline—not in the cells, otherwise you'd end up switching layers as well as the current frame.

Another timeline technique is to click and drag the current-frame marker in the number area. As you drag, you see a quick preview of the animation. This technique is called *scrubbing*. The preview you're given is dependent on how fast you scrub. Naturally, the frame rate is locked when the user watches an animation. If you select Control, Play or just press Enter, you see this animation play at its correct frame rate. To stop, press Enter again. You should also notice the status area near the bottom right of the Timeline. The three numbers are the current frame number, the frame rate, and the current time elapsed (see Figure 9.13).

FIGURE 9.13
The status area in the Timeline contains three important numbers related to timing.

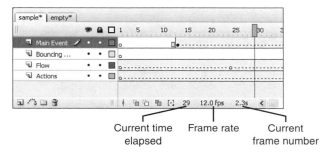

Current time elapsed　　Frame rate　　Current frame number

Frame rate is the rate at which frames are played back for the user, measured in frames per second (fps). A frame rate of 30 fps means that 30 frames are displayed every second. It is easy to confuse frame rate with speed, but they're not necessarily the same. If an entire animation uses 10 frames at 10 fps, it might look identical to the same movement using 20 frames if the frame rate is set to 20 fps. Both of these animations take 1 second to finish.

The current frame number (on the left) indicates the location of the red current-frame marker. It changes while you're playing or scrubbing, reflecting that you can be in only one frame at a time. The frame rate (the middle number) normally indicates the frame rate for the movie on which you are working. However, the number shown can be reduced if, after you play the movie, Flash estimates that it can't actually keep up with the requested frame rate. It's not entirely accurate, but it does provide a good estimate. Double-click this number to open the Document Properties dialog and adjust the Frame Rate field accordingly.

Current time (the third number) indicates how long it takes to reach the frame you're viewing from the start of the movie. For example, how long it takes an animation to play 50 frames depends on the frame rate. At 24 fps, it should take about 2 seconds. At 12 fps, it should take about 4 seconds. The duration of the movie is based on the frame rate.

Frame Rate Versus the Number of Frames

The numbers in the status area are very important. When you design an animation, you should pick a frame rate and stick to it. When you change the frame rate, you're changing it for the entire movie. For example, say I have an animation of a character walking, running, jumping, and sitting still for a few seconds. If the portion where he's walking is too slow and I try to speed it up by increasing the frame rate, that portion might look better. But then the character will run extra fast, his sitting time will go by more quickly—everything will be faster! It's best to leave the frame rate alone and find another way to increase the speed.

There are ways to change the effective speed. Suppose you have an animation of an airplane moving across the sky. You need to decide the effective speed of the airplane according to the size of the airplane and how much sky you're showing. If you move the airplane all the way across the screen in 36 frames, you can't determine whether that's the right speed unless you consider the frame rate. At 12 fps, the airplane takes 3 seconds to move across the sky.

Effective speed is how fast something seems to move. *Actual speed*, in comparison, is absolute and can be measured. If an animation uses 12 frames (at 12 fps), the elapsed time of 1 second is the animation's actual speed. The viewer's psychological impression determines effective speed. Therefore, you can use illusions to increase or decrease an animation's effective speed. If a lot of action and changes occur in those 12 frames, it's effectively fast. If only one slight change occurs, the effective speed is slow. If you extend the animation to take 240 frames, the airplane takes 20 seconds to complete the motion and effectively appears slow because very little is changing from frame to frame. You'll learn how to do these things later, but for now, it's only important to understand how the frame rate and the number of frames affect the effective and actual speeds.

Frame Rates of Different Types of Animation

To put the animation you're about to embark upon into perspective, let's compare some traditional animation media. In a motion picture, the frame rate at which the images appear is 24 fps. Even at this relatively slow rate, you don't notice the moments when the screen is black. Television plays at 30 fps.

In computer animation, the screen doesn't blink between frames, but you do have a choice about what frame rate to use. Technically, the user's monitor will flicker as much or as little as she has it set to flicker, but in any case, it will be much faster than an animation's frame rate. In computer animation, frame rate affects how frequently the onscreen graphic changes or, conversely, how long it pauses before advancing to the next frame. In practice, if you go much below Flash's default setting of 12 fps, your user will start to notice jumpiness, and if it's much higher than 36 fps, it might not perform well on all machines. Remember that traditional movies use 24 fps and look quite smooth.

It might seem that you should always crank up the frame rate as high as you can, which would address the problem of jumpiness. However, it's not that easy. First of all, more frames can mean that your movie has a bigger file size. Also, it often requires a computer that can display images quickly. If your user's machine can't keep up, it slows down the animation and makes it jumpy.

Keyframes and Blank Keyframes

A *keyframe* is simply a frame in which you establish exactly what should appear on the stage at a particular point. A keyframe might include an image, or it might be blank. A blank keyframe is still a keyframe; it's just one in which nothing appears on the stage.

In traditional film animation, every frame is a keyframe—that is, something new appears onscreen each frame. In Flash you can make every frame a keyframe, but you can also take some shortcuts. If the first keyframe occurs on Frame 1 and the next keyframe doesn't occur until Frame 10, there won't be any changes onscreen during Frames 2–9. The keyframe in Frame 1 establishes what will appear in Frame 1, and it doesn't change until the keyframe in Frame 10, which establishes what appears then. This is totally appropriate for something that doesn't need to change every fraction of a second.

Establishing a keyframe is simply a matter of clicking the cell in the Timeline exactly where you want a keyframe to occur. After you click a single cell in the Timeline, select Insert, Timeline, Keyframe (or, better yet, press F6). A couple things happen when you do this. Flash places a keyframe in that frame (indicated by either a solid or hollow circle), and it copies the stage content from the previous keyframe. If at the previous keyframe you have nothing on the stage, a blank keyframe is inserted. If at the previous keyframe you have something drawn on the stage, that shape or symbol instance is copied onto the stage at the new keyframe. This can be convenient because a keyframe gives you a chance to specify both when you want an onscreen change to occur and what the onscreen contents should change to. Often you want just a small change. Creating a keyframe enables you to start with a copy of the previous keyframe's content instead of redrawing it from scratch.

Whatever you draw in a keyframe continues to be displayed until the Timeline arrives at the next keyframe (blank or otherwise). If keyframes are placed one after another, the screen changes with every frame. If the frame rate is 10 fps, you see 10 keyframes in 1 second.

However, keyframes don't have to occur one after another. If you insert keyframes at alternating frames, changes appear five times per second (at 10 fps). For any frames between keyframes, you see the content of the previous keyframe, either an image or a blank screen. Say you want a box to appear onscreen and remain still for 1 second before it moves. In one keyframe you draw a box, and then 10 frames later (1 second at 10 fps) you insert a new keyframe in which you can move the box to a new location.

Tweening

You can put whatever you want in keyframes. The space between two keyframes effectively "holds" the onscreen contents from the first keyframe. Alternatively, you can tell Flash to interpolate the change in a process called *tweening*. For example, suppose that in one keyframe there is an airplane on the left of the stage. The next keyframe shows the airplane on the right side of the stage. Flash can calculate how to move the first image to the second.

Tweening smoothes out a big change by breaking it into little steps. If a circle at the bottom of the screen jumps to the top of the screen 1 second later (at 10 fps), the change appears abrupt. If the two frames are tweened, you see the circle move a little bit (about 1/10 of the total distance) 10 times. The coarse movement is smoothed out with small changes in the in-between frames. Flash calculates these tweened or interpolated frames so you don't have to do all the work.

Tweening really is as simple as drawing two frames and making Flash tween the difference. You'll learn more about tweening later in "Advanced Animation Through Tweening." For now, you just need to realize that Flash will help you by doing some of the tedious work.

Important Flash Document Properties

Now that you're ready to create a movie, you'll need to create a new Flash file, (File, New, Flash File [ActionScript 2.0]). You'll also need to specify a few far-reaching settings early in the creation of any movie. Most of these are found in the Document

Properties dialog box, shown in Figure 9.14, which you access by selecting Modify, Document or double-clicking the bottom of the Timeline (where you see 12.0 fps). You should access the Document Properties dialog box now so you can experiment with a few of its settings. (Notice that most of the same settings appear in the Properties panel if you click the stage or otherwise deselect all objects.)

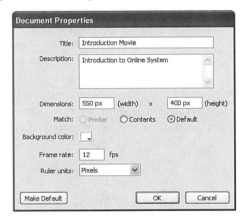

First of all, you need to ensure that Ruler Units is set to Pixels. This is the standard unit of measurement in multimedia and web pages. It's important to set Ruler Units to Pixels because this affects several other dialog boxes (including the Info panel). Next to Background Color, you should see a white swatch that, when clicked, enables you to change the stage color. This isn't actually as useful as you might think because at the time you publish a movie to the Web, you can specify any background color you want and it overrides this setting. Feel free to change the background color any time you want. Maybe gray will be easier on your eyes, or black will make selecting white graphics easier. I often use a bright red background just so it's super clear while I'm editing. Do whatever you want—not only can you change this setting later, but it also affects only the stage color while you're editing.

Two other Document Properties dialog box settings are important to establish early in any project: Frame Rate and Dimensions. Frame Rate specifies the rate—that is, how many frames per second—at which Flash *attempts* to play. I say *attempts* because some of your users might not have a computer fast enough to keep up, so Flash just can't display the specified number of frames in a second. Flash will not exceed the frame rate you specify, but it could get bogged down and not keep up. Dimensions are only important to the degree that they affect the aspect ratio of your stage, as discussed at the start of the chapter, in "The Stage." You need to decide up front on the shape for your stage (sorry, it can't be round). Do you want a wide-screen CinemaScope look, or do you want a square stage? You might even want a vertical rectangle if, for instance, you were building a button bar to appear on the left side of a web page. You need to consider this early on because the stage shape influences how you position graphics and changing it later makes for a lot of repositioning.

People often confuse frame rate with speed, which is more of a visual effect. Animators can use tricks to make something appear to speed across the screen even while using a very low frame rate. For example, if you see a picture of a car on the left side of the screen and then a fraction of a second later, it's on the right side of the screen, which can tell your brain that the car is moving fast. However, such a trick requires only two frames—and at a frame rate of 4 fps, the second frame appears only a quarter second after the first! Frame rate—that is, how many chunks into which each second is broken—controls the visual resolution. Four frames per second can look "chunky"—each change occurs only four times per second. However, 30 fps (equivalent to the frame rate of TV) is such a fine increment that you're not likely to see the steps between discrete frames (although, of course, that's what's really happening). By the way, you can still move a car across the screen in a quarter of a second by using 60 fps—it would just involve 15 frames.

Simple Frame Animations and Tools

As a beginning animator, one of the easiest things for you to do is create a frame-by-frame animation. If you've ever made a flip-book, you already know how to make a frame-by-frame animation. Each page in a flip-book contains a slightly different image so that when you fan through all the pages, the image is animated. That's basically what you can do in Flash. However, instead of drawing something different on each page of a book, you simply draw a different image in each keyframe of the Flash Timeline. This is a very involved form of animation because it doesn't use any of the features like tweening built into Flash.

Imagine that you want to make a walking stick figure. This is done, quite literally, by drawing each frame of the walking animation.

You could accomplish this easily by following these steps:

1. Draw a stick man by using only lines.

2. Single-click just to the right of the keyframe dot in Frame 1 of Layer 1—that is, click in the second frame of Layer 1.

3. Select Insert, Timeline, Keyframe to insert a keyframe in Frame 2 with a copy of the stick man graphic.

4. Make sure that you are editing Frame 2. You should see the red current-frame marker in Frame 2. If it's not there, click in Frame 2 of the Timeline.

5. Make a slight change to the figure, such as bending a leg of the stick man slightly or changing an arm position to look like it's swinging.

6. To preview what you have so far, use the scrub technique. Grab the red current-frame marker and drag it back and forth.

7. To create the third frame, click in Layer 1 right after Frame 2 and select Insert, Timeline, Keyframe to copy the contents of Frame 2 into the new keyframe in Frame 3.

8. Make another slight change to the figure. You now have three frames of animation.

9. Continue to insert keyframes, one at a time. Make an edit to each new frame to keep the arms and legs moving.

This can continue for as long as you want. Keep in mind that Disney's traditional animators made feature-length movies like this!

Previewing an Animation by Using Test Movie

There are three ways to watch an entire animation: scrubbing, playing, and testing. Scrubbing the red current-frame marker is a good way to preview as you work. The only problem with scrubbing is that the speed isn't consistent—it is only as smooth as you scrub. To play an animation, you select Control, Play; use the Play option on the Controller toolbar; or press Enter. However, as you'll see later (when creating buttons the user can click, special effects layers such as masks, and animating using movie clips), playing a movie doesn't always show you *exactly* what your viewers will see, so I strongly recommend that you avoid previewing by using Play. The best way to view an animation is by selecting Control, Test Movie.

Test Movie exports a .swf file into the folder where your file is saved, names this file the same as your file but with a .swf extension, and then launches the Flash Player program so you can view the results. You'll see how this works when you first save your source .fla file into a new, empty folder. After you use Test Movie, the folder contains an additional .swf file.

Editing One Keyframe at a Time

The frame-by-frame animation technique is simple. You just put a keyframe on each frame. An entirely different image appears on each frame—sometimes drastically different, sometimes only slightly different. The beauty is that you can put anything you want in one keyframe because it doesn't matter what's in the other keyframes.

Although frame-by-frame animation is a simple concept, it can be a lot of work. Imagine conventional animation, in which an artist must draw each frame even when only a slight change is necessary. It's detailed, meticulous work and, unfortunately, it's not really any easier in Flash, although Flash provides functions such as Undo that help. You need to realize that this technique is for situations that require it—such as when you're working with something that has lots of details, such as an animation of someone walking. No other Flash animation technique gives you this level of control to change each frame.

Using the Frame View Settings

Just because frame-by-frame animation is a lot of work doesn't mean you can't use a little help. One way to make the process a little easier is by changing the Frame View setting. In Figure 9.15 you can see the Timeline pop-up menu. If you select Preview, each frame in the Timeline is displayed as it appears on the stage. Figure 9.15 shows an animation with Frame View set to Preview. Preview lets you see all the frames of the animation without actually stepping through them. The Preview in Context setting draws the preview in the correct proportions (including blank whitespace).

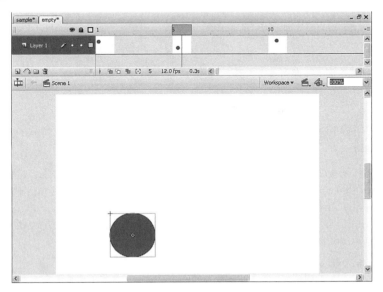

FIGURE 9.15
The Frame View pop-up menu is available to change the size and character of the Timeline. You can make each frame larger or include a visual preview of the contents of the stage in each frame.

Using the Onion Skin Tools

Some of the greatest helpers for frame-by-frame animations are Flash's Onion Skin tools. Flash's Onion Skin feature allows you to edit one keyframe while viewing as many frames before or after the current frame as you want.

Click the Onion Skin button (second from the left) at the bottom of the Timeline (see Figure 9.16). Select Large from the Timeline's pop-up menu. With Onion Skin turned on, you can place the red current-frame marker on any frame you want and edit that frame, and then you see a dim view of the other frames in the animation. Which frames appear depends on where you position the Start Onion Skin and End Onion Skin markers. These markers can be difficult to grab when you try to move them; I often find myself accidentally grabbing the current-frame marker. It's easiest to grab the markers when Timeline View is set to Large.

FIGURE 9.16
When Onion Skin is turned on, you can see the contents of adjacent frames.

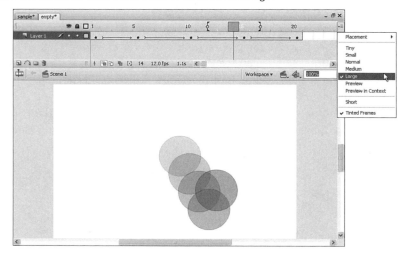

You would probably turn on Onion Skin while creating an animation (instead of after it's done).

To change how many frames are seen at a time, you can move the Start and End Onion Skin markers. By default, the markers are set to Onion 2, meaning you can see two frames ahead and two behind. You can move the markers to several preset positions from the Modify Onion Markers pop-up menu (the rightmost Onion Skin button at the bottom left of the Timeline).

Modify Onion Markers has several preset options:

▶ **Always Show Markers**—This option leaves a faint version of the markers visible in the Timeline even after you turn off Onion Skin.

▶ **Anchor Onion**—This option locks the two markers where they are, no matter where the red current-frame marker is.

▶ **Onion 2**—This option sets the markers to two frames ahead and two frames behind.

▶ **Onion 5**—This option sets the markers to five frames ahead and five frames behind.

▶ **Onion All**—This option moves the Start Onion Skin Marker to Frame 1 and the End Onion Skin Marker to your last frame.

Before we finish with Onion Skin, let's look at two remaining features: Onion Skin Outlines and Edit Multiple Frames (found immediately to the right of the Onion Skin button). You can choose either Onion Skin or Onion Skin Outlines, but not both. Onion Skin Outlines displays the other frames within the Onion markers as outlines instead of as dim images. Outlines can be helpful when the dim view makes images difficult to distinguish.

Edit Multiple Frames is quite interesting. In the previous example, you used onion skinning to see the contents of surrounding keyframes, but you were editing only one frame at a time—the current frame. You could move the stick man's leg close to the faded image in the previous frame without affecting the previous frame. Edit Multiple Frames lets you edit the contents of all the frames within the Start Onion Skin and End Onion Skin markers. Generally, Edit Multiple Frames is useful for editing a finished animation rather than for creating an animation because it is difficult to narrow your focus to a single frame. However, when you want to return to an animation and move the contents of every frame, Edit Multiple Frames is invaluable. In this situation, you just turn on Edit Multiple Frames, select Modify Onion Markers, Onion All, select everything on the stage (or press Ctrl+A), and move everything anywhere you want.

Incorporating Pauses

There's no rule that says you *must* put a keyframe in every frame. If your frame rate is left at the default 12 frames per second (fps) and every frame is a keyframe, the image changes 12 times per second. This might be unnecessary, and it becomes a lot of work when you consider the total number of frames you must draw. What if you don't always want the images to change every 1/12 second? Incorporating pauses is the answer—and it's very easy.

To incorporate a pause, you just follow a keyframe with a non-keyframe frame. If you want a 1-second pause (and you're running at 12 fps), you just follow your keyframe with 12 frames.

There are two ways to create pauses, either as you're making an animation or after you've made one. To incorporate a pause while creating an animation, you either insert a keyframe or insert frames (by pressing F5 or selecting Insert, Timeline, Frame) farther down the Timeline than the next frame.

Creating a pause is slightly different when you want to edit an animation you've already created. To insert a pause (or increase one that already exists), you click the keyframe you want to pause and select Insert, Frame. This effectively pushes out everything that appears later in the Timeline.

Advanced Animation Through Tweening

Creating an animation frame-by-frame can be a lot of work because you have to draw every frame yourself. With tweening, Flash fills in the blank frames between two keyframes. Flash has two types of tweening: motion tweening and shape tweening. Motion tweening animates clip properties such as location, scale, rotation, color, and alpha values. Shape tweening morphs one shape into another.

By the Way

The alpha value of an object is also known as its opacity or transparency. Tweening can make solid objects become transparent and vice versa by changing this value over time.

A basic motion tween is very easy to produce. For example, try animating a circle, making it move across the stage smoothly with only two keyframes:

1. In a new file, draw a circle on the stage.

2. Select the entire circle and choose Modify, Convert to Symbol (or press F8). Name it something appropriate, such as Circle, leave the type set to the default Movie Clip, and click OK.

3. Click 30 or more frames down in the Timeline and select Insert, Timeline, Keyframe.

4. Click on the keyframe in Frame 1; the red current-frame marker moves to Frame 1. Position the circle on the left side of the stage.

5. Click in the last keyframe and notice that the red current-frame marker moves to that frame. Position the circle on the right side of the stage.

6. Try scrubbing. The animation looks pretty abrupt. The circle stays on the left side for 29 frames and then jumps to the right side. To make the movement smoother, you can use tweening to have Flash take care of the in-between frames.

7. Set tweening in the beginning keyframe, in this case in Frame 1. Select the keyframe in Frame 1 and then observe the Properties panel. When a frame is selected, the Properties panel contains a Tween pop-up menu.

8. Select Motion from the Tween pop-up menu. Leave all the default settings, as shown in Figure 9.17. That's all you do! Notice in Figure 9.18 that Flash has drawn a blue background and arrow in the Timeline to represent the interpolated frames—those between two keyframes.

9. Select Control, Test Movie (or press (Cmd-Enter) [Ctrl+Enter]) to see what happens.

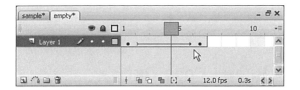

You should, at this point, see how multiple keyframes with tweening could be used to create complex animations using the full suite of Flash graphics tools. In this example, we discussed a bouncing ball, but the complexity is up to you. Let's look at some more things we can do with tweening.

Tweening More than Position

Each symbol you use from your library is a separate instance. Instances can be positioned in different locations, scaled to different sizes, rotated differently, and have their color effects set differently. There are six ways in which instances can be varied: position, scale, rotation, skew, color, and alpha. Flash can tween changes in all these properties.

Skewing an image is also referred to as "shearing." When an image is skewed, the sides remain parallel, but become angled. A rectangle that is skewed, for example, would appear to angle into or out of the screen.

By the Way

Alpha Tweens Affect Performance

Although you can tween the Position, Scale, Rotation, and Alpha effects, it doesn't mean you have to. The Alpha effect forces your audience's computers to work a bit harder because it must take into account how artwork behind an object looks as seen through. The message you're trying to communicate might be overlooked when the user notices everything slowing down to a crawl. I don't want to suggest that you should never tween alpha, but it's the most processor-intensive effect available, and sometimes you can simulate the same effect in other ways. Consider tweening based on the Brightness color effect. If the background is white anyway, this is visually no different from using alpha, but it doesn't slow down the computer as much.

A Motion Tween Shortcut

Because you'll likely use motion tweens a lot, there's a great shortcut to know. Just right-click your starting keyframe (on a Macintosh with a single-button mouse, use Control+click), and then select the Create Motion Tween option from the list that pops up.

Using Ease In and Ease Out

A problem with letting Flash do tweening for you is that the result looks like a computer did it—it's almost too perfect. For example, the bouncing ball from the preceding example moves down at the same rate as it moves up, and the entire animation plays at the same rate.

Flash has a way to address the fact that some kinds of motion accelerate while others decelerate: the Ease In and Ease Out effects. Because every tween is between only two keyframes, you only have to think of two keyframes at a time. *Easing in* (think "ease into animation") means that the motion starts off slow and speeds up at the end. *Easing out* is the opposite—the object starts by going fast and then slows down at the end of its motion.

To add an Ease In effect, just select the first keyframe in a tween animation, then, within the Properties panel, set the Ease slider (a good starting value is 50). Repeat this same action with the final keyframe in the tween animation to ease out of the animation.

To create even more complex ease effects, click the Edit button to the right of the Ease setting and you can graphically edit the acceleration curve of the ease animation.

Making a Shape Tween

Shape tweens are fun because they look really cool and they're easy to create. Compared to motion tweens, they look more dynamic because every attribute—including the shape—animates. Basically, all you do is draw a shape or shapes in two keyframes and set the tweening in the first keyframe to Shape. For example:

1. In a new file, draw a circle on the stage in Frame 1. (No need to convert anything to a symbol because the object changes in every frame anyway.)

2. Insert a keyframe later in the Timeline. This will be the end of the tween, and it will match the beginning. Select this frame.

3. Delete the circle and draw a square.

4. Return to the first keyframe and set Tween in the Properties Panel to Shape.

5. Run the movie and you'll see the circle smoothly transform itself into a square! Cool, huh?

Importing Graphics, Sounds, and Movies

It's rare that all of the content you want to include in a Flash file will be generated entirely in Flash. You might want to include external graphics, sounds, or even embed entire movies. Each of these tasks is performed in a very similar manner, and we'll look at this process now.

Importing Graphics

You've seen how you can create sophisticated custom graphics very quickly in Flash. Despite how powerful Flash's graphic creation tools are, eventually you might want to import graphics created elsewhere. Two good reasons for this are to use photographic images or use existing graphics (instead of re-creating them from scratch).

Importing from a File

The easiest way to incorporate other graphics into Flash is to import them from a file. It's as simple as selecting File, Import, Import to Stage (or Import to Library, if you want the graphic to be available in the Library, but *not* added to your current scene).

Choose All Image Formats from the Files of Type pop-up menu (it's called Enable in the Mac OS version of Flash). This enables you to browse your file system, showing only the files that Flash can successfully import.

Depending on the file type you choose, additional options may be available to you. With Illustrator documents, for example, you can turn pages into keyframes or scenes. Flash just needs to know how you want to handle pages. All the options are fairly easy to interpret and can be controlled during the import process.

Did you Know?

> For bitmap graphics (photos, for example), importing to the stage not only places the graphic on the stage but also puts a master item into the Library. If you import a graphic and then delete the object from the stage, the master will still be in the Library.

Converting a Bitmap to a Vector Graphic

Drawing applications, Flash included, typically deal with one of two types of graphics—vector or bitmap. Vector graphics are defined by their shape rather than a group of pixels—these graphics are usually illustrations or technical drawings. Bitmap graphics, on the other hand, are defined by setting colors for a group of pixels—one at a time. Bitmap graphics are what you get when you take a picture with your digital camera, for example.

If you import a bitmap graphic into Flash, you'll find that you don't have as many options as you do with vector formats. You can't zoom in without the object getting fuzzy, and you can't resize or reshape it cleanly. You may also be limited in the effects that can be applied to the graphic.

Flash provides a built-in tool to convert a bitmap to a vector graphic. To do this, select the object and select Modify, Bitmap, Trace Bitmap. The Trace Bitmap dialog box appears, shown in Figure 9.19.

FIGURE 9.19
Use the Trace Bitmap tool to vectorize an image.

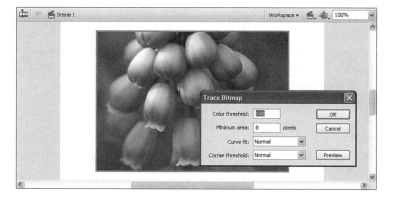

The Trace Bitmap dialog box has several options:

▶ **Color Threshold**—When you're tracing an image, Flash tries to lump areas of the bitmap into single shapes. The Color Threshold option specifies how different two colors can be (in RGB values) and still be considered the same. If you set this option to a high number, you end up with fewer colors and fewer areas.

▶ **Minimum Area**—This option specifies the smallest area Flash will create. For a very detailed image, this number should be set rather low, unless you want a mosaic effect.

▶ **Curve Fit**—This option affects how closely straight and curved areas will be copied. Using the Very Smooth end of the Curve Fit scale is like having a very large pen with which to draw a shape in one quick movement. If you could use a fine pencil and as many strokes as needed, that would be like the other extreme, Pixels or Very Tight.

▶ **Corner Threshold**—This option determines whether corners are left alone or removed.

Click OK (or Preview to see what's going to happen), and within a few seconds, a vector version of the image appears in your stage. Keep in mind that the original graphic is still in the Library if you need to go back to it!

Importing Sounds

Two basic steps are involved in getting audio into a Flash movie. First, you need to import the sound. Then, you need to decide where and how to use it. This is similar to importing graphics. When you import a sound, it's stored in the Library like an imported bitmap. But a sound is not quite a symbol. Rather, the item in the Library contains all the individual properties of the particular sound.

Flash can import digital audio in a variety of file formats, including the popular MP3 and WAV formats.

Importing from a File

As with the graphic formats we looked at earlier, select File, Import, Import to Stage. Choose All Sound Formats from the Files of Type pop-up and then select an audio file to import.

After you select an audio file and click OK in the Import dialog box, you won't see (or hear) anything different. However, the sound has been imported and now resides in the Library. Just open the Library panel to see it. Now that the movie contains the sound file, you can use the sound.

Using Sounds

Now that you've imported sounds into a movie, you can explore how to make them play at the correct times. There's really only one place you can use sounds in Flash: in keyframes. (One exception is adding sounds dynamically by using the Sound object in the ActionScript language.) If you want a sound to play whenever the user places his or her cursor over a button, you still need to place the sound in a keyframe—it's just a keyframe in the button.

Now that you know sounds go in keyframes, you need a way to put them there. When you select a keyframe, the Properties panel provides a way to control what sounds play when you reach the selected keyframe. Flash provides other clues for you to "see" where sounds have been placed. For example, if your Timeline is long enough, you'll see a waveform (a picture of a sound) for the sounds being used.

However, using the Properties panel is the best way to see which sounds have been added to which keyframes. But just like any other panel, the Properties panel displays only the sound used in the *selected* keyframe.

Sync Settings

When you have the Properties panel reflecting sound for the intended keyframe, you can decide exactly how the sound should play. The most fundamental choice you need to make for each use of a sound is its Sync setting. This controls exactly how a particular instance of the sound will play—or, more specifically, the priority of the sound compared to the visual elements in the animation.

▶ **Event**—This is the default setting and, generally, the best performance choice, especially for sound effects and other incidental sounds. When Event is chosen, sounds will start to play when the keyframe is reached and keep playing until they're done. Event sounds might not coincide with visual elements the same way on everyone's machine. Sounds don't play more slowly or quickly (that would make them sound funny), but a machine with slower graphics performance might take longer to display visual elements.

▶ **Start**—This setting is almost the same as Event, except that multiple instances of the same sound are prevented. With Event, a sound can be layered on top of itself, similar to singing a round. Start, on the other hand, plays a sound if it's not already playing.

▶ **Stop**—This setting is a bit different—it's for when you want a specified sound to stop playing. For example, if you import a sound called Background Music and have it playing (by whatever means), when a keyframe is encountered that has the same sound (Background Music) set to Stop, just that sound will stop. Any other sounds already playing will continue. This can be confusing because you use the Properties panel to specify the sound (just as when you want the sound to play), but you specify it as the particular sound you want to stop. Think of Stop as "stop this sound if it's playing."

▶ **Stream**—This setting causes the sound to remain perfectly synchronized with the Timeline. Because, again, you can't have sounds playing slowly if the user's machine can't draw frames quickly enough, with this setting, Flash will skip frames to keep up. Stream sounds start playing when the first frame is reached and continue to play as long as there is space in the Timeline.

Effect Settings

The Properties panel provides some fancy effects you can apply to a selected sound. In the pop-up menu next to Effect are effects such as Fade In and Fade Out, as well as Fade Left to Right and Fade Right to Left. To understand and customize these settings further, you can either select Custom from the list or click the Edit button on the Properties panel to access the Edit Envelope dialog box, shown in Figure 9.20, which lets you select from prebuilt panning effects or create your own.

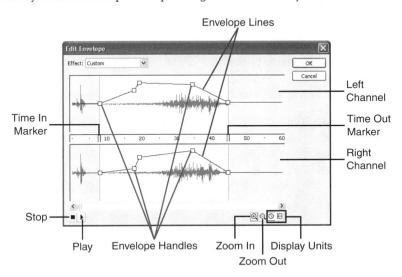

FIGURE 9.20
Create your own effects to apply to sounds.

Here are additional details for the Effect settings that you can modify in the Edit Envelope dialog box:

▶ **Left Channel/Right Channel**—These panes display different wave forms if your original sound was stereo. Even if you use only mono sounds, you'll get the left and right channels so you can still create panning effects. In the case of mono, the same sounds will come out of each speaker—you'll just be able to modify the volume of each.

▶ **Envelope lines**—These indicate the volume level at any particular time in the sound. When the line is at the top, the sound plays at full 100% volume. (Some audio tools are different because they use the middle to indicate 100% and anything higher to indicate amplified or boosted sound, but this is not the case in Flash.) If the envelope line is getting higher as you move to the right, the volume will increase.

▶ **Envelope handles**— These are like keyframes within sound. If you want the envelope lines (indicating volume) to change direction, you need to insert a handle. All you need to do is click anywhere on a line, and a handle will be inserted. No matter which channel you click, a matching handle is placed in the other channel. A handle in one channel must match the moment in time (left to right) of the handle in the other channel. However, the volume (height) can vary between the two.

▶ **Time In marker**—This marker lets you establish the starting point of a sound. You're effectively trimming the extra sound (or silence) at the beginning of the sound file. You're not telling the sound to start any later, but the sound you hear will begin wherever the Time In marker is placed.

▶ **Time Out marker**—This marker lets you trim extra sound off the end of a sound file. Often you'll have a moment of silence at the end of a sound file, and even if you don't hear anything, it still adds to the file size. You can get rid of it by moving the Time Out marker to the left. You won't actually destroy the source sound in your Library, but when you export the movie, the unused portions of the sound won't be used (so your file stays small).

▶ **Stop/Play**—This option lets you preview all the settings you've made. This is important because although the waveform can let you "see" a sound, you ultimately want to judge the effect of a sound with your ears.

▶ **Zoom In/Out**—This option lets you zoom out so a large portion of the sound (130 seconds max) fits in the current window or zoom in for a close up to control precisely how you place the Time In/Out markers or envelope handles.

▶ **Display Units (Time or Frames)**—This option simply changes the units displayed (in the center portion) from time units (seconds) to frame units. Time is not as useful as frames when you want to match sound to a particular frame (where something visual occurs). If the display shows a peak in the music at one second, you have to use frame rate to calculate exactly to which frame that translates. With the display set to Frames, Flash does the calculations for you.

Loop Settings

The Properties panel has an option to either let you specify how many times a sound repeats or have the sound loop forever.

Some sounds loop better than others. Basically, a sound that loops well ends the same way it starts. There's an art to making sounds loop. Although importing a large song and using the Time In and Time Out markers to establish a nice looping sound is possible, it isn't easy. More likely, you'll have to find a sound already prepared by an audio engineer. A professionally prepared sound can loop so seamlessly that you can listen to it and not even notice it's looping; it will just sound like it's endless.

Importing Video

In the not-too-distant past it was impossible to find a website that could display video and ensure that the majority of your viewers could see it. With the inclusion of video support in Flash and the advent of services like YouTube, that has obviously changed.

Importing from a File

Importing video into Flash is really no more involved than importing other media types, such as sound or graphics. It really is as easy as selecting File, Import, Import to Stage (or Library), and then selecting a video.

Again, as with the sound and graphic files, you can limit your selection to supported video types by choosing All Video Formats from the Files of Type/Enable pop-up menu.

You probably are wondering about the Import Video selection under the File menu's Import submenu. Don't worry, this is just another way to get to the same place we are already.

After you've selected the video file and clicked OK, the first of a four-step Video Import dialog box appears, asking where the video file is located. Chances are, you've already picked the file so you can immediately click Next, as seen in Figure 9.21. If you want to use a file off of a remote server, you can click the Already Deployed radio button and provide a URL to the remote video.

FIGURE 9.21
Import your video from your computer or a remote site.

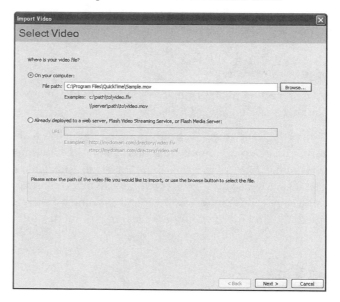

In the second step, seen in Figure 9.22, you choose how you will be deploying the video. You can choose to deploy it as everything from a standalone progressive download from a web server; to a streaming service, such as YouTube; to Flash-supported mobile devices; or you can embed the video in your existing Flash file for playback in the Timeline. This option is probably what you want, unless you're simply interested in creating standalone video files.

By the Way

When you use a QuickTime movie, you can choose to link the video—this does not embed the video and is likely not what you want.

Assuming you're embedding the video, click Next to access the Embedding settings, shown in Figure 9.23.

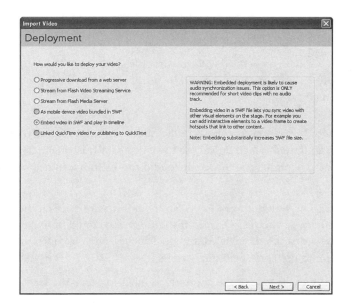

FIGURE 9.22
Choose your deployment method.

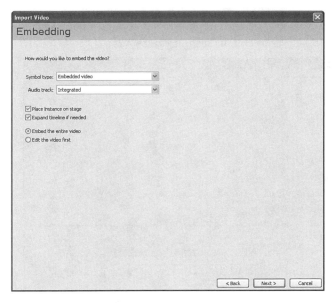

FIGURE 9.23
Choose how the file will be embedded into your Flash project.

Three primary symbol types can be used for embedded video:

▶ **Embedded Video**—Ties the movie to your existing Timeline. This is most likely the embedding type you want.

▶ **Movie Clip**—Movie clips maintain their own internal timeline that is separate from the main Flash Timeline.

▶ **Graphic**—Movies embedded with the graphic symbol type cannot be manipulated with ActionScript (which we'll be using shortly). This is probably *not* the option you want.

You are also given the option of importing the audio track as integrated or separate. An integrated audio track is tied directly to the video as it was when it was imported. If you choose to separate the tracks, the audio can be manipulated independently of the video.

If you want to choose which part of the video to import, click the Edit the Video First radio button, otherwise choose to Embed the entire video. You'll probably find that it's easiest to use a dedicated movie editing package to edit your video prior to importing it than to use Flash's editing options.

Click Next (Continue on Mac OS) to continue to the final step. The last step in the import process lets you set video compression as well as other advanced settings, such as cropping. Although there are dozens of settings, the easiest approach to this part of the process is to choose an appropriate profile using the Flash Video Encoding Profiles pop-up menu, as seen in Figure 9.24.

FIGURE 9.24
Use profiles to quickly pick an appropriate compression setting.

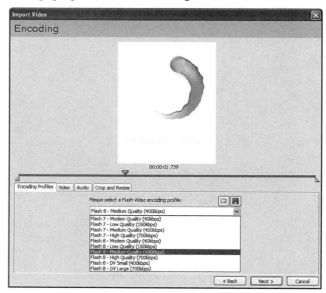

The higher the quality of the profile, the more bandwidth the client will need to display the video smoothly.

Click Next/Continue to finish the import process. It may take several minutes to import your video, depending on the size. After it is complete, you should be back in Flash, with the video you just imported in your Library (or, depending on your selection, already on the stage).

Using Video

To embed a video, you can drag videos from the Library to the stage. If the video exceeds the current length of the Timeline, you'll see a dialog box that asks if you want to extend the Timeline to accommodate the video's total number of frames.

There is a penalty in both file size and performance for using video. If your users are going to be viewing the material over slow connections, incorporating video might not be the best option.

In addition, most of the interesting things you can do with video require some level of ActionScript—such as programmatically starting and stopping video, playing video after certain actions, and so on. Although we'll look briefly at this topic in the section "Using ActionScript and Behaviors to Create Nonlinear Movies," comprehensive ActionScript is beyond the scope of this book.

Creating Buttons for Interactive Animations

You've learned how to create basic drawings and simple animations in Flash, so we can move on to what's possibly the most compelling attribute of Flash: interactivity. A plain linear animation can be quite powerful on its own. When you add interactivity, though, the users are engaged. They become part of the movie. In this section and the next, you'll learn how to add interactivity to movies.

The most straightforward way to add interactivity is by adding buttons. This way, users can click buttons when they feel like interacting—maybe they want to stop and start an animation at will. Or maybe you would like them to be able to skip ahead past an introduction animation.

Making a Button

Creating a button is no more difficult than making a new symbol and choosing a button behavior. To do this, draw any shape you want. Click Modify, Convert to

Symbol and, when prompted (as shown in Figure 9.25), provide a name for the button and select the button type.

FIGURE 9.25
Buttons are
surprisingly
easy to create.

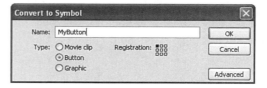

If you test your movie, you'll notice that your mouse cursor now changes when you place it over the button.

Making a button looks easy, doesn't it? Even though you did make a button in the preceding task, it probably falls short of your expectations in two general ways: It doesn't look like a button and it doesn't act like a button. (Currently nothing happens if you click the button while testing the movie.) We'll address the issue of making the button *do* something in the next section, "Using ActionScript and Behaviors to Create Nonlinear Movies." For now, though, let's look at how the button itself can be made more interactive.

Setting Button States

To work with buttons, you must first understand the states that a button can have: Up, Over, Down, and Hit.

The up state contains the visual look of the button in its normal state. Over contains the look for when the user hovers his cursor over the button. Down is how the button looks when the user clicks it. Hit is a special state in which you place a visual representation of what portion of the button you intend to be clickable. This is what the user must "hit" in order to see the over and down states.

Follow these steps to create states for the button:

1. Open the Library panel and double-click the button you created. You're now in the master version of the button symbol.

2. You should also notice that this symbol has four frames named Up, Over, Down, and Hit (see Figure 9.26). They are still four frames—they just all have names. Into each frame, you can draw how you want the button to appear for various states.

FIGURE 9.26
Inside the button symbol are four named frames.

Did you Know?

Buttons can trigger sounds! There are several ways to include sounds in buttons. In the simplest form, a sound can be placed in any of the button state keyframes. For a sound to occur when the user's cursor goes over a button, for example, just put a sound in the over state. Ultimately, however, to create complicated sounds and effects, you need to learn about ActionScript.

Defining a Button's Hit State

The hit state is never visibly seen by the user. It defines where the user must position her cursor to show a button's over state or where she must click to see the button's down state. Imagine that you had a doughnut-shaped button. If you didn't set a hit state, the user wouldn't be allowed to click anywhere in the hole. However, if you inserted a keyframe and drew a solid circle (no doughnut hole) in the Hit frame, the user could click anywhere within the solid circle. This can also be useful when you want a small button but you don't want to frustrate the user by requiring her to have the precision of a surgeon. You should strive to make the hit state big enough to easily click even if that means that it's bigger than the button itself.

Did you Know?

Dozens of premade buttons can be added to your project by dragging and dropping from the Buttons panel found in the Common Libraries group, accessed by choosing Window, Common Libraries, Buttons from the menu bar.

Using ActionScript and Behaviors to Create Nonlinear Movies

Flash's programming language is called *ActionScript*. Like any programming language, ActionScript lets you write instructions that your movie will follow. Without ActionScript, your movie will play the same way every time. If you want the user to be able to stop and start the movie, for example, you need ActionScript.

By the Way

The scripts that we will be looking at are ActionScript 2.0 compatible. As a Flash beginner, you should use ActionScript 2.0 rather than 3.0 until you are familiar with the scripting process and ready to work in a more advanced environment.

The topic of scripting is very deep. We can't cover it all in this book. Rather, we'll cover the basic concept as well as look at typical applications for scripting. This way, you'll build a good foundation on which to grow at your own pace. If you want to learn more about ActionScript, you may want to look at *Sams Teach Yourself Flash MX ActionScript in 24 Hours.*

Scripting is nothing more than writing instructions. Each instruction tells Flash to do something very specific. For example, it tells Flash to "play," "stop," or "set that movie clip's alpha to 50%." By keeping each piece of ActionScript very specific, you can easily piece together more advanced instructions. But at the core, each "sentence" (or line of code) is a single instruction.

The Actions Panel

All your ActionScript is typed into the Actions panel. Open the Actions panel and follow along as we explore. Select Window, Actions, and make sure you fully expand the panel, as seen in Figure 9.27.

FIGURE 9.27
The Actions panel has several components.

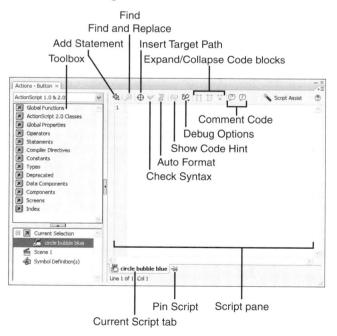

The Actions panel has the following features:

▶ **Toolbox**—The Toolbox list provides access to all installed actions. It is organized like folders.

▶ **Script pane**—In the Script pane, your actions appear in order of execution.

▶ **Current Script tab**—The Current Script tab indicates which script is currently being edited. Compare this to how the Properties panel shows you the currently selected instance.

▶ **Pin Script**—The Pin Script button adds a tab for a particular script so you don't have to first select the object or layer into which you want to add a script. Normally, the Actions panel acts like other panels—always reflecting the settings for the currently selected item (in this case, the script for the selected keyframe or object, such as a button).

▶ **Options toolbar**—The Options toolbar includes the following buttons:

 ▶ **Add Statement**—This button, which I call the "plus button" throughout the rest of this book, pops up a menu that provides the same script elements found in the Toolbox. The menu also shows the key combination for each script that has one.

 ▶ **Find and Find and Replace**— These buttons let you search scripts as you would in a word processing program.

 ▶ **Insert Target Path**—This button helps you address specific objects, such as particular clips. You'll learn that scripts can apply to individual clips (say you want to play or stop just one clip—you have to target that particular clip). This button helps you specify a target clip.

 ▶ **Check Syntax**—This button ensures that your ActionScript has no errors. (This won't guarantee that the movie will behave as you had in mind—only that you have no show-stopping errors.)

 ▶ **Auto Format**—This button cleans up your code by adding indentation where appropriate. This makes it much easier to read.

 ▶ **Show Code Hint**—This button retriggers the code-completion helper that appears as a ToolTip to help you complete ActionScript (when Flash knows what you're about to type).

 ▶ **Debug Options**—This button enables you to add and remove *break points*—where you purposefully make Flash pause on a specified line of code so you can investigate how it's playing (or, most likely, not playing the way you expected). You can also add and remove breakpoints by clicking in the gutter to the left of any line of code. You'll see a red dot appear to the left of the line of code.

▶ **Expand/Collapse Code Blocks**—Expand and collapse related chunks of code to clean up the display.

▶ **Comment Code**—Add and remove comments from blocks of ActionScript code.

Syntax is unique to each programming language. Every piece of ActionScript has a very specific syntax that must be followed. As an analogy, consider how every email address has to have the form *name*@*domain*.*something* or it won't work. Flash has no mercy for invalid syntax—you'll see errors appear in the Output window until you resolve the errors. Even after you perfect the script, the movie might not play exactly as you had in mind. Luckily, there are plenty of ways to ensure that your scripts have perfect syntax.

You can easily add an action from the Toolbox by double-clicking or dragging it to the right side of the Actions panel (the Script pane). You can build a complex set of instructions, one line at a time. A *statement* is a code sentence that uses only words from the ActionScript language.

Again, *actions* are instructions. Flash will follow each line of code in sequence. Some actions are complete pieces of instruction, with no additional modifications on your part. For example, you can add a `stop` action, and when Flash encounters it, the playback head will stop advancing. However, many actions require that you provide additional details (called *parameters*). For example, the action `gotoAndPlay` (which goes to a frame and starts playing) requires that you provide the additional detail about to which frame number or frame label you want to go.

Specifying Actions and Using Parameters

The easiest way to understand ActionScript is by performing some actions and using parameters. You'll see that some actions are quite simple. The following example is a quick exercise that uses actions and parameters to make the last few frames of an animation loop. After you complete it, we'll step back to analyze what you did in the example:

1. In a new file, use the Text tool to create a text block containing the word *Welcome*. Make sure the text type is Static in the Properties panel. Select the block and convert it to a symbol. Make it a movie clip and name it Welcome Text.

2. Position the movie clip instance in the center of the screen, and insert one keyframe at Frame 20 and another at Frame 30.

3. Move the current-frame marker to Frame 1 and move Welcome Text all the way off the stage to the left. Set motion tweening for both Frame 1 and Frame 20. In Frame 20, use the Properties panel to make the tween rotate one time clockwise on its way from Frame 20 to Frame 30. Test the movie. Notice that the whole movie loops over and over. Instead of leaving the animation as is, you're going to make the rotation part (from Frame 20 to Frame 30) loop forever.

4. You can add actions to any keyframe, but instead of mixing scripts with your animation, you can just make a whole new layer exclusively for actions. Name the single existing layer Animation and then choose Insert, Layer and name the new layer Actions. Make sure the current layer is Actions (you'll see a pencil next to the layer's name in the Timeline). Select Frame 30 in your Actions layer, insert a keyframe (by pressing F6), and then access the Actions panel. You're going to set an action to execute when the playback head reaches Frame 30.

5. To insert a `gotoAndPlay` action, select Global Functions, Timeline Control and then double-click `gotoAndPlay`. You should see a `gotoAndPlay` action added to your script in the Script pane on the right (see Figure 9.28). Because this action requires parameters, a code hint appears to help guide you. If it goes away, just click inside the parentheses following `gotoAndPlay` and click the Show Code Hint button.

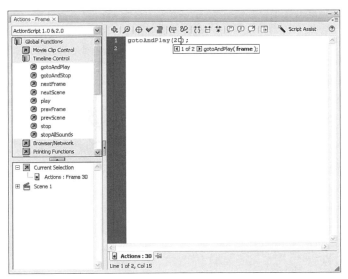

FIGURE 9.28
Right after you insert gotoAndPlay, the Actions panel is populated as shown here.

6. You always type parameters inside the parentheses. In this case, type **20** because that's the frame number to which you want to go and play. Therefore, the finished action in the script area should read `gotoAndPlay(20);`.

7. Test the movie (don't just play in the authoring environment). It plays once, and then every time it gets to Frame 30, it goes back to Frame 20 and plays again.

As easy as the preceding example was, there is one thing in particular that could make it better. Consider the amount of work involved if you changed the location of the keyframes. For example, what if the second keyframe (Frame 20) had to move to Frame 25? Of course, the initial tween would take longer to play, and the rotation would be quicker, but the loop would also stop working properly. To fix it, you would need to remember to edit the action in Frame 30 so that it read `gotoAndPlay(25);`. You would have to repeat this fix every time you changed the location of the keyframe where the rotation starts.

Frame Labels

Naturally, there's a better way. Instead of making the destination of `gotoAndPlay` an explicit frame number, you can change the parameters to make the destination a named frame label, which will be the same for the frame no matter where it is located in the Timeline.

To set a frame label, simply click the frame in the Timeline, and then view the Properties panel. In the Frame field, type in a name that makes sense for what you're doing. In the previous script, for example, you might have named Frame 20 "LoopStart."

After a frame is named, it can be referred to in actions by that name. The `gotoAndPlay(20)` that we used previously could be changed to simply `gotoAndPlay("LoopStart")`.

Frame Actions

You just saw how placing one action in a keyframe and changing its parameters makes the playback head jump to a different frame. Step back a second and consider what else you've learned. Actions are instructions that you want Flash to follow. Actions do things. You can modify actions by changing their parameters. This is all good information; however, if actions are instructions, exactly when does Flash *follow* those instructions?

The answer depends on where you put the actions. You can put actions both in keyframes and on any object type, such as button instances, movie clip instances, and components. In the preceding example you placed an action in a keyframe. In that case, the action was executed (that is, the instruction was followed) when the playback head reached that frame. If you put an action in Frame 10, it would not be followed until the playback head reached Frame 10.

With an action in a keyframe, the user doesn't do anything but wait for the playback head to reach the appropriate frame to see the action happen. Although this isn't exactly interactivity, it's quite powerful. For example, often it's useful to place a stop action in the first frame so the movie initially appears paused and won't play until a play action is encountered (usually when the user clicks a button). Another example might be when you want to stop in the middle of an animation. All you need is a keyframe and a stop action. There are many more types of keyframe actions, which are good for when you want something to happen at a certain moment in the animation—not just when a user clicks.

Button Actions

Putting an action in a keyframe causes the action to execute when that frame is reached. However, putting an action on an instance of a button makes the action execute when the user clicks the button. The decision of whether to put an action in a keyframe or a button is simple. If you want an action to occur when a particular frame is reached, put it in a keyframe. If you want an action to occur when the user acts (for example, when he clicks a button), put the action in an instance of the button.

Keyframe actions are pretty straightforward: You just assign them to keyframes. Button actions, however, require that you specify to which mouse event you want the action to respond. Do you want the action to respond when the user presses the button or when the user releases the button? Maybe you want the action to execute when the user rolls over the button. This level of detail gives you the power to make an action perform exactly as you want.

Mouse events are specific situations that refer to exactly how the user is interacting with a button. For example, one mouse event is press and another is release. When you specify to which mouse event you want an action to respond, you are specifying exactly when the action is to execute. Only in actions attached to objects do you need this extra level of specificity because actions in keyframes simply execute when the keyframe is reached. All mouse events include the word on followed by the actual event name in parentheses (for example, on(press)).

Again, the best way to see how mouse events work is to try it out. Let's add to the preceding example buttons that enable the user to stop and continue the animation while it plays:

1. Either use the file created in the previous examples or make a new file with a motion tween over several frames (make sure you can see something moving while the animation plays).

2. Insert a new layer for the buttons. You don't want to place buttons in the layer that has the animation; that would affect the tween. Name the new layer Buttons.

3. Into the new Buttons layer, draw a rectangle that will become a button. Select it, and then convert it to a symbol. Name it MyButton and make sure the type is set to Button.

4. You're going to need two buttons, so either copy and paste the instance that is already on the stage or drag another instance of the MyButton symbol from the Library onto the stage in the Buttons layer. Apply a Tint color style to each instance—one red (for Stop) and one green (for Play). You do so by selecting the button instance on the stage and using the Properties panel to select Tint from the Color pop-up menu and then selecting a color and percentage.

5. Give each button a memorable instance name (for instance, Green and Red). Use the Properties panel to set the instance names.

6. Now you need to attach an action to each button individually. Select the red button and access the Actions panel. The tab should read Red and have an icon of a button. This way you know you're editing the script for that button instance. Click the plus button and select Global Functions, Timeline Control, Stop.

7. Unlike a keyframe action, which can appear as a single line of code, a button action requires at least two extra lines of code: one before and one after the main script so the script is wrapped inside an event. Think of the main script (in this case, stop()) as the meat of a sandwich, but it's not complete without pieces of bread above and below the code. Any code attached to a button has to be surrounded by an on event. Therefore, place your cursor in front of the s in stop and then type the following:

```
on(press){
```

Then press Enter.

8. Click after the last line of code (that is, after `stop()`), press Enter, and type this:

```
}
```

The resulting script looks like this:

```
on(press){
 stop();
}
```

Notice that you should indent the second line for clarity. This is a very good habit to adopt. You can always clean up your code by pressing the Auto Format button in the Actions panel.

9. The preceding steps go through every last detail. If you know you're going to be adding code to a button, you can start by defining the event and then coming back to actions. For the green button, you'll do just that. Select the green button and open the Actions panel. Confirm that the green button appears in the current script tab at the bottom of the Actions panel. Next find the on action in the Toolbox, under Global Functions, Movie Clip Control, On. Insert it into your code and notice not only that both pieces of bread appear (the `on(){` and `}`), but that a list pops up, from which you can select the `press` event. Go ahead and double-click `press`.

10. As for the action of this script, you have to be sure to place it between the two curly braces. Click at the end of Line 1 and press Enter. Now add the `play` action found under Global Functions, Timeline Control, Play.

11. Test the movie, and you'll find that when you press the buttons, the movie will play and stop.

For almost all interactive elements you create in Flash, you'll always need both parts: the event and the actual actions. In the case of scripts placed in keyframes, you don't specify any events because keyframe scripts are executed when Flash reaches the correct frames.

Movie Clip Actions

You've seen how to place actions in keyframes and on button instances. Most of the actions you'll encounter are likely to fall into one of those two cases. However, there's a third place where you can attach actions: in instances of movie clips. It's a little confusing because, unlike with buttons, you can put actions inside a master movie clip in the Library. However, the rule that you can only put actions in keyframes, button instances, and movie clip instances remains—so if you put any actions *inside* a movie clip, you have to put them in one of those three places (keyframes, nested buttons, or nested clips) inside the clip. We've already discussed putting actions on buttons and in keyframes—and those techniques will work inside master movie clips. But now you're going to see how actions can also be placed on instances of movie clips.

Actions on movie clips are powerful. It would get complicated to fully explore this feature now, but you can do an exercise that gives you a taste. These steps show you how to attach actions right onto clip instances:

1. Create a movie clip that contains several frames and some kind of animation inside the clip (so you can see whether it's playing).

2. Place this movie clip on the stage and test the movie (to verify that it's animating). Your main Timeline should have only one frame.

3. Back in Flash, select the instance of the movie clip on the stage and open the Actions panel. (Confirm that you have the movie clip selected by looking at the current script tab.)

4. In the Toolbox insert onClipEvent, which is listed under Global Functions, Movie Clip Control. The code and code hint appear.

5. Like buttons requiring that you use on events, clips require that you use onClipEvent events. Select or type load. This event will trigger when the clip first loads.

6. Between the two curly braces insert a stop action. The resulting code so far should look like this:

```
onClipEvent(load){
 stop();
}
```

Feel free to type it by hand, but be sure to type it *exactly*.

7. You will add two more actions that respond to the mouseDown and mouseUp events. For this example, when the user clicks mouseDown, the movie clip should start to play. When the user stops clicking (that is, when mouseUp occurs), the movie clip should stop. You can add all that to the script for the selected clip. The separate events, however, must appear as independent sandwiches (well, starting and ending curly braces). To add the additional actions, click once after the closing curly brace and then press Enter. Either type or use the Toolbox to add two more events so that the entire script now looks like this:

```
onClipEvent(load){
  stop();
}
onClipEvent(mouseDown){
  play();
}
onClipEvent(mouseUp){
  stop();
}
```

8. Test the movie. It's sophisticated, despite the simplicity of the script. Go back and reread the script (in the Script area of the Actions panel) attached to the movie clip instance.

There are a few important things to note about the preceding example. First, the movie clip events mouseDown and mouseUp respond to any mouse click—not just to clicks on the movie clip itself. If you want something that responds to clicks right on a graphic, using a regular button is easier.

Also, the actions you attach to a movie clip instance apply only to that instance. It might be more explicit if you precede stop() and play() in all cases in the preceding example with this., as in this.stop() and this.play(). This makes more sense when you think about it because it means just that one movie clip will stop or play. You can prove this to yourself several ways. Drag another instance of your movie clip from the Library (and don't attach any actions to this instance). When you test the movie, the stop and play actions apply to (or "target") only the clip with the actions attached.

Finally, this example shows that you can write code to respond to various events (in this case, load, mouseDown, and mouseUp). For each one, you have the two pieces of bread plus the meat in the middle. What I haven't mentioned yet is that you can stack the sandwich with many layers of meat. That is, for one event, you can trigger several lines of code. For example, when the mouseDown event occurs, you could have a sound start playing in addition to triggering the play() action. As long as you put your code between the two curly braces, one event can trigger as many lines of code as you want. (This is also true with buttons and on events.)

The basic things to remember are that just as with buttons, actions on movie clip instances are wrapped inside events. Buttons respond to the on event, whereas movie clips respond to the onClipEvent. Finally, actions attached to movie clip instances affect only the particular instances to which they're attached.

Using Behaviors

You have enough of the basics of scripting down to move on to behaviors. Behaviors are intended to make programming easier for novices, but in my opinion, you'll get a lot more out of them if you understand what they're doing. Behaviors simply insert several lines of ActionScript in one swoop. For scripts that require you to specify parameters, the behavior will prompt you for data. Another interesting feature of behaviors is that even after you've inserted a complete script, you can come back and make edits to it without touching the code. That is, you can use the Behaviors panel as your interface to edit the underlying code.

Because Behaviors are inserting ActionScript, be sure to keep your Actions panel open and watch what occurs in the Actions panel as you make changes—this will help you understand what is going on in your project and may give you some additional insight into ActionScript syntax.

Open the Behaviors panel, which should resemble Figure 9.29.

FIGURE 9.29
The Behaviors panel is used to add functionality to components without messy scripting.

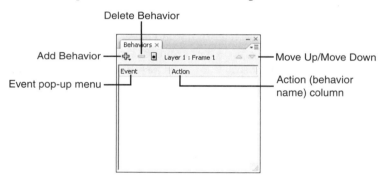

Delete Behavior

Add Behavior

Event pop-up menu

Move Up/Move Down

Action (behavior name) column

The Behaviors panel has the following features:

▶ **Add Behavior**—You always select a behavior to add by clicking the Add Behavior (plus) button. This reveals a hierarchical menu of all installed behaviors.

▶ **Delete Behavior**—The Delete Behavior button lets you remove a behavior. Alternatively, you can just select and delete any row containing a behavior that you want to remove.

▶ **Move Up and Move Down**— These buttons let you reorder multiple rows of behaviors (you can add more than one).

▶ **Event**—The Event pop-up menu enables you to specify a trigger for any added behavior.

▶ **Action column**—The Action column simply presents the name of any added behavior.

The whole idea of the Behaviors panel is that it will insert the ActionScript code for you. Most behaviors prompt you for additional details so parameters can be set. Also, if you need to re-edit a behavior, you can do it through this panel. Actually, you can tweak any behavior by editing the resulting code by using the Actions panel. If you edit the code through the Actions panel, however, you not only potentially break it, but the Behaviors panel can't access code after you've changed it.

Using the getURL **Action**

Whereas the gotoAndPlay action jumps the playback head to another frame, getURL jumps the user to another web page. If you're familiar with how a hyperlink works in HTML, you should know that getURL is the same thing. With gotoAndPlay, you need to specify as a parameter the frame to which you are navigating. With getURL, you need to specify to what URL you want to navigate.

URL stands for *uniform resource locator* and is the address for any web page. If you want to use the getURL action to jump to a website, for example, you need to know the URL.

The following example teaches you how both getURL and the Behaviors panel work. You'll build a hyperlink in this example. Here are the steps:

1. In a new file, create a Button symbol called myButton and place an instance on the stage. Give this instance the name go.

2. With the button instance selected, open both the Actions panel and the Behaviors panel (by pressing Shift+F3). Move the Actions panel to the side because you're only going to use it to watch what's happening behind the scenes.

3. Make sure the button is selected by ensuring that you see myButton, <go> in the Behaviors panel.

4. Click the plus button in the Behaviors panel and select Web, Go to Web Page. Into the URL field that appears in the dialog box, type in the URL of your favorite website (including the "http://" part). (Leave the Open In option set to the default, _self.)

5. Test the movie. Or, better yet, select File, Publish Preview, Default or press (Cmd-F12) [Ctrl+F12] so you can watch this in a browser. Just click the button in the Flash movie and, if you're connected to the Internet, you'll hyperlink to the page whose address you entered.

You can see that the ActionScript produced by the preceding example is the same as if you had created it using the steps in one of the earlier examples. That is, you can also select getURL in the Actions panel list under Global Functions, Browser/Network. The getURL action is nearly the same as gotoAndPlay(), except that the parameter needs to be a URL. If you want to change the event that triggers this behavior, click in the Event field (by default set to On Release) in the Behaviors panel, and you can select from the other events available to buttons, as Figure 9.30 shows.

FIGURE 9.30
The Behaviors panel lets you change the event trigger without affecting the underlying code.

You can also change the destination URL by double-clicking in the Action column in the Behaviors panel. That redisplays the dialog box that appeared in the first place. You can actually do all these modifications (change the event, change the URL, and even delete the whole behavior) through the Actions panel. You get the same results either way.

Behaviors are simply a tool that guides you through ActionScript. But they can become more trouble than they're worth, especially when you know exactly what you want to do. Sort of like cookie cutters, they're great for holidays, but sometimes you just have to use your fingers and shape the cookie yourself.

Publishing Your Animation

Flash's Publish feature makes the process of preparing a movie for the Web a snap. Just select File, Publish. Publish will not only export a .swf file, but it will also create the HTML file that's necessary.

The HTML file specifies where the Flash movie (that is, the .swf file) is located and how to display it onscreen. This is almost the same as how it specifies a static image, such as a .gif or a .jpg. In the case of the .jpg or .gif image, additional information can be included—parameters such as the height and width of the image. Similarly, the HTML referring to a .swf file can include parameters such as width, height, whether the movie loops, whether it should be paused at the start, and more.

If you want to set these sorts of options manually before you publish, simply choose File, Publish Settings. From this dialog, shown in Figure 9.31, you can control how the Flash animation is embedded in the web page as well as control whether aspects of the Flash .swf file generate themselves, such as compression, sound quality, and password protection.

FIGURE 9.31
Fine-tune your finished movie's settings using the Publish Settings option.

Of course, you can always take your finished .swf file and use it directly in Dreamweaver CS3, so don't feel like you're stuck with the HTML files generated by this publication process.

Summary

Flash is a large application development environment with everything from drawing tools to a full programming language. It can take years to master, but almost guarantees a ton of fun along the way.

In this chapter you learned how to find your way around Flash; create graphics; create frame and tween-based animations; import sounds, graphics, and movies; and even add interactive elements through ActionScript. As Flash continues to grow in popularity and power, you'll find that this foundation of skills will help you develop the next generation of Internet applications.

CHAPTER 10

Using Adobe Dreamweaver CS3

Over the past six years, Dreamweaver has become the standard for building, maintaining, and working with websites. Known for its intuitive toolset, cross-platform–feature parity, and wide range of supported server technologies, Dreamweaver is to web publishing as InDesign is to print. Adobe's acquisition of Dreamweaver strengthens the platform by combining it with the best graphics tools available.

Dreamweaver makes it simple to construct anything from a single web page to a site consisting of thousands of pages across hundreds of folders. It frees web developers from the drudgery of site management and allows them to concentrate on the creative aspects of site design and information presentation. For the "hardcore" developer that requires hands-on access to HTML, Dreamweaver provides code-level editing and validation that are second to none.

> **What's New in Dreamweaver CS3?**
>
> If you're familiar with Dreamweaver MX, you'll be right at home with Dreamweaver CS3. Adobe has refined the interface, combined features from its Adobe GoLive product with Dreamweaver CS3, and introduced advanced new dynamic website development features and a JavaScript-based (Ajax) effects generation feature known as Spry.

By the Way

This chapter will cover everything you need to know to create websites in Dreamweaver. We'll start by defining a new project, then work our way through adding design elements, media, and more!

Defining Your Web Project

Let's get started. Opening Dreamweaver brings up the typical Quick Start welcome screen. Here you can create a new document, open a recently edited page or site, or create a new site from one of Adobe's built-in templates. If you prefer to use this interface for getting to your files, feel free, but our focus will be on using the standard menu items to access functionality. In fact, if you never want to see the welcome screen again, just click the Don't Show Again check box.

Creating New Documents

The New command is conveniently found in the File menu. Don't let the simplicity of the single word *new* fool you, though, because Dreamweaver can create a host of document types—everything from XHTML pages with a variety of prebuilt layouts to plain old text (TXT) files. XML, CSS, SMIL, JavaScript, QuickTime, Perl, PHP, MMS, and other Web-related file formats are documents Dreamweaver can handle with ease. This chapter covers only the basic file types, but be aware that Dreamweaver has a depth and breadth beyond what is discussed here.

Also located in the File menu are the Open and Open Recent commands. The Open Recent submenu is especially helpful because it lists not only recently opened sites, but also individual HTML pages and other types of documents you might have opened recently. At the very bottom of the Open Recent submenu is the option Reopen on Startup, which reopens all of your recent files each time Dreamweaver starts up.

Editing Individual Files

When you need to quickly work on a file or two, Dreamweaver can be used in a pinch just by opening the existing file using File, Open, or by creating a new file using methods we've just described. Working in this mode too much, however, can lead to problems.

The Web works by linking different pieces of content together. Imagine that you start by creating one page, add in a few images, and then add another page, linking them together. Do this a few more times and you've just created a website. Unfortunately, you're stuck without being able to organize the content. If you move pages into a folder, the links will be lost and you'll have a bunch of manual cleanup to do just to get things working again.

To get around this problem, Dreamweaver defines the notion of a site. A *site* is any collection of content that you want to use together on one or more web pages. When pages are created and managed within a site, Dreamweaver takes care of keeping your links intact for you. Move your files to a new folder? No problem— Dreamweaver makes sure your links change appropriately.

Creating a Site

From your computer's perspective, a site is simply a directory where all of the web files will be created. From the Site menu, choose Manage Sites. Figure 10.1 shows the Manage Sites dialog box.

FIGURE 10.1
Define and
manage your
Dreamweaver
CS3 sites.

By choosing Manage Sites rather than New Site, you open a simple manager for all of the sites that you set up on your system. Here you can create a new site, edit/duplicate existing site definitions, import or export sites, and, of course, remove sites. Click the New button and choose Site to start a new site definition.

When you click New, you are also given the option of defining an FTP or RDS server rather than a site. These options open a simple network connection window where you can enter information necessary to connect to an existing hosted website and make changes directly to the files that are already online. This isn't recommended, as you lose all of Dreamweaver's site management features, but is an option for those who just want to touch up some pages on a remote site.

The process of defining a site walks you through a wizard that collects some information about your website. If you aren't positive of something, you can always go back and edit it later, so don't worry about it too much. Figure 10.2 shows step one of the Site Definition wizard.

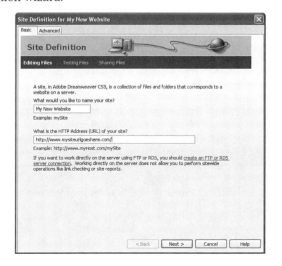

FIGURE 10.2
The Site
Definition dialog
box requires a
site name.

First, decide what you want to name your site, and type it into the Site Name field. This is an arbitrary name that is only used to identify the site to you; it won't show up on any of the web pages. You are also prompted for the URL of the site. If you don't yet know, just leave it blank. Click Next to move on.

Dreamweaver now prompts you to see if you want to work with a server technology (to build dynamic database-driven pages). Because this is beyond the scope of this book, choose No, I Do Not Want to Use a Server Technology, and then click Next.

On the third screen of the Site Definition wizard, things get a bit complicated. Here you need to decide whether you're going to be editing files directly on a connected server volume (a mapped network drive—*never* a good idea), or locally and then uploading them to a remote server. The local option is what you want, even if you aren't ready to connect to a server. Click the Edit Copies Locally button, and then click the folder icon to choose where your site files will be saved. After making your choice, click Next, as shown in Figure 10.3.

FIGURE 10.3
Choose to edit files locally.

Dreamweaver is fully capable of connecting to and uploading files to servers using RDS, FTP, SFTP, WebDAV, and other protocols. We'll look at setting up these connections later in "Transferring Files to and from Remote Sites."

Finally, Dreamweaver wants to know how it is going to connect to a remote server. Choose None, and then click Next.

Your site is now defined. Dreamweaver displays a summary of your settings. Just click Done and you're ready to start building. Any new pages you create will be added to and managed within this site definition.

Site Files

After you've saved one or more site definitions, you can view the contents of the site from the Files panel within the Files panel group, as seen in Figure 10.4. This presents a Windows Explorer–like view of the files that are currently available within your site. If you have multiple sites defined, switch between them quickly using the pop-up menu in the upper-left corner of the panel.

After your site is selected, you can double-click files to open them, drag them to move them, and so on. New files and folders can be created directly within the panel using the Files panel groups flyout menu (the upper right corner of the group panel) or by right-clicking in the file listing. It's a convenient way to organize things without having to leave Dreamweaver.

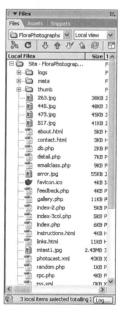

FIGURE 10.4
The Files panel is used to view and manipulate files that are associated with your website.

Dreamweaver makes extensive use of contextual menus. Right-clicking (Ctrl-clicking if you still have a single-button mouse) on items in the file list enables you to perform many basic file functions on the selected object, such as deleting, renaming, and so on.

Did you Know?

The best thing about the Site Files view is that it is an "intelligent" means of managing your files. Unlike the file system on your computer, when you drag a file from one folder to another in your site, the Dreamweaver CS3 file manager understands that this move might have consequences. It automatically scans through your documents and makes sure that any links to or from the document being moved will still work. With these conveniences (and others you'll learn about later), you're likely to find that this panel quickly becomes one of your most frequently visited screens.

By the *Way*

> As an added bonus, you can drag and drop files directly from Windows Explorer or the Mac OS Finder into the Site Files area. They are immediately imported into your website.

Importing Existing Sites

Unlike GoLive, Dreamweaver does not have an official site import feature, but it is still very easy to do. To import an existing site that is located on a remote server, you configure your site definition as you did earlier, but you specify the full details of the connection to your remote server in the Sharing Files area of the Site Definition dialog box.

When a site definition has a remote server attached, you can copy the files from the remote server into your local site definition using, you guessed it, the Files panel. We'll look more closely at this in the "Transferring Files to and from Remote Sites" section later.

Navigating the Dreamweaver Workspace

As you work with your CS3 suite, you'll appreciate the similarity between the different applications. Dreamweaver, as you've seen, has a main window (where you'll do your web page composition) as well as a number of different panel groups, each containing panels that provide additional features. Chances are, you aren't going to use all of these all the time, but it's good to get a sense for what there is, and where it is. Let's explore the Dreamweaver CS3 workspace now.

To begin, let's create a new blank document by clicking "Create New... HTML" from the Welcome window, or by choosing File, New, HTML from the menubar.

Document Window

When you start Dreamweaver CS3, the largest area on your screen is the Document window. This is where you compose your web pages in the What You See Is What You Get (WYSIWYG) interface. As you build your page, you'll immediately see the results of each change, just as it would appear in a web browser.

Three parts make up the Document window. The top of the window contains the toolbar, which holds shortcuts to many common commands and functions (you'll learn about these as needed). If you open multiple documents in Dreamweaver, they'll open in separate tabs also located along the top of the window (just like most popular web browsers). The middle is the content area, and the status bar is at the bottom.

Manipulating Content

The Document window is where you will do most of your web page editing. To add to your page layout, you can type directly into the Document window or use the Insert panel or Insert menu to add text, graphics, or links to the page. The flashing cursor in the Document window shows where the current insert point is located. You can move this point by clicking with your mouse or using the arrow keypad to move it around. Wherever the cursor is, that's where your text or object will be inserted.

Anything that has been added to the Document window can easily be removed, cut, copied, or pasted—much like your standard word processing software. You can select text by clicking and dragging your cursor over the letters. To select an object such as an image, click it once. You can choose multiple items by moving the insertion point to the beginning of the group of objects you want to select, and then holding Shift and clicking where you want the selection to end. Single selected objects are designated by a darkened outline, whereas multiple objects are darkened completely.

After an object is selected, you can use the Copy, Cut, Paste, and Clear commands under the Edit menu to move, duplicate, or delete the selection. The Backspace key also works in a pinch to delete a selection. Two additional copy-and-paste methods are located in the Edit menu—Copy HTML and Paste HTML. These are rather counterintuitive operations that might not perform exactly how you'd expect. As you might know, HTML is the underlying language that forms web pages. Simple tags define the way a page looks when it is presented in a browser. Each tag usually has a start tag and an end tag to define what a particular style applies to.

For example, the bold tag is used to make text appear bold in your web browser. In the following sentence, the word *bold* is defined using HTML tags to appear in a bold typeface onscreen:

I like to emphasize words with `<b>bold</b>`.

The Copy HTML selection will copy the underlying HTML behind what you see onscreen. You can then paste the HTML into other applications. If you simply used the Copy command, you'd end up just pasting the text version of what you see onscreen.

Paste HTML works similarly with the Paste operation. If you've copied HTML code from another program, you can use the Paste HTML function to paste it into Dreamweaver with all the styles intact. The standard Paste operation would end up pasting the HTML code itself. A good rule of thumb is to use these special forms of Copy and Paste only when working with external programs; otherwise you might find the results confusing. The tags themselves will be pasted as part of the onscreen text, rather than being recognized as HTML.

Dreamweaver has provided several shortcuts that make selecting objects even easier. To select a line of text or an object, click in front of the object near the left window border. The cursor changes to an alternate arrow style to show that it is in the line-select mode. You can extend this technique to select multiple objects by clicking and dragging down the left border of the screen.

Status Bar

At the bottom of the Document window is the status bar. This provides a few simple controls for interacting with the document view.

The left side of the status bar contains a listing of the HTML tags surrounding the current cursor position. As you work with more complex web page designs, you'll appreciate how quickly this can help you determine exactly where you are in the document.

Another component in the status bar is the current size of the Document window in pixels (width × height). As you're almost certainly aware, websites often are designed without any attention paid to the size of the screen on which they will display. You can quickly set several preview sizes by clicking and holding on the display of the current window size in the status bar. A pop-up menu appears with a list of common preset sizes that you can choose, including the maximum window size for WebTV viewers.

On the far right of the status bar is an estimation of the page size and the time it will take to download. Most site developers target a particular class of user—dial-in/DSL/LAN browsers, and so on. Creating beautiful pages that take 10 minutes to download is not a good idea. The default speed that is used to estimate the download time is a 56kbps modem. You can adjust the speed in the Dreamweaver status bar preferences, accessed by pressing Command-U (Mac) or Control-U (Windows).

Toolbar

The final portion of your document area is the toolbar. Located directly above the Document window itself, the toolbar contains quick-click shortcuts for switching between HTML, split HTML/Design, Design, and several preview modes, as well as a very convenient way to set the title of the current document and validate that the document is made with correct HTML. You'll learn more about these features later in the chapter.

Insert Panel

Arguably, the most important of the myriad of Dreamweaver panel groups on your screen is the Insert group. This is a floating window that appears above your Document window. As you design pages, you'll frequently refer to this panel, shown in Figure 10.5, and its toolbox of web elements.

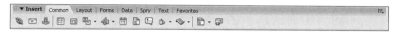

FIGURE 10.5
The Insert panel group is your web design toolbox.

Looking at the Insert panel, you'll see several categories of elements that you can work with, represented by tabs. In its vertical orientation, the tabs are replaced by a single pop-up menu at the top of the panel. Using either the tabs or the pop-up menu, you can access these types of tools:

- ▶ **Common**—This is the most common of the design elements. This includes images, tables, embedded objects, and composite constructs such as navigation bars and image rollovers. This is the default palette shown.

- ▶ **Layout**—Tables, layers, and other elements for creating complex page layouts.

- ▶ **Forms**—Text fields, radio buttons, and everything you need to put together input forms.

- ▶ **Data**—When creating dynamic websites, this panel contains several tools for tying into databases and accessing other server-side features.

- ▶ **Spry**—Elements that use Adobe's Ajax (JavaScript) features to create dynamic onscreen effects, such as collapsible lists, sorting tables, and so forth.

- ▶ **Text**—Common text formatting features, such as headings, paragraphs, and lists.

- ▶ **Favorites**—Right-clicking when Favorites is selected allows you to customize this panel with any of hundreds of available shortcuts, including those from any of the other Insert panels.

Properties Panel

Each element that you add to a web page, be it image, text, or any other object, has properties that can change how it looks in a web browser. Text can be set to certain colors; images can be altered to different widths or heights. Rather than create a different configuration dialog box for each object that you can edit, a single panel, called the Properties panel, handles everything. Located under the document area, this panel is context sensitive. Whatever item is currently selected in your design can be configured through the Properties panel. As you switch from one element to another, the contents of the Properties panel update automatically. Try, for example, selecting some text that you've typed into your document design window. Figure 10.6 shows the properties for basic page text.

FIGURE 10.6
The Properties panel shows the attributes that can be modified for the selected object.

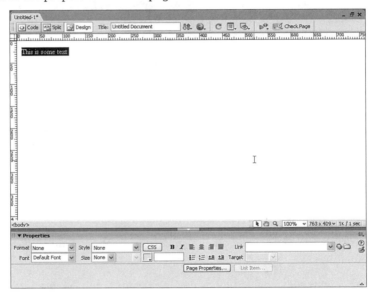

Simple and Expert Modes

The Properties panel itself has a few different modes that can be activated depending on the level of detail with which you want to work. If you're a beginner, you might want to view the Properties panel in the simple mode. To do this, collapse the window to its smallest size by clicking the up arrow in the lower-right corner of the window. If the arrow is pointing down, the window is already collapsed, and clicking the arrow toggles the window into expert mode, providing several additional options.

Getting HTML Help

If you don't have a perfect encyclopedic memory of HTML tags, you can access an extensive help system in the Properties panel—just click the Help icon located in the upper-right corner of the Properties panel. This launches the help system and displays information about the attributes you are editing. You'll find this is an excellent way to get context-sensitive information about an object without resorting to a reference manual.

Quick Tag Editor

Another useful feature of the Properties panel is the Quick Tag Editor. Clicking the button directly below the Help button launches the Quick Tag Editor. The Quick Tag Editor simply brings up a pop-up window that contains the HTML for the tag being edited. You can change any of the HTML in the tag directly. Although this might not seem like a very big feature, sometimes you know exactly what you want to change on a tag, but you don't want to search through the source code or deal with going through an interface to find it. The Quick Tag Editor gives you exactly what you want and doesn't force you to use the point and click tools to make your changes.

Other Panel Groups

The other panels used in the Dreamweaver CS3 environment are important, but will not be as heavily used as what we've seen to this point. To get a sense for what other tools are available, let's review the panel groups and the panels they contain. Keep in mind that you *can* rearrange panels and panel groups. So if your system doesn't match exactly, someone has probably been customizing things a bit. You can revert back to the default layout by choosing Window, Workspace Layout, Default from the menu.

Not all panel groups are visible initially. If you don't see one of the groups listed here, look under the Window menu.

Application Panel Group

The Application panel group contains these tools:

- ▶ **Databases**—Databases provide the information used inside a dynamic site. The Databases panel is used to define and view databases connected to the current site.

- ▶ **Bindings**—Defines and edits connections to live data sources (for instance, databases).

▶ **Server Behaviors**—Also necessary for dynamic sites, Server Behaviors control how information is processed by the remote web server.

▶ **Components**—Used to add JavaBeans or web services to the application. This panel is mainly of use to advanced developers.

Frames Panel Group

The Frames panel group contains this tool:

▶ **Frames**—If you're creating a website that uses frames, you'll probably want an easy way to control them. The Frames panel lets you select and modify individual frame attributes.

Files Panel Group

The Files panel group contains these tools:

▶ **Files**—The Files panel contains the tools you need to keep track of your website's files and synchronize them with remote servers.

▶ **Map**—Although part of the Files panel, the Map is an entirely separate tool, accessed from the flyout menu. One of the hardest parts about maintaining a site is keeping track of how the pages connect and the paths that the users can take to reach different pieces of information. Dreamweaver can generate a map of your website for easy reference.

▶ **Assets**—Site assets are all the images, colors, and other objects in use on your site. You do not need to manually create the Assets panel—Dreamweaver will update it for you. The Assets panel is an excellent way to keep track of everything on your site.

▶ **Snippets**—The Snippets panel holds small code fragments that you can use with your site.

Tag Panel Group

The Tag panel group contains these tools:

▶ **Attributes**—A hierarchical list of all the attributes that can be set for your HTML tags and styles.

▶ **Behaviors**—The Behaviors panel is used to add JavaScript actions to objects on a web page. The behaviors are generated automatically, without any need for knowledge of the JavaScript language.

Timelines Panel Group

The Timelines panel group contains this tool:

> ▶ **Timelines**—Through the use of JavaScript and layers, portions of a web page can be animated over time. The Timeline panel enables you to visually set the position of layers against time.

CSS Panel Group

The CSS panel group contains these tools:

> ▶ **CSS Styles**—Cascading Style Sheets (CSS) are the World Wide Web Consortium (W3C) standard for controlling the look and feel of your website down to the pixel size of the font being used and the margins around your elements. This panel contains all the defined styles and allows you to edit and apply them.

> ▶ **AP Elements**—Lists and allows selection of any absolutely positioned (AP) elements. AP elements can exist on top of one another or even be entirely invisible. As such, it's often difficult to find what you want to edit. The AP Elements panel shows you a list of all these items in one place.

History Panel Group

The History panel group contains this tool:

> ▶ **History**—If you've used History to fix some boo-boos in Photoshop, you'll recognize the History panel immediately. The History contains a list of all the changes you've made to the web document. You can immediately back up to any state that the document has been in since it was last saved. The history can hold between 2 and 99,999 steps, with the default being 50. You can reset this value in the General section of the Dreamweaver preferences (Command-U or Control-U).

Results Panel Group

The Results panel group contains these tools:

> ▶ **Search**—Conducts a search on the entire site, identifying the matched files in the panel.

> ▶ **Reference**—The Reference panel is an extremely detailed reference for CSS, HTML, and JavaScript. If you're interested in the technology behind the code you create, everything you need to know is right here.

▶ **Validation**—Want to see how close your documents are to true HTML standards? Using the Validation panel, you can check for how well your document validates against popular web standards. Not many web pages are fully standards compliant, but it's a good goal to have.

▶ **Browser Compatibility Check**—No matter how well your document follows web standards, it may still have problems in certain browsers. The browser compatibility check identifies potential problems before your site is launched.

▶ **Link Checker**—The link checker automatically scans your entire site for broken links. Any identified errors are found and presented for correction.

▶ **Site Reports**—Site Reports runs a series of tests on your website looking for problems, as well as identifying what editors are currently working on files.

▶ **FTP Log**—Need to check on FTP file transfers to and from your site? This panel might help your diagnose connection errors.

Managing Your Workspace Layout

Don't think the panel layout is ideal for your particular needs? No problem—you can rearrange everything in Dreamweaver CS3.

You can collapse panel groups into a single line or expand them to show the entire panel by using the disclosure arrow in front of the panel name. These groups are then listed as part of the complete panel collection, usually located down the right side of your screen. You can break the collection into smaller groups by clicking on the dotted drag handle in front of the group name and dragging the group out of the main collection. Dragging the group back to the main collection will add it back to the list.

If you want to take things even further, you can drag individual panels from one group to another to create new hybrid groups. Clicking the pop-up panel menu button at the top-right corner of each panel provides additional features for renaming groups, maximizing panels, closing group panels, and special functions for the frontmost panel.

To clean up your view quickly, you can deselect individual panels under the Window menu or use the View, Hide Panels (F4) command to hide all of them at once. If you're more interested in arranging things neatly rather than hiding them, choose the Tile or Cascade options. Dreamweaver will attempt to arrange the floating windows as best it can.

To jump between some predefined layouts that might suit your working style, look under Window, Workspace. Here you'll find layouts for coders, designers, multi-monitor setups, and even options for saving and switching between your own Dreamweaver CS3 layouts.

Did you Know?

Creating and Editing Basic Pages

You're now ready to start creating and editing basic pages. To begin, make sure that you have a site created and selected.

To create a new page, choose New from the File menu. The Category selection allows you to choose between blank documents, templates, and stationary. You want to start with a Blank Page, so be sure that it is highlighted. Next, in the page type list, pick HTML. If you want to use a predefined page layout, select an option from the Layout column. Finally, click the Create button.

In the lower-right corner of the New Page dialog, you can choose the HTML/XHTML standard to which you plan to conform. It is important to choose correctly, as your document will be validated against this setting. Visit http://htmlhelp.com/tools/validator/doctype.html for information on choosing a document type.

By the Way

Your new document will open in the workspace. (You could also create a new file in the Files panel using the Files panel menu or contextual menu, as mentioned earlier.)

Before doing anything else, choose Save As from the File menu, enter in the appropriate name for your home page, and save the file into your website directory.

Until a file is saved, Dreamweaver may not recognize that it is part of a site and might miswrite links to other documents.

Watch Out!

You should now have a blank HTML document open in your editor, waiting anxiously for content.

Setting a Page Title

When you make a new page, Dreamweaver CS3 automatically puts the words Untitled Document in the Title field. This will appear at the top of the browser window when the page is viewed and will also be used as the default bookmark name should your visitors want to come back later.

Before adding anything to the body of your page, you'll want to change these words to something that better indicates the content you expect to be in the page. Click the Title field at the top of the page to select the default title, and then simply type in the new title (see Figure 10.7).

FIGURE 10.7
Your first step in creating a page should be setting an appropriate title.

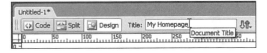

With your title in place, you're ready to begin building your page. You'll have your choice of several editing views. Let's take a look at the editing views and how they are used.

Choosing an Editing View and Using View Controls

Not everyone approaches building a web page the same way. Some people have visual minds and like to work as they would in a page-layout application. Other folks prefer to hand-code their HTML. Fortunately, Dreamweaver has a set of tools to satisfy everyone.

When editing HTML, you'll notice three buttons in the upper-left corner of the editing area (Code, Split, and Design). Those buttons represent the various page-editing views (see Figure 10.8). Each mode has unique features, so you will probably find yourself using a combination of editing views as you become more experienced with the application.

FIGURE 10.8
Use these three buttons to switch between the different editing views.

Common Controls

There are several controls along the top of the editing window that you can make use of at any time regardless of the editing view that you are in. You've already seen the Title Editor; each of the other buttons hides a pop-up menu with several features. Let's review these buttons now, from left to right:

> ▶ **File Management**—After you've configured your site definition with a server for deployment, you'll be able to use these buttons to send the file you are working on to the remote server, fetch files from the server, and more. You can do all of this from the Files panel as well, but this button is a convenient shortcut.

▶ **Preview/Debug in Browser**—Dreamweaver uses a real embedded web browser engine to display your documents in real-time as you create them, but obviously this is only one potential view and there are half a dozen browsers that you might want to check your creation in. The Preview button will allow you to view the current page in any browser on your system. If a browser is now already in the list, just click the button and choose Edit Browser List to easily edit the available browsers, as shown in Figure 10.9.

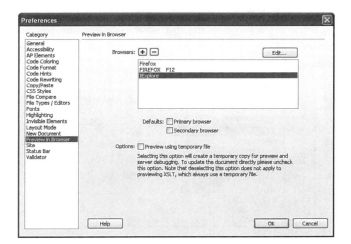

FIGURE 10.9
Configure Dreamweaver to use any browsers that are on your system.

When you use the Preview button, you'll notice that there is an option to preview in Device Central. Device Central is an external application that displays your web page as it will appear on a variety of cell phone and handheld device browsers.

Did you Know?

▶ **Refresh Design View (Design/Split)**—If you've made a change to the code that isn't being reflected yet in the Design or Split views, click this button to force Dreamweaver to update the screen.

▶ **View Options**—The View Options button opens a menu that displays several settings that are specific to the view in which you are working. In Code view, for instance, this button can turn on and off line numbers and word wrap. In the Design view, it shows and hides tools such as rulers and grids.

▶ **Visual Aids (Design/Split)**—When working in one of the visual modes, these settings are used to activate the display of elements such as table borders and visual displays of width and height values—pieces of information that are helpful, but might be distracting when trying to view your designs onscreen.

▶ **Validate Markup**—Checks to see if the code in the document is valid according to the type of document you are creating (HTML, XHTML, ColdFusion, and so forth). If you're only using the design tools, your documents should always validate because Dreamweaver will obey the appropriate standards. If you're coding by hand, however, there might be errors introduced into the code. This is the tool that can help you find them.

▶ **Check Page**—One of the most useful features of Dreamweaver CS3 is its capability to check your page against a variety of browsers to find common problems. Using the Settings command, which displays the Target Browsers dialog shown in Figure 10.10, you can configure the versions of the various browsers that will be tested.

FIGURE 10.10
Check for potential browser problems across a range of browser platforms and versions.

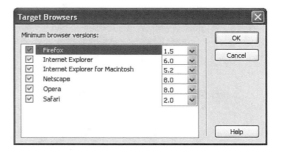

To use the Check Page functionality, you do *not* need to have the browsers installed on your system. Windows systems can check against Mac OS X Safari, and Mac users can check their sites against Internet Explorer.

Of course, nothing can take the place of checking your pages in real live web browsers, but the Check Page tool is an invaluable asset when you don't have direct access to a particular browser.

By the Way

Now that you know what the common controls are for, let's review the different views available and the features specific to them.

Code View

Code view is where the HTML code that makes up a page is visible. The code is fully editable, and changes made here are reflected in the other modes. Dreamweaver's Source Code Editor is very powerful, with features such as code formatting, element collapsing, and code completion. If you're in raw HTML, as seen in Figure 10.11, this is the place to be.

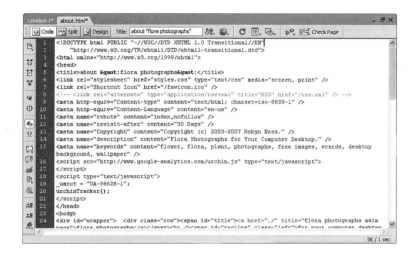

FIGURE 10.11
The Code view is perfect for HTML coding by hand.

Down the left side of the window, you'll find several tools specific to this mode:

▶ **Open Documents**—Choose which source code file you're working on if you currently have several open.

▶ **Collapse Full Tag**—If you've spent time working with HTML, you'll know that tags generally come in pairs. For example, a document's title and page description can be found with the <head> and </head> tags. Sometimes you don't necessarily need everything in between the tags to be visible onscreen. By clicking inside a tag, such as <head>, and then activating this tool, it will collapse the tags into a single space-saving line.

▶ **Collapse Selection**—Just like the Collapse Full Tag tool, this feature collapses multiple lines of text into a single line. This variation, however, collapses any group of lines you select, not just a pair of tags.

▶ **Expand All**—Expands all of the currently collapsed tags and selections so that all code is visible.

▶ **Select Parent Tag**—Selects the text between the parent tag of a given tag. The <title></title> tags, for example, are children tags of the <head></head> tags. If you use this tool while your cursor is in the <title> tag, it automatically selects everything in the <head> tag set.

▶ **Balance Braces**—Often, when programming or using CSS, you'll need to use braces {} to start and stop blocks of code. If you're in the middle of a block of code and want to see everything enclosed within the pair of braces that you're in, you can click the Balance Braces button to select all text within your current set of braces.

▶ **Line Numbers**—Toggles line numbers on and off within the editor.

▶ **Highlight Invalid Code**—Toggles highlighting of bad code on and off. While useful, invalid code highlighting can be troublesome when you're making edits and temporarily have code that registers as invalid.

▶ **Apply Comment**—Adds comment tags to a selected block of HTML code. Choose from HTML comments or comments specific to a programming language, such as ColdFusion Markup Language.

▶ **Remove Comment**—Removes the comment tags from the currently selected block of text.

▶ **Wrap Tag**—Wraps the currently selected block of text within a tag of your choosing.

▶ **Recent Snippets**—Access recently used snippets of code from your Snippets library.

▶ **Move or Convert CSS**—Moves a selected CSS block to an external stylesheet, or converts inline CSS into a block-style CSS rule.

▶ **Indent Code**—Indent a selected group of lines.

▶ **Outdent Code**—Outdent (the opposite of indenting) a selected group of lines.

▶ **Apply Source Formatting**—As much as we might like to think we write pretty code, few of us really do. The Apply Source Formatting feature automatically formats your code according to the hierarchy of HTML tags and rules of the programming language you're using (if any).

One of the most useful features of the Code Editor is code completion. Code completion is one of those things that you won't think you'll need until you actually use it. The process is simple—just start typing a valid tag or function from a programming language, and a list of matching tags appears, as seen in Figure 10.12.

FIGURE 10.12
Code completion can help you enter code manually without having to type everything out!

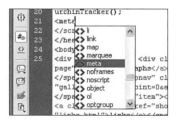

Use your cursor keys (or your mouse) to select the tag you want to enter, and then press Return. The tag is automatically completed for you.

A tool that works hand-in-hand with the Code Editor is the Attributes panel, found in the Tag panel group. This panel is context sensitive. Wherever your cursor is located, the panel will display all of the available attributes for the tags that affect your current position.

For example, if you place your cursor in the <body> tag (or within content directly located within the <body></body> tags), the Attributes panel will look similar to what is shown in Figure 10.13.

FIGURE 10.13
Set specific tag attributes easily.

Here, the general attributes for the <body> tag are shown and can be edited by clicking in the column to the right of their name. For example, to set the bgcolor (background color) for the body tag, you'd click the box to the right of bgcolor. This will open a small color chooser window where you can pick the color you want.

Besides just showing general attributes, the panel can also be used to control attributes that are specific to certain browsers, set attributes that control CSS styles and accessibility features, and so on. Just click the + button to the right of each attribute group to show the potential options for the tag you are editing.

Split View

The second editing mode, Split view, gives you the ability to work directly with the code or with a visual representation of the page simultaneously. In this view, shown in Figure 10.14, the editing area is split into two parts. The upper half provides the same features as the Code Editor and can be used to directly enter and edit HTML or other programming information.

FIGURE 10.14
The Split view provides access to the code and visual design areas simultaneously.

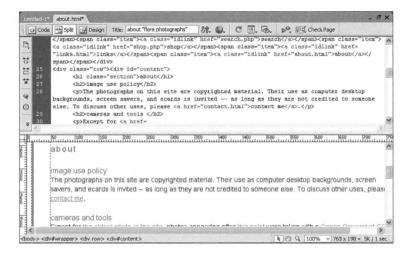

The lower portion of the view shows the live design layout. You can use Dreamweaver's visual tools to create and edit content in this area. As you make changes in one area, they are immediately reflected in the other. This gives you an easy way to test out different styles and tags and see their effects without having to preview the page in your browser, or jump directly into a design-only view.

Design View

WYSIWYG web editors provide a visual process for designing pages rather than requiring the developer to write HTML syntax. The Design view is the purely visual mode that works like a page-layout program. You can drag images onto the page, type text, and use layout grids, tables, and layers to position elements just the way you like them, all without writing a line of HTML code. Figure 10.15 shows the Design view with rulers visible.

Design View Options

By default, the Design view has two view options active—rulers and guides. If you've used the other CS3 programs, you're probably already familiar with what these are. The rulers provide a measurement in pixels, inches, or centimeters across and down the editor. The guides are horizontal or vertical markers that you can set up to help place content precisely within the design area.

To add a guide, just click and drag from within a ruler. For example, to add a guide at 250 pixels from the left side of the page, you'd place your cursor in the ruler at the left side of the editor (anywhere in the ruler area will do), and then click and drag into the design area. As you drag, a vertical line is drawn that extends through

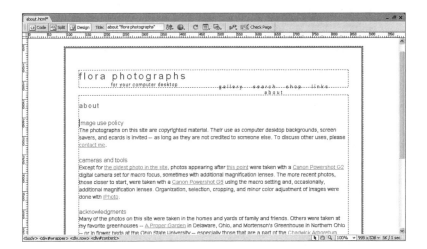

FIGURE 10.15
The Design
view works just
like a traditional
page layout
application.

the editor. Simply continue dragging until it reaches the 250 pixel point, and then let go. The guide is invisible in the actual HTML page, but can be used to precisely align elements that you're adding to the design.

Another helpful alignment tool that you might want to activate is the grid. To do this, use the View Options button at the top of the Design area. This button can be used to toggle any of the view elements on or off, should you find them distracting.

Using Page Properties to Add a Tracing Image

Another feature of the Design mode that can help you turn your web visions into reality is the tracing image. A tracing image is just what it sounds like—an image of what you want to create that can be placed in the design view for the purpose of tracing the layout into a working design.

To add a tracing image to the Design view, choose Modify, Page Properties. When the Page Properties dialog box appears, click Tracing Image. Your screen should now resemble Figure 10.16.

Click the Browse button to find and choose a graphics file to use as a tracing image, and then use the transparency slide to choose how opaque the image will appear in the design view. If you find the image too distracting or too faded, you can always re-open these settings and change the transparency at any time.

FIGURE 10.16
Adding a tracing image can simplify the process of converting a purely visual design into an actual working HTML design.

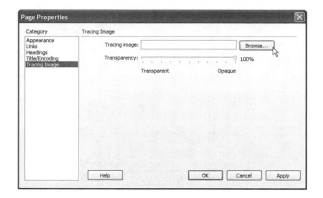

After the tracing image has been added, you can quickly turn it on and off using the View Options button, just as with the rulers, grid, and guides.

You can also use the Page Properties dialog to designate an actual background image for a page, not just a tracing image. To do this, just choose the Appearance category within the Page Properties dialog.

Images used in the background of HTML pages tile when they are displayed, meaning that they repeat. Small images are usually designed to tile seamlessly, giving the appearance of one large image, similar to the way wallpaper looks. If you prefer to use a large image that you don't want to repeat, you should consider using CSS to define the background image for the page. We'll look more closely at CSS in the section "Using Cascading Style Sheets," later in this chapter.

Accessing the Head Content

Although you can see the content, or body area, of your page design visually, there is a portion of your page that is important, yet hidden from view—the head.

The difference between these two areas is that the body portion is what loads into the browser window, whereas the head portion is used to give directions to the browser. The head section is where you put metatags, such as the keywords or description metatags that search engines use to index your site, links to external CSS and JavaScript pages, and more. A whole set of objects in the Common panel of the Insert group is devoted to the head portion of the page. You can select any head object to add it to the page, and then configure it using the Properties panel. But, if this is a purely visual design view, how do you see the head elements?

Once again, we turn to the View Options—this time, choosing Head Content. This makes a small bar visible across the top of the design area. Within the bar are icons representing different pieces of head content, such as the page title and content type. When one of these elements is selected, its properties are visible and editable within the Properties panel. Figure 10.17 shows the head content area visible with the Page Title icon selected.

This gives you complete access to the hidden portion of your web design without needing to access the source code!

FIGURE 10.17
Use the buttons in the head area to set the hidden meta information for a page without touching the source code.

Adding and Modifying Page Content

Now that the page is created and you've seen your view options, let's take a look at adding and editing some actual page content. We're going to be working in the Design view, because the ability to work visually makes web design a much more fluid process.

The first thing to try is just adding some text into the design area. Click inside the editor and start typing. As you'd expect, the text you enter appears onscreen—this is exactly what your visitors are going to see in your browser. Because you're presumably already familiar with using a text editor, we'll skip the details on how to move the cursor around and copy and paste—this should all work just as you'd expect.

Modifying Text Styles with the Properties Panel

What you probably want to do, however, is start styling the text content that you enter. To do this, look no further than the Properties panel, shown in Figure 10.18.

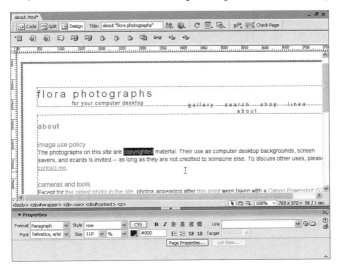

FIGURE 10.18
The Properties panel helps control the appearance of whatever you're currently editing.

The controls visible when entering text should seem familiar—fonts, text sizes, alignment, ordered and unordered list formats, indenting, outdenting, and colors. Almost all the tools you'd expect in a common word processor are available for your use.

To set the style for a specific piece of text, just select the text in the Design view, and then click to apply the styles. If no selection is made when you apply a style, whatever styles you choose will be used when you enter more content.

Let's take a closer look at two of the Properties panel tools that might require a bit more explanation: Colors and Links.

Setting Colors

If you've opened the color chooser in Dreamweaver (usually represented by a small square with a triangle in the lower-right corner), you'll notice that it is very different from choosing a color in an application like Photoshop.

Initially, a web-safe color palette is displayed that enables you to pick a color from the 212 web-safe colors available. For more variety, however, you can choose alternative color options by clicking the pop-up menu arrow in the upper-right corner of the color palette when it is being displayed.

Two other options can also make life easier if you find yourself feeling too constrained by the web color palette: the eyedropper and the system color pickers.

To use the eyedropper, just click the color square—your cursor changes to an eyedropper. Wherever you move and click the eyedropper, that color will be selected. This enables you to choose a color from anywhere on the screen, including your desktop background. If, at any time, you want to return to the default color setting, click the default color icon (a square with a line through it) in the upper-right corner of the Color panel.

A more precise way of choosing colors is by using the system's Color Pickers. Once again, open the web-safe palette and click the right-most icon in upper-right corner. This will bring up the Color Picker that is native to your system.

Web-safe colors are guaranteed to display correctly on 256-color systems. Using web-safe colors is the only way to ensure that your images will look even remotely correct on an 8-bit system.

Today's computers ship with graphics cards that run in either 16- or 24-bit color—eliminating the need to worry about selecting colors from the web-safe palette. If you are designing a site using new technologies targeted for the most recent browsers, you really don't need to worry about choosing web-safe colors. In a few years, they'll be nothing but a distant memory.

Setting Links

A *link* is a hot spot—usually a few underlined words—that, when clicked, takes viewers to a new page, or to a specific location on a long scrolling page.

Because there are a number of ways to create these links, let's review a few that you might find useful.

The first method of adding a link is to position your cursor where it should appear, and then click the Hyperlink object in the Insert panel. You should see a dialog box similar to that shown in Figure 10.19.

FIGURE 10.19
The Hyperlink tool inserts everything you need for a link.

Use the Text field to set the text of the link that is displayed onscreen in the browser. Next, in the Link field, type the filename that should be displayed when the link is clicked. Alternatively, click the folder icon at the end of the field and choose a file directly from your site directory.

Any time you see a folder icon at the end of a URL or file path field, you can click the icon and use your standard system file chooser to graphically pick the file.

Remember that you'll also be asked whether to use absolute or relative linking. Relative linking is the easiest to manage in most cases, as it keeps track of the files relative to one another. Absolute linking bases the links on the top level of the website, making it less flexible when you want to move files around.

Did you Know?

Leave the Target field empty, unless you want to open the link in a new window or a frame (which we'll look at later in "Advanced Layout with Frames"). The remaining settings, as follows, are useful and can be defined however you'd like:

▶ **Title**—Link titles do not show up in the page itself, but appear as tooltips in many browsers.

▶ **Access Key**—This is a keyboard shortcut that can be used to access the link directly.

▶ **Tab Index**—Setting a tab index chooses the order in which the link will be highlighted when users press Tab to navigate the page.

When you've finished filling in the dialog box, click OK to create the link and add it to the web page.

Perhaps it's just me, but this seems like an incredible hassle, just to add a link or two to a page. Luckily, as we hinted at earlier, Dreamweaver provides a myriad of other ways to link documents together…some of which are much faster.

The second way to create a link is by entering your link text directly into the Design view. After you've typed out what you want to be clickable, select the text with your cursor.

Next, using the Link field in the Properties panel, enter in the filename to link to and press Enter. Congratulations, you've just created another link!

For the third linking method, we'll try something a bit more exciting. Again, enter and select a few words in the Design view. This time, however, instead of manually entering the file to link to, open and position your Files panel so that you can see the file you want to use with the link. Now look at the Properties panel. Just to the right of the Link field you should see a little crosshairs icon.

This is the Point-to-File icon, used to target a particular file. Click and hold on the crosshairs icon and drag to the file you want to link. As you drag, an arrow will be drawn from the crosshairs to the file in the Site window, as demonstrated in Figure 10.20. That's it; you've just created a link by pointing to a file! Pretty nifty, huh?

FIGURE 10.20
Use the crosshairs to choose a file from the Files panel.

There are actually even more ways to make links with Dreamweaver CS3. Using the Insert menu, or selecting the link-to-be-text and using the contextual menus, will also suffice. You can go back at any time and edit existing links through the Modify menu's Change Link option, or, of course, by editing the Link field in the Properties window.

Working with Images

Now that you understand the basics of working with text content and the Properties panel, let's take a look at another type of content you'll want to add—images. Most websites, for better or worse, are graphics intensive, making use of images to convey information visually and to create compelling user interfaces.

Adding an Image

To insert an image, make sure your cursor is located where you want the image to appear, and then click the Image button in the Common panel of the Insert panel group, or choose Image from the Insert menu. Next, select the image from your site directory, as shown in Figure 10.21.

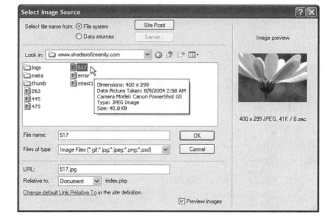

FIGURE 10.21
Choose an image to insert into an HTML page.

You'll see a few options related to dynamic data when selecting the image from your drive. You can ignore these as they pertain to dynamic programming, which we won't be getting into. One option you will want to take a look at is the Relative To: setting. This pop-up menu determines how Dreamweaver writes the links to the image. Usually you want to use the Relative to Document setting. This means that the links are created relative to one another. If an image is located two directories above the current document, the link in the document is set to look for an image two directories above it, no matter where you happen to store the file. Linking that is relative to the site root references the files based on the top of the website—moving the linked files anywhere else within the site breaks the link.

If you choose an image outside of your folder, Dreamweaver gives you the option of copying it into your site. You can also specify a URL to an image that is located remotely. Unfortunately, Dreamweaver only displays local images, so the design view might become a bit confusing if you link all your images into the site via remote URLs.

Did you Know?

> To save yourself some time, you can open the Files panel, navigate to the image file you want, and then drag its icon into the document where you'd like to see it inserted.

Watch Out!

> If linking to a remote image via a URL, be sure you have properly secured the rights to display the image and use of the remote server to transfer the image. If not, you might be breaking copyright law and inadvertently stealing service.

If you want to insert an image, but you don't have one ready yet (waiting on the graphic designers again, huh?), you can insert a placeholder using the Image Placeholder object rather than an image. You can drag the handles (black squares) around the placeholder to size it in your document view. Later, you can assign an image file to the placeholder by selecting it and providing an image filename or URL in the Properties panel.

Image Attributes

As with any HTML object that is inserted into a page, you can set certain attributes for an image. This is done by selecting the image in the Design view and then turning to our trusted friend, the Properties panel. As with the text content, there are a number of attributes that can be controlled for images. Figure 10.22 shows the image properties available in Dreamweaver CS3.

FIGURE 10.22
Image attributes are set through the Properties panel, just like text attributes.

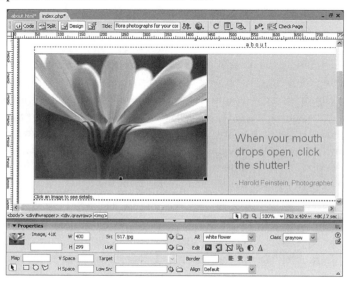

From left to right, these are the properties that can be set for images on your page:

- **Name**—Directly below the image size is a name that can be used to refer to it programmatically. This is typically used in JavaScript.

- **Width/Height**—The W and H fields set the width and height of the image as it will appear on the page.

- **Src**—The URL to the image that will be displayed.

- **Link**—If an image is to be used as a link, you can quickly add all the appropriate <a href> tags around it by just typing in the destination URL in this field.

- **Alt**—Alternative text to be displayed in case the image can't be displayed or to be read aloud by browsers for the visually impaired. You should try to use alt attributes whenever possible.

- **Class**—The name of a style sheet class that should be applied, if any style sheets are defined.

- **V Space/H Space**—Set vertical and horizontal padding around the image.

- **Target**—The target window or frame to be set as the target if the image is being used as a link. This should usually be left blank.

- **Low Src**—Rarely used, this sets a URL to a low resolution (usually black and white) version of the image. This allows a version of the image to be displayed quickly, while the high-resolution version loads.

- **Border**—Sets a border around the image.

- **Justification**—The three justification alignment buttons in the lower-right of the Properties panel control where the image is placed in relation to the HTML text around it.

- **Align**—Determines where an image will lie in relation to objects that are next to it.

Using the Alignment properties to position text and graphics is beneficial when creating web pages that must be accessible to a variety of computers and browsers. If you are positioning text exactly (with tables or layers—something you'll learn about later in "Advanced Layout with Tables"), you inevitably create pages that display poorly on low resolution screens or on displays that have different font settings. Using Alignment properties allows the images and text themselves to drive the display of the page. If text is too long, it will wrap around the image and fill the screen (or the parent object) as much as necessary.

To change the size of an image (or other HTML object that supports resizing), select it within the Document window, and then use the small square handles on the sides of the element to shrink or expand it.

It is important to note that resizing an image does not make its file size smaller. Even when you resize a 1024×1024 image down to a 10×10 icon, the browser must still load the large image to display it. To actually resize the image, you'll need to use the Resample button in the Properties panel.

Don't worry—we'll look at tools for editing photos shortly.

If you don't have complex image alignment requirements, allow the text to wrap around images on your pages. Any time you can design a page to take advantage of the cross-platform and cross-browser nature of HTML, it's a good thing.

Remember to fill in the alt attributes for as many images on your site as possible if you intend it to be viewable from text-only browser systems and accessible to screen readers.

Creating Image Links

Linked images are common on the Web. When the user clicks a linked image, the browser loads the linked web page. With an image selected, you can add a hyperlink in a couple ways:

- ▶ Type a URL into the Link box in the Properties panel.

- ▶ Browse for the linked page by selecting the Browse icon beside the Link box.

- ▶ Use the Point-to-File icon to link to a file. The Point-to-File icon enables you to simply drag the file over to the Files panel to create a link.

To enter a known URL as an image link, select an image on your web page and make sure the Properties panel is open. Enter a URL in the Link box underneath the Src box.

Notice that when you enter a URL in the Link box, the Border property automatically changes to 0. This is so that you do not have the hyperlink highlight as a border around the image. If you prefer to have a highlighted border, set the border to a value greater than 0. You can also set a border for an image that isn't linked to anything. The border will then appear as a black box around the image.

After you save the web page, preview it in a browser. When you click the image that has the hyperlink, your browser should go to the hyperlinked page.

Adjusting Alignment

The Align pop-up menu in the Properties panel controls how objects that are located beside an image align with it. Align is very different from the text alignment settings you used previously. You use the text alignment settings to align an image in the center, to the left, or to the right of the screen. You use the Align pop-up menu to affect how *other* objects align with an image. In Figure 10.23, for instance, the image is aligned to the right of the text because Right is selected in the Align pop-up menu.

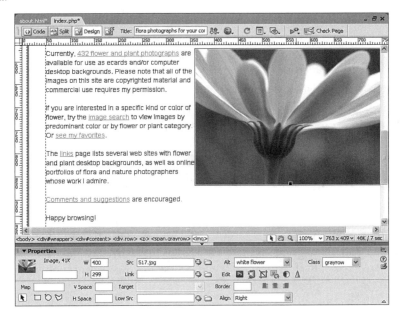

FIGURE 10.23
You can change how an image aligns with adjacent objects in the Align pop-up menu.

Change the Align setting of the image so that all the text appears to the left, beside the image. To do this, select Right from the Align pop-up menu in the Properties Panel. Why select Right? The image will be on the right. Remember that the Align options apply to the image but affect other elements within its vicinity. The alignment choices are described in Table 10.1.

TABLE 10.1   Image Alignment Options in the Properties Panel

Align Option	Description
Default	Baseline-aligns the image, but this depends on the browser.
Baseline	Aligns the bottom of the image with the bottom of the element.
Top	Aligns the image with the highest element. Additional lines of text wrap beneath the image.
Middle	Aligns the baseline of the text with the middle of the image. Additional lines of text wrap beneath the image.
Bottom	Aligns the baseline of the text at the bottom of the image.
TextTop	Aligns the image with the highest text (not the highest element, as with the Top option). Additional lines of text wrap beneath the image.
Absolute Middle	Aligns the middle of the image with the middle of the text beside it.
Absolute Bottom	Aligns the bottom of the highest element with the bottom of the image.
Left	Aligns the image to the left of other elements.
Right	Aligns the image to the right of other elements.

To increase the distance between the image and other page elements, set the V Space and H Space. V stands for vertical and H stands for horizontal. To add space to the right and left of an image, put a value in the H Space text box. Horizontal space is added to both the right and the left of the image. Vertical space is added to both the top and the bottom of the image.

Editing Images

With Dreamweaver CS3, you can easily edit images that you've placed in your documents. Within the Edit section of the Properties panel, you'll see six buttons that can be used to edit your images directly (sort of) in Dreamweaver. Changes you make with these tools are permanent, so be careful what you do!

These controls are

▶ **Edit**—Opens the selected image in Photoshop for editing (or in another application set in the File Types/Editors section of the Dreamweaver CS3 preferences).

▶ **Optimize**—Opens the selected image in the Dreamweaver optimization window.

▶ **Crop**—Lets you trim off unwanted portions of the image and saves the smaller file. This command works within Dreamweaver, enabling you to save the cropped image.

▶ **Resample**—This command becomes active after you've resized an image in Dreamweaver. It optimizes an image by adding or removing pixels in the image. This command works within Dreamweaver.

▶ **Brightness and Contrast**—Changes the brightness and contrast of an image to correct an image that is too bright or too dark. This command works within Dreamweaver.

▶ **Sharpen**—Sharpens a blurry image. This command works within Dreamweaver.

You can access all these image-editing commands from the Properties panel when you have an image selected. Make sure you have a backup copy of any images you modify because Dreamweaver changes the actual image file.

Although they aren't as full featured as Illustrator or Photoshop, these controls enable you to perform common image-editing tasks without leaving the comfort of the web design app.

One of the most compelling features of Dreamweaver is its integration with the other applications in the Creative Suite. It is possible to use your native Photoshop, Flash, Fireworks, and Illustrator documents in your web pages. Dreamweaver accepts the native files and compresses them to an appropriate web format. But the magic begins when the source file is edited because those edits are automatically reflected in the Web-ready version of the image.

Take a native Photoshop or Fireworks file and drag it into an open HTML page. To accommodate the image file, Dreamweaver brings up the Save for Web dialog box, which enables you to determine an appropriate web file format for the image; adjust compression settings; resize the image, if necessary; and then save the resulting GIF, JPEG, or PNG file into your website. During the Save process, Dreamweaver helpfully assigns the Web-friendly version of the image a filename based on the source file.

When created, the object retains a link back to the original document, and it will be updated if the original is changed. When viewed in the Properties panel, editable CS3 objects have a small icon in the lower-right corner of their preview.

To reopen the source file in Photoshop or the application that created it, just double-click on the file. Edit the source file in its originating application, save it, and then flip back to Dreamweaver. The target image automatically updates without requiring you to do a thing.

Did you Know?

Adding Rollover Images

Dreamweaver CS3 makes it easy to implement rollover images by using the Rollover Image object. A rollover is an image that swaps to another image when the viewer's cursor is over it. You need two image files with exactly the same dimensions to create a rollover.

To create a rollover image, follow these steps:

1. Place the insertion point where you want the rollover image to appear.

2. Select the Rollover Image object from the Common panel of the Insert panel group or select Insert, Image Objects, Rollover Image. The Insert Rollover Image dialog box appears.

3. Type a name for the image in the Image Name text field.

4. Select both the original image file and the rollover image file by clicking the Browse buttons next to those options and selecting the image files.

5. Check the Preload Rollover Image check box if you'd like the rollover image downloaded into the viewer's browser cache when the page first loads. With a preloaded image, there is less chance that the viewer will have to wait for the rollover image to download when she moves the cursor over the image.

6. Add Alternate text that describes the image. This helps the visually-impaired to browse and understand your site.

7. Add a link to the rollover image by clicking the Browse button next to When Clicked, Go to URL or type in the external URL or named anchor.

8. The Insert Rollover Image dialog box should look as shown in Figure 10.24. Click the OK button.

FIGURE 10.24
A rollover image swaps one image for another when the viewer's cursor is over the image. You need to enter both image paths into the Insert Rollover Image dialog box.

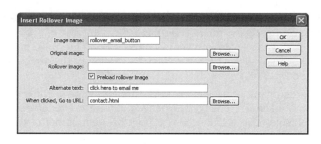

Make Button State Images the Same Size

Rollover and button images require that the up, over, and down images be all the same size. Otherwise, the over and down images will stretch to the size of the original up image and will be distorted.

Creating a Navigation Bar with Rollover Images and Links

What if you wanted to create a bunch of rollover images as a navigation bar? And what if you wanted each of them to have a down button state, too? You could create all these buttons individually, or you could use the Dreamweaver Insert Navigation Bar dialog box to create all the buttons at once.

You simulate a button by swapping images that are the same size but look slightly different. Each image represents a *button state*. The default button state is up. The down state appears when the user clicks the mouse on the button; the down state image usually modifies the up state image so that it looks pressed down. The over state appears when the user passes his mouse over the button. The navigation bar can also add an over when down state, which appears when the user rolls the mouse over the button when it is already in the down state. You must add an up state image to a navigation bar, but all the other button states are optional.

To create a navigation bar, follow these steps:

1. Select the Navigation Bar object from the Common panel or select Insert, Image Objects, Navigation Bar. The Insert Navigation Bar dialog box appears.

2. An initial, unnamed button element is visible. Change the element name to the name of your first button. (If you simply go to the next step, Dreamweaver will automatically give your button the same name as the name of the image file.)

3. Browse to load a button up image, a button over image, and a button down image. You can also enter an over while down image. All these images must be the same size.

4. Enter a hyperlink in the When Clicked, Go to URL box. Type in a URL or browse to a web page. The Target pop-up menu next to the URL box enables you to target a specific frame. You'll explore frames later in "Advanced Layout with Frames."

5. Check the Preload Images check box if you want the images to be automatically preloaded when the page first loads. Check the Show Down Image Initially check box if you want the button to appear pressed in at first.

6. Add additional buttons by clicking the plus button at the top of the dialog box and repeating steps 2–5. Rearrange the order of the buttons by using the arrow buttons at the top of the Insert Navigation Bar dialog box. To delete a button, click the minus button.

7. At the bottom of the Insert Navigation Bar dialog box, choose to insert the navigation bar either horizontally or vertically into the web page. Select the Use Tables check box if you'd like the navigation bar to be created in a table. (The section "Advanced Page Layout by Using Tables" explains how to use tables for layout.) The table layout occurs here for you automatically.

8. When you are finished adding buttons, click OK.

To test the buttons, save your file and preview it in a browser. If you've made a mistake, don't fret! You can edit the navigation bar by selecting the Navigation Bar object again.

By the Way

> You can have only one navigation bar per web page.

Creating Image Maps

An *image map* is an image that has regions, called hotspots, defined as hyperlinks. When a viewer clicks a hotspot, it acts just like any other hyperlink. Instead of adding one hyperlink to an entire image, you can define a number of hotspots on different portions of an image. You can even create hotspots in different shapes.

Image maps are useful for presenting graphical menus that the viewer can click to select regions of a single image. For instance, you could create an image out of a picture of North America. You could draw hotspots around the different countries in North America. When the viewer clicked a country's hotspot, she could jump to a web page with information on that country.

When an image is selected, you see four image map tools in the lower corner of the expanded Properties panel. These four tools are used to define image map hotspots. The arrow is the Pointer Hotspot tool, which is used to select or move the hotspots. There are three image map hotspot tools: One tool draws rectangles, one draws ovals, and one draws polygons.

To create an image map, follow these steps:

1. Insert an image into a web page. The image must be selected for the image map tools to appear in the Properties panel.

2. Give the map a name in the Map Name text box, as shown in Figure 10.25. The name needs to be unique from other map names in the page.

Map Name text box

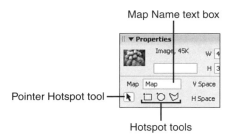

Pointer Hotspot tool

Hotspot tools

FIGURE 10.25
Give an image map a name and use the hotspot tools to draw hotspots within an image map.

3. Select one of the hotspot tools. You'll spend the next minutes exploring each of the hotspot tools in depth.

4. With a newly drawn hotspot selected, type a URL in the Link box, or click the Browse icon to browse to a local web page. You can also link a hotspot to a named anchor by entering a pound sign followed by the anchor name.

5. Enter alternative text for the hotspot in the Alt text box; some browsers display this text as a tooltip.

6. Optionally, select a window target from the Target pop-up menu in the Properties panel. Setting a target window will open a new browser window when the link is clicked. Most of the time, you probably won't select a target.

You set all the image properties for an image map just as you would an ordinary image. You can set the vertical space, horizontal space, alt text, border, and alignment. If you copy and paste the image map into another web page, all the image map properties come along, too.

Adding a Rectangular Hotspot to an Image Map

To add a rectangular hotspot to your image map, first select the Rectangle Hotspot tool. Click and drag the crosshair cursor to make a rectangle the dimensions of the hotspot you want to create. When you release the mouse, a highlighted box appears over the image, as in Figure 10.26. With the hotspot selected, enter a URL into the Link box in the Properties panel.

FIGURE 10.26
Create a rectangle and link it to a URL. Now it's a hotspot!

Rectangular hotspot

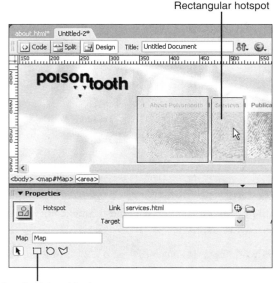

Rectangle Hotspot tool

To move or adjust the size of the hotspot, you need to first select the Pointer Hotspot tool. You can't use the other hotspot tools to adjust the hotspot, or you will end up creating another hotspot. Click the hotspot with the Pointer Hotspot tool and either move the hotspot to another location or resize the hotspot by using the resizing handles.

In the web page HTML, the rectangular hotspot is defined by two sets of x and y coordinates. The upper-left corner of the rectangle is recorded as the first two coordinates in the code and the lower-right corner of the rectangle is recorded as the last two coordinates. The coordinates are in pixels, and they are relative to the image, not to the web page.

Adding a Circular Hotspot to an Image Map

A circular area might better define some areas in your image map than a rectangular one. You create a circular hotspot just as you create a rectangular one. Select the Oval Hotspot tool and then click and drag to create the hotspot—press Shift as you draw to make the hotspot a perfect circle. Reposition or resize the hotspot by using the Pointer Hotspot tool.

You can understand why you can have only a circle and not an ellipse when you see how the circular hotspot coordinates are defined. A circle is defined by three values: The circle's radius and the x and y values that define the circle's center.

Adding an Irregular Hotspot to an Image Map

Sometimes the area you'd like to turn into a hotspot just isn't circular or rectangular. The Polygon Hotspot tool enables you to create any shape you want to define as an irregular hotspot.

You use the Polygon Hotspot tool a little differently than you use the Oval or Rectangle Hotspot tools. First, select the Polygon Hotspot tool from the Properties panel. Instead of clicking and dragging to create a shape, click once for every point in the polygon, as shown in Figure 10.27. You should move around the area you want to define as a hotspot in either a clockwise or counterclockwise manner; clicking randomly may create an odd polygon. When you are finished creating the points of the polygon, select the Pointer Hotspot tool to complete the polygon. You select the Pointer Hotspot tool to deselect the Polygon Hotspot tool so you don't accidentally add stray points on the screen. Or you can double-click when you are finished drawing the polygon.

Polygon hotspot

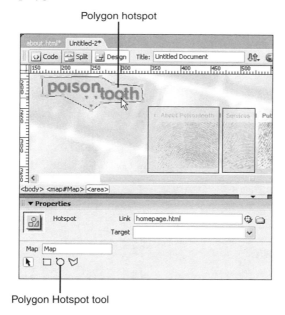

Polygon Hotspot tool

FIGURE 10.27
To create an irregular hotspot with the Polygon Hotspot tool, click once for every point and double-click to finish.

A polygon is defined by as many x and y coordinates, each representing one of the corner points, as you need to define the hotspot shape.

Aligning Hotspots

Dreamweaver has built-in alignment tools that you can use to align the hotspots in an image map. First, you need to select the hotspots you want to align. To select all the hotspots in an image map, use the keyboard shortcut Ctrl+A in Windows or Command+A on the Macintosh. Or you can hold down Shift as you click hotspots to add them to the selection. You can tell when hotspots are selected because you can see the resizing handles.

Sometimes it is difficult to finely align hotspots with your mouse. You can use the arrow keys to move a hotspot or multiple hotspots one pixel at a time. The Arrange submenu under the Modify menu contains commands to align hotspots, as shown in Figure 10.28. You can align multiple hotspots on the left, right, top, or bottom. You can make multiple hotspots the same height by using the Make Same Height command or the same width by using the Make Same Width command.

FIGURE 10.28
The Modify menu's Arrange submenu has commands for aligning hotspots.

Hotspots can overlap each other. Whichever hotspot is on top (usually the one created first) will be the link triggered by clicking on the overlapping area. You can change the stacking order of hotspots by using the commands located in the Arrange submenu of the Modify menu. You might want to create overlapping hotspots on purpose as part of the design of an image map. For instance, you might use a circular hotspot over part of a rectangular hotspot. Alternatively, the overlapping might simply be a consequence of the limited shapes you have available to define the hotspots.

It's difficult to tell which hotspot is on top of another hotspot. If you've recently created the image map, you know which hotspot was created first and is therefore on top. You can manipulate the stacking order of the hotspots by selecting Modify, Arrange, Bring to Front or Send to Back. If a hotspot overlaps another and needs to be on top, select the Bring to Front command.

Advanced Layout with Tables

Using the tools you've seen to this point, you can create web pages with styled text and images. Although these pieces make up most of the sites you'll create (or visit!) you don't have the tools you'll need to create compelling layouts. There are three approaches we'll look at for laying out information on the screen—tables, frames, and CSS layers.

Basic Tables

Tables give web developers the ability to make page elements appear in a specific place onscreen. Dreamweaver enables you to work in Layout view so you can draw table elements directly onto the Document window. This makes it easy to create tables for page layout. Let's start, however, with just adding a table and using it as you would in something like Microsoft Word.

To insert a table into your web page, follow these steps:

1. Place the insertion point in your web page where you want the table to be inserted.

2. Select the Table button in the Common panel (Insert panel group) or choose Insert, Table. The Table dialog box appears, as shown in Figure 10.29.

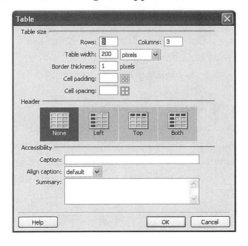

FIGURE 10.29
The Table dialog box allows you to set the initial values of the table. You can always edit these values in the Properties panel later.

3. Accept the default values or enter your own values into the Rows and Columns text boxes. By default, Dreamweaver creates a 3 by 3 table.

4. If you'd like a border to be drawn around the table, choose the number of pixels wide the border should be. For no border, enter 0.

5. Set the amount of space between the content contained in a cell and the border of the cell—the cell padding.

6. Use Cell Spacing to set the amount of space, horizontal and vertical, between two cells.

7. If you'd like to have headings for the columns or rows in your table, make the appropriate choice in the Header section of the Table dialog. The contents of header cells appear bold and centered by default.

8. Finally, configure your accessibility options. You can add a caption for a table that appears in the browser and is visible to everyone. You can set the alignment for the caption so that it appears above, below, to the left, or to the right of the table. You should always add a summary for your table. The summary is read by screen readers and helps the visually impaired user evaluate whether to progress through the table data or skip the information.

9. When you're done setting values in this dialog box, click OK.

A table with the attributes you've specified is inserted into the document.

Adding and Modifying Table Content

When you have your table structure determined, you can start adding text or images to the table. You can also fine-tune the structure as you work in Dreamweaver by using the Properties panel and selecting table cells or entire tables.

To enter content, click in a table cell, type, and then tab to the next cell. You can press Shift+Tab to move backward through the table cells. When you reach the rightmost cell in the bottom row, pressing Tab creates a new row.

Adding and Removing Rows and Columns

To remove a row or column from a table, use the context menu that pops up when you right-click (Control+click on the Mac) a table cell. Right-click (Control+click on the Mac) a table cell and select Table; a submenu appears, with a number of commands to add and remove rows, columns, or both. Select one of these commands to make a change to the table.

Use the icons in the Layout panel of the Insert panel group to add rows either above or below the current row or to add columns to the left or the right of the current column. You can also add or remove rows and columns by editing the table properties in the Properties panel. Adjust the number of rows and columns in the Properties panel with an entire table selected to add or remove groups of cells.

When you use the Properties panel to adjust the number of rows and columns, Dreamweaver inserts a new column to the far right of the table. It inserts a new row at the bottom of the table. If you remove columns or rows in the Properties panel, the columns are removed from the right side and the rows are removed from the bottom. You lose any data that is in the removed columns or rows.

By the Way

Changing Widths and Heights

You can change column width and row height by dragging the cell borders or by entering values in the Properties panel. If you prefer to "eyeball" the size, position the cursor over a cell border until the cursor turns into the double-line cursor. Drag the double-line cursor to change the column width or row height.

Use the W (width) and H (height) boxes in the Properties panel to give exact values to widths and heights. Values are expressed in either pixel or percentage values. A percentage value changes your table size as the size of the browser window changes, whereas a pixel value always displays the table at a constant size.

Just as you can change the size of cells, rows, and columns, you can change the size of an entire table. With the entire table selected, drag the resizing handles to make the table a different size. If you have not given width and height values to cells, rows, and columns, the cells distribute themselves proportionally when the entire table size is changed. Or use the W and H boxes in the Properties panel, with the entire table selected, to give the table either pixel or percentage size values.

When your table is selected, you'll notice a gray bar appear below it. Within this bar are pop-up menus below each column, and a central pop-up menu in the middle. You can use these menus to quickly clear the width of a column, or of the entire table.

You can also clear the cell heights and clear the cell and convert all the values between pixels and percentages in the Properties panel, as seen in Figure 10.30.

FIGURE 10.30
When an entire table is selected, the Properties panel has buttons available to clear the row height and the column width. There are also buttons available to convert dimension values to pixels or percentage.

Clear buttons

Convert buttons

Merging and Splitting Table Cells

You might want some rows or columns in your table to have fewer cells than other rows. For example, you might want the top row of a table to have a title that is centered over all the columns. How do you accomplish that?

You can increase or decrease the column span and row span by either *splitting* or *merging* cells. To merge an entire row so it appears as one cell, select the row and click the Merge button in the Properties panel or right-click anywhere on the row and select the Merge Cells command from the Table submenu of the context menu. Now the content of the entire row can be positioned over all the columns.

Use the Split Cell command to add additional rows or columns to a cell. The Split button is beside the Merge button in the Properties panel. Select the Split button or right-click (or Control+click) in the cell and select the Split Cell command from the Table submenu of the context menu, and the Split Cell dialog box appears, as shown in Figure 10.31. Enter the number of rows or columns you would like the cell to be split into and click OK. Now a single cell is split into multiple cells.

FIGURE 10.31
The Split Cell dialog box enables you to split a single cell into multiple columns or rows.

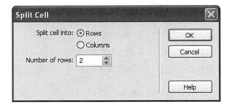

Setting Table Alignment and Colors

You can align the contents of a cell or a group of cells vertically—from top to bottom. The Vert pop-up menu in the Properties panel sets the vertical alignment for the contents of an individual cell or a group of cells.

Align the contents of a cell or a group of cells horizontally—from left to right—with the Horz pop-up menu.

There are several places you can add color to a table:

- ▶ A background color for a table cell or group of cells
- ▶ A background color for the entire table
- ▶ A border color for a table cell or group of cells
- ▶ A border color for the entire table

Figure 10.32 shows the different table colors in the Properties panel. Cell properties always have priority over the same properties in the table. For instance, if you applied blue as the table background color and then applied red to an individual cell, the one cell would be red and all the other cells would be blue. Set the table background and table border in the Properties panel. The Brdr Color setting determines the border color of the entire table.

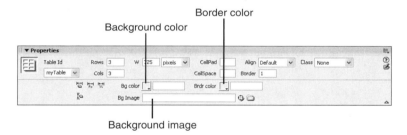

Border color

Background color

Background image

FIGURE 10.32
Adding colors in the Properties panel controls the table border and table background color attributes.

You can add a background image to a table cell or an entire table. Enter the URL for a background image in the box labeled Bg Image in the Properties panel. You can enter a pixel value in the Border text box to see a border; however, you don't usually add borders to a layout table. If you add a border color and don't see the border, you might have the border size set to zero. Set the cell background and cell border colors in the Properties panel with a cell or group of cells selected.

Using Layout Tables

Traditionally, designing tables for page layout has been a complicated task. Making changes or creating the perfect number of cells has required web developers to combine various rows and columns to get pages to look the way they want them to. Dreamweaver includes Layout view, which enables you to easily draw, move, and edit table cells.

To turn on Layout view, select View, Table Mode, Layout Mode. When you turn on Layout view, two layout buttons on the Layout panel (Insert panel group) become active. One of these buttons, Draw Layout Table, draws a layout table; the other, Draw Layout Cell, draws an individual layout cell (a table cell). A *layout table* looks just like a regular HTML table in the web browser, but it looks slightly different in Dreamweaver. In Dreamweaver, you can manipulate layout tables and layout table cells by clicking and dragging them into position on the page.

Adding a Layout Table and Layout Cells

Dreamweaver's Layout view enables you to draw onto the Document window a design that will appear in table cells. You create areas for content, menus, and other elements of a web page by selecting the Draw Layout Cell command and drawing cells for each page element.

To create a layout, follow these steps:

1. Select the Layout Mode from the Table Mode options in the View menu.

2. Select the Draw Layout Cell button in the Layout panel of the Insert panel group.

3. Draw cells in the Document window for page elements, as shown in Figure 10.33. A layout table is automatically created to hold the layout cells.

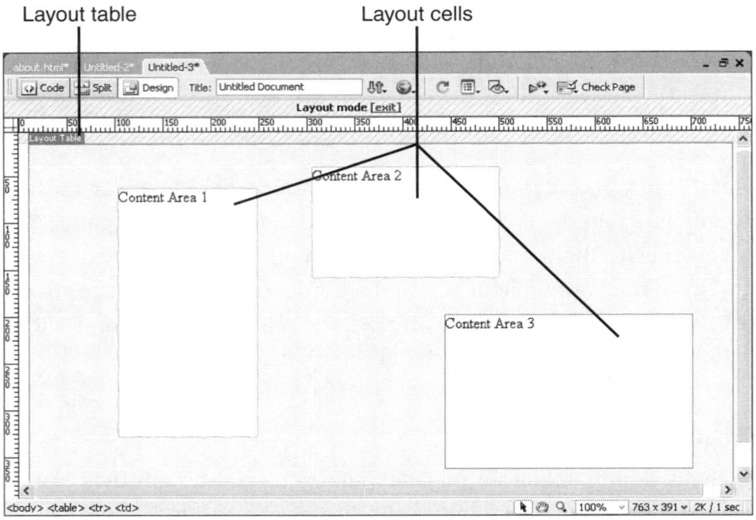

FIGURE 10.33
In Layout view, you can draw table cells in the Document window. The cells are contained within a layout table.

Layout table   Layout cells

4. Alternatively, you can draw the layout table first, and then draw cells within it.

5. After your design is onscreen, you can click the borders of the layout cells and use the handles to resize the layout.

To quickly select a cell to edit its properties, hold down Ctrl and click (Command+click on the Mac) within the cell. As shown in Figure 10.34, the Properties panel presents the Width, Height, Bg (background color), Horz (horizontal alignment), Vert (vertical alignment), and No Wrap properties. These properties are exactly the same table cell properties that you learned about earlier. There's one additional property, Autostretch, which is unique to layout tables.

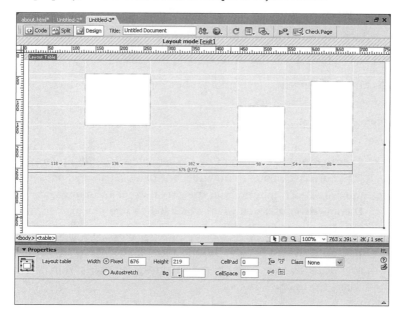

FIGURE 10.34
In Layout view, the Properties panel displays layout cell properties.

Autostretching Content to Fit the Page

Autostretch enables a column to stretch to fill all the available space in the browser window. No matter what size the browser window is, the table will span the entire window. When you turn on Autostretch for a specific cell, all the cells in that column will be stretched. This setting is particularly useful for cells that contain the main content of the page. The menus can stay the same width, but the content can stretch to take up all the available space. Or you can place a stretched cell on the right side of a table and stretch the background colors over the width of the screen, no matter what the user's resolution.

Sometimes it's difficult to see the edges of tables when they don't have a border. You can turn on the Expanded Tables view, in the Layout panel, to display borders within Dreamweaver. This doesn't actually add borders to the web page. It simply displays borders in Dreamweaver so the table is easier to see.

Dreamweaver automatically adds spacer images to table cells to make sure they remain the size that you intend in all browsers. The spacer image trick is an old trick used by web developers to ensure that table cells don't collapse when viewed in certain browsers. A transparent one-pixel GIF is stretched to a specific width. This image is not visible in the browser. The GIF maintains the width of all the cells that are *not* in the autostretched column. If you do not add a spacer image, any columns without an image to hold their size might collapse.

To turn on Autostretch, follow these steps:

1. Select a cell by holding Ctrl while clicking the cell.

2. Select the Autostretch radio button in the Properties Panel. The Choose Spacer Image dialog box appears.

3. In the Choose Spacer Image dialog box, you have three choices:

   ▶ **Create a Spacer Image File**—When you select this option, Dreamweaver creates an invisible one-pixel GIF image, adds it to the top cell of each column, and stretches it to the column width. Dreamweaver asks you where you'd like to store the spacer.gif image that Dreamweaver creates.

   ▶ **Use an Existing Spacer Image File**—If you've already created a spacer image, select this option. Dreamweaver asks you to navigate to where the image is stored.

   ▶ **Don't Use Spacer Images for Autostretch Tables**—If you select this option, Dreamweaver warns you that your cells may collapse and not maintain the widths you have set.

Advanced Layout with Frames

Love 'em or hate 'em, many people seem to have strong opinions about frames. Creating a web page with frames enables you to contain multiple web pages in a single browser window. The user can select a link in one frame that loads content into another existing frame, enabling the user to stay in the same browser window.

Adding Frameset Objects

Frames consist of individual web pages—one for each frame—held together by a web page that contains the frameset. The *frameset* defines the size and position of the individual frames. You can either load an existing web page into a frame or create a new web page. The frameset is like the glue that holds all the frames together. The frameset web page isn't visible to the user; the user sees only the content held in the frames defined by the frameset.

The quickest way to create frames in Dreamweaver is to use the prebuilt frames objects that are available in the Frames menu in the Layout panel of the Insert panel group. The Layout panel has several common frame configurations that can quickly get you going with a set of frames.

If one of these prebuilt configurations fits the way you want your frames to look, you'll have a head start by using the frames objects. You can fine-tune the frame settings by using the methods we'll look at shortly.

With a new web page open, add a frameset object by either clicking an icon from the Frames menu in the Layout panel of the Insert panel group or selecting Insert, HTML, Frames. The framesets in these frames templates all have the borders turned off and have default names set—we'll look at how to change the frame names, borders, and default content in a second.

Creating Arbitrary Frames

To create frames from scratch, use the Visual Aids menu in the Document window's toolbar to turn on Frame Borders, or select View, Visual Aids, Frame Borders. Dreamweaver CS3 adds a set of borders surrounding the page. These borders don't represent how the finished page will look in the browser.

To create frames, drag from the frame borders into your design—just like adding guidelines. After they are added, you can move these borders to resize your frames. When you are ready to turn them off, simply select View, Visual Aids, Frame Borders again to toggle the setting off.

Now you can immediately start entering content into the individual frame areas by clicking in them and using the design tools. What's different from using a table, however, is that in the case of frames, the content for each frame comes from a separate HTML file. If you add a new set of frames and then start adding content, each frame saves as an individual HTML file.

Resizing Frames

Simply drag the frame borders in Dreamweaver to resize a frame. If you want finer control over the size of a frame, you can set frame sizes in the Properties panel while the frameset is selected, as shown in Figure 10.35. You can select the rows or columns in the frameset by clicking the small visual representation in the Properties panel. Often, the first frame has an *absolute* value (either pixel or percentage), whereas the second frame is defined as relative. When a frame is defined as *relative*, it takes up the remaining space either horizontally or vertically.

FIGURE 10.35
Use the small visual representation of the frameset to change frame sizes.

Setting Frame Names and HTML Sources

When you Alt+click (or Option+click on the Mac) within a frame, the properties for that frame are available in the Properties panel, as shown in Figure 10.36.

FIGURE 10.36
The Properties panel presents frame attributes, such as Frame Name, when an individual frame is selected.

Here, you can choose the HTML file that will initially be displayed in the frame using the Src field.

This is also where you give each frame a unique name. It's important that each frame have a name. This is not a filename; this is an actual name for a frame. The frame name is used to target the frame, making a web page load into the frame when a link is clicked in another frame. Click on each frame in the Frames panel and type a name in the Frame Name box in the Properties panel. You can name the top frame `banner`, the left frame `toc` (for table of contents), and the right frame `main`.

Setting the Scrolling and Resize Attributes

Each frame has its own scrolling attributes displayed in the Properties panel when a frame is selected in the Frames panel. There are four settings in the Scroll pop-up menu of the Properties panel.

▶ **Yes**—This setting turns scrollbars on, whether the content requires them. Both vertical and horizontal scrollbars might appear, depending on the browser.

▶ **No**—This setting turns scrollbars off, whether the content requires them. If viewers cannot see all the content in the frame, they have no way to scroll to see it.

▶ **Auto**—This setting turns the scrollbars on if the content of the frame is larger than what is visible in the browser window. If all the content is visible, the scrollbars are off. This setting turns on only the necessary scrollbars, horizontal or vertical, and is usually a better choice than the Yes setting.

▶ **Default**—For most browsers, this setting is the same as Auto.

Select the No Resize check box in the Properties panel if you do not want the user to be able to resize your frames. Checking this check box keeps the user from resizing the frame size in the browser window. Allowing users to resize the frames can sometimes help them maintain the readability of your web page, but it also might ruin your page design. If a frame-based web page is well designed, taking into account how the page will look at various monitor resolutions, users shouldn't have to resize the frames.

Setting Borders

The default look for frame borders is a gray shaded border between the frames. You might not want your frame-based web page to be so obviously "framed." While you're surfing the Web, it's sometimes difficult to identify websites that use frames because they have turned off the frame borders or colored them to blend with the site design.

Using the Properties panel, you can turn borders on and off, set the border color, and change the border width. Border attributes are a little tricky because some of them are set in the frame, some are set in the frameset, and some can be set in both places. Setting properties in an individual frame overrides the same properties set in the frameset. If you set attributes for frames but they don't seem to work, check to make sure you have set the attributes in all the framesets; you might be working with a nested frame that is affected by *two* sets of frameset attributes.

Set the border width in the frameset. The easiest way to select the frameset and display the frameset attributes in the Properties panel is to select a frame and then use the tag selector in the lower-left corner of the design window to choose the frameset tag. You can also click the frame borders to select the frameset.

Targeting Linked Pages to Open in a Specific Frame

The most useful feature of frames is their capability to load content in one frame after a user clicks a link in another frame. The frameset is the parent, and the frames or framesets it contains are its children. Understanding these concepts helps you understand *targeting*. You can load a web page into a frame or window by targeting it. You add the target attribute to a hyperlink to send the linked content into a specific window or frame.

There are four reserved target names:

▶ **_top**—This opens a linked web page in the entire browser window.

▶ **_self**—This opens a linked web page in the same window or frame that contains the link. This is the default setting.

▶ **_parent**—This opens a linked web page in the parent frameset. If the parent frameset is not nested, the linked page will fill the entire browser window.

▶ **_blank**—This opens a linked web page in a new browser window.

The Target pop-up menu in the Properties panel lists all the reserved target names, plus the names of any of the frames you created that are currently open in the Document window. Creating a hyperlink and selecting a frame name from the Target pop-up menu causes the linked page to load in that window. If no target is entered, the linked page loads in the frame that contains the link.

Advanced Layout with Layers and CSS

Earlier you saw how easy it was to lay out content using the Dreamweaver CS3 layout tables. Layout tables simulate the next feature we'll been looking at—layout with layers, or, to be more precise, layout with absolute positioned DIVs through CSS. An HTML <div> tag (or DIV) behaves just like a layer in a graphics program. It can hold content and sit behind or in front of other layers. It is used to divide content into logical sections within a web page.

An *AP DIV* is an "absolute position" DIV that uses special CSS styles to size and place it anywhere on a page with pixel-perfect precision. For our purposes, we'll call these layers, but the appropriate technical term is DIV.

Creating a Layer

To create a layer (or an AP DIV), select the Draw AP Div tool in the Layout panel (Insert panel group), and then just click and drag in the design area. Alternatively, choose Insert, Layout Objects, AP Div to insert a layer, as seen in Figure 10.37.

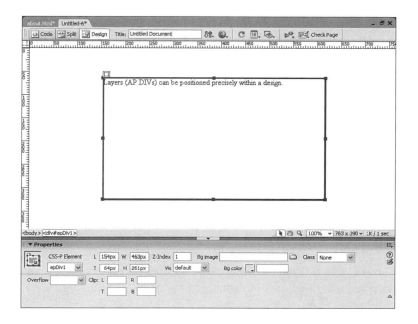

FIGURE 10.37
Add a layer to
your design.

If the Layer object is grayed out in the Insert bar, you are currently in Table Layout view. Be sure to exit this view before attempting to use an AP DIV.

Positioning Layers

You'll notice the resizing handles on each border of your layer. You can drag these handles to make a layer bigger or smaller. You can also set the width and height of the layer in the Properties panel. The W and H properties in the Properties panel are the width and height of the layer. The default measurement unit is pixels.

A layer has a selection handle in the upper-left corner. You can reposition a layer by picking it up and moving it with this handle. To select multiple layers, hold down the Shift key while clicking layers to add them to the selection. You can also use the arrow keys on your keyboard to move a selected layer.

Layers provide a good reason to activate the grids and guides in the Design view. These visual aids help align your layer elements precisely on the page.

You can use the drag handle to drag a layer anywhere on the screen, or you can use the Properties panel to set the exact positioning of a layer. The L and T properties stand for the left, the offset from the left edge of the page, and top, the offset from the top edge of the page. These positions are relative to the entire browser window. You can move a layer either by dragging it (with its selection handle) or by positioning it exactly by entering values in the L (left) and T (top) boxes.

> It's a good idea to always name your layers. If you have multiple layers, names help you identify specific layers. You can specify a name in the CSS-P field in the Properties panel.

Layer Content

A layer is treated just like a mini web page. Almost anything that you can add to a web page can be added to the content of a DIV. Just click inside the DIV area and use the same Dreamweaver tools that you've been using up to this point. You can even add other layers into an existing layer.

When a layer is selected, you'll be able to set background colors and images for the layer using the Properties panel—this should be getting quite familiar by now, so we won't get into the details on this process.

Using the AP Elements Panel

Another useful tool for working with layers is the AP Elements panel. To set a layer name, for example, double-click the name in the AP Elements panel's Name column. It becomes editable and you can type in a new name, as shown in Figure 10.38.

Notice that when you select a layer in the AP Elements panel, the layer is selected in the Document window also, making it simple to manage large numbers of layers.

FIGURE 10.38
You can edit the name of a layer in the AP Elements panel by double-clicking the name and changing it.

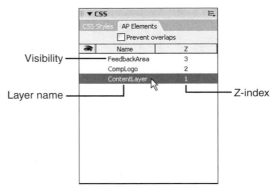

Notice that you can select a check box at the top of the Layers panel to prevent layers from overlapping. If you find that you cannot place your layers on top of one another, this check box is probably selected.

The main reason you would want to prevent overlaps is if you were going to eventually convert the layers into a table; a table cannot have overlapping elements. You can export a table as a series of layers by using the Tables to Layers command (by selecting Modify, Convert, Convert Tables to Layers). You can also use the Layers to Table command (by selecting Modify, Convert, Convert Layers to Table) to turn the layers in your page into a layout table.

Setting the Z-Index

Not only can you position layers in exact places on the page, you can also allow layers to overlap one another. So, which layer is on top? The stacking order decides which layer is on top of other layers. The *z-index* value, in turn, determines the stacking order. The z-index can be either a negative or a positive number.

The layer with the highest z-index is the one on the top. The term *z-index* comes from the coordinate system that you used back in geometry class—remember x and y coordinates? Well, the z-index is the third coordinate that is necessary to describe three-dimensional space. Imagine an arrow coming out of the paper or screen toward you and another going back into the screen or paper. That is the z-index.

To change the z-index, double-click the Z column in the AP Elements panel and type a new value.

Layer Visibility

Layers have a visibility attribute that can be set to Visible, Hidden, Inherit, or Default. The AP Elements panel represents visibility with a picture of an eye. The eye beside a layer is open when the layer is set to Visible. It's closed when the layer is set to Hidden. The Inherit setting does not have an eye representation. The eye is a toggle that moves through the Default, Visible, and Hidden settings and then goes back to Default.

To access all the visibility attributes, use the Vis pop-up menu in the middle of the Properties panel when a layer is selected. These are the visibility settings:

▶ **Visible**—A layer set to Visible appears on the web page upon loading.

▶ **Hidden**—A layer set to Hidden does not appear on the web page. You can later make the layer visible by using the Show-Hide Layer behavior.

▶ **Inherit**—A layer set to Inherit has the same visibility as its parent. Imagine you have one layer inside another (a child layer inside a parent layer). If the parent is set to Hidden and the child is to Inherit, it will also be hidden.

▶ **Default**—The Default setting is actually the same as Inherit in most browsers.

Using Cascading Style Sheets

Initially, web pages were designed using tags that not only defined types of content (headers, paragraphs, tables, and so forth), but the appearance of those elements as well. This, unfortunately, was counter to one of the goals of the Web—to separate content from design and let the output device render the output to the best of its capability. Enter CSS.

Those of you familiar with paragraph and character styles in page-layout applications will probably grasp the basics of CSS readily, but the scope of CSS falls well beyond altering font faces, sizes, and colors. CSS can be used to position elements, not merely text, on a page. In fact, if you have played with layers, you were working with CSS because a layer actually writes a <DIV> tag, which defines an area, and that area is positioned (and can be styled) with CSS.

Internal Versus External

Ever wonder why they're called Cascading Style Sheets instead of simply style sheets? It's because you can define styles in several ways, which at times could result in conflicting styles. The method of resolving this conflict is called precedence. For example, you can define a style internally, meaning that it's written into a page, or externally, meaning that the style is defined in a separate document and linked to the page. In such a case, any conflicting styles in the internally defined styles take precedence over those defined in the external styles. Likewise, a style can be written inline, which means that it is applied to only one element on a page rather than the whole page, like an internal style. In this case, the inline style takes precedence over the internal style.

So if you have an external style sheet that defines a piece of text as red, and there is no internal or inline style on that text, the text appears red. If you also have an internal style declaring that text to be blue, the internal style would win and the text would be blue. But if you also had an inline style defining the text as green, the inline style would triumph over the others and the text would appear green.

Creating Tag Styles

Let's start by creating an internal CSS. Open a blank page, and then open the CSS Styles panel in the CSS panel group. The editor employs two buttons at the top, All and Current. The All button displays all the styles currently defined while Current shows only the styles applied to the current object.

To define a style, click the + page icon at the bottom right of the panel. A New CSS Rule dialog box appears, as shown in Figure 10.39.

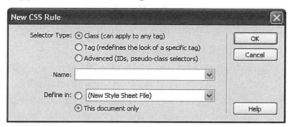

FIGURE 10.39
Choose the type of style and where you want it defined.

Now, choose whether you are adding a tag style, a class style, or an ID style. Let's concentrate on tag styles first. *Tag*, in this case, refers to an HTML tag, which is a markup element. Say, for example, that you want to create a style that would make all your hyperlinks appear with no underline, but you want the underline to show up when the visitor puts his mouse over the link. You would need to define a style for the <a> tag, which is the tag used to make a link, and define two variations of the tag, one for each mouse state, off the link and over the link.

First, click the Tag radio button. Next, use the Tag pop-up menu to choose the tag you want to modify—in this case, a. Finally, click the In This Document Only radio button (this saves the style as an internal style), and then click OK.

Dreamweaver now takes you into the CSS Editor. The left half of the editor displays categories for all of the different style attributes, as seen in Figure 10.40.

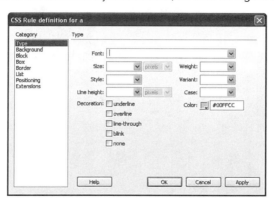

FIGURE 10.40
Edit the available attributes for your styled object.

To choose a color for your link, click the Type category and use the Color selector to pick a link color. To make sure that no link is displayed, ensure that Underline is not chosen in the text decoration settings. Click OK and your style is defined!

Next, let's see how you can define the color of a link when the mouse is hovering over it. In this case, follow the same procedure you just did, but choose Advanced as the selector type and a:hover as the style to define, and click OK.

Within the category, choose Type. Pick a color for the mouseover state of your link, and then click the Decoration Underline button. Click OK to save your style. Your page links will now change color and underline when you mouse over them. It's that simple!

To test out the styles you defined, preview the page, and put your mouse over the link. Remember, when you create a tag style, that style attaches to every instance of that tag in the page, or in all pages referenced by an external style sheet. In some instances, you might want to define a style that you can apply only where needed. In that case, you need a class style.

Creating a Class Style

Defining a class style is not much different from defining a tag style, but unlike a tag style, which automatically adheres to every occurrence of a specific HTML tag in a page, a class style needs to be manually applied wherever it is desired. Class style names begin with a period (.) and won't work properly without it. Let's try one. Click the New Class button at the bottom of the CSS Styles panel. In the New CSS Rule dialog, choose a selector type of Class and change the name of the selector to .body-class. Click OK.

Make sure that the Type category is selected. Choose white for the color and set the type size as 16 pixels. Click the Font button and choose Trebuchet. Next, click the Background category, and choose navy for the background color.

Now click the Box category, and in the Padding section, type **5** into the Top field, making sure the Same for All box is checked. When you click out of the input field, the attribute automatically fills in for all four sides, as shown in Figure 10.41.

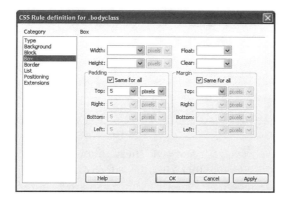

FIGURE 10.41
Define every-
thing from col-
ors to borders
and margins.

The CSS Editor uses pixels by default in all the input fields. If you'd like to change to points, picas, inches, ems, percentage, or another unit, click the pop-up menu next to the field and make your selection.

By the
Way

Click the Border category, and make sure that Border is active. Type **2** into the width field, type "lime" in the color field (or choose a nice color from the pop-up color swatches!) and Solid from the Style pop-up menu. Save your changes and go over to your HTML page. Type the words **try it!** and select them. In the Properties panel, use the Style pop-up menu to choose the style you've defined. It should immediately be visible in your design and in previews of your page.

External CSS

Although internal style sheets are useful, the external version has the real power. When you reference an external style sheet from multiple pages in a site, all it takes is an edit to that one CSS document to make a quick site-wide change.

You can create a new external style sheet by going through the same steps you've already seen to define a new style, but by clicking the radio button next to New Style Sheet File in the New CSS Rule dialog, as seen in Figure 10.42.

You'll be prompted for a name and a location to save the file. Choose any appropriate location within your site structure. After it is created, the style definition continues as you've already seen. After an external style sheet has been defined, it is selectable from the Define In pop-up menu.

FIGURE 10.42
Create a new
external style
sheet.

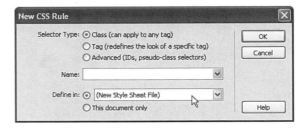

To link your HTML pages to your new style sheet, simply open up the HTML file you want to link to the CSS file, and then click the Attach Style Sheet button (it looks like a chain) in the CSS Styles panel. Choose Add As Link, browse for the CSS file, and click OK to apply.

Entire books are devoted to CSS, but hopefully this section will get you started. CSS is somewhat addictive. When you realize its incredible power, you'll never want to go back to the old way of styling your pages again!

Transferring Files to and from Remote Sites

Finished websites reside on a web server where many people access the web pages. While you are working on your websites, you will want to move them onto the server for testing. At the end of the project, you'll need to move your web pages to a public server so other people can look at them. There are different ways to move the files onto a server and different methods for ensuring that the version of the files is correct and not accidentally overwritten.

When working in Dreamweaver, you don't need FTP transfer software or any other software to move your files onto the remote server. This capability is built right into Dreamweaver! It's more convenient to set up your remote site and transfer files while working in Dreamweaver than to jump out to another application.

Adding Your Remote Site Connection

You define a remote site by editing the website definition (which you get to by selecting Site, Manage Sites). Select a site and click the Edit button to launch the Site Definition dialog box for the selected website. In the Basic tab, click the Next button until you reach the Sharing Files section of the Site Definition Wizard, as shown in Figure 10.43.

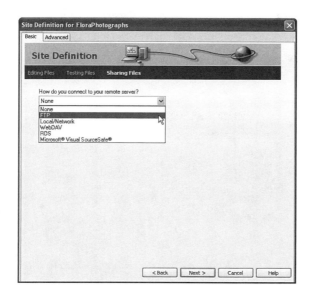

FIGURE 10.43
You set up the
remote site defi-
nition in the
Sharing Files
section of the
Site Definition
Wizard.

You can choose five transfer methods from the pop-up menu:

▶ FTP

▶ Local/Network

▶ WebDAV

▶ RDS

▶ Microsoft Visual SourceSafe

The transfer method you select depends on where your remote site is located. The
site may be on your company's intranet, and if so, you can transfer the local site up
to the remote site by using a LAN, or Local/Network, connection. The site may be at
your ISP, the folks who provide you with an Internet or a web hosting service. In this
case, you will probably connect to its servers by using FTP. SourceSafe, RDS, and
WebDAV connections are less common than the others but are sometimes used in
professional web development environments.

Setting FTP Information

You should select FTP access, as shown in Figure 10.44, if you need to transfer files
over the Web to a remote server. The server could be physically located in your
building, or it could be on the other side of the world. You need to enter the name of
the FTP server into the text field What Is the Hostname or FTP Address of Your Web
Server? Often this is in the following format: ftp.domain.com.

FIGURE 10.44
You need to set
the FTP informa-
tion, including
the server
address.

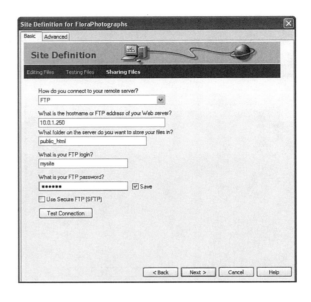

Enter the correct directory in the text field What Folder on the Server Do You Want
to Store Your Files In? You might need to get the path for this directory from your
web or network administrator. If you are unsure what the root directory is on the
remote site, try leaving the What Folder? field blank. The FTP server might put you
in the correct directory because your account may be configured that way.

You need a login and a password to access the FTP server—enter these in the appropriate fields. Dreamweaver saves your password by default. If other people have
access to Dreamweaver on your computer and you don't want them to access your
FTP account, deselect the Save check box.

If you're using secure FTP (SFTP), which encrypts all traffic between your computer
and the remote hosting computer, click Use Secure FTP.

Click the Test Connection button to make sure that you've entered everything correctly and are successfully connecting to the FTP server.

You can troubleshoot FTP connection problems by first closing the Site Definition
dialog box and then selecting Window, Results and clicking the FTP Log tab. The
FTP log lists the reason you didn't connect successfully. For instance, if the log states
that the password was incorrect or the directory you are targeting doesn't exist, you
can change these in the Site Definition Wizard and try again.

If you are behind a firewall or using a proxy server, you might have difficulties with
FTP. Consult the network administrator about which settings you need to choose

when setting up FTP. If you go through a firewall to access the Internet, you might need to edit the advanced FTP settings, located by clicking the Advanced tab in the Site Definition dialog.

Setting LAN Information

You should select Local/Network in the Site Definition Wizard if the server is on a computer that you can connect to directly by using a network. If you can access files on the server the same way you access your hard drive, moving files to and from it with ease, you have LAN access. You need to know the correct web-accessible directory; your web administrator should be able to give you that information.

Set up LAN access to the remote server by entering the path to the remote directory. Use the Browse icon to browse to the directory or type in the path. Checking the Refresh Remote File List Automatically box (in the Advanced tab) might slow down Dreamweaver's performance a bit, but you will always have an up-to-date reflection of the remote site.

Setting RDS and Source Safe Access

Using the RDS and Visual SourceSafe options require specific information from your network administrator. Depending on how these services are configured, your setup may change. Consult your administrator before attempting setup of these features.

WebDAV

Another standard is WebDAV (sometimes just called DAV); the version-control information for WebDAV is set up similarly to a SourceSafe database. *WebDAV* stands for World Wide Web Distributed Authoring and Versioning, and it is a group of standards governing Web collaboration that is an extension to HTTP. Again, you'll need to consult with your network administrator to identify if this feature is available and how to configure it on your system.

Check In/Check Out

After you define the remote site and click Next, Dreamweaver asks if you'd like to enable Check In/Check Out. Because you overwrite files when you transfer them from the local site to the remote site, you need to be careful if multiple people are working on the same site. You can use Check In/Check Out functionality so you do not overwrite files that others have recently edited and uploaded to the remote site.

Using the Site Advanced Tab

Click the Advanced tab of the Site Definition dialog box to see a different view of your remote site's settings. The Remote Info category, shown in Figure 10.45, displays the login information, along with firewall and other settings. You can click back and forth between the Basic and Advanced tabs if you like.

FIGURE 10.45
The Advanced tab shows all the remote site's settings.

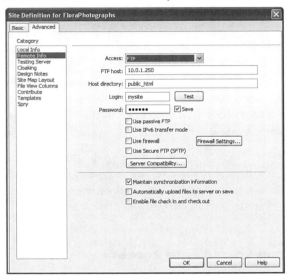

You can close the Site Definition dialog box by clicking OK to save your settings. Next you'll try connecting to the remote server and transferring your files.

If you are having problems connecting to the server when using FTP (you'll receive a message from Dreamweaver), you might want to select Use Passive FTP on the Advanced tab of the Site Definition dialog box. This often solves transfer problems, especially when you are transferring files from behind a firewall.

The File Transfer Interface

The Files panel enables you to transfer files to and from the remote site you've defined. You can transfer files to your local site by clicking the Get File(s) button, and you can transfer files to the remote site by clicking the Put File(s) button. Unfortunately, the full view of your files is hidden until you click the Expand button in the upper-right corner of the file panel. After it is expanded, the panel shows a view of both your local and remote sites, as seen in Figure 10.46. When you want to collapse the expanded Files panel, click the Expand/Collapse button again.

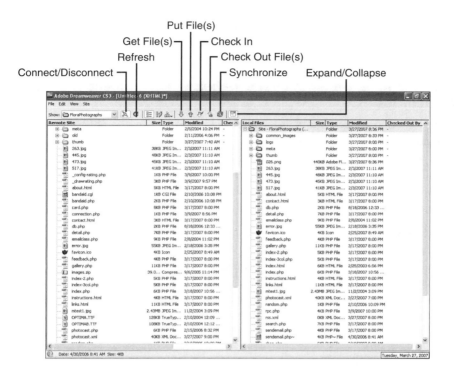

FIGURE 10.46
The buttons at the top of the Files panel help you transfer files between the local and remote sites.

You'll want to pay close attention to these buttons at the top of the Files panel:

▶ **Connect/Disconnect**— This button establishes a connection to an FTP server. The button has a little green light that is lit when you are connected to the FTP server. This button is always lit when you have LAN access to your remote site.

▶ **Refresh**—This button manually refreshes the list of files in the Files panel.

▶ **Get File(s)**—This button retrieves files from the remote site and moves them to your local site.

▶ **Put File(s)**—This button places files from your local site onto the remote site.

▶ **Check out File(s)**—This button retrieves files from the remote site, moves them to your local site, and marks them as Checked Out.

▶ **Check in File(s)**—This button places files from your local site onto the remote site and marks them as Checked In.

▶ **Synchronize**—Find changes on the local or remote sites and synchronize the corresponding site copy.

▶ **Expand/Collapse**—Changes the panel display from a fullscreen view of your files to a mini listing of just the local or remote files.

Understanding Dreamweaver's Website Management Capabilities

Use the Check In/Check Out tools in Dreamweaver to ensure that only one person is working on a file at a time. When you have a file checked out, no one else can check out that file until you check it back in, just like when you have a DVD or video checked out from the video store. Dreamweaver marks the file as checked out by you so that your collaborators know who to bug if they also need to make changes to the file!

When you check out a file from the remote site, Dreamweaver retrieves a copy of that file from the remote server to ensure that you have the most up-to-date version of the file in your local site. When Dreamweaver gets the file, it overwrites the file that exists on your local drive. The checked-out file appears to Dreamweaver users with your name beside it on the remote server, signaling to your collaborators that you have checked it out. The file has a green check mark beside it in your local site, showing that you currently have that file checked out.

Getting and Putting Files

To get or put files, first make sure the correct site is selected in the Site pop-up menu of the Files panel. If you access your site via FTP, click the Connect button. If you are already connected or are accessing the files on a LAN, skip this step.

To get or check out files, follow these steps:

1. Select the files you want to transfer to your local site. You can also select an entire folder to transfer all of its contents.

2. Click the Get File(s) button, or click the Check Out button if you have Check In/Check Out enabled for this site.

3. Dreamweaver might display a dialog box, asking if you would also like to download dependent files. *Dependent files* are images and other assets that are linked to the files you are transferring. You can disable this dialog box by checking the Don't Ask Me Again box. I prefer to transfer the asset files manually instead of having Dreamweaver do it automatically.

To put or check in files, follow these steps:

1. Select the files you want to transfer to the remote site.

2. Click the Put File(s) button, or click the Check In button if you have Check In/Check Out enabled for this site. If you transfer a file that is currently open, Dreamweaver prompts you to save the file before you put it on the remote site.

3. Dreamweaver might display a dialog box, asking if you would also like to upload dependent files. You can disable this dialog box by checking the Don't Ask Me Again box.

Importing an Existing Website

When a website already exists at a remote site, you need to define the website in Dreamweaver, connect to the remote site, and download all the files in the site to work on it. Remember, you can edit only files that are located on your own machine. You can download and edit an existing site even if it wasn't created with Dreamweaver.

Downloading a site for the first time might take some time, depending on how you are accessing the site and what your network connection speed is. After you initially download all the files, however, you should need only to download any files that change.

To import an existing website, all you need to do is mirror the existing site on your local drive. There is no conversion process, and the files will remain unchanged in Dreamweaver. To import an existing website, follow these steps:

1. Set up both your local and remote info in the Site Definition dialog box.

2. Get all the files on the remote site by selecting the top entry in the remote site of the Files panel. Selecting the top entry, the root folder, selects the entire site. If you select a file, you get only that file instead of the entire site.

3. Click the Get File(s) button to transfer all the files on the remote site to your local site.

After the files have transferred you can access and edit the files locally, and then use the file controls to upload changes back to the server as needed.

Reusing Content in a Website by Using the Library

When designing web pages, you can create library items from objects that you use often. If you update a library item, it updates everywhere throughout your site. This is very handy!

Library items help you maintain consistency in a website. They also allow you to share design elements with other web developers. When you are in the design phase of a website, you should be thinking about common elements that would be appropriate to create as Dreamweaver library items.

You can turn all sorts of objects into library items. For instance, a navigation bar that is present in many of the pages in your website would be an excellent candidate for a library item. When you need to add a new button to the navigation bar, it is simple to add the button to the original library item and then update your entire site automatically with the change.

Creating a Library Item

You can create a library item, save it to the Library category of the Assets panel, and then apply it to any web page within your website. Anyone working on the same website can use the library item, and you can use library items created by others. You can include a library item in a web page multiple times. Library items can be created from any object contained in the body of the web page, such as forms, tables, text, Java applets, layers, and images.

You need to define a website before Dreamweaver can insert a library item. Dreamweaver creates a directory called Library in the root of your website where it stores all the library items. When you insert a library item into your web page, Dreamweaver inserts into the page a copy of everything contained in the library item.

> Library items differ from Dreamweaver templates because *library items* are portions of a page, whereas a *template* is an entire page. Libraries and templates are similar, though, because both can automatically update all the linked items and pages.

Using the Library Category of the Assets Panel

When you are creating and applying library items, you open the Library category of the Assets panel, shown in Figure 10.47. The Library category of the Assets panel shows all the library items that exist in the current website. Each website that you create can have a different set of library items.

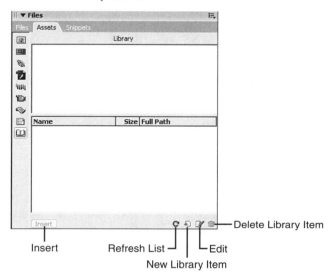

Insert

Refresh List

New Library Item

Edit

Delete Library Item

FIGURE 10.47
The Library category of the Assets panel displays all the library items in the current website. There are buttons at the bottom of the panel to insert, create, open, and delete library items.

The Library category of the Assets panel is divided into two halves. The bottom half lists the names of the library items in the website. The top half displays the contents of a library item that you have selected in the bottom half. The buttons at the bottom of the panel include the following:

▶ **Insert**—You click this button to insert the currently selected library item at the location of the insertion point in the web page.

▶ **Refresh List**—You click this button to refresh the list in the Assets panel. This is useful for refreshing the list after you've added a new item.

▶ **New Library Item**— You click this button to create a new, blank library item.

▶ **Edit**—You click this button to open the library item in its own Dreamweaver Document window for editing.

▶ **Delete Library Item**—You click this button to remove the original library item from the library. This doesn't affect any instances of the library item (although the item can no longer be updated throughout the site).

Creating a Library Item

There are two ways to create library items:

- ▶ **From an existing object or group of objects**—After you decide to create a library item out of a group of objects on a web page, you select the objects and save them into the library.

- ▶ **From scratch, as a new, empty library item**—You can create a new library item, open it up, and add objects to it just as if it were a regular web page.

Creating a Library Item from Existing Content

You create a library item from an existing object or group of objects on your web page as follows:

1. Select an object or a group of objects. Select multiple objects either by dragging your cursor over them or by holding down the Shift key and clicking objects to add to the selection.

2. To add the selection to the library, drag and drop it onto the bottom half of the Library category of the Assets panel. Alternatively, select Modify, Library, Add Object to Library.

3. Give the library object a meaningful name. The Name field is selected immediately after you create the library item; at any time, you can reselect the name with a long single-click on the name field.

When you select a library item name, you see the contents of the library item in the top half of the Library category of the Assets panel, as shown in Figure 10.48. The contents might look different from how they will look in the web page because the Library category of the Assets panel is small, and the objects wrap. Also, because the library item is only a portion of a web page, it appears with no page background color.

Creating a Library Item from Scratch

To create a library item from scratch, follow these steps:

1. Click the New Library Item button at the bottom of the Library category of the Assets panel. Dreamweaver creates a new, blank library item. A message telling you how to add content to the blank library item appears in the top half of the Library category of the Assets panel.

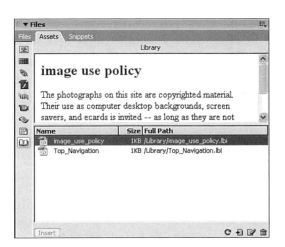

FIGURE 10.48
The Library category of the Assets panel displays a preview of a single library item in its top half and the names of all the library items in the bottom half.

2. Give the library item a name. For example, create a copyright statement that will go at the bottom of each of your web pages. The name Copyright would be a good choice.

3. Double-click the library item in the Library category of the Assets panel. Dreamweaver opens the library item in a separate Document window. You can tell that you have a library item open because Dreamweaver displays <<Library Item>> along with the name of the library item in the title bar as well as using the extension .lbi, as shown in Figure 10.49.

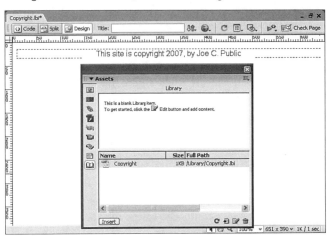

FIGURE 10.49
To add content to a library item, you open it in a separate Dreamweaver Document window. The window shows <<Library Item>> in the title bar.

4. Insert objects into the library item's Document window just as you would in any web page. Insert the copyright symbol (from the Text category in the Insert bar or by selecting Insert, HTML, Special Characters), a year, and a name.

5. Close the Document window and save the library item. Your changes are reflected in the Library category of the Assets panel.

Adding a Library Item to a Page

After you have created a library item, you simply drag it from the list in the Library category of the Assets panel and drop it onto your web page. You can pick up the library item and move it to a different location in the Document window. You will not be able to select individual objects contained in the inserted library item. When you click any of the objects, you select the entire library item; the group of objects in a library item is essentially one object in your web page.

When you insert a library item into a web page, a copy of its contents is inserted. You no longer need to have the original library item present. When you upload your web page onto a remote website, you do not need to upload the Library directory. It is a good idea to keep the directory, though, in case you want to make changes to library items throughout the website.

Consider uploading the library onto your server so others can use the library items, too. When collaborating with a group, you can share a library so that everyone creates consistent web pages using the same library items.

The Properties panel, as shown in Figure 10.50, displays the library item attributes when a library item is selected in the Document window. The Src box displays the name of the library item (which you cannot change here). Three buttons in the Properties panel help you manage the library item:

▶ **Open**—This button opens the library item you want to edit.

▶ **Detach from Original**—This button breaks the link between this instance of a library item and the original item. If the original library item is changed, a detached item will not be updated. If you detach a library item from its original, the individual objects contained in the item will be editable.

▶ **Re-create**—This button overwrites the original library item with the currently selected instance of the library item. This is useful if the original library item has been inadvertently edited or lost.

FIGURE 10.50
The Properties panel contains buttons to manage a library item. You can detach the item from its original or overwrite the item as the original.

You can apply a highlight to library items so that they are easy to see in the Document window. The highlight appears only in Dreamweaver and not in the browser. In addition, the highlight appears only if Invisible Elements is checked in the View menu. You set the highlight color in the Highlighting category in the Dreamweaver Preferences dialog box.

Making Changes to a Library Item

You edit a library item by opening that item to add or change objects in the Document window. Don't worry about the page background color when editing library items; the item appears on the background color of the page in which it is inserted. After you've inserted your previously created library item into a page, open the library item to edit it. Apply different formatting to some of the objects in the item.

After you are finished editing, save the library item. Dreamweaver asks you whether you want to update all the documents in the website that contain the library item, as shown in Figure 10.51. Click Update to automatically update all linked library items.

FIGURE 10.51
Click Update to begin updating all the library items in your entire website that are linked to the selected library item.

After updating, a dialog box displays statistics on how many files were examined, how many were updated, and how many could not be updated. Check the Show Log check box if you want to see these statistics. Click Close to close the Update Pages dialog box.

Check out Web Pages to Update

Certain library items in a website might not be updated if you do not have those items checked out. When you have Check In/Check Out turned on in your website, files that are not checked out to you are marked as read-only. Dreamweaver will not be able to update any library items in files marked read-only. Make sure you have all the appropriate files checked out before you update a library item.

You can manually update linked library items at any time. Right-click on the library item in the Library category of the Assets panel and select either the Update Current Page command to update the current web page or the Update Site command to update the entire website. The Update Current Page command acts immediately, and no dialog box appears. When you issue the Update Site command, the Update Pages dialog box appears. Click the Start button to begin updating all the linked library items in the website.

Summary

Dreamweaver CS3 provides all the features you need (and more!) to be a successful web designer. The inclusion of Dreamweaver in Adobe's software lineup makes it the most complete solution for implementing a website from start to finish. Dreamweaver CS3 adopts the look and feel of the rest of CS3 while keeping the features that have made Dreamweaver a popular product in its own right.

In this chapter you learned how to create and manage sites, add and style most common types of content, and create cascading style sheets, rollover images, and even complex layouts using tables and absolutely positioned layers.

CHAPTER 11

Using Adobe Acrobat 8 Professional

Have you ever tried to send a document to someone, only to find that it can't be read on her system? Dealing with compatibility issues across software products and different systems can be a nightmare. The Portable Document Format (PDF or .pdf), is easily read by any computer system and used extensively on the Web. If you don't have a PDF viewer (Adobe's is called "Reader"), you can download one free. Many web designers use Acrobat to create their PDF files, add forms to their websites, and add a reviewing/commenting system to multiple-page documents. Additionally, designers and printers can use Acrobat 8.0 Professional to preflight and touch up files for final printing.

What's New in Acrobat 8 Professional?

By the Way

Acrobat 8.0 has received a facelift. The new 8.0 interface is much more consistent with the rest of the CS3 suite, utilizing palettes just like what you'll be using in the rest of the Adobe applications. You'll also find a nice Getting Started welcome screen that will give you a jumpstart to the features that you use most.

Acrobat 8.0 improves on virtually all of its existing features, including forms, reviewing, digital signatures, and so on. With these new additions, Acrobat is easier to use and more flexible than ever before.

Introduction to Acrobat

PDF is a file format that is used universally as a standard for file transmission. PDF is perfect for use across multiple platforms as well. Regardless of the system they are viewed on, Adobe PDF files retain all the original file information, such as fonts, graphics, and text formatting. What you see on Windows matches on Mac OS X, Linux, and so on. Mac OS X, in fact, uses PDF natively for generating its onscreen display.

PDF files are small and easily transferred anywhere to anyone with Internet access. Many companies today use PDF files for enabling web surfers to send in job or membership applications, and for internally passing information for review between departments and to other divisions.

Viewing PDF Files

To get started with Acrobat, let's begin by reading a PDF file. To open a PDF file, you can choose File, Open; double-click a PDF file; or drag the PDF file icon to the Acrobat program icon.

Did you Know?

> Another way to open files is by using the Organizer feature. The Organizer lets you easily find files, create collections of files, and preview the contents of PDF files (see Figure 11.1). Similar in concept to what Bridge offers the other Suite applications, Organizer is specifically created for working with PDF files. To open files through the Organizer, use File, Organizer. If you've created PDF collections, you can even access files within the collections directly from the Organizer submenus.

FIGURE 11.1
The Organizer provides a nice way to find and open files.

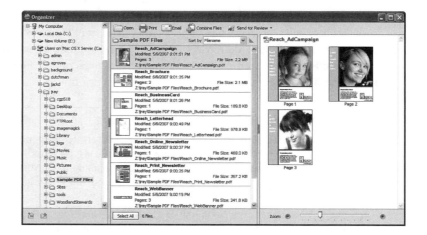

Setting File View Modes

After you have a file open, you can choose from several viewing options. In Full Screen mode, for example, you see only the document—no menus, toolbars, or windows.

To view a PDF file in Full Screen mode, choose Full Screen View from the Window menu, or press (Cmd+L) [Ctrl+L]. Pressing the key command a second time toggles between Full Screen mode and default mode. You can also press the Esc key in Full Screen mode to return to default mode.

If you prefer to keep things in a window, but get rid of some of the clutter, switch to Reading Mode (View, Reading Mode). This keeps the PDF file in a window, but removes all the toolbars.

Another option is to view a single page or continuous pages of a PDF file. One nice advantage to viewing continuous pages is that you can set it up to view facing pages to read your documents as you would a book. This is a perfect setting for reading e-books with Acrobat.

To view a PDF document in continuous facing pages, choose Two-Up Continuous from the Page Layout submenu of the View menu. To go back to Single Page view, you can choose from the Page Layout submenu or click the Single Page or Single Page Continuous button in the toolbar, shown in Figure 11.2.

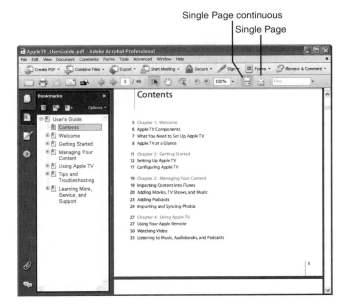

FIGURE 11.2
Choose single page at a time, or single page continuous.

Navigation Tools

Now that you have opened a PDF file and set how you want to look at it, navigating the document is the next step. Getting around the page quickly and efficiently is easy using the various Acrobat toolbars, which can be enabled and disabled from the View, Toolbars submenu.

Zoom Tools

Acrobat offers various tools to zoom in, zoom out, and move around your PDF file. The Select and Zoom toolbar houses the Zoom In and Zoom Out buttons, preset zoom levels, and an area to enter the level of the zoom. In addition, you can use the Marquee Zoom tool (the magnifying glass with a superimposed rectangle) to quickly zoom in and out.

With the Marquee Zoom tool selected, click to zoom in, or hold down (Option) [Alt] and click to zoom out. This tool also enables you to zoom in or out on a specific area by clicking and dragging to create a selection marquee, as seen in Figure 11.3.

FIGURE 11.3
Use the
Marquee
Zoom tool
to zoom in
and out.

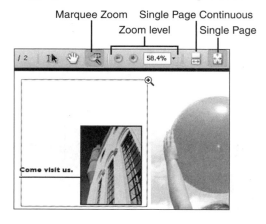

Additional zoom options are available under the View, Zoom submenu.

Page Navigation

To move around within a page, use the Hand tool. The Hand tool acts as your hand does in real life with paper. Need to look at the bottom of a page? Click and drag up. Need to look at the top? Click and drag down.

To navigate between pages, click the forward and backward buttons in the Page Navigation toolbar, as seen in Figure 11.4.

FIGURE 11.4
Use the arrows
and page
number field
to navigate the
PDF.

To go to a specific page, enter a number in the Page Number field and press the Return or Enter key. You will automatically go to the page you requested.

If you prefer to jump to the end or beginning, use the View, Go To submenu to quickly skip through the document or between multiple open documents.

Adding Additional Toolbar Navigation Buttons

By default, you can't see all of the different navigation elements in the Acrobat toolbars. To access advanced controls, go to Tools, Customize Toolbars. You'll find a myriad of additional options that you can add to the existing toolbars, such as:

▶ **Dynamic Zoom**—Click and drag with the Dynamic Zoom tool to zoom in or out on an image.

▶ **Loupe Tool**—Magnifies a selected area of the document; similar to looking through a magnifying glass.

▶ **First Page**—Jump to the first page in the document.

▶ **Last Page**—Jump to the last page in the document.

You can also add toolbars (or additional controls to existing toolbars) by right-clicking a toolbar in the Acrobat window.

Other Panels

In addition to the navigation tools in the Acrobat toolbar, you can add panels to your workspace to enhance your navigation and document-viewing options.

Pages

Managing your PDF document's pages is quick and easy in Acrobat Professional. Jump to a specific page by entering the page in the status bar. Go to the beginning or end of the document by clicking the arrow button in the status bar. In addition to the page-by-page navigation, you can use the Pages panel.

The Pages panel shows a thumbnail view of each page in the PDF document. Use the Pages panel to delete pages, rearrange pages, or jump to a certain page by double-clicking on it. To access the Pages panel, click the icon of two overlapping pages in the top-left corner of the document window, as seen in Figure 11.5.

Bookmarks

The Bookmarks panel works just like the bookmarks in your web browser. Use this panel to bookmark specific pages in a PDF file, or to jump to a previously specified bookmark. To access the Bookmarks panel, click the button of the page with a bookmark ribbon overlaid on it. A list of bookmarks within the document (if any) appears, as demonstrated in Figure 11.6.

FIGURE 11.5
Use the Pages panel to navigate through thumbnails of your pages.

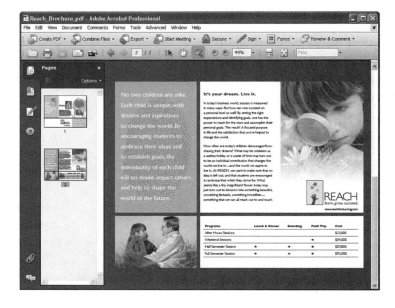

FIGURE 11.6
The Bookmarks panel displays any bookmarks set within the document.

Layers

Layers capability in Acrobat? Well, if there were layers in the original Adobe application used to create a PDF file, there might be layers in Acrobat. Let's say you create this fantastic multilevel floor plan in Illustrator and you want to send it out for reviews. Save the Illustrator file as a PDF file with layers and all, and you'll see those same layers in Acrobat. To see the layers in Acrobat, click the Layers panel button (two stacked squares).

Signatures

Click the pen and paper button to open the Signatures panel where you can quickly verify any digital signatures that are added to the document.

How To

The How To panel, shown in Figure 11.7, provides a great way to learn about common features of Acrobat. This integrated help feature is unique to Acrobat and should be your first stop when looking for help. Access the How To panel by clicking the question-mark icon in the middle of the left side of your Acrobat window.

FIGURE 11.7
For quick help, turn to the How To panel.

Attachments

Near the bottom left of the Acrobat window is the Attachments (paperclip) button. Clicking this button opens the Attachments panel, where you can add file attachments to the PDF file and view any attachments that have already been added.

Comments

As you'll learn later in "Using Comments and Markup," you can add and read comments to and from a PDF file. The Comments panel provides a convenient way to both view and reply to comments in the file you are currently viewing.

Managing Multiple Windows

Work with multiple PDF documents by arranging the pages in various ways. Choose from tiling your multiple windows horizontally or vertically. To bring the active window (the one you are currently working on) to the front, choose Cascade from the Window menu. The active window is placed in front, and the window title is black. All other windows show a gray window title to let you know that they are not active.

Creating PDF Files

Of course, viewing PDF files is great, but you also need to be able to create them. With Acrobat Professional, you can create a PDF file from one file, many different files, a web page or pages, scanned images, or Microsoft Office applications, with just a single button click.

Creating a PDF File from One or More Files

Create a PDF document from a file by choosing File, Create PDF, From File. You can also choose Create PDF, From File from the Welcome screen when Acrobat first opens or from the Create PDF pop-up menu in the Acrobat toolbar.

When prompted, simply find the file on your computer and choose Open. When you open the file, you must save the file to make it into a PDF. The file types you can open in Acrobat to create a PDF file from include BMP, CompuServe GIF, HTML, JPEG, JPEG 2000, Microsoft Word, PCX, PNG, PostScript/EPS, text file, and TIFF.

To create a PDF file from multiple files, choose From Multiple Files from the menu, Welcome screen, or pop-up choices in the Create PDF button on the toolbar. This launches the Combine Files dialog box, as seen in Figure 11.8.

Under the Choose Files area, click the Add Files button to select your files. You can do this multiple times to get all of your files if they aren't in the same folder. If they are in the same folder but are not contiguous, hold the (Cmd) [Ctrl] key to select the noncontiguous files. To select a folder full of files, use the Add Folder button, or use the Add Open Files to select from files you currently have open.

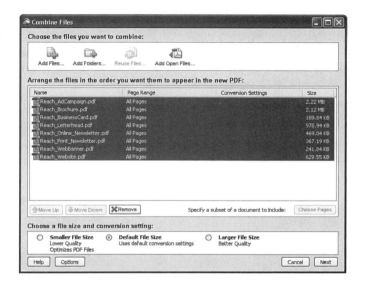

FIGURE 11.8
Combine multiple files into a single PDF file.

When the files are selected, you can arrange them in the Files to Combine area by dragging and dropping them in the order you want. You can also change the order in Acrobat. Then click OK to bind all the pages in one PDF file.

Creating a PDF File from Microsoft Applications

One valuable feature is one-click PDF creation from Microsoft applications. In Microsoft Office applications, an Adobe toolbar is available with a Convert to Adobe PDF button. If the Convert to Adobe PDF button isn't showing, find it under View, Toolbars, Adobe Acrobat PDFMaker.

In Internet Explorer, go to the website you want to convert to a PDF, and click the Convert Current Web Page to PDF File button. This launches the Convert Web Page to PDF dialog box. Enter a name for the PDF file and click the Save button to convert the current web page to a PDF file.

Creating a PDF File from a Web Page

Downloading a web page or a whole website into Acrobat is an easy task. Create a PDF file from a web page by choosing From Web Page from the Create PDF button in the menu bar; choose File, Create PDF, From Web Page; or create the file from the Welcome screen.

Enter the URL of the website you want to download into the URL field. You can also set how many levels of the website you want to convert (see Figure 11.9). Keep in mind that if you choose to convert the whole website or many levels of the website, the result could be a huge PDF file. You might want to limit the PDF file to staying within the same directory on the server and not following links to other servers by activating the Stay on same path and Stay on same server options.

FIGURE 11.9
Set the options for the website you want to convert.

You can convert HTML pages that include forms, links, frames, Flash, JPEG or GIF graphics, tables, and text files into PDF pages. To fine-tune what is converted, click the Settings button.

> Most websites are built hierarchically in different levels. You might have certain links on a home page, which constitutes one layer, but clicking on any of those links could reveal a whole new set of links, which would be another level deeper into the site.

After the web page is converted into a PDF file, you can edit and enhance it as you see fit.

Creating a PDF File from a Scanner

Sometimes the PDF file you want to create might be based on an existing printed document. In these cases, if you have a scanner connected and configured on your computer, you can choose Create PDF, From Scanner, as seen in Figure 11.10.

For typewritten documents, you can even set Acrobat to run the scans through optical character recognition (OCR), converting them back into text, rather than just an image.

FIGURE 11.10
Create PDFs
directly from
printed
documents.

Editing and Manipulating PDF Files

After you have converted files into a PDF, you can edit and alter the files as you want. Not only can you edit the text in the PDF file, but you also can add comments, stamps, headers and footers, watermarks, backgrounds, sound, movie clips, and more.

The basic tools for manipulating existing PDFs are the Hand tool and the Select tool (for text, tables, and images). Use the Hand tool to move your page around. The Select tool simply selects text, tables, or objects so you can copy and paste.

> If you can't find a tool, choose Tools, Customize Toolbar and make sure the tool is enabled within one of the visible toolbars.

Did you Know?

The more advanced editing features include the Select Object, Article, Crop, Link, Movie, 3D, Sound, TouchUp Text, TouchUp Object, and various other tools. To view the Advanced Editing tools, choose Tools, Advanced Editing, Show Advanced Editing Toolbar. Many of the advanced editing tools are covered throughout this chapter.

TouchUp Tools

The TouchUp tools enable you to edit an object as well as text. Use the TouchUp Object tool to edit an existing object. With the TouchUp Object tool, you can do only basic edits, such as copying, deleting, and altering properties. If you need to do more extensive editing, you need to edit in the program with which the object was created. When you double-click a placed object with the TouchUp Object tool, the original application launches, enabling you to edit the object. When you save, the saved version updates in your PDF file.

The TouchUp Text tool lets you edit text in a PDF document. You first select the text using the TouchUp Text tool, and then you enter the new text in the highlighted area, as seen in Figure 11.11. This works only if the font was initially embedded in the PDF file or if you have the font on your system.

FIGURE 11.11
Use the TouchUp Text tool to edit PDF text.

The TouchUp Reading Order tool provides the capability to change the reading order of sections within a PDF document, as well as adding alternative text to images and form fields.

Checking Spelling

You can check the spelling in form fields or comments of any PDF file. To check the spelling of the form fields and comments, choose Edit, Check Spelling, In Comments. You can also edit the dictionary to include odd words that might not be recognized by default. You can have Acrobat automatically check the spelling as you are typing comments or form fields.

Using Comments and Markup

Adding comments or basic edits is a breeze in Acrobat. The Comments and Markup toolbar (or menu) is used to add notes, highlights, or other markings to a PDF document to indicate changes. Comments can be as simple as a sticky note, or as complex as a long explanation. You can also add text edit marks or proofreader marks to the PDF file. Sound and movie attachments can be included, as well as stamps to indicate approval, rejection, and more.

The tools include Sticky Note, Text Edits, Stamp, Highlight Text, Cross Out Text, Underline Text, several drawing tools, Text Box, Pencil, and Attachment. These tools can be found under Tools, Comment and Markup, and can be added to an onscreen toolbar by choosing Tools, Comment and Markup, Show Comment and Markup Toolbar.

To make finding comments (and comment tools) easy, you can enable the Comment panel, which displays a list of all the comments in a document. To open this view, shown in Figure 11.12, click the comment bubble icon in the lower-left corner of your window.

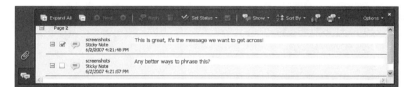

FIGURE 11.12
Enable the Comment panel.

Adding Text Edits

Text edits modify the textual content of the PDF file.

To insert a text edit, first choose the Text Edit tools from the Comment and Markup toolbar. Choose the Text Edits tool and highlight the text on which you want to show edits. Then choose from Insert Text at Cursor, Replace Selected Text, Highlight Selected Text, Add Note to Selected Text, Cross Out Text for Deletion, and Underline Selected Text, as seen in Figure 11.13. When you choose any of the text edit functions, they automatically change the selected text to your chosen text edits.

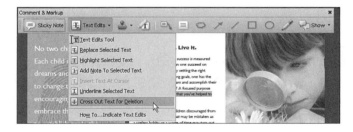

FIGURE 11.13
Text edits change the PDF content itself.

Adding Sticky Notes

Many people simply write a comment on a sticky note and slap it on a printed document. I have even seen sticky notes stuck on a computer screen! To add a sticky note without the mess to your PDF file, choose the Sticky Note tool from the

Comment and Markup toolbar. Click and drag to make the note the needed size. Don't worry, the note won't show up as a huge yellow page covering your PDF. When the note isn't active, it is a small symbol. You can also resize your note at any time. After creating the note, enter the text for your note, as demonstrated in Figure 11.14.

FIGURE 11.14
Sticky notes are a convenient way to mark up a document.

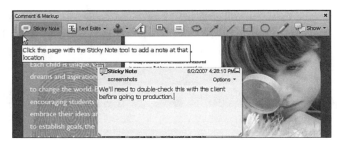

Reading Notes

Obviously, notes are only good if you can read them! To read a note that you or someone else have added to a PDF, first choose the Hand tool. Next, let the Hand tool rest over the note, and you'll see a pop-up of what the note says. You can also double-click the note to open the note completely. To close the note, click the box in the upper-right corner of the Note text box. Double-clicking the note symbol again also closes the note.

Additionally, you can click the Options pop-up menu in the Sticky Note box to perform a variety of tasks, including replying to the comment (creating a thread), setting the status of the comment, and changing the properties of the note itself, such as color and opacity.

Stamp Tool

Another interesting tool is the Stamp feature. Using a virtual rubber stamp, you can stamp a document approved, disapproved, or even create your own stamps.

To add a stamp to a document, you can choose a stamp from the menu, or you can create and use your own stamp. When choosing from the Stamp menu, choose from Dynamic, Sign Here, or Standard Business. Under Dynamic, you can choose from Approved, Confidential, Received, Reviewed, and Revised. In the Sign Here stamp submenu, you'll find Rejected, Accepted, Initial Here, Sign Here, and Witness. The Standard Business stamps are Approved, Completed, Confidential, Draft, Final, For Comment, For Public Release, Information Only, Not Approved, Not for Public Release, Preliminary Results, and Void. Under each of those stamp submenus, you can see a preview of what the stamp looks like, as shown in Figure 11.15.

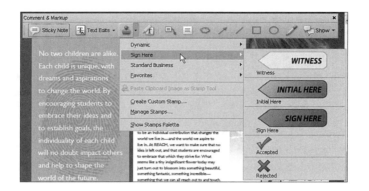

FIGURE 11.15
Preview the different stamp options.

Under the Stamp menu, you'll see the commands Create Custom Stamp, Add Current Stamp to Favorites (in the Favorites submenu), and Manage Stamps. Before choosing Create Custom Stamp, you first must have created the stamp image in another program, such as Adobe Illustrator or Adobe Photoshop. Then you can follow the steps under the Create Custom Stamp command. Alternatively, if you have an image in your clipboard that you'd like to use as a stamp, choosing the Paste Clipboard Image As Stamp Tool command lets you quickly create a custom stamp.

Advanced Comment and Markup Tools

In addition to the basic tools we've seen, Acrobat provides access to other comment and markup tools. You can access these additional tools under the Tools, Comment and Markup submenu, or by choosing Tools, Customize Toolbar and adding the tools to the existing Comment and Markup toolbar. The Advanced Commenting tools fall into the categories of Drawing, Text Box, Pencil, and Attachment.

Under the Drawing tools, you'll find the Rectangle, Oval, Arrow, Line, Cloud, Polygon, and Polygon Line tools. Use the Drawing tools to add a visual markup to your PDF file. The tools can create a dramatic marking to really show your editing ideas. With the Drawing tools, you can add notes as well.

The Text Box tool lets you create a box in which you enter text. You can enhance the text box by accessing the properties of the box. To access the properties, right-click the text box with the Text Box tool as the active tool and choose Properties from the context menu. Under the Properties, change the border color, style, background color, opacity, and border thickness.

The Pencil tool is handy for adding free-form sketching and shapes to a PDF document. The partner to the Pencil tool is the Pencil Eraser tool. Use the Pencil Eraser tool to remove any sections of the lines you have drawn. The Pencil Eraser tool removes only lines drawn with the Pencil tool, not those drawn with any other drawing tools.

Add attachments to your PDF file with the Attachment tools. The Attach a File as a Comment tool allows you to choose any file and add it as an attachment to the PDF file. The Record Audio Comment tool, on the other hand, provides the capability to record and attach a sound file.

To attach a sound to a PDF file, first select the Record Audio Comment tool. Click the cursor on the PDF file where you want the sound symbol to appear. This launches the Record Sound dialog box. You can either record your sound or notes verbally, or choose a sound stored on your computer.

By the Way

> To attach a more advanced sound, such as music from your iPod, you need to use the Advanced Editing tools discussed later in "Using Sound and Video."

Importing and Exporting Comments

Assume that copies of your PDF document get sent to your colleagues for commenting. Once they're done, you might want to import their comments (from all the individual PDF files) and then export your own comments.

To import comments, you first must have the document open into which you want to import the comments. Then choose Import Comments from the Comments menu. This launches the Import Comments dialog box, where you choose the PDF file on your computer. The comments then show up in the comment window and are added into the document as well.

To export your comments, first make sure you have the file with your comments open. Choose Export Comments from the Comment menu. Choose the Save As Type (PDF or XPDF) option, and save the file on your computer.

Summarizing Comments

The Summarizing feature enables you to create a PDF file with all the comments shown and organized by date, author, and type. To use this feature, choose Summarize Comments from the Comments menu or from the Options menu in the Comments panel. You then set how the comments will be organized and displayed. Choose by date, author, type, and page. In the Summarize Options dialog box, you can choose to include the original PDF file with the comments (this might be a large file) or just the comments (see Figure 11.16).

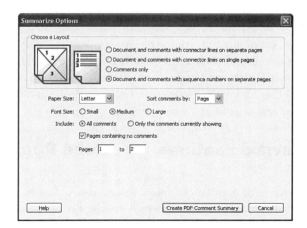

FIGURE 11.16
Choose your
summarization
options.

Additionally, you can choose Comments, Print with Comments Summary to print the comments in a PDF file. This is useful when you need to make corrections to your source file in, say, InDesign.

Reviewing PDF Documents

Acrobat has added the option for you to include others in a reviewing process with PDF documents. You can send a PDF document to your coworkers to get their comments on a file. Use email to start your review or your web browser to host the review. This is a great way to get instant feedback without waiting for the postal or delivery systems to send paper files back and forth. You can set up an email-based review.

Email-Based Review

Setting up an email-based review is a fairly easy task. First open the PDF file you want to be reviewed. Choose Attach for Email Review under the Review and Comment menu of the Tasks toolbar. Then follow the step-by-step process to enter the email addresses of the reviewers and add your email address, and your email program takes care of the rest. Acrobat enters instructions in the email on how to review. Simply click the Send button (if necessary), and the review process is under way.

Review Tracker

Acrobat also has the capability to track the reviews. Under the Review and Comment menu of the Tasks toolbar is the Review Tracker command. Under the Review Tracker, choose which review you want to track. You'll see the list of any documents you have set up for review. The Review Tracker can also be used to invite more people to your review or send a reminder.

Enabling Review Features for Adobe Reader Users

The commercial versions of Acrobat can mark up and review PDF files, but those who have the free Adobe Reader don't have that capability—until now, that is. You can choose Comments, Enable for Commenting in Adobe Reader to allow Adobe Reader users to review and comment on your PDF file.

Using Sound and Movies

To go beyond just plain text and graphical markup, sounds and video can be added to your document. These capabilities can be found in the Advanced Editing tools. The Advanced Editing tools, found under the Tools menu, are Select Object, Article, Crop, Link, Sound, 3D, Movie, TouchUp Text, TouchUp Object, and TouchUp Reading Order. The addition of sound or a movie clip nudges the simple, boring PDF to the next level.

You can select the tools directly from this menu, or turn on the Advanced Editing toolbar from the same menu.

Adding Sound

Add sound clips to any PDF file using the Advanced Editing toolbar. Sound can be played when the sound button is clicked or when a certain action is performed. Use any sounds that can be played in Flash, RealOne, QuickTime, and Windows Media Player. If you are recording your own sounds, make sure you have a microphone attached to your computer. You can add a sound by dragging out a sound button, or you can add sound to a page action or a form field.

Adding Movies

Movies can be added to any PDF document. Unlike attachments, movies are considered an editing feature. You'll find the Movie tool under the Advanced Editing toolbar. Just as you use other applications to access your sound clips, you need other applications to access your video clips. Adding a movie clip to a PDF file is done just as you would add a sound clip. Keep in mind that the larger the movie is, the larger your PDF file will be.

Creating Interactivity

Acrobat lets you create amazing interactive documents using various tools. We have already discussed the Sound and Movie tools. Bookmarks, Flash, links, actions, and buttons are all used to create interactive PDF documents. You can make any PDF form interactive as well. Interactivity just lets you go where no static document has ever gone before.

Adding Bookmarks

Just as you would create a bookmark in your web browser, you can create bookmarks in your PDF documents. This is quite handy for large PDF files with numerous pages. You can access often-used pages quickly with bookmarks.

To create a bookmark, first open the Bookmarks panel by clicking the Bookmarks (page with ribbon) button on the left side of the Acrobat window or via the View, Navigation menu.

Next, go to the page you want to bookmark. Then choose New Bookmark from the Options menu on the Bookmarks panel (or by clicking the bookmark page with a star on it), as seen in Figure 11.17. I suggest entering a name for the page you are bookmarking that lets you know what the page is about.

FIGURE 11.17
Bookmarks make it easy to navigate through files.

In large PDF files, the bookmarks are really nice for navigating in the document. Bookmarks organize your PDF files. You can also access the New Bookmark option by (Ctrl-clicking) [right+clicking] the PDF page you want to bookmark and choosing New Bookmark from the contextual menu.

Accessing the Pages panel lets you view the whole PDF page in a mini preview. This is also a way of navigating to a certain page, but you really won't know which page is which unless they have very different layouts. That is why bookmarks are so handy for navigating exactly to the area you want.

At any time, you can rename, rearrange, or remove bookmarks. By dragging a bookmark above or below another bookmark, you can change the order of the bookmarks. You can also drag a bookmark within a bookmark as a subset of the other bookmark.

Linking and Actions

The Link tool is used to create a button link to other pages in the PDF file. You can also link to other documents or websites on the Internet. Within the link, you can set the properties of the button as you can for the Sound and Movie buttons. You can not only set the properties, but also add an action to the link.

You can choose Actions in the Link Properties dialog box (not in the Create Link dialog box). Some of the actions you can choose from are Go to a Page View, Open a File, Read an Article, Execute a Menu Item, Set Layer Visibility, Show/Hide a Field, Submit a Form, Reset a Form, Import Form Data, Run a JavaScript, Play Media (Acrobat 5 Compatible), Play a Sound, Play Media (Acrobat 6 Compatible), and Open a Web Link. So when you set a link, it can do multiple things.

To set an action to a link, follow these steps:

1. Using the Link tool, drag out a button area for the link.

2. Enter the type of link in the Create Link dialog box.

3. Click OK. Ctrl+click the link with the Link tool to access the Link Properties dialog box.

4. In the Link Properties dialog box, click the Actions tab.

5. Choose an action from the pop-up menu and click OK.

After the link is added, use the Hand tool to click the button to see the action activated.

JavaScript Support

JavaScript enables you to add more cross-platform interactivity to your PDF forms that you just can't get with Acrobat alone. Use JavaScript with forms, links, and page actions. For those of you who are wondering what JavaScript is, it is a coding language for HTML pages. Use it in Acrobat forms for adding up items, costs, and so forth.

To access a JavaScript, choose a button's properties and choose Run a JavaScript from the pop-up menu. Select the desired JavaScript and choose Edit to access the JavaScript Editor. In this editor, you can alter the JavaScript code. Click OK when you are done. For more information on JavaScript, see Moncur, Micheal. *Sams Teach Yourself JavaScript in 24 Hours, 4th Edition* (Sams Publishing: 0-672-32879-8 2006).

Ensuring Accessibility

Acrobat has added accessibility functions to make using Acrobat easier for vision- and motor-challenged people. The features added include the capability of reading out loud, visibility, autoscrolling, keyboard shortcuts, and creating accessible PDF documents.

The Read Out Loud settings are found in Acrobat's Reading preferences. You can set the volume, voice type, pitch, words per minute, reading order, and screen reader options.

Visibility can be enhanced by changing the document's color options in the Accessibility area of Acrobat's Preferences. Other visual enhancements are to increase the magnification in the Default Zoom area of Page Display Preferences.

Under the View menu, you can set the page to automatically scroll. Use the number keys to control the scroll speed (9 being fast scrolling and 0 being slow scrolling). You can also use the up and down arrows for autoscrolling. The right and left arrows take you to the next page and the previous page.

Memorizing keyboard shortcuts is always a great way to enhance your productivity, whether or not you have special needs.

To make your PDF document accessible, Acrobat creates a report on the accessibility of your file. Open the PDF file that you want to make accessible, and click Advanced, Accessibility, Add Tags to Document. Before making your file accessible, you might want to run a quick check (choose Advanced, Accessibility, Quick Check) to see whether you need to fix any problems.

Did you Know?

Using Forms

Forms are probably the most sought-after feature in Acrobat. Use Acrobat to create interactive PDF forms that you can access on a website. Forms are created with data fields to be filled out. Form fields can include buttons, check boxes, combo boxes, list boxes, radio buttons, signature fields, and text fields. Acrobat includes a Forms palette and Form tools. Forms are so popular because you can save form data within Acrobat Standard or Reader. Your only limitation is that you cannot edit in Standard or Reader. Forms are the best way to get information on your client or from your website.

Creating Forms

When you first decide to create a form, you'll need to figure out the type of data you'll require. After you determine the data, the form fields are easy to add. Use a design program to create your actual form. When choosing a size, keep in mind the computer screen and how it will be seen. In the design program, create the text, labels, and any graphic elements.

Typically, you start by designing a form in another application, such as Adobe Illustrator or Microsoft Word. When you've created a PDF file for the form you started in the other program, use the Form tools to create form fields to complete your PDF form.

After you create the form's graphic appearance, save the file as a PDF and open it in Acrobat to add the actual form fields.

Form Elements

The form elements come in various appearances and functions. Each function is used for specific effects. Buttons are used to create an action. You click a button and something happens, such as going to another page or seeing different fields appear. Check boxes are used to narrow selections. A combo box is used like a pop-up menu—you see a list of choices and pick one from the box. The list box is similar to the combo box—you choose one option from the menu. Radio buttons are used to choose an option. You pick one option by clicking the radio button next to it. In the Signature field, you enter a digital signature or, in a printed form, sign your name. The text fields are used to enter such things as names, addresses, items, costs, and totals.

To start a form, add the Forms toolbar to your display.

By the Way

An alternative way to create forms is by using Adobe LiveCycle Designer (Windows Only). To use this feature, click the Forms toolbar button and choose Create a New Form. You are prompted to choose from a variety of existing templates, to import from a spreadsheet, to scan from a paper form, or use a PDF file that has the form base already created in another graphic program.

You are then taken into LiveCycle Designer, which contains extensive tools for precisely laying out PDF forms (see Figure 11.18).

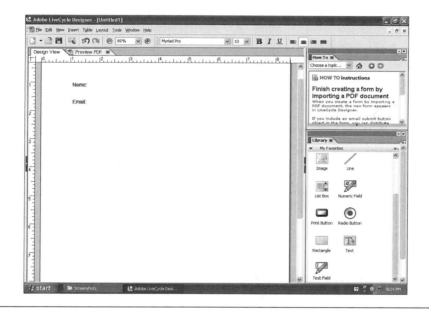

FIGURE 11.18
LiveCycle Designer can be used to lay out complex forms.

Text Fields

To create a text field, use the Text Field tool from the Forms toolbar. Drag out a box to the size that you want the text field to be. This launches the Text Field Properties dialog box, shown in Figure 11.19.

FIGURE 11.19
Edit the proper-
ties for form
text fields.

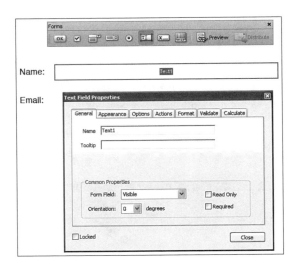

These are the tabs in the Text Field Properties dialog box:

▶ **General**—Under the General properties, set the name of the field and the Tooltips. Tooltips are the little notes that come up when you rest your cursor over an item such as the text field. The Form Field properties you set are whether the box is visible, hidden, visible but not printable, or hidden but printable. Set the orientation to 0º, 90º, 180º, or 270º. Also choose whether to check the Read Only and Required check boxes.

▶ **Appearance**—In the Appearance tab, set the Border Color, Fill Color, Line Thickness, and Line Style. Under Text, choose the Font, Font Size, and Text Color.

▶ **Options**—Choose the alignment for the text field in the Options tab. Enter a default value. Check or uncheck the following boxes: Multiline, Scroll Long Text, Allow Rich Text Formatting, Limit of Characters, Password, Field Is Used for File Selection, Check Spelling, and Comb of Characters.

▶ **Actions**—Set an action for the text field just as you would in a link. Choose your action and the settings.

▶ **Format**—Choose from a format category pop-up: None, Number, Percentage, Date, Time, Special, or Custom.

▶ **Validate**—Check the radio button to specify whether the field value is vali-dated, to indicate whether a field value is within a certain range, or to run a custom validation script.

▶ **Calculate**—Under the Calculate tab, choose whether the field value is calculated and, if it is, whether it is the sum, product, average, minimum, or maximum of a group of fields that you pick. You can also choose a simplified field notation or a custom calculation script.

Set the General, Appearance, Options, Actions, Format, Validate, and Calculate tabs to your liking, and then click the Close button to set the text field.

Buttons

Probably one of the most fun things to do with Acrobat is to create interactive buttons. Acrobat has a Button tool in the Advanced Editing toolbar. Use the Button tool to drag out the size of the button. Enter the properties that you want for the button. Be sure to make an action for the button, or the point of having a button is lost. If you want a more exciting look for your button, use Adobe Illustrator to create a fantastic button and then use Acrobat to activate it.

Add options to your buttons by altering their look and how they act in the Options tab of the Button Properties dialog box. Choose the Icon and Label states: Label Only, Icon Only, Icon Top Label Bottom, Label Top Icon Bottom, Icon Left Label Right, Label Left Icon Right, and Label over Icon.

List Boxes and Combo Boxes

Use the combo box to list various choices for the form field. A list box is very similar to a combo box, in that it offers choices in menu pull-down form. The big difference between the two is that you use the combo box for adding text, whereas a list box can't be used to add text. The combo box is also great for fewer choices. The options you'll find in the list and combo boxes are Item, Export Value, Add, Delete, Up/Down, Sort Items, Multiple Selection (List Box Only), Check Spelling, Item List, and Commit Selected Value Immediately.

Radio Buttons and Check Boxes

Radio buttons and check boxes are used for selecting or deselecting certain variables. The options you'll find under radio buttons and check boxes are Button/Check Box Style, Export Value, Button/Check Box Is Checked by Default, and Buttons with the Same Name and Value Are Selected in Unison.

Performing Calculations

Calculations are great for figuring out a total of items, determining total cost, adding in taxes, and so on. As with spreadsheet programs, you can set up a range of calculations in the Field Properties dialog box. The calculations you can set are adding, multiplying, averaging, and figuring out the minimum and maximum.

To set a calculation field, first pick the type of calculation and then select which fields you want to calculate. To set the field for calculation, use the Text Field tool to create the box for the calculation. In the Text Field Properties dialog box, click the Calculate tab. In the Calculate tab, seen in Figure 11.20, choose from Sum (+), Product (x), Average, Minimum, or Maximum. After you set your value, click the Pick button. This launches the Field Selection dialog box. This dialog box lists all the fields used in your PDF file. Here you can choose which fields will be calculated.

FIGURE 11.20
Plan your
calculations.

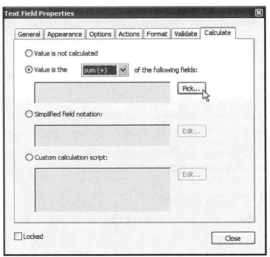

Importing and Exporting Form Data

Now that you are getting the hang of forms, you'll need to know how you can import and export the data from the forms. The key to getting your data is having your field names match word for word. To export your PDF data, choose Forms, Manage Forms, Export Forms Data. Enter a name for your form data file and click Save.

Import your form data by choosing Forms, Manage Forms, Import Forms Data. Locate your file and click Select. Make sure you have the correct and matching file open so the data will be brought in to the file.

Security

Use Acrobat's security to protect your files from unwanted access. When you create a PDF file, it isn't protected until you set the protection. Security commands are located in a submenu of the Advanced menu. Under the Security submenu, choose Show Security Properties, and then click Security. You can now choose from different security methods, as seen in Figure 11.21.

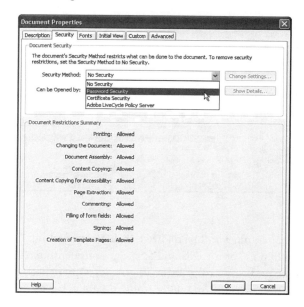

FIGURE 11.21
Set the security policies for your document.

Restricting Opening and Editing

The most common form of security is password security, found in the Security Method pop-up menu. After choosing Password Security, a dialog box appears with the options for protecting your document.

Within this dialog box, you can set the Compatibility version of Acrobat. The lower the version is, the lower the encryption level. The higher the version of Acrobat it is, the higher the encryption level.

You can check the box to require a password to open the document. When you choose this option, you are asked to enter a password. If you choose this option, you always have to use a password to open the document.

Permissions options include using a password to restrict printing and editing of the PDF file and its security settings. With the Permissions check box, you set the password and choose whether you allow no printing, low-resolution printing, or high-resolution printing, as seen in Figure 11.22.

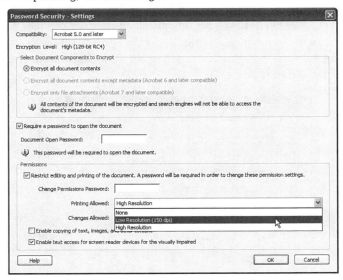

You also set whether changes will be allowed, including Inserting, Deleting, and Rotating Pages; Filling in Form Fields and Signing; Commenting, Filling in Form Fields, and Signing; and Any Except Extracting Pages. Other check boxes include Enable copying of text, images, and other content; Enable text access for screen reader devices for the visually impaired; and Enable Plain-Text Metadata.

You have three tries to open a password-protected PDF file. After three tries, the document closes, and you have to reopen it to try the password again.

Encrypting for Certain Identities

If you choose the certificate security method, the Certificate Security dialog box launches. From here, you are walked through the process of adding authorized recipients to the PDF file.

Digital Signatures

More than ever, people want to use digital signatures to replace hand signatures. Using a digital signature saves a ton of time and money because you don't have to ship physical documents back and forth. A digital signature can be an actual handwritten name, text, or a graphic symbol. When you have a digital signature, you can verify that the signature is authentic.

Acrobat has a Self-Sign Security feature that will create your own signed security certificate. To begin the signing process, choose Advanced, Security Settings. Click the Add ID button to start creating your signature.

When the Add Digital ID dialog appears, click the Create a Self-Signed Digital ID for Use with Acrobat radio button, and then click Next. Enter the digital ID information as prompted in Figure 11.23, and then click Next.

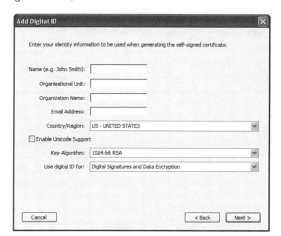

FIGURE 11.23
Self-sign your documents.

Continue through the Add Digital ID wizard, and, when finished, you'll have a digital signature that can be used for signing your documents.

Modifying Signature Appearance

If you'd prefer that your signature appear differently from what the default Adobe signature looks like, you can import graphics and make other modifications. In Acrobat's Preferences dialog box, select Security from the list on the left. Click the New button to add your scanned signature. This launches the Configure Signature Appearance dialog box. In this dialog box, enter a title; under Configure Graphic, choose the imported graphic button, and then click File. In the Select Picture dialog box, click the Browse button, choose your image file, and then click OK. In the Select Picture dialog box, you see a small preview of your signature. Click OK three times while clicking your heels together, and you have a saved digital signature.

Digitally Signing Your Document

The signature you have saved can now be applied to any PDF document.

To sign your PDF document with your digital signature, choose Advanced, Sign and Certify, Place Signature. Next, drag out a box to hold your signature. The Digital Signature Properties dialog box comes up. Select the appearance for the box. Enter your password and then click the Sign button. Your digital signature appears in the box you dragged out, as seen in Figure 11.24.

FIGURE 11.24
Sign your documents.

Certified PDF

After you digitally sign a document, you might want to certify the PDF document. Doing this lets you exercise some control over the editing of the file. To certify your PDF, follow these steps:

1. Choose Save As Certified Document under the File menu. The Save As Certified Document dialog box comes up.

2. In this dialog box, you are told that you need a digital ID to certify the document. You can get a digital ID from an Adobe Partner, or click OK if you already have a digital ID. After you click OK, you set the allowable actions.

3. Drag out the area where you want the certification to appear on your document.

4. Choose your ID appearance, and enter a password.

5. At the bottom of the window, use the Permitted Changes pop-up menu to determine what the user can do after the document is certified.

These Permitted Changes settings take effect only after you save and close the document. It is also a good idea to lock the certifying signature so it can't be cleared or deleted by anyone.

6. Click the Sign button.

7. Enter a name and location, and click Save.

PDF Presentations

Presentations are not limited to PowerPoint or Apple Keynote. Believe it or not, Acrobat can be used for a slideshow presentation. You even get to use fancy transitions between the slides!

One really nice perk of using Acrobat to create a slideshow is that you can send the file to anyone and that person can view it. You need only Adobe Reader (available free online at www.adobe.com) to view the slideshow.

Creating a Slideshow

To create a slideshow presentation with Acrobat, first pick the files you want to be in the slideshow. Make sure that all the files are PDFs. In fact, you can use the Create PDF from Multiple Files function to convert the files and open them together as one bound PDF file as described in "Creating PDF Files."

Using the Create PDF from Multiple Files function, arrange the files in the order in which you want them to appear in the slide show, as seen in Figure 11.25. When you have all the files arranged, click OK. Choose to merge the files into a single PDF file, and then click the Create button.

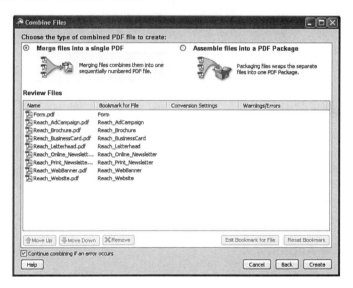

FIGURE 11.25
Arrange the PDF files into the order you want.

Full Screen Preferences

Creating a slideshow is pretty easy. Now let's clean it up by editing the Full Screen preferences. Choose Acrobat, Preferences (Macintosh) or Edit, Preferences (Windows), or press (Cmd-K) [Ctrl+K]. Choose Full Screen from the choices on the left. Here is where you can set how the slideshow functions, as seen in Figure 11.26.

FIGURE 11.26
Set your
slideshow
options.

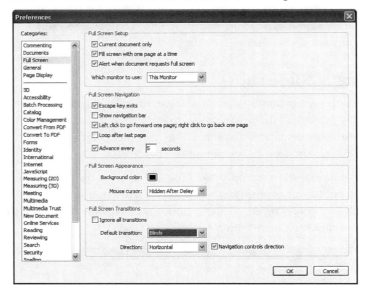

Full Screen Navigation

Enter a value in seconds for how quickly or slowly the slides automatically advance. Check the Loop after last page box to have the slideshow run continually. Keep the Escape key exits box checked so you can quickly get out if you forget the keyboard shortcut. The last option in this area is Left click to go forward one page; right click to go back. These are just nice keyboard commands to navigate your slideshow manually.

Full Screen Appearance

Under this Full Screen preference, you can specify the visibility of the mouse cursor, and background color.

Full Screen Transitions

Transitions are a wonderful way to advance from one page of your slideshow to the next. Use transitions to enhance your presentation. When choosing a transition, keep in mind what your slides look like. For example, if you have mostly text or tables, using a dissolve transition looks rather sloppy and confusing. When you choose a transition, it is used between all slide transitions; you can't choose a different one for each slide. If you are looking for variety, choose the Random transition. This option randomly uses the various transitions between slides.

If some day you decide you don't want the transitions anymore, go to Full Screen Preferences and check the Ignore all transitions option, or choose No transition from the Default transition pop-up menu. Remember that you can also change the background color from the default black to any color you want.

Printing and Saving PDF Files

After creating a fantastic PDF document, you need to make sure that it is saved. Actually, you should be saving periodically so you don't ever lose any information. Saving a PDF file is routine and easy. Choose Save from the File menu to save over the original file, or choose Save As to save the file with a different name. Another choice is Save As Certified Document; this option was discussed earlier in the "Certified PDF" section.

You might wonder about printing your PDF file. As with any other file, you can print your PDF documents.

Saving

When you create a PDF file using most methods, the first time you choose Save you get the Save As dialog box. You don't have to save every file as a PDF. These are the file format choices:

▶ **PDF**—Portable Document Format, or PDF, is easily read by any user who has Adobe Reader (the free program is found at www.adobe.com).

▶ **EPS**—Encapsulated PostScript is used when working with design or page-layout programs.

▶ **HTML**—Use this file type to save documents as text for the Web.

▶ **Graphic formats**—You can save a PDF file as these graphic-type formats: JPEG, JPEG 2000, PNG, and TIFF. When you save a PDF file as any of these formats, you lose the text-editing capability.

▶ **PostScript**—Similar to EPS, PostScript is mostly used to change the printing options of a file.

▶ **RTF**—Rich Text Format lets you use the file in a word-processing application.

▶ **Word**—Use this format to save the file so you can take it back into Microsoft Word.

▶ **Text**—Use this format for plain or accessible text. The text file format retains the text but not the text's formatting.

▶ **XML**—Use this format and XML Data Package Files for forms and to manage document workflows.

Saving a file as anything other than a PDF can offer many options under the Save As dialog box. If you choose to change the default settings under any of the other formats, click the Settings button to see your options, as demonstrated in Figure 11.27.

FIGURE 11.27
Set any additional options for your file format.

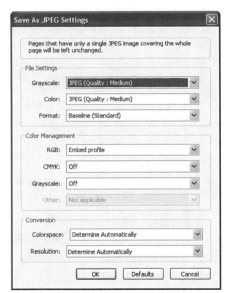

Reverting

The Revert command under the File menu takes the document you are working on back to the last saved version. If you realize that you have made some errors and Undo just won't get you back, choose Revert to revert to the last saved version of the document.

Printing

Print any PDF file by choosing the Print command under the File menu. This launches the Print dialog box. In the Print dialog box, choose the options for Printer, Presets, and Copies and Pages. If you are connected to multiple printers, choose the printer you want to use from the pop-up menu. Choose from standard presets, or if you have saved your own presets, choose one of your own. On Mac OS under Copies and Pages, you have more options from which to choose:

- ▶ **Copies and View**—In this area, choose All Pages, Current View, Current Page, or From [page number] To [page number].

- ▶ **Subset**—In the Subset area, choose from All Pages in Range, Even Pages, and Odd Pages.

- ▶ **Print What**—Use this setting to choose Document, Document and Comments, or Form Fields Only.

- ▶ **Page Scaling**—With Page Scaling, choose None, Fit to Paper, Shrink Large Pages, Tile Large Pages, or Tile All Pages.

- ▶ **Auto-Rotate and Center**—This check box rotates the page to fit the paper and centers the document on the page.

The Printing Tips button launches the troubleshooting area on printing for Acrobat at Adobe's website.

Advanced Printing Options

In the Advanced Print Setup dialog box (click the Advanced button to get there), choose from the following: Output, Marks and Bleeds, Transparency Flattening, and PostScript Options. Each area allows you to do the following:

- ▶ Under the Output options are Color, Screening, Flip, Printer Profile, Apply Working Color Spaces, Apply Proof Settings, Simulate Overprinting, Use Maximum Available JPEG 2000 Image Resolution, Emit Trap Annotations, and Ink Manager.

- ▶ In the Marks and Bleeds setup, choose Emit Printer Marks or All Marks. The Marks Style pop-up menu lets you pick the style of printer's marks. Check or uncheck Crop Marks, Trim Marks, Bleed Marks, Registration Marks, Color Bars, and Page Information.

- ▶ In the Transparency Flattening area, you set the Quality/Speed slider (higher for vector-based images and lower for raster-based images). Enter the rasterization resolution for line art, text, gradients, and meshes in pixels per inch. The other options you can check or uncheck are Convert All Text to Outlines, Convert All Strokes to Outlines, and Clip Complex Regions.

▶ The PostScript Options you can choose are Font and Resource Policy, Print Method, Download Asian Fonts, Emit Undercolor Removal/Black Generation, Emit Halftones, Emit Transfer Functions, Emit PS Form Objects, and Discolored Background Correction.

Printing Color Separations

Use Adobe Acrobat to print your color separations for a color PDF document. In the Print dialog box, click the Advanced button to access your color separation options. Under the Color pop-up menu in the Output options, choose Separations. You can even get as specific as choosing which plates to print. When printing with separations, you get one black, one cyan, one yellow, and one magenta file. Printing separations lets you see whether the different plates register (line up) with each other. If the plates are off in any way, you'll get gaps in the printing and might need to use trapping to fix any problems.

If you want to see what the separations will look like before printing, choose Advanced, Print Production, Output Preview. This launches the Output Preview dialog box (shown in Figure 11.28) where you can see each plate on its own by unchecking the other plates. The preview is directly on your PDF document.

FIGURE 11.28
View a preview of your separations.

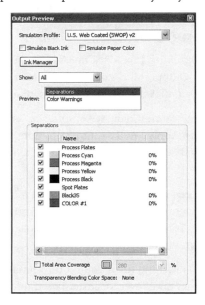

The Output Preview dialog box can help identify ink coverage limits and also high-light areas in your file that are set to overprint.

Preflight

Preflight refers to the analyzing of a document for printing. Preflighting checks for any problems before sending a file to the print shop or service bureau.

Choose Preflight from the Advanced, Print Production submenu to activate the Preflight command. This launches the Preflight dialog box. Under this list, you can choose a preset profile, or you can edit a preset profile by choosing the file and click-ing the Edit button. After you have chosen your profile, click the Analyze button to check the file.

You can choose from a bunch of preflight profiles. Click one and click Edit to see the rules and conditions of that particular profile. Each profile has certain rules and conditions.

After you have either chosen or created the preflight profile, click the Analyze but-ton to check the current file. It might take a few minutes to analyze the file, depend-ing on the file size. After the file is analyzed, the results appear in the dialog box. Any problems with the file are listed, based on the rules of the profile that you chose earlier. Then with the results listed, you can decide whether and how to fix the files.

Creating PDF/X-1a–Compliant Files

When you have a preflight validated file, you can create a PDF/X-compliant file. Use this when sending out a file for a professional print job. PDF/X is a form of the PDF created by the International Standards Organization. The intent is to increase the reliability of printing and streamline the process by getting rid of unneeded information in a PDF document.

Acrobat Distiller

Included with Acrobat is Distiller. Distiller is used to convert a PostScript file (created by another application) into a PDF file. To convert a PostScript file to a PDF docu-ment using Distiller, you can simply drag the PostScript file on top of the Distiller icon, or with Distiller active, open the PostScript file. You can also adjust the settings in Distiller to output the PDF file the way you want.

Acrobat Distiller can be launched as a separate application, or you can start it in Acrobat under the Advanced menu.

Summary

In this chapter you learned about Adobe Acrobat 8 and PDF files—*the* standard for viewing styled documents on multiple platforms. Acrobat provides many tools for manipulating PDFs, including commenting, editing, sticky notes, and more. Using the Acrobat tools, you can even create electronic forms that can be filled in using the free Acrobat reader software. Acrobat integrates with OCR software and Microsoft Office to provide a seamless and convenient way to get all of your documents—electronic or on paper—into a standard digital format.

PART III

The Projects

CHAPTER 12

Creating a Corporate Identity

In this chapter, you'll create a logo, a business card, a letterhead, and a standard #10 envelope for a fictitious company, REACH. This company provides goal-setting workshops and tutoring for children and teens, encouraging them to achieve their dreams through focused effort. There are many other tutoring companies out there, and REACH has hired you to give it an identity that will set it apart from others and that will clearly define its niche in the market. In an effort to communicate its vision, REACH has decided to use the tag line "Learn. Grow. Succeed."

I've chosen to use images from iStock Photo. If you would like to work along with these projects, you can download these images from http://www.istockphoto.com/teachyourselfcs3.php.

By the Way

Creating a Version Cue Project

Start by creating a new Version Cue project. Launch Bridge and choose Tools, Version Cue, New Project (see Figure 12.1). Name your project reach, add a description in the Project Info field, and check the Share This Project with Others option before clicking the OK button.

FIGURE 12.1
Creating a new Version Cue project from within Bridge.

Creating the Logo

The first step is to create a logo for REACH. It's best to create logos in Illustrator because vector art is scalable to any size. It's also easier to repurpose the art for print or Web use, as well as to easily apply spot colors, if necessary.

The logo you're going to create for REACH will consist of a type treatment and an illustration. Launch Adobe Illustrator CS3 and create a basic CMYK document.

Choosing a Typeface

Choosing a typeface is obviously one of the most important parts of designing a logo. Although it might be fun trying to find a totally unique font to use, remember that a logo has to be clear and readable. It's not just by coincidence that so many logos are set in fonts such as Helvetica or Garamond. You can always add little tweaks to the type afterward to give it a unique look, if necessary.

Press T to select the Type tool and type REACH. Try applying different fonts to the type to get the look you want (see Figure 12.2). I chose Gill Sans Light because I think it gives a clean, confident look. (If Gill Sans Light isn't available on your system, Myriad Pro Regular is another good choice.)

In the Character panel, change the type size to 72 point. Set the tracking amount to –18 to pull the letters toward each other and turn on Optical Kerning (see Figure 12.3); letters aligned in this way will work well with the illustration you're going to be adding.

Next, start a new line of text and type the tag line **learn. grow. succeed**. Change the tag line to a font size of 24 point, with tracking of 50 and leading of 25 point. Also, turn off Optical Kerning for the tag line text. This treatment makes the tag line a nice counterpoint to the larger, uppercase company name text.

Now you'll want to convert the text to outlines. This is usually a good idea with a logo, making it easier to send the logo to others without worrying about fonts. The last thing you would want is to have your logo look completely different just because the person who opened it on another computer didn't have your exact font. To convert the text to outlines, select the Type object and choose Type, Create Outlines. The typography part of the logo is now complete.

FIGURE 12.2
I usually stack different type treatments and then eliminate the ones that don't work, leaving me with a choice few to make a final decision.

FIGURE 12.3
Setting the tracking and the kerning so the characters look better as a unit.

Creating an Illustration

To add a graphic element to the logo, you can create an illustration that can quickly help identify what REACH does or represents. Because the company represents reaching for your dreams, here you'll create the image of a hand reaching for the stars. Rather than attempt to actually draw a hand and stars, you'll employ Illustrator's Live Trace feature to help create a realistic illustration that will surely draw attention. Remember that because you're creating this in Illustrator, it will be easy to repurpose this design element for other needs.

It's always a good idea to plan your art in advance and try to anticipate ways it will be used—and build it to work for all uses. You never know where or when the art might be needed.

Did you Know?

To create a hand and three stars to echo the three words in REACH's tag line, you first place an image into Illustrator with which to work. Choose File, Place, and navigate to the folder of images and locate the file iStock_000001106412Large.jpg, which is a photograph that matches our concept (see Figure 12.4). The image, as it appears in your document, is too big for your needs here. With the image still selected, double-click the Scale tool, enter a value of 15% in the Uniform field, and click OK (see Figure 12.5). Position the scaled image to the left of the text.

FIGURE 12.4
The image of a
hand and three
stars.

FIGURE 12.5
Scaling the
placed image.

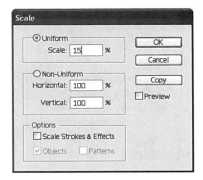

Using raster images in a logo is usually not a great idea because if the logo needs to be scaled up in size, you will lose resolution and detail. The Live Trace feature in Illustrator enables you to convert this pixel-based image into a vector-based image and also enables you to customize the look of the image. Select the image, click the Tracing Presets and Options icon in the Control panel, and choose Comic Art.

The result of the Live Trace (see Figure 12.6) is a more stylized image because of the posterization that occurs as a result of a reduction to fewer colors.

This is a very good trace of the hand, and lowest of the three stars, but there is some clean up to do to remove the smudge at the upper right and fix the other two stars. To do this, you'll need to expand the paths so you can work with sections of the trace individually. Click Expand in the Control panel and watch the selection switch to paths with points (see Figure 12.7).

FIGURE 12.6
Applying the Comic Art preset in Live Trace to the hand and stars image.

FIGURE 12.7
Expanding a traced object allows you to edit points along its paths.

To remove unwanted points, choose the Direct Selection tool, select the mess of points at the upper right, and press Delete on your keyboard. Do the same for the top two stars. Don't worry—you'll replace them with copies of the bottom star. Also delete the corner points at the upper left, lower left, and lower right.

As long as you're cleaning up, now is a good time to point out that Live Trace makes both shaded and white shapes, which can be confusing when you start moving and changing the tracings. To remove them, switch to the Selection tool, select the traced objects, and choose Object, Ungroup. Select the shaded shapes and nudge them of the way, and then click areas where there might be white shapes and delete them.

All of the pieces of the traced image are grouped and you will need to use the Direct Selection tool to move individual parts. However, you can use the regular Selection tool if you ungroup the object.

Did you
Know?

Now that you have a clean area to work in, select the remaining star and double-click the Selection tool, which brings up the Move dialog box. Click the Copy button (see Figure 12.8). Using the Direct Selection tool, position the new star approximately where one of the originals was. Then press (Cmd-D) [Ctrl+D] to duplicate the last transformation, which gives you a total of three stars. Position the final star roughly where you want it.

FIGURE 12.8
Moving a copy
of a star.

Let's vary the angle of the stars, as they were in the original image. Select the top star and choose Object, Transform, Rotate from the menu and set the Angle property to 340. Select the other new star and set its angle to 15.

You will now change the appearance of the traced object by using different shades of gray instead of black. Choose Swatch Library from the Swatches panel (see Figure 12.9), and open the Metal library. Now that the library is open in your document, you can use these colors for your traced objects.

FIGURE 12.9
Opening a
swatch library
from the
Swatches
panel.

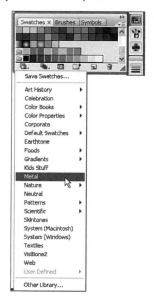

Select the star at the top and click a deep gray in the Swatches library. Set the star just below it to a medium gray and the bottom star to a light gray. For the reaching hand, echo the dark gray of the top star to bring visual coherence (see Figure 12.10).

FIGURE 12.10
The stars and hand are changed to shades of gray in the Metal swatches library.

Now, you'll create a border by clicking once on the artboard with the Rectangle tool. Specify a width of 1.5 inches and a height of 2 inches, and press the D key to fill it white with a black stroke. Change the width of the stroke to 4 points and change the fill to a very soft gray. Send it to the back of the stacking order and position it behind the hand and stars (see Figure 12.11).

FIGURE 12.11
Positioning the border behind the hand and stars.

The hand is overlapping the box more than we'd like, so we'll need a clipping mask to hide the part we don't want. Fortunately, our rectangle is exactly what we need. Duplicate it and carefully position it on top of the original rectangle with the extra area of the hand shape sticking out; notice that the new rectangle is at the top of the stack. Then, hold down the Shift key and select both the new rectangle and the hand. Choose Object, Clipping Mask, Make from the menu bar. The hand now fits neatly in the box (see Figure 12.12).

FIGURE 12.12
Mask the vector
hand shape
with a clipping
mask for
neater edges.

To complete the logo, position the text you created earlier to the right of the rectangle (see Figure 12.13).

FIGURE 12.13
The completed
logo.

Saving the Logo

Choose File, Save and click the Use Adobe Dialog button (if the button reads Use OS Dialog, you're already using the Adobe dialog box). This dialog box gives you direct access to your Version Cue project. Navigate to the Reach Version Cue project (start by clicking on the Version Cue icon listed on the left side of the dialog box) and save the file as a native Illustrator document (.ai). Give it a comment describing what it is. If you have enough RAM, you can leave Illustrator running, but if your computer has less than 512MB of RAM, quit Illustrator so you won't be slowed down when working in other applications.

Preparing a Photo

The next step in our project is preparing a photo to use as a background on the letterhead and business card. The client wants something that will grab a reader's attention (what client doesn't?), and using a photograph adds some punch. Locate photo iStock_000000289745Large.jpg and open it in Photoshop.

Adjusting the Image

Although the image looks pretty good, I'd like to convert it to true grayscale and make a few small adjustments. Choose Image, Adjustments, Desaturate to remove any hint of color.

Next, let's lighten up the shadows to give a softer image. Choose Image, Adjustments, Shadow/Highlight. I think the default Shadows setting of 50% is too low, so drag the slider up to 100% (see Figure 12.14).

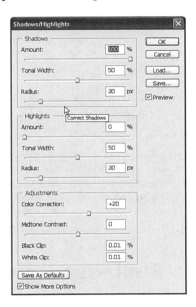

FIGURE 12.14
Applying the Shadow/ Highlight filter to enhance the shadows and the highlights of the image.

The photo still seems a bit too harsh for the calm, confident mood you're after. Blur the edges to give a more soothing feeling. Choose Filter, Blur, Smart Blur and use a threshold of 30 and a radius setting of 3 pixels (see Figure. 12.15).

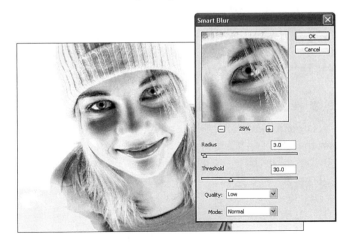

FIGURE 12.15
Smart Blur softens edges.

> Just as the Blur filters can soften a photo, the Sharpen filters can create sharper edges. Sharpening a photograph can give it the pop it needs to grab attention.

Finally, convert the image to the CMYK color space by choosing Image, Mode, CMYK Color.

Saving the Image

You're done with the image for now, so you can save it to your Version Cue project. Choose File, Save As and navigate to your REACH project. Save the image as a native Photoshop file (.psd) and add a comment.

> I know it takes an extra few seconds to add a comment to a file when you save it using Version Cue, but remember that a few seconds now can save you several minutes later when you're trying to find a particular file. It also helps when other people in your department need to use your files for other projects.

Designing the Business Card

Now that the design elements are complete, you can lay out and design the stationery. Although it's possible to create business cards inside Illustrator (and, in some cases, it makes sense to do so), for this example, you will use InDesign. Start by launching InDesign CS3.

> I like to start designing the business card first because it's normally used most often and because the business card is small and thus forces you to think and design clearly. If you create other items first, you might find that your design won't work in such a small space.

Creating a New Document

Create a new document, setting the Page Size to Custom, the Orientation to Landscape, and the Width to 3.5 inches and the Height to 2 inches. Set your margins to 0.125 inches all around and click the More Options button to set a Bleed of 0.125 inches all around as well (see Figure 12.16).

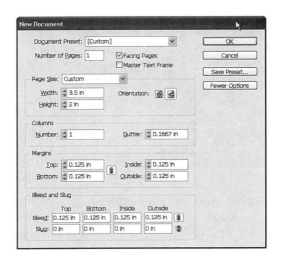

FIGURE 12.16
Setting up a
new document
in InDesign.

> Because business cards are so common, you can save a document preset with these specifications to use again later. Simply click the Save Preset button and specify a name. The next time you want to create a business card, you'll be able to choose the preset from the Document Preset pop-up menu.

Did you Know?

Place the Photoshop file from Version Cue (see Figure 12.17). You'll have the image bleed off the card, so use the Scale tool to resize the image to fit within the card's outside edges. Use the Selection tool to resize the picture frame to form neat edges.

FIGURE 12.17
Placing the
image. Note
that the placing
preview is mere-
ly a thumbnail
image of the
original.

Now you can place the Illustrator logo from the Version Cue project. Scale the logo so it fits nicely within the card (see Figure 12.18).

FIGURE 12.18
Scaling and
positioning the
logo over the
photo.

Enter the additional text information on the card. I used 8-point Gill Sans Light on 10-point leading to type 15-285 Learning Lane, Lake Success, NY 11020, 516.555.8000, www.reachforlearning.com. Bold the phone number and position the type under the logo (see Figure 12.19). Feel free to add your name and make yourself the CEO of the company, if you'd like. So you can see the outcome better, choose View, Display Performance, High Quality Display.

FIGURE 12.19
Adding the infor-
mational text to
the card.

Although the card is shaping up nicely, the image in the background is demanding too much attention. Changing the opacity of the image will result in a more subtle background. Select the image with the Selection tool, and change the Opacity setting in the Control panel to a value of 25%.

Did you Know?

If desired, you can edit an image you've placed in InDesign by selecting it and opening the Links panel. Click the Edit Original icon to automatically open the image in Photoshop.

Although the faded image looks good, it might be more effective to bring out the face along the left side with a gray overlay. Use the Rectangle tool to create a shape over the left one-third of the card. Change the fill color to black, and then change the Opacity setting in the Control panel to 25% (see Figure 12.20). The face is now nicely highlighted.

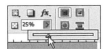

FIGURE 12.20
Change the Opacity to allow the image behind to show through.

To create additional emphasis, use the Rectangle tool to create an 80% black bar between the face and the logo on the card.

Finish the business card with a great quote. Create a new text frame and type The wisest mind has something yet to learn.. Then set it to 16-point Gill Sans Regular with leading of 16 and tracking of –10. Position the quote over the photo on the left side of the card as four rows of text, and make the text white so it shows over the gray background. Then, add the attribution line George Santayana on a separate line as 6-point type.

Press the W key on your keyboard to view the final business card in Preview mode (see Figure 12.21). Save the file into your Version Cue project and remember to add a comment.

FIGURE 12.21
The final business card.

Designing the Letterhead

Next you'll design the letterhead, which is very similar in design to the business card you just made. Create a new document in InDesign that is set to letter size 8.5 × 11 with a margin of 0.375 inches all around and a bleed of 0.125 inches all around as well.

Rather than redoing all the work you did for the business card, simply open the business card file and copy all the contents from it. Then switch back to the letterhead document and paste.

Scale the photo to 510% and position it so it fits correctly, bleeding off the edges of the page. Use the shaded sidebar with quote on the left edge, like in the business card. Select the gray rectangle and size it to 2 inches wide (plus extra for the bleed), and then select and size the dark gray bar to 1/8-inch wide and the height of the document and place it along the right side of the gray rectangle. Resize your quote text to 22-point with leading of 26, and make the text size for the attribution 12 point.

Scale the logo to 160% and position it. Next, select the address text, change it to 10-point type on 12-point leading, and position it in the bottom-left corner. Copy and paste the web address into a new text frame and position it to the right of the street address and phone number. The letterhead is now complete (see Figure 12.22), so save it into Version Cue and add a comment to the file.

FIGURE 12.22
The business card elements carry over to the letterhead.

Designing the Envelope

Finally, you'll create a standard #10 envelope. Create a new InDesign file, set to 9.5 inches wide and 4.125 inches tall. Set the margins to 0.375 inches; you don't need a bleed because you won't be using the photo or background colors in this design.

Did you Know?

As I mentioned earlier with the business card, you might consider saving the envelope settings as a document preset so you can quickly create standard envelopes in the future.

First, copy and paste the logo and the text from the letterhead file and remove the phone number (not necessary for an envelope). Position the text and the logo in the upper-left corner of the envelope and save the file to your Version Cue project with a comment to complete the envelope (see Figure 12.23).

FIGURE 12.23
The final #10
envelope.

Congratulations, you've just created a complete corporate identity!

Summary

In this chapter, you learned many tricks for using CS3 to create a logo as well as a business card and stationery to reinforce the corporate identity. To create the logo, you used Adobe Illustrator to make a vector version of an image using the Live Trace feature. You then created vector shapes to frame your logo and cleaned up the edges with a clipping mask. You also learned how to convert text to outlines to preserve its shape regardless of font availability. For the business card and stationery, you used InDesign to lay out print documents for a business card, letterhead, and envelope. You then placed your new logo, inserted and scaled an image (that you had edited in Photoshop), and applied and styled text.

CHAPTER 13

Creating a Brochure

In this chapter, you'll create a trifold brochure (also called a "slim jim") for REACH. You created the company's corporate identity in the preceding chapter, and you can use some of those assets for this project as well.

> If you're following along using Version Cue, you'll use the same REACH project you created for the preceding chapter.

By the Way

Planning the Layout in InDesign

A trifold brochure; is an 8.5 × 11–inch sheet of paper that's folded twice. The result is a brochure that has six panels and can fit inside a standard #10 envelope. (Note that these sizes follow U.S. standards.) When you are laying out the brochure in InDesign, you'll need to arrange the panels so that the job will look correct when it is folded and printed.

Launch InDesign and create a new document. In the New Document dialog box, specify the following options (see Figure 13.1):

- ▶ Set the number of pages to 2.
- ▶ Uncheck the Facing Pages option.
- ▶ Specify a letter-size page (8.5 × 11 inches) with an orientation set to landscape (wide).
- ▶ Set your number of columns to 3 and specify a gutter of 0.5 inches.
- ▶ Set the margins to 0.25 inches all around and set the bleeds to 0.125 inches all around.

Click OK. Save the file into your Version Cue project with a comment.

New Document
Document Preset: [Custom]
Number of Pages: 2
Facing Pages
Master Text Frame
OK
Cancel
Save Preset...
Fewer Options
Page Size: Letter
Width: 11 in
Height: 8.5 in
Orientation:
Columns
Number: 3
Gutter: 0.5 in
Margins
Top: 0.25 in
Bottom: 0.25 in
Left: 0.25 in
Right: 0.25 in
Bleed and Slug
Top
Bottom
Left
Right
Bleed: 0.125 in
0.125 in
0.125 in
0.125 in
Slug: 0 in
0 in
0 in
0 in

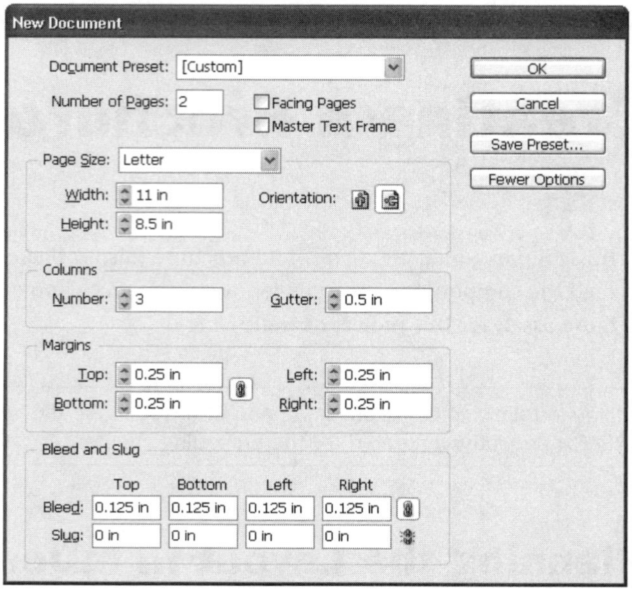

FIGURE 13.1 Specifying the document settings for the brochure.

Importing the Text

Before beginning the actual design and layout, I like to label the individual panels, making it easier to visualize the final piece (see Figure 13.2). Most important, this step keeps you from accidentally mixing up the panels.

Flap
Back
Front
Inside 1
Inside 2
Inside 3

FIGURE 13.2 Labeling the panels in the layout. You'll delete these later in the project.

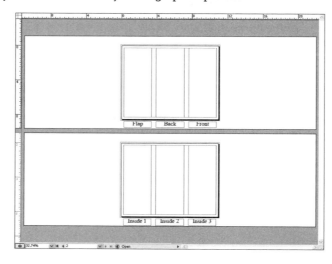

Before continuing, plan the content for each panel. The front panel will show eye-catching graphics to attract attention. The inside panels will present details about REACH and its services. The flap will contain an inspiring quote, and the back will contain an invitation to visit. (On brochures that are intended for mailing, the back panel is an addressing space and is mostly blank.)

The next step is to bring in the text. For many jobs, you'll receive text files from a word-processing program (Microsoft Word, for example). Of course, at times you'll also receive text that you'll have to copy and paste from an email, and there will be plenty of times when you'll type the text directly into InDesign. I'm going to place a Word file and then break up the text as needed. Place a file by choosing Place from the File menu and navigating to the text file.

> If you are creating a sample layout and don't have the real content, simply draw a text frame and choose Type, Fill with Placeholder Text.

Did you Know?

After placing the text frame on the panel where it should start (in our case, the second inside panel because of the ordering of the sections in the text file), choose the Selection tool and click on the out-port box of the frame and then click in the panel where the text continues (see Figure 13.3). This threads the text so that it flows from one panel to the next.

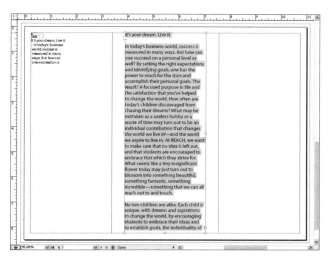

FIGURE 13.3
Threading the text across two panels.

The sections of text for this project were written to fit on specific panels of the brochure, so we want to choose where the text splits. To force threaded text to break to the next threaded panel at a chosen point, press Shift+Enter. Break before the second paragraph of text so it appears in the first inside panel. The quote and invitation to visit are to appear on the flap and back, respectively, so force those blocks of text to break to new frames and thread the text to the flap and back panels (see Figure 13.4). Choose the Selection tool to reposition or resize the text frames so all the text is visible.

FIGURE 13.4
Separate sections of content into their panels.

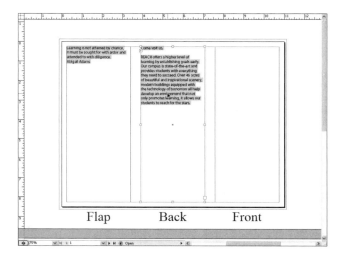

Flap   Back   Front

Preparing Images

You'll be using several photos in the brochure, so return to your iStock photo lightbox as you did in the preceding chapter's project.

As in the previous chapter, images are from iStock Photo. If you would like to work along with these projects, you can download these images from http://www.istockphoto.com/teachyourselfcs3.php.

In this brochure, you're going to use five images, which we'll convert to grayscale to match our logo and identity pieces. The images are

▶ A child holding a ball (iStock_000000277310Medium.jpg)

▶ A building (iStock_000000212151Medium.jpg)

▶ A photo of a tree (iStock_000000337933Small.jpg)

- ► A father and child (iStock_000001208679Large.jpg)

- ► A child with a magnifying glass (iStock_000000676021Large.jpg).

> All of our photos are in good condition, but if it's needed, Photoshop's Healing Brush makes it easy to blend away imperfections, such as dust specks, scratches, or other small flaws. To use this tool, select the Healing Brush tool and set your brush size. Next, (Option-click) [Alt+click] on a clean area of the photo and then draw over the imperfection to remove it. Use the Blur tool or the Clone tool to touch up any edges, and press (Cmd-D) [Ctrl+D] to release the selection.

To begin, open all the images in Photoshop. As we will desaturate all the images, let's create an action to automate the process. Also, although we want to use black-and-white images for this piece, in the future we might want the option to use these images in color, so let's use adjustment layers that can be made visible or invisible, depending on which effects are needed.

To create actions in Photoshop, choose Windows, Actions from the menu to launch the Actions panel. Click Create New Action at the bottom of the panel, type a descriptive name such as REACH_bw, and click Record. At this point, any changes you make in the current file will be recorded so you can "play" them in another file (see Figure 13.5). Choose New Fill or Adjustment Layer, Hue and Saturation from the bottom of the Layers panel. When you are done with the steps you want to automate, click Stop Playing/Recording at the bottom of the Actions panel. Run this action for the remaining images and save them as Photoshop files (.psd).

FIGURE 13.5
Record an action to apply a set of changes to other images.

Before quitting Photoshop, you're going to create a fade-out on the bottom edge of the photo of the child with a magnifying glass. Double-click on the Background layer to make it editable—click OK in the New Layer dialog. Then, select the Gradient tool, set the Gradient picker to Foreground to Transparent, press the Q key to enter Quick Mask mode, and create a fade that starts just above the flower and ends just below the flower. Press Q again to exit Quick Mask mode, and a selection area will appear over the lower portion of the image (see Figure 13.6). Choose Layer, Layer Mask, Hide Selection to execute the fade.

FIGURE 13.6
Create a Quick Mask gradient selection over the lower edge of the photo.

You should now see the checkerboard transparency grid fading on the right side of the image (see Figure 13.7). When you drop this file into an InDesign layout later in the project, InDesign will see and recognize this transparency as well. Save the image.

FIGURE 13.7
The image with the transparent fade layer mask applied.

Save your images to your project folder and return to InDesign.

Designing the Cover

Switch back to InDesign, and you'll begin designing the brochure, starting with the three cover panels. In our previous project, we used gray bars and backgrounds to add visual interest. You are going to carry those design elements forward. Start by dragging a guide six inches from the top of the page. Next, let's use the Rectangle tool to create a 1/8-inch wide band below the guide and set the color to 80% black using the Color panel—be sure to set the stroke weight to 0 unless you want an outline. Then, use the Rectangle tool to create gray backgrounds on the bottom of the front panel and top of the flap panel. (Create these rectangles to extend exactly halfway into the gutters so they will end on the folds.) Set the color to 12% black, and choose Object, Arrange, Send to Back so these rectangles won't interfere with other objects (see Figure 13.8).

Make sure rulers and guides are visible, or you won't be able to place guides precisely. Also, if needed, you can change the ruler units to inches under the Units and Increments Preferences.

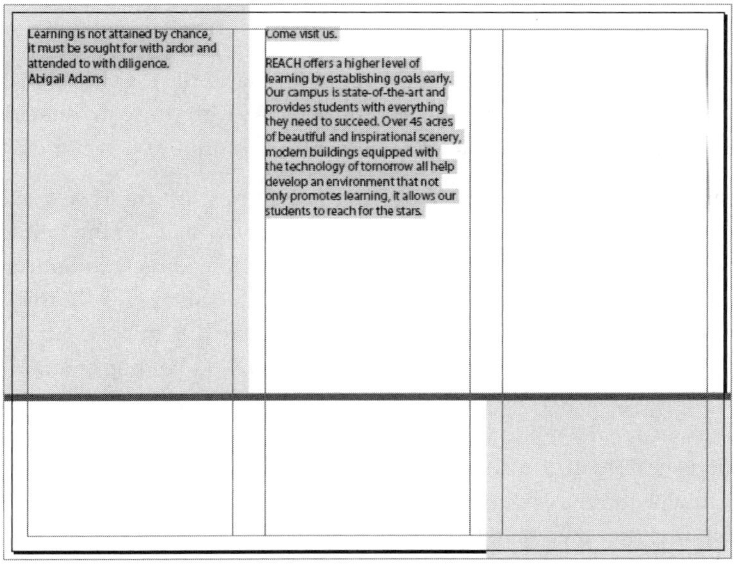

By the Way

FIGURE 13.8
Rectangles of varying degrees of black add visual interest.

Now that we have some structure, it's time to design the front panel. Press (Cmd-D) [Ctrl+D], locate the image of the child holding a ball, and place it on the front panel. Adjust the picture frame and scale the image to fit within the cover, extending halfway into the gutter to account for the fold (see Figure 13.9). Remember to allow the image to bleed off the right and top edges of the page.

FIGURE 13.9
The image, correctly scaled and positioned on the front panel.

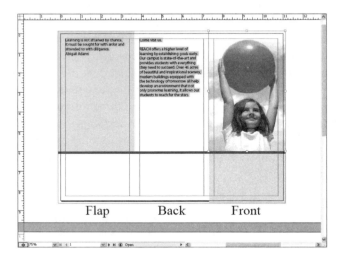

Flap   Back   Front

Text Effects

At the bottom of the front panel, there is space for the words "Success is within reach"—this slogan emphasizes REACH's message. As with the logo, this slogan may be reused across several pieces, so let's create it in Illustrator as a vector graphic.

Open Illustrator and create a new document. Press T to select the Type tool and type the phrase, pressing Return after the words *Success* and *within*. Set the font to Gill Sans, and make the first two lines 30 point on 36-point leading with optical kerning. Change only the word *reach* to 90 point with 60-point leading and -22 tracking. (Press the spacebar twice at the beginning of the middle line to break up the harshness of the left edge.) To make the text stand out more, add a drop shadow by using the Selection tool to select the text, and choose Effects, Stylize, Drop Shadow from the menu. Specify a blending mode of Multiply, 100% for Opacity, and 0 for the X and Y offsets (see Figure 13.10), and then click OK. Change the text color to white so the drop shadow produces the effect. Finally, select the type object and choose Type, Create Outlines and then save the slogan to your project folder.

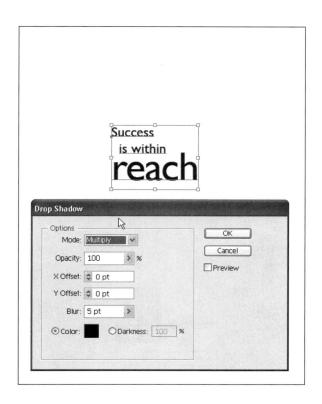

FIGURE 13.10
Specifying the
drop shadow
for the text.

Return to InDesign and place your slogan at the bottom of the front panel (see Figure 13.11).

FIGURE 13.11
The additional
text completed
and in position.

Additional Images and Text Styling

The back panel, which will be visible when the brochure is folded, is an invitation to visit. To begin, set the text to 12-point Gill Sans, with a style of Light and a leading of 16 to give some openness to the text. Make the heading 16-point Gill Sans Bold.

Now that you have your text in place, let's add the photo of REACH's main building. Place the image and scale it to approximately 1.5 inches wide. For emphasis, give the photo an outline by setting a 2-point black stroke. Now, position and integrate the text to start about in the middle of the image. Put a few line breaks between the heading and the remaining text and add a 2-point black line below the heading to connect it to the image—hold down the Shift key while dragging to create a perfectly straight line (see Figure 13.12).

FIGURE 13.12
The text on the back panel integrates with the image.

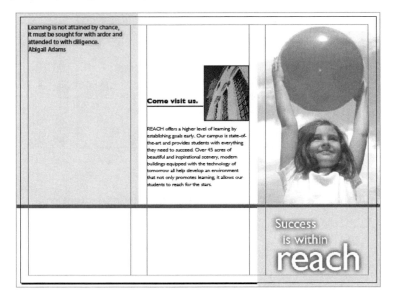

For the flap, you'll use an inspiring quote and the tree photograph you'll prepare in Photoshop. To style the quote, set the text to 22-point Gill Sans. (If you'd like, set the quote's source smaller.) Using the Type tool, select the text and change the color to white in the Color panel.

Now, consider the photo treatment. To soften the edges, you'll create an oval shape with vignette (faded) edges. Choose the Ellipse Frame tool to create a frame area for the image. Keeping the frame selected, place the image in the frame. The image is much too large for the frame, so choose Object, Fitting, Fill Frame Proportionally to fit the image to the frame size. To soften the edges of the framed object, choose

Objects, Effects, Basic Feature and set the Feather Width to .25 inches. Position the framed image in the panel where you want it to appear.

Creating a Text Wrap

The next step is to wrap the text around the oval-shaped image. First, select the quote text and bring it to the front of the stack. Then, hold down the Shift key to select both the text and the image, and choose Window, Text Wrap to open the Text Wrap panel (see Figure 13.13). Click the Wrap Around Object Shape option, and position the text frame so that the text wraps nicely (see Figure 13.14). You can continue to position the text as needed.

FIGURE 13.13
Opening the Text Wrap panel.

FIGURE 13.14
The styled text wrapped around the oval-shaped image frame.

Adding the Logo

Finally, you'll add the logo to the bottom of the back panel. Press (Cmd-D) [Ctrl+D] to place the REACH logo. Double-click the Scale tool and scale to 50%. Position the logo. Switch to High Quality Display so you can better see what you're doing.

As a finishing step, use the Type tool to add the web address for REACH. Set the font to Gill Sans and the size to 10 points, and position below the logo text.

One side of the brochure is now complete (see Figure 13.15).

**Did you
Know?**

To hide the artboard around your canvas, switch the Screen Mode to Preview. If the Selection tool is active, you can do this by simply pressing the W key. Your canvas will be framed in a neutral gray and any objects not inside the canvas will be hidden, as shown in Figure 13.15.

FIGURE 13.15
One side of
the brochure,
completed.

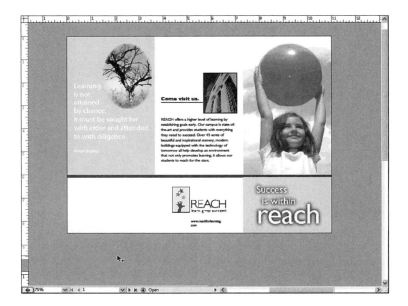

Designing the Inside of the Brochure

Now let's move to the inside of the brochure. Switch to page 2 of your InDesign document.

As with the cover, set a horizontal guide to the 6-inch mark. Return to the cover, copy the horizontal gray bar, and return to the second page and choose Edit, Paste in Place. Next, set the first panel apart with a vertical, 80% black, 1/8-inch wide bar, positioned in the gutter between columns. Then, create a 30% black rectangular background for the entire first panel, remembering to extend it halfway into the gutter and to send it to back.

Next, select the text in the left panel, and choose white for the color to make it more readable against the medium-gray background. Set the font to Gill Sans with a size of 20 point and a leading of 34 point to give it a more spacious feel.

In the bottom of the left panel, place the image of father and child. Scale and crop it so that it fits in the first panel (see Figure 13.16).

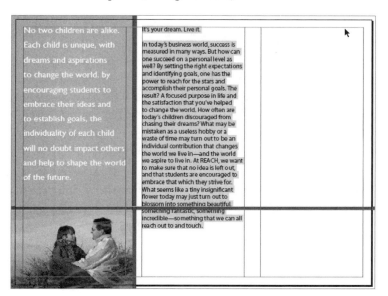

FIGURE 13.16
The image, scaled, cropped, and in position.

Adding a Background

You'll use the graphic of a fingerprint to add a background to the left panel and fill out the design. The fingerprint motif reinforces the individualized attention REACH offers its students.

Place the image outside the page margins to avoid accidentally placing it inside another object on the canvas. (If you try to place it inside the page margins, you are likely to place it inside another object—making it very hard to resize and position!) Now, use the Scale tool to size it—hold down the Shift key to preserve the proportions. Then position it in the left panel. Keep the object selected. Open the Effects panel and choose a blending mode of Multiply so the white background drops out. Also, decrease its opacity to 30% so the image blends into the background of the page to make the text easier to read. After you've positioned it, send it back in the stacking order by pressing (Cmd-[) [Ctrl+[] until the text is visible (see Figure 13.17).

FIGURE 13.17
The fingerprint
background
appears behind
the quote.

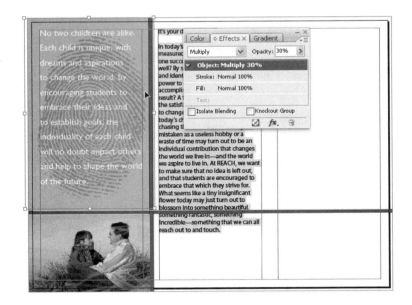

Styling Text

Now you'll style and lay out the text for the rest of the inside of the brochure.

To apply styles consistently, let's create a couple of paragraph styles based on the text we styled for the back panel. Return to the first page and place your cursor in the body text from the back panel. Open the Paragraph Styles panel—if it's not visible, you can show it by choosing Window, Type and Tables, Paragraph Styles from the menu bar. From the Paragraph Style panel, choose New Paragraph Style from the panel menu to open the Paragraph Style Options window (see Figure 13.18). Choose Basic Character Formats and give the style a name of Body. The settings should show the options set for the brochure text selected—Gill Sans Light, 12-point type on 16-point leading. Click OK to create the style.

Follow the same steps to create an additional style for the headline. Now, return to the second panel of the second page. Select the unstyled body copy and click the Body style to apply it. Apply the Heading style for the header as well (see Figure 13.19) and save the file.

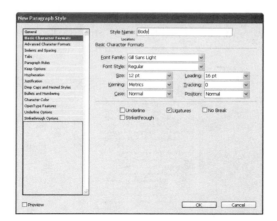

FIGURE 13.18
Defining a paragraph style for the body copy.

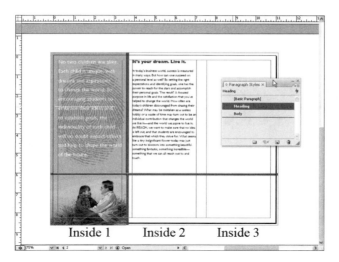

FIGURE 13.19
The text, styled and moved into position.

Inserting Tables

There's something special planned for the inside-bottom of the brochure—a data table comparing REACH's programs. Let's place a data table from Microsoft Word or Excel, and then format it. (If you want to work along, create a table in Word with five rows and five columns, including the header row and column.)

To place a Microsoft Word table, simply use the Place command to import the file (see Figure 13.20). Notice that the table is squeezed into one column, but it needs to span both columns. To fix this, select the Type tool and resize the table by dragging the right table border. To resize columns proportionally as you resize the table, hold down the Shift key while dragging the right table border. You can also resize the table vertically and keep the relative sizes of the rows by holding down the Shift key and dragging the bottom table border. Before continuing, let's apply the Body style to see how the text fits.

FIGURE 13.20
Placing a table from Microsoft Word.

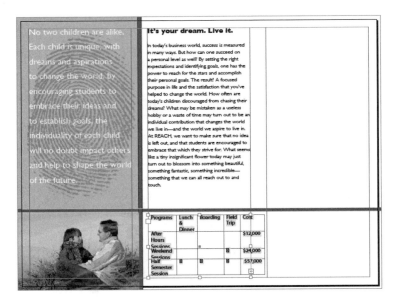

To resize the left column so the text doesn't wrap, hold down the Shift key and drag its right column—this will take up space from the adjacent column, rather than resizing the entire table. Also, select the four right-most columns and choose Table, Distribute Columns Evenly (see Figure 13.21).

FIGURE 13.21
The columns to the right of the programs are distributed evenly and the rows are spaced apart vertically.

Programs	Lunch & Dinner	Boarding	Field Trip	Cost
After Hours Sessions				$12,000
Weekend Sessions			☒	$24,000
Half Semester Session	☒	☒	☒	$57,000
Full Semester Session	☒	☒	☒	$92,000

One other thing to correct—there are strange characters in the four right-most columns. In the original file that you placed, they had been star-shaped glyphs to mark which options were available, but the copywriter might have used an uncommon font that is not available to you. To change them, select the fonts and choose a font with special characters, such as Webdings or Wingdings, and choose a pleasing shape. Alternately, use a typical character font and press (Option-8) [Alt+8] to get a circle bullet character. Size the special characters as needed.

The table is almost done, but let's make it easier to scan. To set the column headers apart from the rest of the text, change them to be Gill Sans, size 12, and bold. Next, let's use only horizontal lines between table cells. To remove extra lines, choose Tables, Table Options, Table Setup and set the Table Border to 0. Then, in the Column Strokes section, change the Weight setting to 0 for both the First and Next columns and click OK. To give some padding between the horizontal lines that remain and the text, choose Tables, Cell Options, Text and set the Vertical Justification to Align Center. The table is now easy to read at a glance (see Figure 13.22).

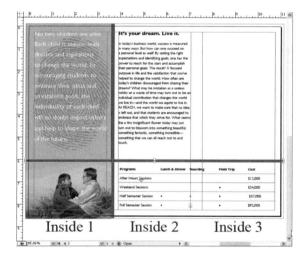

FIGURE 13.22
The table is complete.

Finishing Touches

As the last step, complete the right-most panel with graphics. Place the image of a child with a magnifying glass and scale it to end a little more than halfway down the panel. Crop the image by positioning the object frame to bleed off the panel on the top and right and to end midway between panels on the left. Then, place the logo just below it (see Figure 13.23).

Congratulations, you've just completed a trifold brochure! You can either print a proof or create a PDF file to send to your manager or client for comments or approval.

FIGURE 13.23
The completed
inside of the
brochure.

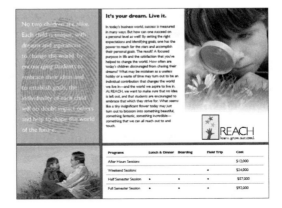

Summary

This chapter focused on the creation of a reasonably complex print publication—a trifold brochure. By the end of the chapter, not only did you use advanced layout techniques in InDesign, but you also explored the text formatting capabilities of InDesign. You're well on your way to being a CS3 professional!

CHAPTER 14

Creating an Ad Campaign

In this chapter, you will create a print advertising campaign for the REACH company. After designing the ads, you'll create a PDF file to send to the client for comments. Next you'll pretend you're the client, and use Acrobat to make comments on the campaign (you'll be your own critic!). Then you'll go back to InDesign and see how to generate a PDF/X-1a–compliant file, which is an ISO standard format used in the advertising industry.

Choosing and Preparing Images in Photoshop

All those sayings that you hear people repeat endlessly, such as "Image is everything" or "A picture speaks a thousand words," prove quite true in the world of advertising. Advertisers know that they have only a few precious seconds to attract people's attention before they move on to something else.

In this campaign, you're going to create a series of three ads; each will display a photograph with the caption "It's your dream. Live it." The photos will be large, will have people in them, and will convey a strong message of what REACH has to offer. Locate photos in the iStockPhoto lightbox using the same method as before and download them. I've chosen images of confident-looking children and young people (iStock_000000359619Large.jpg, iStock_000000813871Large.jpg, and iStock_000000439439Large.jpg). Open all three images in Photoshop (see Figure 14.1).

FIGURE 14.1
The three
images that
you'll use
for the ad
campaign.

As the ad campaign pieces will be black and white like the images in the previous chapter, use the action you created on them to get them prepared. When all your images are saved into your project folder, quit Photoshop.

Setting Up Pages in InDesign

Launch InDesign and create a new file. In the New Document dialog box (see Figure 14.2), specify the following options:

▶ Set the number of pages to 3.

▶ Uncheck the Facing Pages option.

▶ Specify a letter-size page (8.5 × 11) with an orientation set to Portrait (tall).

▶ Set your margins to 0.25 inches.

▶ Set your bleed to 0.125 inches all around.

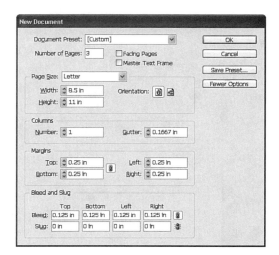

FIGURE 14.2
Specifying New
Document
options.

You might be wondering how I knew to set up all these specific options before even starting to design the piece. I'm psychic. The truth is, I started out with a letter-size document with default margin and column settings, and then made changes as I designed the piece using the Layout, Margins and Columns, and File, Document Setup settings. To make it easier to follow along, I've already given you the final settings, but when you're creating your own projects, you'll probably use the method I just described.

By the Way

Setting Up a Master Page

Because you want the ads to appear as a series, they will all be similar in layout; only the content will be different in each ad. Instead of applying the same design elements to different pages, you'll use a master page that will contain the common elements. This is beneficial not only when creating the files, but also when making edits. For example, when the client asks for the logo to be made larger, you can make the change on the master page; all the other pages are updated automatically.

Double-click on A-Master in the Pages panel to switch to that master page (see Figure 14.3). Start by dragging a horizontal guide to the 8-inch mark, which you will need later. Drag another horizontal guide to the 10.5-inch mark, which will be the baseline for the logo. Then drag a vertical guide to the 2-inch mark to mark a sidebar (see Figure 14.4).

FIGURE 14.3
Switching to the
A-Master page.

FIGURE 14.4
Placing guides
for alignment.

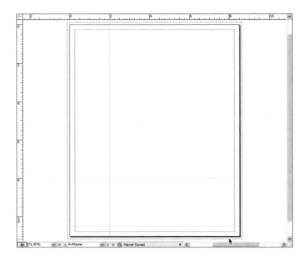

Adding Common Design Elements

Now that you have the guides in place, choose File, Place and import the REACH logo from your project folder. Use the Control panel to scale the logo by 50%. Position the logo so it rests along the baseline you created, against the right margin of the page. Below the logo, use the Type tool to add REACH's URL in 10-point Gill Sans Light.

To bring in design elements you used in the brochure project, let's add some background color and color bars to set off the sections of the ad. Choose the Rectangle tool and create a background for the entire sidebar and change its fill to 30% black. Then, create a vertical bar, 1/8-inch wide, positioned to the left of the vertical guide. Set its fill to 80% black. Create a horizontal bar, also 1/8-inch wide and 80% black, and place it just above the 6-inch guide. Send it to back so it doesn't overlap the gray sidebar.

Adding Text

Next, let's add the text to the master, as it will be the same in all the ads. As mentioned in the preceding chapter, you can place a text file, or you can just type the text yourself inside InDesign. Add the body copy for the ad, and create a paragraph style using Gill Sans Light, 11.5-point text on 16-point leading, with tracking of –10. Apply the paragraph style to the body text, and position it to the left of the logo.

The final element to be added to the master is the headline. At the top of the text box, type the words It's your dream. Live it.. Set the headline text to Gill Sans Pro Bold, 14-point text on 16-point leading, with Optical kerning turned on. Color the text black (see Figure 14.5).

FIGURE 14.5
Style and position the copy.

> InDesign always has master page elements at the bottom of the stacking order. If you want to position a headline over a photo that isn't on the master, you will have to create it in the page instead of in the master.

By the Way

You've completed the master page.

Placing the Photos

Now the fun begins. Switch back to page 1 of your document. Place the photo of the girl with pigtails in her hair that you prepared in Photoshop, and scale and position it so the image fills the entire upper-right portion of the ad. The bottom of the picture box should meet the horizontal guide at 8 inches and the vertical guide at 2 inches—the top and right side should bleed off the page. If needed, use the Selection tool to position the image's frame to crop it to fit inside the guides (see Figure 14.6).

FIGURE 14.6
The image posi-
tioned, cropped,
and scaled.

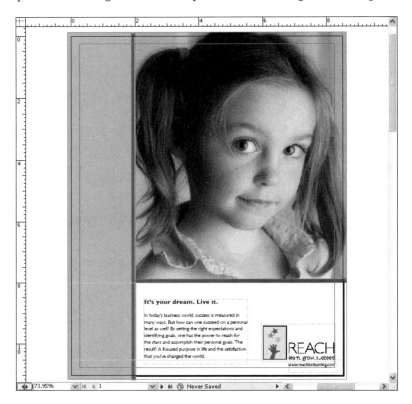

The last thing to add is a thought-provoking statement in the sidebar on the left side. Create a type frame and type Teach them how they can reach even high-er.. Then, size and position the frame over the sidebar. Set the font to 36-point Gill Sans Light with 48-point leading and optical kerning. Change the text color to white (see Figure 14.7).

FIGURE 14.7
The first ad is complete!

Now that you've completed the first ad, save the file into your Version Cue project.

You'll create the two other ads to complete the campaign, which will be quite easy because of how you set up the first ad. While still on page 1, switch to the Selection tool (the black arrow) and choose Edit, Select All; copy all the contents with (Cmd-C) [Ctrl+C]. Next, switch to page 2 of the document and choose Edit, Paste in Place. This pastes all the items into the exact position that they were in on page 1. For this second ad in the campaign, you want to use a different photo. Open the Links panel (see Figure 14.8), and highlight the image that appears in page 2. Click Relink and navigate to one of the other photos your prepared earlier in this chapter. Adjust or recrop the image as necessary. Repeat the process for the third ad in the campaign. Change the text in the sidebar of each ad (see Figure 14.9) to a new inviting quote. Save a version of the updated file to your project folder.

FIGURE 14.8
The InDesign
Links panel lets
you relink
placed files.

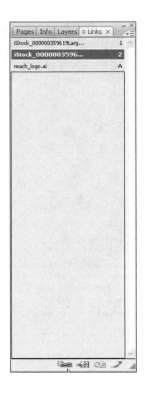

FIGURE 14.9
The remaining
pages in the ad
campaign.

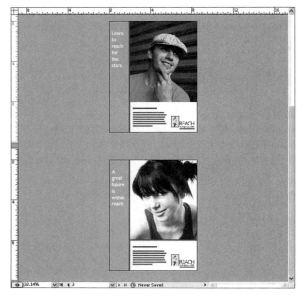

Exporting a PDF File for Review

Now that the designs are complete, you can send off the campaign for approval. Whereas in the past you might have created large (and expensive) proofs to present to your client (and then waited for faxed corrections), today's fast-paced world demands the use of email and PDF files.

Choose File, Export and select Adobe PDF as the format. Then choose a location in which to save your PDF file, and click Save. Because you want this PDF to be print-ready in case the client loves it as-is, choose Press Quality in the Export PDF dialog box (see Figure 14.10), and click Export.

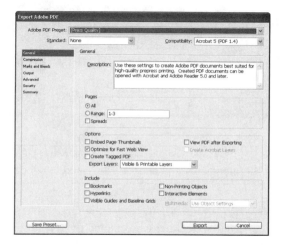

FIGURE 14.10
Choosing the Press Quality preset, which optimizes the PDF file for printing.

> Where quality matters, you may want to choose High Quality Print in order to pre-serve any special fonts, but not be quite as large a file as created for Press Quality. If file size is a consideration, you can choose Smallest File Size from the Export PDF Dialog box. However, if you have used uncommon fonts, others might not see a faithful representation of your design because the fonts are not embed-ded in order to decrease the file size.

Did you Know?

You can then send an email to your manager or client and attach the PDF file that you just created to your email.

Adding Comments to the File in Acrobat

Are you up for a little role-playing adventure? I am. Let's make believe that you're now the manager or client who just received the PDF of the ad campaign. Double-click on the PDF file to open the file in Adobe Acrobat 8 Professional (see Figure 14.11).

FIGURE 14.11
Viewing the file
in Acrobat.

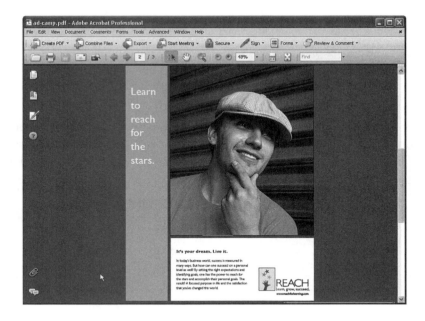

Did you Know?

If the PDF file opened in the Adobe Reader (the free viewer), close it. Then manually launch Acrobat 8 Professional and choose File, Open to choose the PDF file.

Step through the three pages of the PDF file to see the three ads. You like them (and make a mental note to give the designer who created them a raise), but a few small things have to be changed. First, the logo is too small (of course), so click on the Review and Comments button in the toolbar to show the Comments and Markup toolbar. Click the Sticky Note tool and then click on the logo to create a comment tied to that area of the page. In the note that pops up, write that you'd like to see the logo enlarged. Now click on the headline to add a second note. You'd like this text to have larger letters. Add that comment into the new note you just created. Finally, click on the Stamp tool in the Comments and Markup toolbar and choose the Dynamic, Reviewed option to stamp your action on the document (see Figure 14.12). Save the PDF file and email it back to your very hard-working designer, who really does deserve that raise.

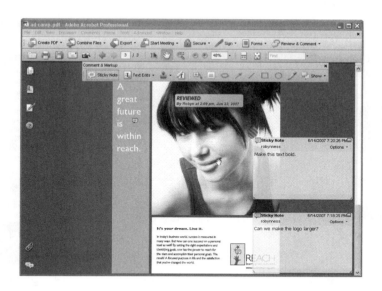

FIGURE 14.12
The PDF file
with the com-
ments added.
(Note that the
Comment and
Markup toolbar
is also open.)

Making Changes in InDesign

Turning back into a designer, you check your email to see that you got the PDF file back. You open it and read the comments (and roll your eyes at the "bigger logo" comment), and then open the source InDesign file.

Change the headline as requested, but you can see that the logo can't really be made any larger, so you leave it as is.

Exporting It As a PDF/X-1a–Compliant File

To send the ad to the publisher, you'll want to export a PDF/X-1a–compliant file. With the file still open in InDesign, choose File, Adobe PDF Presets, [PDF/X-1a:2001] to export your file as a PDF/X-1a–compliant file (see Figure 14.13).

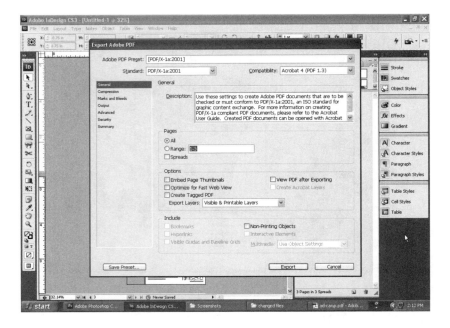

Congratulations! You've just created an ad campaign.

Summary

In a short span of about 10 pages, you created a professional ad campaign! This project chapter guided you through the process of using Acrobat, InDesign, and Photoshop to pull together the components for an ad campaign for the fictitious REACH company.

CHAPTER 15

Creating a Web Banner

In this chapter, you'll create a web banner that the REACH company can use to help promote itself online. Things that are important to ad banner advertising are a clear message, eye-catching graphics, and a small file size. With Adobe Creative Suite 3, you have all the tools necessary to achieve those goals. You'll use Illustrator to create a layered file and Flash to animate it.

> We're using Illustrator for the graphics in this project, but Photoshop also works nicely for creating web graphics. In fact, we'll be using Photoshop in the next chapter.
>
> ***By the Way***

Creating a New Illustrator File

Begin by launching Illustrator and creating a new file. In the New Document dialog box, set a width of 468 pixels and a height of 60 pixels. Show the advanced settings and change the Color Mode to RGB and the Raster Effects resolution to Screen (see Figure 15.1).

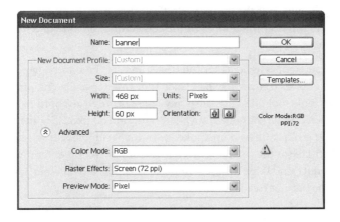

FIGURE 15.1
Creating a new document in Illustrator CS3.

Like it or not, designing for the Web is very much a "by the numbers" process. You're usually concerned with exact pixel dimensions, exact colors, exact positioning, and more. As you'll see throughout this project, you'll be performing tasks with exact values. Especially with web graphics, it's a discipline that will undoubtedly result in better-looking graphics and, ultimately, more free time on your hands.

Next, you'll set up a few things in Illustrator to make the task of designing web graphics easier and more precise:

▶ If needed, choose View, Pixel Preview. This enables you to view your art as it would appear in a web browser, with correct antialiasing applied.

▶ Press (Cmd-R) [Ctrl+R] to turn on your rulers if they're not already visible. This assists you in positioning items.

▶ Finally, open your Transform panel by choosing it from the Window menu. The Transform panel helps you edit and position graphics perfectly.

With your file set up this way, you can be assured that you'll be creating high-quality web graphics. Now would also be a good time to save your file into your Version Cue project with the name of your choice.

Adding the Images

You're going to split the banner into three sections. The animation that you'll create will rotate through the images in the center, and the logo and tag line will remain the same.

Before you create elements for the three areas of the banner, you'll first create a rectangle to use as a mask for the image that will appear in the center section. Select the Rectangle tool and click once anywhere on your artboard to create a rectangle numerically. Enter 150 pixels for the Width and 60 pixels for the Height. Give the rectangle a black fill and no stroke. With the rectangle still selected, click on the lower-left box of the proxy in the Transform panel, and enter a value of 200 for the x coordinate and 0 for the y coordinate. This positions the black rectangle perfectly inside the banner (see Figure 15.2).

FIGURE 15.2
Drawing and positioning a rectangle numerically using the Transform panel.

Double-click on Layer 1 in your Layers palette and rename the layer Background. This rectangle will serve as the background for the banner. Create three new layers in your document. Name them Image 1, Image 2, and Image 3 (see Figure 15.3).

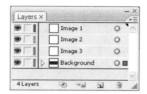

FIGURE 15.3
Creating three new layers in the document.

> Using layers when creating web graphics that will eventually be animated is extremely important because you can switch between layers to see what the different states of the animation will look like. By taking the extra few seconds to organize your art in Illustrator in the design stage, you can save a lot more time later in the animation and optimization stages.

Did you Know?

Select the rectangle that you created earlier. If you look at the Layers panel, you'll see a dot appear on the Background layer. Dragging this dot into the Image 1 layer while holding the (Option) [Alt] key moves a copy of the selected rectangle to that layer. (A plus sign appears to indicate that you're copying artwork from one layer to another.) Use this method to copy rectangles to layers Image 2 and Image 3, respectively (see Figure 15.4).

Now you're ready to bring in the images. For the three images, you'll reuse the images from the ad campaign in the previous chapter. However, because the web is a colorful environment, use the full-color versions of the photos rather than the black-and-white versions you prepared for the print pieces.

FIGURE 15.4
The Layers panel shows that all the layers include copies of the original rectangle.

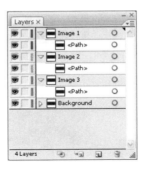

Navigate to the folder of the stock photos you've been using for all your projects and find the original versions. Select the three images of confident young people (iStock_000000359619Large.jpg, iStock_000000813871Large.jpg, and iStock_000000439439Large.jpg), and drag them all into your Illustrator document. In your Illustrator file, you'll want to move the images onto their correct layers and set up masks as well, which you can do directly from the Layers panel.

Click on the disclosure triangles for each of the layers you created to view the contents of the file. Drag each of the images so that they all appear on a different layer, each beneath the rectangles you created (see Figure 15.5).

FIGURE 15.5
The Layers panel indicates the hierarchy for the entire Illustrator file.

Now you'll resize and position the images. Select the image in the first layer and click on the Lock icon in the Transform panel, which constrains the proportion when scaling. Specify 200 pixels for Width and press Enter. Click on the lower-left box of the proxy in the Transform panel, and enter a value of 180 for the x coordinate and –125 for the y coordinate (see Figure 15.6).

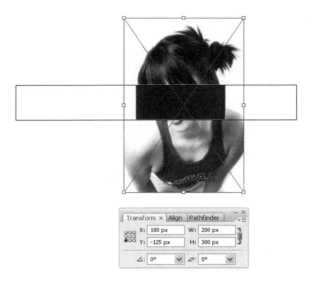

FIGURE 15.6
The first photo, after being scaled and positioned.

Click on the Image 1 layer in the Layers panel to highlight that layer, and then click on the Make/Release Clipping Mask button at the bottom of the panel (see Figure 15.7). You'll notice that the rectangle now becomes a mask for the photo in that layer. You can move the image vertically to get the best cropping for the image.

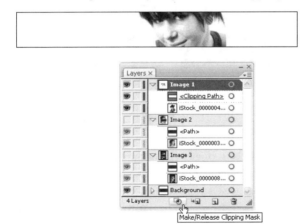

FIGURE 15.7
Setting a layer clipping mask for the Image 1 layer.

Hide the Image 1 layer (by clicking on the eyeball) to make it easier to see and work with the next layer. Repeat the steps to resize, position, and mask the images on the Image 2 and Image 3 layers. You will have to adjust the values in the Transform panel to scale and position the images to get similar face sizes across the three images.

Choosing a Web-Safe Color

Now that the center section of the banner is complete for all three versions, let's complete the edges. Hide the image layers so you can focus on the Background layer.

The rectangle on the Background layer will appear behind the images, but we'd like to place it on the left side. Select it and change the values in the Transform panel to make it 200 pixels wide and positioned up against the edges of the canvas. The rectangle is filled with black, which won't work well in your design. Looking at the images used, you decide that a periwinkle blue would make an excellent color for the background. (It's the color of the tank top worn in one of the photos, and will also look nice with the other images.) Make sure the layer with this color is visible. Then select the Eyedropper tool and Shift-click on a blue part to sample a color.

Open your Color panel and you'll see that the color you sampled appears there. You'll also notice a small cube, which indicates that the color you've sampled is not a Web-safe color. Click on the cube to have Illustrator change the color you sampled to the closest Web-safe color equivalent (see Figure 15.8).

FIGURE 15.8
Converting the sampled color to the closest Web-safe color.

Hide the layers for the three images to reveal the rectangle on the Background layer. Click on the rectangle and fill it with the Web-safe color you just created.

Before continuing, let's bring in one of the design elements you've used in previous projects—color bars. Create a new topmost layer and name it Color Bars. In that layer, create a rectangle 60 pixels tall and 8 pixels wide and fill with black. Be sure to remove any stroke around the rectangle. Position it using the Transform panel. Click on the lower-left box of the proxy, and enter a value of 200 for the x coordinate and 0 for the y coordinate. Show the objects in the Color Bars layer and copy and paste the color bar to make an exact duplicate. Then, select the copy, and use the Transform panel to position it 345 pixels from the left edge (see Figure 15.9).

FIGURE 15.9
Create and position color bars to divide the sections.

Adding the Tag Line

Create a new layer and name it Tag Line. Select the Type tool and click on your artboard to create a point text object (don't click on an existing shape). Enter the text It's your dream.. Style the text with 18-point Gill Sans Bold. Color the text white and position it on the left edge of the background. Then, create a separate text object with the line Live it.. Style the text to 36-point Gill Sans Bold, color the text black, and position it below the first line (see Figure 15.10).

FIGURE 15.10
Styling the text and placing it into position.

Adding the Logo

Create a new layer and name it Logo. Position it at the very bottom of the layers panel. Then choose File, Place and browse to the REACH logo file you created way back in the first project. Select the Scale tool and size the logo fit in the banner, approximately 33% of full size. Position it on the right side of the canvas. You'll also want to create a clipping mask around the logo, in case the background edges interfere with the elements behind it. (Refer to the steps for masking an image in "Adding the Images" above.) The logo appears correctly scaled and in position (see Figure 15.11).

FIGURE 15.11
The REACH logo, scaled and in the correct position.

Save the Illustrator file to your hard drive.

Preparing the Layers

The file is nearly complete, but you need to put your objects and layers in order so you can bring them into Flash to complete the animation.

If you have a simple animation that doesn't use clipping masks, you can export them as a Flash animation directly from Illustrator. Illustrator will export individual layers as frames of an animation, but each layer needs to contain the full design—otherwise, the animation will show only one object at a time as it cycles through the layers. This method won't work in our case because if we were to include all the design elements on the image layers, which use clipping masks, the masks would affect not only the images, but also objects that need to be visible.

This is easy to do by copying and pasting between applications. Use the Layers panel to make all layers visible, and then select all by using the Selection tool to trace a rectangle containing all the objects on the page. The Layers panel will show that everything is selected by displaying colorful squares (see Figure 15.12). Choose Edit, Copy from the menu bar.

FIGURE 15.12
Make all the layers visible and select them in the Layers panel.

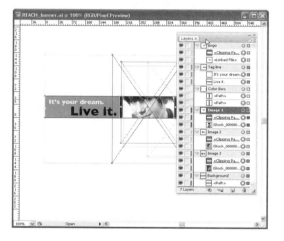

Creating a Flash Animation

Now you're ready to bring your layers into Flash. Open Flash and create a new file of the correct size by choosing Templates, Advertising from the New Document dialog (see Figure 15.13). Select the option 468×60 (Banner). With the new document open, choose Edit, Paste in Center. When prompted, choose the option Paste Using AI File Importer Preferences and wait for Flash to bring in the Illustrator layers. The layers appear in the order they existed in the Illustrator document (see Figure 15.14).

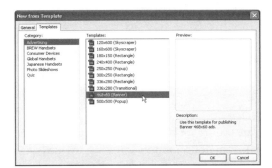

FIGURE 15.13
Templates allow
you to choose
from common
preset sizes.

FIGURE 15.14
The layers from
Illustrator
appear in Flash.

With your layers prepared, you are ready to create your animation effects. For this animation, you will need a total of three keyframes, which divide the timeline into three sections—one for displaying each image layer. Note that the remaining layers will be visible for the entire animation.

Let's start by creating a keyframe at Frame 60 that includes the layers that don't change. To do this, hold down the (Cmd) [Ctrl] key and click the frames representing them at Frame 60 (see Figure 15.15). Then, choose Insert, Timeline, Keyframe.

I've chosen 60 frames for this animation because it's neatly divisible by 3. You can choose more or fewer frames, or even change the frame rate under Modify, Document in the menu, if you want to change the rate of change in the animation.

FIGURE 15.15
Insert a keyframe containing only the layers that don't change.

Next, you need to create frames for the image layers at even intervals in the timeline. To do this, insert keyframes containing only the image layers at Frame 20, Frame 40, and Frame 60. Hold down the Shift key and select the boxes for the first and last image for Frame 20—holding down the Shift key selects the range so the middle image will also be selected. Then, insert a keyframe as before. Repeat this process for Frame 40 and Frame 60 so your timeline shows all layers (see Figure 15.16).

FIGURE 15.16
Keyframes containing the image layers split the timeline into thirds.

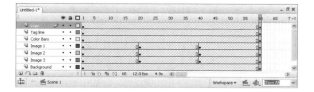

Although you want one image to show for each section of the timeline, you currently have them all used in each section—which means the top image will be the only one that is viewable. To achieve the desired effect of changing images, you need to selectively delete the frames containing the unneeded images from each of the three sections you've created. In the first section, select the frames for images 2 and 3 and press the Delete key to remove them. For the second section delete the frames for images 1 and 3, and for the final section delete the frames for images 1 and 2 (see Figure 15.17). (To quickly delete all the frames for a layer prior to a keyframe, select the white rectangle preceding it.) Drag the playhead at the top of the timeline for a quick preview of the effect.

The final step is to export the movie by choosing File, Export, Export Movie from the menu. Name your file, choose a location to save the file, and then click Save. In the next dialog box, choose which version of Flash you want to support and click OK (see Figure 15.18).

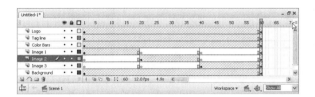

FIGURE 15.17
Remove frames for images that aren't to be shown.

Now, double-click the saved file to test the animation.

As is often said, timing is everything—and in animation, timing is key. You want to make sure that the animation pauses long enough so people can read the text and see the name of the company.

By the Way

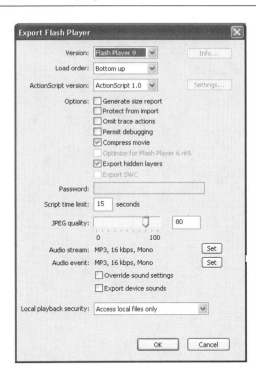

FIGURE 15.18
When exporting, you can choose from a wide range of options—most importantly, which version of Flash.

Congratulations, you've just created an animated web ad banner!

Summary

In this chapter, you used Illustrator and Flash to create an animated web graphic. As you work with the CS3 suite, you'll find that this is a powerful application combination for creating web animations. By practicing with the Illustrator tools and the Flash timeline, you'll be creating dynamic web presentations in no time.

CHAPTER 16

Creating a Web Page

In this chapter, you'll create a single web page for the REACH company. Other pages will be linked to this page, so you'll create navigation links that allow users to visit the other pages in the site. You'll also utilize some other elements that you created in previous projects.

Although you'll be building the web page itself in Dreamweaver using HTML and CSS, most web designs include images—and it's much easier to plan the outcome you want by creating a visual mockup before beginning to build the site. Any needed graphics can be created from the mockup. Some web designers use Illustrator or Fireworks for this purpose; others choose Photoshop. It's a matter of personal taste.

Creating Web Graphics

You'll be using Photoshop to sketch your page layout and create graphical elements for use in your site. The layout concept is a three-column page with a header and a footer that span all columns. To provide continuity with REACH's existing ad campaign and materials, you'll reuse colors, design motifs, and several of the graphics and photos you've already prepared. Also, as with the animated web banner from the previous chapter, you'll be working in color.

> As in previous chapters, I've chosen to use images from iStock Photo. **By the Way**
> If you would like to work along with these projects, you can download
> these images from http://www.istockphoto.com/teachyourselfcs3.php.

Header Graphic

Let's start by creating a header graphic to span the top of the page and set the tone for the rest of the design. If it isn't already open, launch Photoshop and create a new document 765 pixels wide by 125 pixels high. Choose Fill from the Edit menu and make the background color #666699, which is the same web-safe color you used in the web banner in Chapter 15, "Creating a Web Banner." Next, place the three images used in the web banner project, scaling them so the faces aren't too small. If needed, double-click the images to turn off the black and white adjustment layers so the color versions of the images appear.

Before continuing, set guides to evenly space the images in the header. If needed, turn on Rulers under the View menu. Set the guides by choosing the Move tool and clicking and dragging the left ruler for vertical guides or the top ruler for horizontal guides. Starting at the right edge of the canvas, create three 110-pixel wide sections with 10 pixels between them. Then, add guides for 10-pixel margins at the top and bottom. Then, position the faces in the images to show in the nearly-square areas created by the guides (see Figure 16.1). Don't worry that the images overlap each other—layer masks can fix that.

FIGURE 16.1
Position your images carefully so the faces are lined up in the grid of guides.

When working with web graphics, you'll want to switch Photoshop's ruler units to pixels in the application preferences.

Next, to apply a layer mask to an image, select the image's layer and then switch to the Rectangular Marquee tool. Draw a shape over the area of the image that you want to remain visible. The guides you set create neat edges for marking the area. Click Add Layer Mask at the bottom of the Layers panel, and the edges of the image outside the rectangle selected seem to disappear (see Figure 16.2). (Note, however, that the edges of the photo aren't really gone, and you can reposition the image within the mask.) Repeat masking for the remaining two images.

FIGURE 16.2
Use a layer mask to hide the edges of a photo.

You set up guides to carefully position the images and masks because, although you can move both images and layer masks, it is tricky to position them. In this case, it saves time to mark the edges ahead of time.

Next, you will insert the logo—and for that, you'll want a white background. Create a new layer, use the Rectangular Marquee tool to select the unfinished left side of the canvas inside the top and bottom guides, and fill with white. Then, place the REACH logo and scale it to fit inside the top and bottom guides with some extra white space at the left, top, and bottom (see Figure 16.3).

FIGURE 16.3
Place and scale the logo on the white background on the left half of the canvas.

The header design is coming along well, but it still needs something. Place the image of a child holding a magnifying glass, which was used in the brochure project (see Chapter 13, "Creating a Brochure"). Scale it so the face is slightly larger than the faces in the other three photos. You'll want to use a color version of the photo, so double-click its layer to open the original file in Photoshop and turn off the layer you applied to create a black-and-white image for the brochure. Next, set a layer mask to hide the top and bottom edges of the photo as you did previously.

Let's soften the grid-like appearance of the header by having this photo fade to white along the left edge near the logo. Before continuing, make sure your foreground color is set to white, and create a new layer. Then, choose the Gradient tool, set the Gradient Picker to Foreground and choose Transparent, and drag your cursor from left to right across the left side of the photo to create a white gradient (see Figure 16.4). Position the gradient to fade the edge of the photo, and create a layer mask on the gradient layer. (If needed, change the layer order to bring the logo to the top.)

FIGURE 16.4
The photo fades to white to blend with the logo area.

Congratulations, your header graphic is complete!

Page Design

Before continuing, let's do some project organization. It's a good practice to organize your layers into folders so you can easily find different sections in the design document. In the Layers panel, create a new folder, name it Header, and select and move all the existing layers into it. You can then collapse the folder to take up less room.

You can also clear the guides used to create the header so it won't be confusing if you add guides for other areas of the page.

Now, you will sketch out the rest of the page in Photoshop so you'll know what to build in Dreamweaver. To do this, you need more space on the canvas, so set the background color to white and then choose Image, Canvas Size from the menu, anchor the existing content to the top center, and set the height to 550 pixels (see Figure 16.5).

FIGURE 16.5
Resize the height of the canvas to make room for the rest of the page.

> **Watch Out!**
>
> Keep in mind that what you are sketching is merely an idea of how a web page will look. Web pages, unlike print pieces, are designed to be fluid. If text changes, the length of the page changes. If a user changes his preferred font size, the length and positioning of page elements change. If you find yourself positioning text very carefully, it might be a sign that your design is not well-suited for the fluidity of the Web!

In the fresh area of the canvas, you'll be mapping out a three-column layout with a single-column footer. The left column will hold the site navigation, the middle column will contain the majority of the content, and the right column will hold some additional text. (Creating a secondary content column on the right breaks up the wide expanse for easier reading and for more visual interest in the page.)

Use a horizontal guide to mark the bottom of the header and place one 30 pixels from the bottom for the footer. Next, create some guides to show the columns and footer. Create vertical guides at 165 pixels and 525 pixels to indicate columns that are 165, 360, and 240 pixels wide. Finally, put in extra guides to mark the left margins for these columns so their content won't be pushed up against the edges.

Now let's create the footer. Choose the Rectangular Marquee tool and select a 10-pixel tall area the entire width of the canvas. Then create a new layer and fill the area with #666699. Position this color bar 30 pixels from the bottom of the canvas to mark the top of the footer. Next, use the Text tool to type `© Copyright 2007,` `Reach Learning Center. All rights reserved.`. Select your text and open the Character panel to set the font size to 10 point and the font face to Arial.

Did you Know?

Most of the text you add in Photoshop won't be used directly in this website—it is used to give an idea of what the final site will look like. When you build the site in Dreamweaver, you'll use real text that is selectable and searchable, unlike image-based text.

You'll need to consider the font used for the web text. The font chosen has to be available on the site visitors' computers for it to appear as you intended on their screens. For that reason, you'll want to use common fonts for most of the text in your site mockup. In the section "Main Content," you'll learn one way to use images with fancy fonts in place of text titles and headings.

The header and footer are complete, so turn your attention to the navigation. To start, give the navigation area a background color—create a new layer and use the Rectangular Marquee tool to select the column between the header and the footer. Fill with #666699 and, to soften it, change the opacity to 50%. Now, let's add the navigation text. Create a new layer, choose the Text tool, and type `Home,` `Enrollment, Campus, Schedule, Alumni,` and `Contact Us` on separate lines. Set the text color to black, the font to 15-point Arial, and apply underline to mimic typical linked text. Set the leading to 24-point to give some space between the lines. For extra emphasis, create graphic bullets, such as arrows. The Webdings font includes an arrow (in place of the 4) that will do nicely. Apply the arrow in front of each navigation item (see Figure 16.6).

Moving to the middle column, paste in some text for the main page. Once again, use a common font, such as Arial. Set the size to 12 point and set the leading to 14 point to give a feeling of openness despite all the text. Position the text to give white space around it—I'm using about 15 pixels of padding to the left and right and on the top.

FIGURE 16.6
Use dingbats,
such as arrows,
to make
a bulleted list.

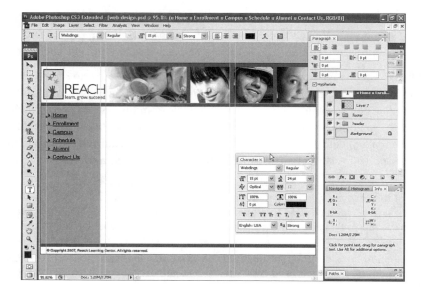

Let's try something interesting with header text for the middle column. In the other REACH projects, you've used the Gill Sans font, which is not a common web font. However, you can use it on a website if you use an image of the text in place of real web text. (Image text is harder to update and takes more time to create than regular text. However, it's a nice way to use special fonts for headings.) At the top of your middle column, type It's your dream. Live it., set the font to Gill Sans, and then bold the text. Set the size to 15 point and, to give a bit more readability by separating the letters, set the tracking to 12 point. This single line of text will receive special attention when it's time to build the site in Dreamweaver.

For the right column, the goal is to create visual interest, so use supplementary text and an image. Type a few lines of text and in the Character panel, set the font to 11-point Arial, bold it, and apply a leading of 16 to visually set it apart from the other text. Next, place the image of the father and child from the brochure. Once again, use a color version, so double-click the photo layer to open the original file and turn off the black-and-white adjustment layer. Position the image below the text.

Break up the linearity of the left edge in the right column by shifting the text and adding the fingerprint graphic, also used in the brochure. Scale the placed image to fit neatly next to the text (see Figure 16.7).

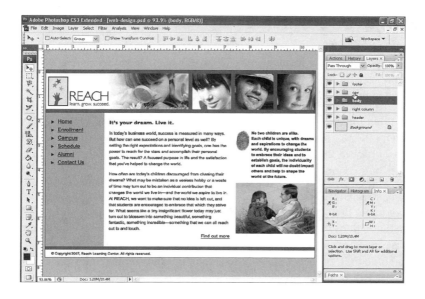

FIGURE 16.7
Shift the text in the right column and add a graphic element to create visual interest.

The page is almost done, but continuity is a good thing in designing an identity. Let's bring in the secondary tag line, "Success is within reach," that we created for the brochure. Place the file and position it in the navigation column below the links (see Figure 16.8).

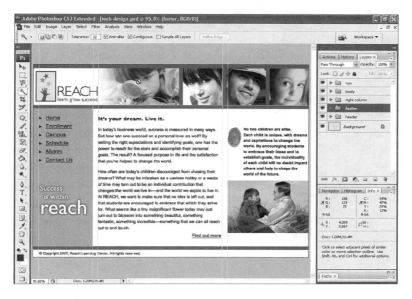

FIGURE 16.8
Add another element to the navigation column.

Creating Web Graphics

Your design is complete, but you're not yet ready to open Dreamweaver. You still need to prepare graphics for use in the website. Note that you won't be using the whole image as it looks in Photoshop, just pieces of it—you'll want most of the site to use real text, not images, so it can be searched and easily changed.

Let's take a moment to understand what you'll need for graphics for the site before you prepare them. The images needed to create a web version of this design are the header graphic, an image bullet for the navigation items, a background color for the navigation column, an image to replace the content heading, the image of the father and child, the thumbprint image, and the secondary tag line graphic.

How do you get these specific graphics? The best way is to use Photoshop's Slice tool to select the regions of the page that you need as distinct graphics. For instance, you would use the Slice tool to select the header graphic, an image bullet, the replacement heading text, the father-and-child photo, the thumbprint, and the secondary tag line (see Figure 16.9). Notice that the guide you set to lay out the page helps align the slices—that's because the Snap setting (in the View menu) is active. Also, notice that auto-slices appear in areas that aren't in the slices you've defined.

FIGURE 16.9
Select slices that you'll need for your website.

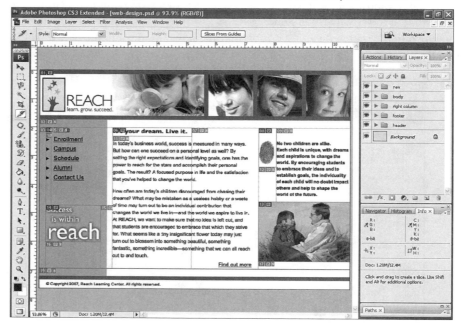

You'll also want to create a 765-pixel-wide, very short slice that will be used as a background to create the left column. Although this graphic can be as short as one pixel tall, it can be repeated vertically to fill an entire page, which is a very economical way to use background graphics. This will make more sense when you start building the site.

With slices in place, it's time to save the slices as web graphics. Choose Save for Web and Devices from the File menu. A window appears to show previews of your graphics and settings for choosing what kind of graphics to create (see Figure 16.10). Use the Slice Select tool to pick each slice and customize the options in the settings on the right side. (If you need to reposition the preview, switch to the Hand tool at the upper left. Switch back to the Slice Select tool to work with slice settings.) Set the header and the image of father and child to JPEG format, which uses more colors and is better for photographs. Set the quality to 40 and the blur to 1 to lessen any jagged edges. Set all the remaining slices to GIFs, which use a limited number of colors and are better for text and solid fields of color. Also, give your slices meaningful names by double-clicking each to open their Slice Type settings.

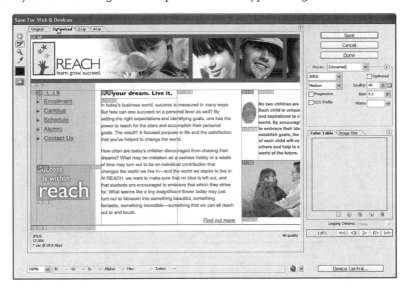

FIGURE 16.10
Choose options for your slices.

When done setting slice options, click Save at the upper right. A folder appears on your computer, containing the slices you set, as well as auto slices that complete the rest of the page. As you won't need the auto slices (the ones named with the original file name plus a number instead of the names you applied), locate them in the folder and delete them.

Creating a Site in Dreamweaver

Now that you have web-ready graphics, it's time to create the web page. Before working in Dreamweaver, use your operating system to create a new folder called reach_site and move the images file with your site images into it.

Then open Dreamweaver and create a new site. As you learned in Chapter 10, "Using Adobe Dreamweaver CS3," defining a site to work with is critical because web pages contain references to images and other files, and those references are dependent on the relative position between files. When defining the site, follow the screens in the basic setup to provide the name of the site (but skip the URL of the site), and click Next. On the next screen, select None for Server Technology and click Next. Choose Edit Local, locate the folder you created for your site files, and click Next. Set None for how you want to connect to a server and click Next. Review the settings (see Figure 16.11) and click Done.

FIGURE 16.11
Confirm your
site definition
settings and
click Done.

Choosing and Modifying a Layout

With a site defined, go ahead and create a new document. Choose File, New from the menu. In the New Document window (see Figure 16.12), select Blank Page, HTML, and 3 column fixed, header and footer in the Layout panel. Set Layout CSS to Create New File, and click Create. (Keep the suggested name thrColFixHdr.css for the CSS filename.) Then, save your new document as index.html in the reach_site folder. The main page of most websites is named index.html or index.htm because that is where most web servers are configured to point when users don't specify a page name.

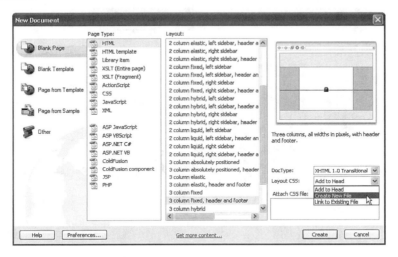

FIGURE 16.12
Choose a layout and set the Layout CSS to Create New File.

> **By the Way**
>
> Setting the Layout CSS option to Create New File means that the rules controlling the layout of your page are centralized in one file that you can use across your whole site. This increases the power of CSS, allowing a single rule change to affect all pages in a site. For example, if you decide to change fonts, you can do so with a change to a single file instead of updating every page.

The page layout that Dreamweaver provides is a good starting point, but you can modify it to fit your design. The width is set to 780 pixels, but 765 pixels is a more commonly used size. To change the width, click anywhere on the layout and then select <div#container> from the Tag selector at the lower left of your window (see Figure 16.13). Double-click the width setting in the CSS Styles panel to open the CSS Rule Definition window (see Figure 16.14) where you can change the width to 765 pixels. Click OK.

> **Did you Know?**
>
> One of the challenges of designing for the Web is that web pages interact with window size. You will be centering your design in the middle of the screen, flush to the top. But you could also push the site to the upper left, or create a design that changes size with the window. Designs that change with the window size are especially challenging because there is such a wide range of screen sizes available—it is difficult to create a design that looks good at both 765 pixels wide and up to double that width!

FIGURE 16.13
Click in the design window and use the tag selector at the lower left to precisely select a section of the page code. The CSS Styles for the selected element will show in the CSS Styles panel.

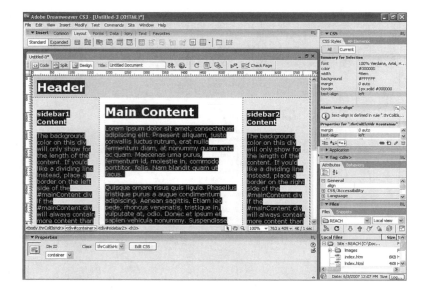

FIGURE 16.14
Change the width of your page to 765 pixels.

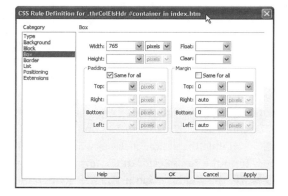

Notice that a file named thrColFixHdr.css opened when you began editing the layout width. That's because the rules for the page layout are stored in that file. You must save that file before quitting Dreamweaver and before previewing your pages in a browser in order for your design rules to take effect.

Now let's put the header image in the header of the page. Delete the text HEADER from the top section and, with your cursor in place, choose Image from the Image pop-up menu in the Insert panel's Common tab (see Figure 16.15). A dialog box opens to your images folder where you can select the graphic. In the Image Tag Accessibility Attributes window that appears, enter Alt text to give a short text description of the image for devices that don't display images, such as text-only browsers and screen readers used by blind people. Your image appears in the page (see Figure 16.16), but it is not positioned against the edges of the header space as desired. To change this, click the image and select <div#header> from the Tag Selector at the lower left of Dreamweaver's main window. Double-click the padding setting in the CSS Styles panel and, in the CSS Rule Definition window that appears, check the Same for All option and set all the padding to 0 (see Figure 16.17).

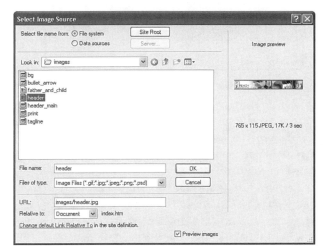

FIGURE 16.15
Use the Insert panel's Common tab to insert an image.

FIGURE 16.16
The image is in the page, but extra padding around it needs to be changed.

FIGURE 16.17
Set the padding
to 0 to allow
the image to
reach the
boundaries of
the header.

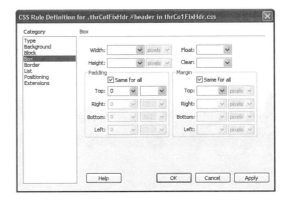

Now create the footer. To start, type the copyright statement. (To get the copyright symbol, choose Insert, HTML, Special Characters, Copyright.) Footer text is typically quite small, so create a special style for it. To do this, click the footer text, click <p> in the tag selector, and then choose New CSS Rule in the CSS Styles panel. A dialog box appears where you can define the kind of style you are creating. You see Dreamweaver's best guess for the selector you want to define, based on the position of your cursor in the page (see Figure 16.18). In this case, you do want an Advanced selector (one targeted to paragraphs in the footer), so click OK to open the CSS Rule Definition window. In the Type settings, set the font size to 80% and click OK.

FIGURE 16.18
The New CSS
Rule dialog
makes its best
guess about the
selector you're
trying to create.

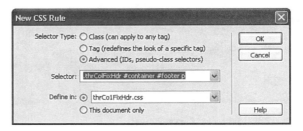

By the
Way
Dreamweaver's three types of selectors are Class, Tag, and Advanced. Tag (called a *type selector* in official CSS documentation) is the easiest to understand—it's a style that applies to any instance of a given HTML element, such as heading levels or bulleted list items. In contrast, class selectors allow you to create a style that can be applied to anything on the page; however, you have to specifically apply it for it to take effect. (For instance, you could create a class style for a specific text color and then apply it anywhere in the document.) Advanced tags, as you've just seen, are used for more precise application than the first two types, including selectors that define a specific section of a page (officially called *ID selectors*) and selectors for which the effect of a Tag or Class style is confined to a specific section of the page (officially called *descendant selectors*).

Now you'll change the background color of the footer and give it a top border. To do this, select anything in the footer, choose <div#footer> from the Tag selector, and double-click Background in the CSS Styles panel to open the CSS Rules Definition window. Change the background color to white, and then switch to the Border rules to make a blue top border to match the blue in the header graphic. Uncheck Same for All, set Top to Solid, set a width of 10 pixels, and choose color #666699. Your footer is now complete.

Before you work with more text, let's set a general font for the entire page. Click anywhere in the page and select <body.thrColFixHdr> from the Tag selector. Double-click Font in the CSS Styles panel to edit the settings. Set the font to Arial, Helvetica, Sans Serif with a size of 90% and the line-height to 1.25 em.

> The CSS font options require some explanation. As mentioned previously when you were designing your page in Photoshop, the font for web text must be available on visitors' computers. CSS rules allow you to set alternate fonts in case your first choice isn't available. The setting you just made says your preferred font is Arial, but you'll also accept Helvetica, or if necessary, the default sans-serif font on the system. (By the way, em is a relative size equal to the width of an *m* in the current font size.)

Navigation—The Left Sidebar

You're now ready to focus your attention on the left sidebar and navigation links. Delete the placeholder text (and set the Format to none in the Properties panel), and type the list of pages: Home, Enrollment, Campus, Schedule, Alumni, and Contact Us. Press the Return key between each item to place each on its own line, and then select all the items and click the Unordered List button on the Properties panel. (From a structural perspective, navigation is an unordered [or un-numbered] list.) Now, click anywhere in the list, select <ul> from the tag selector, and click New CSS Rule in the CSS Styles panel. Click OK. The CSS Rule Definition window opens. Open the List setting, and browse for the bullet image you created in Photoshop. Click OK. Your list now shows arrows instead of dots for bullets (see Figure 16.19). (Don't worry that the bullets have a background color—when you're done they will blend in!)

You'll need to work on the padding, width, and background of the left sidebar. As with the header, some padding is in place that you want to change. Click anywhere in the left column, select <div#sidebar1> from the tag selector, and double-click Padding from the CSS Styles panel. Change the padding to 5 pixels all around. Then, change the width of the left sidebar to 165 pixels. You'll also take out the background color under Background rules because it doesn't fill all the way to the

FIGURE 16.19
Image bullets can be defined in CSS.

footer like you want. (We'll come back to how to get a column effect later.) You can quickly clear a color by clicking the clear option in the Color Picker—the clear option is a red diagonal line across a white box.

Next, let's change the line spacing between the items in your list. Click the list of navigation items, select <ul> from the lower left, and click Edit Style in the CSS Styles panel. Under the Type rules, set the line height to 1.7 and choose ems from the menu. Click OK.

But wait, you still need to add the most important part of navigation—links. To link each item in the navigation, select it and type the filename of the page it will eventually link to in the Link field of the Properties panel (see Figure 16.20). Remember, the link will be broken if the filename doesn't match the link provided!

FIGURE 16.20
Make the text link to pages that will be in the site by selecting the text and typing the filenames in the Link field.

Finally, you want the secondary tag line to appear below the navigation links for extra visual impact. To insert it, place your cursor at the end of the bulleted list and press Return twice. Then use the Images tool in the Insert Common panel to browse to the image. Make your Alt text "Success is within reach."

Main Content

The navigation is complete, so you can move on to the main content. Flow in the text for the page. (If you'd like, you can work with the filler text, but take out the second-level header that you don't need. However, make sure the first line of text is set as an <h1> header.) The font size isn't quite what you're after, so change the font size for <div#mainContent> to 85%. Next, add the line Find out more to the end of the text, link it to the same page as Contact Us, and align the text to the right using the Properties panel. Although the text is complete (see Figure 16.21), the white space to the left is a bit overwhelming. Change the Box rules of <div#mainContent> to a 170-pixel left margin and click OK. This moves the left edge of the text closer to the left sidebar (see Figure 16.22).

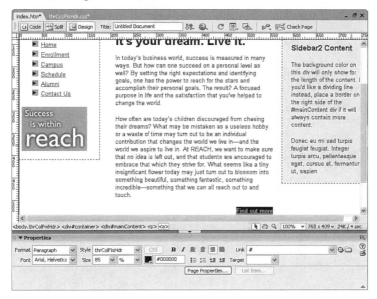

FIGURE 16.21
Text aligns left by default, but you can align it to the right (or center it) in the Properties panel.

FIGURE 16.22
Decreasing the
left margin of
the main con-
tent improves
the look of
the page.

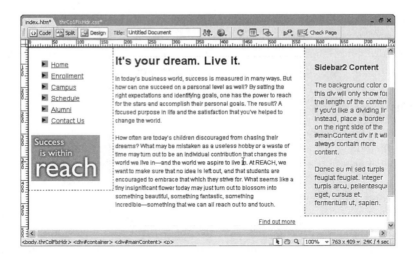

Although this web layout appears to have three columns, CSS designs aren't like tables (with defined rows and columns). The center "column" is really the space left over after the left sidebar is floated to its left and the right sidebar is floated to its right.

By the Way

There's one last thing to do in the main content—apply the image header in place of the <h1> text header. It is a better practice to use real heading levels than images for text, so you're going to get the best of both worlds: you'll have a real text header, but hide it off the edge of the screen and use the image in its place. That way, search engines and screen readers have access to the text content, but other devices will show the pretty image header on screen.

To replace the header text, select it and choose <h1> in the tag selector. Then create a new CSS style. You're going to create a Class style, so delete Dreamweaver's guess at a name and change the radio button to Class. Type .replace_text as the name and click OK. (Class styles' names always begin with a . to show they are Classes.) Then, open the Box rules, uncheck the Same for All box under Margin and set the left margin to × 9000 pixel, which will move the header text far outside the viewable region of the screen. Next, open the Background rules and browse to the replacement image you created. Be sure to set No Repeat. Click OK to add your new rules. Note that nothing has changed yet in your document because you need to apply the replace_text style to the <h1> text. To do this, select the <h1> text and, from the Styles menu in the Properties panel, choose replace_text. Your text headline is now replaced with image-based text (see Figure 16.23).

FIGURE 16.23
Use CSS to replace page headers with image text.

Print Style Sheets

Images set as backgrounds in CSS will not appear when a page is printed. When using image headers, it's a good practice to create a print style sheet so all important elements of the page will appear when printed.

In a print style sheet, the header can be set to regular text instead of the image header used on screen. To create a print style sheet, create a new document of the CSS type and save it to your site folder as print.css. Then open your original CSS file, copy and paste the rules to the new sheet, and remove any rules that won't make sense in print, especially any backgrounds, such as the image header you just applied. (You might want to wait until you are done with your project so the rules on the screen and print versions are somewhat parallel.)

To link the print style sheet to your HTML document, open your HTML document and click Attach Style Sheet at the bottom of the CSS Styles panel, and then browse to your file (see Figure 16.24). Set the Media type to Print, and click OK. Now, when the page is printed, different rules apply than those used to show the page on screen.

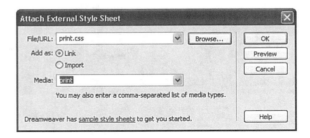

Right Sidebar

You'll now focus on the right sidebar. To start, remove the background color by edit-ing the Background rules for <div#sidebar2> and switch to Box rules to set the width to 225 pixels (so the 225-pixel-wide photo will fit). Set the left padding to 15 and the right padding to 0. Next add your text and style it. Click the right sidebar and choose <div#sidebar2> from the tag selector and then edit the Type rules to have a size of 85%, a font weight of bold, and a line height of 1.5 ems.

As you recall from the Photoshop design file, you used the fingerprint graphic to the left of the right column text. To make room, give extra padding on the left of the text. Click the right column text, click <p> in the tag selector, and click New CSS Style in the CSS Styles panel. Click OK, switch to the Box rules, uncheck the Same for All box under Padding, and set the left padding to 25 pixels to make room for the graphic. As long as you're here, change the right padding to 10 pixels to keep the text from touching the right edge. To insert the fingerprint, edit the Background rules for <div#sidebar2> and browse to the fingerprint graphic you created. Set No Repeat so the graphic appears only once. Click OK to see the changes (see Figure 16.25).

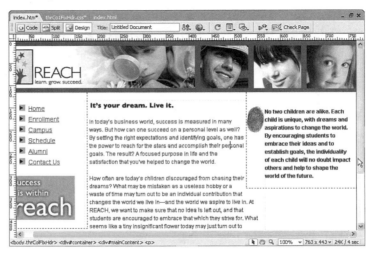

Let's finish the right sidebar by adding the photo of the father and child. You will insert this photo directly in the page, rather than setting it as a background as you did for the fingerprint. Place your cursor at the end of your text and press Enter, and then use the Image button on the Insert panel's Common tab to insert the image. Remember to type descriptive Alt text. If the image is aligned with the left margin of the text above it, the image has been inserted into a paragraph style. You don't want this, so select the image, choose <p> from the lower left (if it appears), and choose None from the Format menu in the Properties panel. The image will shift to the left because the margin set for <p> in the right sidebar no longer applies (see Figure 16.26).

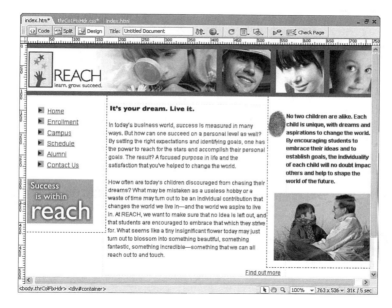

FIGURE 16.26
The page is nearly complete.

Faux Column CSS Effect

The page is nearly complete, but the last thing to do is to make a background appear in the navigation column. Recall that the original left sidebar background didn't fill all the way to the footer because the background color set for a DIV only fills as far as the content goes. If you have a short column, a background color will stop short.

To achieve the desired column effect, you'll use a CSS trick called faux columns to apply a background graphic that appears to fill the left sidebar. To create a faux column, you need to set a repeating background for the entire container section of the page, not just the <div#sidebar1> area. (That's because the container of the page will be the longest item of the page and the column has no risk of running short.) Note that, although the background will be set for virtually the entire page, the very top and bottom will be covered by the header and footer and the background image will show up only in the central content area of the page.

To set the background, click anywhere in the page, choose <div#container> at the lower left, and click Edit Style. Go to the Background rules, and choose the background graphic you created in Photoshop. Set the Repeat to Repeat-y, which repeats the graphic along the y-axis of the page (vertically). Click OK to see the result.

Previewing in a Browser

Although the design view in Dreamweaver is often accurate, you won't know what your page will really look like to web visitors until you test it an array of browsers. (Professional web designers know that different browsers render HTML by a different set of guidelines—what you see in Internet Explorer might not be what you see in Firefox or Safari for the Mac.)

To preview from Dreamweaver, make sure all your site files (including CSS files) are saved and click Preview/Debug in Browser at the top of the document window. Then, choose an available browser to see what your page will look like (see Figure 16.27). Note that the list of browsers depends on the browsers installed on your computer.

FIGURE 16.27
Preview in a browser to see your finished page—notice that the background "column" appears in the left sidebar.

Congratulations, you've created a web page!

Summary

To create your web page, you learned how to sketch and prepare your graphics in Photoshop, including how to export them as web graphics. You then built your page in Dreamweaver. Starting from a prepared layout, you modified the CSS rules to match your design. You learned how to insert images, make links, create custom bullets, and change margins and padding. You learned how to style and size text. You also learned some advanced tricks, like replacing header text with images and creating "faux" columns using background images, and how to create a style sheet especially for print versions of your page.

Output: Sending Your Files to Print

Getting It Printed

Creating artwork on your computer is really only half the process. It's not like you'll be inviting everyone to your home or office to see what you've created on your screen—a client might not be too keen on that. Rather, after your design is complete and approved, you'll need to send it to a printer to create the final piece.

Naturally, each job is different. In some cases, your final product will be a website or a PDF, but most jobs require a printed piece as the final product. This chapter specifically covers jobs that are printed by an offset printer.

> Plenty of jobs are simply run off on a copying machine or even a laser printer. For the most part, this chapter does not address those kinds of jobs, although some concepts do apply.

By the Way

The Love-Hate Relationship Between Designers and Printers

Ask some printers what they think of graphic designers, and they might answer, "They are the root of all evil." Other printers get along with designers just fine, so what's all the fuss about? In reality, the issue stems from designers who aren't familiar with the printing process, its capabilities, or its limitations.

The biggest complaint from printers is that designers create art that is very difficult to print—and in many cases, they design art that can't be printed reliably at all.

As a designer, you have only to gain by learning more about the printing process and applying that knowledge to the art you design. For example, don't create 5-point white text that knocks out of a process color background. Find out how close you can come to the edge of a page (a printer needs "gripper" space), or if you are creating art that will come to the edge of the page, be sure to add a bleed (extending the art past the edge of the page).

Undoubtedly, there's a gray line between what a designer is responsible for and what a printer is responsible for. But when it comes to getting a job done and there's money on the line—and a client waiting to get the product—you want to make sure that the job is done correctly. And the better shape a file is in when you hand it off to a printer, the happier everyone will be in the end.

I know that many printers value a designer who knows what they are doing, and will even refer design work to them when their clients ask whether they know any good designers. Turns out, I've gotten more than just design jobs referred to me over the years—my father-in-law is a printer....

Understanding the Printing Process

When trying to understand graphics, printing, and the technology that makes it all possible, I like to make a comparison to how some of the greatest professional athletes look at the sports they play.

Sandy Koufax is considered one of the greatest left-handed pitchers of all time, and what made him unique is that he understood the underlying physics of what makes a baseball curve, rise, or sink. He likened the human body to a catapult and understood the dynamics of throwing a baseball.

Tiger Woods is arguably the greatest golf player in history—and for good reason. Besides having talent, Tiger studies the physics of the game and understands why a certain club gives more lift than others, or how the direction the grass grows affects a particular shot.

The point I'm trying to make is that the more you know about your field, the better you can be at it, no matter what you do. In graphic design specifically, knowing about printing makes you a better designer.

Many of today's printers are utilizing digital workflows to save costs and improve quality and turnaround time. Some printers have a CTP (computer-to-plate) system, which eliminates the need to create film, basically creating plates directly from a computer file. Although these methods present other challenges to printers (trapping, imposition, and so on), use of such a method also puts the responsibility on the designer to create art files that are free of problems (okay, so at least with as few problems as possible).

Understanding Transparency

The transparency features in Illustrator and InDesign have gotten a bad rap since they were initially introduced—and rightfully so. The technology was too new for the older systems that most printers were using, and, above all, there was very little information on how it worked, leaving many printers and designers to struggle with the settings. Most people didn't even know that transparency existed, and printers who suggested that users save their files as older Illustrator files ended up causing even more issues. At the end of the day, it was all quite messy.

But transparency has come quite a way since then. Illustrator, InDesign, and Acrobat now all share the same flattening technology (necessary to process files with transparency), and, more important, the transparency features and settings across all of these applications are identical. Adobe has also been extremely proactive in helping print service providers and printers learn about transparency, and numerous guides and whitepapers are also available (I reference these later).

A Designer's Checklist

Although it's impossible to list everything that might go wrong in a job, several issues come up more often. As a checklist for yourself when you're creating files or preparing them to send to a printer, here are some common issues to be aware of:

- ▶ **Make sure that everything is CMYK**—Make sure that you haven't accidentally created artwork in RGB mode. Many times you might use stock photography that you've downloaded from a website—and those images are almost always in RGB. Remember that almost all images from a digital camera are RGB and must be converted to CMYK in Photoshop before they can be sent to the printer.

- ▶ **Remember your fonts**—When you send your files to your printer, make sure that you've included copies of all the fonts you've used in the file. Additionally, try to avoid using off-brand fonts that you've found somewhere on the Internet, or fonts from those "10,000 fonts for $9.99" collections because they usually end up causing problems.

- ▶ **Use spot and process colors correctly**—If you're printing a job as a four-color process (CMYK), don't provide your printer with a file made up of spot colors. Likewise, if you're printing a spot-color job, don't provide your printer with a file that uses process colors. Some jobs combine both spot and process colors as well. If you aren't sure, talk to your printer.

▶ **Make sure that images are high resolution**—Sometimes designers use low-resolution images in their design but forget to replace them with high-resolution versions of the images before they send their files to the printer. Sometimes designers copy files from a website, and those images are almost always 72dpi low-resolution images. Make sure that photos taken with a digital camera are also of sufficient resolution.

▶ **Check Illustrator resolution settings**—If you've applied any effects in Illustrator (they appear in the Effects menu), those effects might need to be rasterized at print time. Drop shadows, feathers, Gaussian blurs, and some mapped 3D artwork are examples of effects that get rasterized at print time. To ensure best results, make sure that the Document Raster Effects Setting is set to 300dpi.

▶ **Check Transparency Flattener settings**—In many cases, if you've used native Illustrator CS and InDesign CS files—and PDF 1.4 files or higher—your printer will determine the correct flattener settings. But at times you might be working with EPS files, or your printer might ask you to export older format files. In those cases, you'll be supplying files to your printer that are already flattened. Flattened files can't be changed, so if they aren't correct, the printer can't fix them.

▶ **Check your stroke weights**—Just because Illustrator and InDesign allow you to specify extremely thin lines, that doesn't mean a printing press will be able to reproduce them. In general, never specify a stroke weight that's less than 0.25 point. Pay attention to logos or other art that is scaled: A logo that has a 1-point stroke that is scaled down to 20% in your InDesign layout will end up with a 0.2-point stroke.

▶ **Check your tints**—Specify tints that won't cause problems on press. Tints lower than 5% or higher than 95% are usually problematic. The truth is, each printing press is different, and printers know what their presses can handle; it's best to ask your printer for suggestions.

▶ **Add bleed or gripper space**—If your design includes art or a background that is supposed to print all the way to the edge of a page, you have to specify a *bleed*, which is basically extending the art outside the boundaries of the page. This ensures that no whitespace will show when the page is trimmed to the correct size. Where art doesn't come all the way to the edge of the page, you have to leave a certain amount of space, called *gripper space*, along the edges of your page (you can use margin settings to help you stay out of these areas).

By the Way

> In case you were wondering, pages with a bleed don't usually need gripper space because they are printed on larger pages that are trimmed down to the page size you specify.

▶ **Perform general file cleanup**—Throughout the design process, you might choose from many colors, fonts, symbols, and so forth. When your job is complete, it's best to "clean up" your file by deleting unused swatches, brushes, or symbols. Use the Find Font feature in InDesign or Illustrator to make sure that you don't have empty objects with additional fonts in your file.

▶ **Provide a dummy**—I'm not referring to the kind of dummy that a ventriloquist uses. A dummy is a printed mockup that shows a printer how a job should look when it's printed and folded. It doesn't have to be in color or even full size, but it should give the printer a good visual of what you expect. Creating a dummy also helps you, the designer, because you can make sure that the panels fold correctly and are the right size.

InDesign's Package Feature

InDesign's Package feature is a great way to prepare a project to hand off to your printer. This feature (found in InDesign's File menu) creates a folder that contains a copy of your file, along with all the fonts and linked images that are used in your file. It also enables you to easily create a text file with instructions that you can pass on to your printer.

I've found that it's also good practice to send along a PDF version of your file so that the printer can see what the file looks like and compare it to what he sees in InDesign, making sure that everything is correct.

InDesign and Acrobat's Separation Preview Feature

Both InDesign and Acrobat Professional enable you to view color separations onscreen and also feature a densitometer reading for checking ink coverage. To make sure that your process or spot colors are separating correctly, these are invaluable tools that should be used. If you aren't sure what you should be looking for when viewing separations, speak to your printer.

Resources

Plenty of material on this topic is available, and it would only benefit you to find some time to learn more about the printing process, as well as understand how art goes from the computer monitor to the printed page (and everything that happens in between).

Here's a list of some resources that I find useful on this subject. Visit www.designresponsibly.com for the latest updated list.

▶ *A Designer's Guide to Transparency for Print Output*, by Adobe Systems Incorporated (www.adobe.com/products/indesign/pdfs/transparency_guide.pdf)

▶ *Adobe InDesign CS Printing Guide for Service Providers*, by Adobe Systems Incorporated (partners.adobe.com/public/asn/en/print_resource_center/IDCS_PrintGuide.pdf)

▶ *Adobe Illustrator CS Printing Guide for Service Providers*, by Adobe Systems Incorporated (partners.adobe.com/public/asn/en/print_resource_center/AICS_PrintGuide6.pdf)

▶ *Adobe Acrobat 6.0 Professional Output Guide for Print Service Providers*, by Adobe Systems Incorporated (partners.adobe.com/public/asn/en/print_resource_center/Acrobat6fOutputGuide.pdf)

▶ *Professional Printing with Adobe Illustrator CS*, by Adobe Systems Incorporated (www.adobe.com/products/creativesuite/pdfs/ilcsproprint.pdf)

▶ *Pocket Pal: A Graphic Arts Production Handbook*, 19th Edition, by Frank Romano Jr. (International Paper)

▶ *Real World Color Management*, 2nd edition, by Bruce Fraser, Fred Bunting, and Chris Murphy (Peachpit Press)

Finally—and I can't emphasize this enough—talk to your printer. An open line of communication between designer and printer is crucial and can save time, energy, money, and sanity. If possible, arrange to spend a day or two at a printer and see the process for yourself. Learn about the issues that come up and how they are addressed. The information you will learn will prove more valuable than you can imagine.

Index

How can we make this index more useful? Email us at indexes@samspublishing.com

How can we make this index more useful? Email us at indexes@samspublishing.com

U - V

W

save as .gif   transparent (no background)
  in photoshop

Rich Black   60   40   40   100

Create PDF   (from Heather)
    Press Quality
    unclick # rely on system

    unclick # ask

    Paper Quality Color

    Layout - Portrait

Open PDF   Advanced
                Print Production
                Output Preview
                    does it show
                      SPOT under process?
                    fix if it does

~~~~~~   ~~~~~~~

RICH BLACK   60 40 40 100
~~~~~~~~~~~~~~~~~~~~~~~

    In Illustrator (from Alna Eno - how to
    select all   get crisp edges)
    Type
        Outline

~~~~~   ~~~~~~~~

THIS BOOK IS SAFARI ENABLED

INCLUDES FREE 45-DAY ACCESS TO THE ONLINE EDITION

The Safari® Enabled icon on the cover of your favorite technology book means the book is available through Safari Bookshelf. When you buy this book, you get free access to the online edition for 45 days.

Safari Bookshelf is an electronic reference library that lets you easily search thousands of technical books, find code samples, download chapters, and access technical information whenever and wherever you need it.

TO GAIN 45-DAY SAFARI ENABLED ACCESS TO THIS BOOK:

- Go to **http://www.samspublishing.com/safarienabled**
- Complete the brief registration form
- Enter the coupon code found in the front of this book on the "Copyright" page

If you have difficulty registering on Safari Bookshelf or accessing the online edition, please e-mail customer-service@safaribooksonline.com.